WILLIAM TYNDALE

WILLIAM TYNDALE
(from Holland's Heroologia, 1620)

Frontispiece

WILLIAM TYNDALE

By

J. F. MOZLEY, M.A.

GREENWOOD PRESS, PUBLISHERS
WESTPORT, CONNECTICUT

Originally published in 1937
by The Macmillan Company, New York

First Greenwood Reprinting 1971

Library of Congress Catalogue Card Number 70-109801

SBN 8371-4292-X

Printed in the United States of America

PREFACE

It is full time that a new life of Tyndale were written. Demaus laid a good and true foundation sixty-six years ago, but much knowledge has been gained since then, and lurks in state papers and learned magazines. Even in the case of records that have long been known, a closer study of the text reveals many fresh facts, and sweeps away certain hoary fables that have gathered about the memory of the reformer. When I began to study Tyndale for myself two and a half years ago, I speedily discovered the state of the matter. Here is a man who has never yet received his due, whose reputation has been at the mercy of ignorance and partizanship: and so I determined to enter the field.

The building up of the life of Tyndale demands care: for so much of the evidence consists of small points, often standing alone—casual notices in ancient letters, bibliographical details, and the like. Nevertheless, if the task is properly performed, these small points are found to fit into one another, and to form a single self-consistent whole. In the latter stages of this investigation several new facts have come before me, and it has been gratifying to observe how easily and naturally they fit into the plan laid down. There is still much to be discovered; but I hope that I may claim to have carried the study of Tyndale a long stage forward.

Many persons, both within and without my family, have given me help. I thank them all; I only name them when their expert authority is needed to establish the points in question. For myself I can say that my labour in making this book will be richly rewarded, if it leads to a truer and fairer estimate of a great Englishman and a great Christian man.

J. F. Mozley.

May 3, 1937.

v

THE AUTHORITIES

Edward Halle's *Chronicle*, 1548.

John Foxe's *Acts and Monuments*, 1563, 1570, etc.
  Foxe's account of Tyndale has been triumphantly vindicated by modern discoveries.

The Whole Works of W. Tyndall, John Frith and Doctor Barnes, 1573, edited by Foxe and printed by Daye. [Quoted as Daye's folio.]

Tyndale's Works, edited by H. Walter for the Parker Society, 1848–50, 3 volumes:—
  I Doctrinal Treatises, II Expositions, III Answer to More.

Works of Sir Thomas More, 1557.

Letters and Papers of the Reign of Henry VIII, edited by Brewer and Gairdner. [*L. & P.*] Most of the letters quoted can be found in this collection under their dates.

The first printed English New Testament, E. Arber, 1871.

Records of the English Bible, A. W. Pollard, 1911.
  These last two books print many of the original documents.

William Tyndale, Robert Demaus, 1871 and 1886—an excellent book.

CONTENTS

ILLUSTRATIONS

CHAPTER I

WILLIAM TYNDALE, otherwise named Hutchins, translator of the English bible, was born some half-dozen years before the close of the fifteenth century. The exact year is uncertain, and can only be calculated from the dates of his Oxford university degrees. Since he proceeded master of arts on July 2nd, 1515, and since that degree was rarely taken, and very likely could not legally be taken, before reaching the age of twenty years, we thus obtain 1495 as the latest possible date of his birth. Beyond this it cannot be pushed back far, and perhaps 1494 is as probable a date as any.

Nor is the *place* of his birth known to us. Halle's *Chronicle* merely says that he was born " about the borders of Wales," and Foxe follows with the same phrase. But happily a strong and unbroken local tradition throws light into the gloom and enables us at least to fix the district. In the western parts of Gloucestershire, where the range of the Cotswolds falls into the vale of Berkeley, with the river Severn flowing beyond, there was settled for three hundred years a family named Tyndale or Hutchins, which has always claimed the great translator for its own: and since the county of Monmouth beyond the Severn was then, and for long afterwards, reckoned to Wales, the tradition tallies exactly with the words of Halle. The headquarters of this family were at Melksham Court, a big manor house in Stinchcombe, which lies just beneath the western spur of the Cotswolds. Here—so the court rolls of the manor tell us— there dwelt in 1478 one Tebeta Hutchins, who was succeeded within a dozen years by Richard Hutchins or Tyndale, perhaps her son, and so the succession went down from generation to generation, until the estate was given up in the third quarter of the eighteenth century. Moreover, during the first hundred years of this period another branch of the family resided in a part of the same village called Southend, a name still to be found on the ordnance map.   This Southend farm was held in 1478 by a second Richard Tyndale or Hutchins, who also transmitted it to his progeny; and thus the two branches continue side by side until 1591, when the two sisters, who have inherited Southend, remove on their marriage into another county, and sell their Stinchcombe properties to their kinsman of Melksham Court.

Many writers state confidently that William Tyndale was the younger brother of this Richard of Melksham Court. This is most unlikely.   Richard, since he was in possession of a small holding, named Holder's Croft, in 1478, and was a collector of the parliamentary subsidy in 1492, can hardly have been born later than 1460, at least thirty years before the birth of our hero.   Nor can William be the *son* of Richard; for the latter already had a son William, who was ordained by 1502, and died in 1523.   Can he then be the son of the other Richard of Southend?   No; for he had a son John, who died many years before our reformer's brother of that name.   The fact is, William Tyndale cannot be fitted, as son or brother, into the Stinchcombe lines at all: and yet he clearly belongs to them, for he uses the same double name as they.   The most likely guess would be, that William was nephew to one of the Richards, both of whom died before 1507, and that his father was settled somewhere in the neighbourhood.

And in fact two villages near by claim the honour of his birth, and their inhabitants proudly point out the house to the visitor.   The first is North Nibley, two miles south of Stinchcombe, lying on the lower slopes of the hills.   Here in a big farmhouse, named Hunt's Court, dwelt for more than 250 years, down to 1784, a line of Tyndales.   But this house came into the possession of the family too late to be the birthplace of William.   It passed to them with Alice Hunt, the heiress of Hunt's Court, who married Thomas Tyndale, the son and successor of Richard Tyndale of Melksham Court, and this marriage cannot be placed before 1505.   Besides, their son William, who seems to have been put into Hunt's

Court by his parents, and who was at one time confounded with our reformer, is now proved by a legal document to have outlived him by at least seven years. Nibley therefore must be ruled out, and the noble monument, which now stands on Nibley knoll overlooking the village, had better have been erected on the more central and no less lofty eminence of Stinchcombe hill, above the ancient manor house, which, though it may not have seen his birth, was at least the chief home of his family.

But a fresh claimant has arisen in recent years, and has been received with a good deal of favour. This is Slymbridge, a village right down in the vale of Berkeley, three or four miles distant from Stinchcombe to the north. Outside this village there is an old farmhouse, dating probably from before Tyndale's birth, named Hurst farm, and here resided for thirty years from 1516 onwards one Edward Tyndale, who held the important post of receiver for the lordship of Berkeley. William Lord Berkeley had died in 1492, and to spite his brother, with whom he had quarrelled, had bequeathed his estates to the king and his heirs male; and in royal ownership they remained until the accession of queen Mary. A local receiver of rents and other revenues had to be appointed, and from 1519 until his death in 1546 this receiver was Edward Tyndale. He had previously been for two years woodward, or keeper of the forests, on the Berkeley estates in Gloucestershire and Somerset. He was evidently an able man, and rapidly made his way in the world. He became also steward and auditor of Tewkesbury abbey, and leased from that foundation the manor of Pull Court just over the Worcestershire border; and he held besides the manor of Burnet in Somerset, close to Bristol. His will is still extant, and shows him to have been a man of some wealth. He was doubtless akin to the Stinchcombe family; for he is found, and so is his son, acting as witness, trustee and the like to their legal documents: but more than that, he turns out to be a brother of our William.

We learn this from a letter, first unearthed by Demaus, written in January 1533 by Stokesley bishop of London to Thomas Cromwell. In it he begs that a certain farm in

Gloucestershire, named Greenhampster, may be given to an old servant of his, and not to the other candidate who is in the field. This other suitor, he says, " hath a kinsman called Edward Tyndale, brother to Tyndale the arch-heretic, and under-receiver of the lordship of Berkeley, which may, and daily doth, promote his kinsfolks there by the king's farms." If his servant is worsted, adds Stokesley in a subsequent letter, it will be a discredit to himself, and an occasion of boasting to " Tyndale and others of his sect "; and to clinch the matter he sends a gift of twenty nobles, for the minister of state was notoriously open to bribes. Now Stokesley had himself been rector of Slymbridge from 1509 onwards. He was a fellow of Magdalen college, Oxford, and the living was in the gift of that foundation; and indeed to this day the expenses of the Mayday singing on the top of the college tower are said to be borne by the rectory of Slymbridge. He seems to have held the living for twenty-one years, but he cannot have resided much; for he had other preferments, and was also frequently employed on the king's business. Still he must sometimes have visited the place—indeed, this old servant may well have been employed there—and at all events he is likely to have been well informed about the neighbourhood. Here then is our first piece of direct evidence concerning our reformer's family. He was brother to Edward; and doubtless a younger brother: for Edward can hardly have been born later than 1492, to hold the responsible position of collector of revenues in three counties by 1519. There was a third brother also, John, of whom we shall hear later that he was a merchant in London, and came into trouble for his Lutheran propensities. Nor was Edward without sympathy with reform; for he possessed certain prohibited books, and bequeathed them in his will.*

But though Edward lived at Hurst farm for so many years, there is nothing to show that he was born there. He only

* The will gives a mark to Margaret, daughter of Henry Tyndall, in addition to the pound lately given her as appointed by her uncle Griffith Tyndall. It may be that these were two other brothers of Edward. Edward was twice wedded and had thirteen children. He left his " great lute " to his son, and his " best bow " to the vicar of Tewkesbury.

took over the lease in 1516, and the previous owner had not been named Tyndale. It is true that in 1485 the Southend Tyndales came into ownership of a property, which is described as " part of Kingston's or Rivers' lands in the manor of Hurst in Slymbridge "; but Demaus is wrong in supposing that this belonged to Hurst farm. It was part of the manor of Hurst, but it belonged to the neighbouring farm which still bears the name of Kingston, lying between Hurst and the river: and the tenants, who thereafter held it, appear—so far as we hear their names—not to have been members of the family. Thus there is no shred of evidence that Tyndale's father ever resided at Slymbridge. One thing only we can say : if he did so, it is easy to explain why William went to Magdalen hall, Oxford; for that house, though independent of Magdalen college, was closely connected with it, standing on ground rented from it, and drawing its principals from among its fellows. That is the only evidence which Slymbridge can boast, and very slender it is. The matter therefore of Tyndale's birthplace must be left undecided.

The double name of the family has never been explained. That the real name was Tyndale and not Hutchins, seems proved by the fact that both William and his Gloucestershire kinsmen begin to drop the latter name about the year 1525, and at length it entirely disappears. The family tradition, expressed in a letter of 1663 from a descendant of Edward Tyndale to his cousin at Stinchcombe, states that a certain Tyndale came out of the north during the wars of the Roses —that is, presumably from Tyndale in Northumberland— changed his name to Hutchins for safety, came to Gloucestershire, married there, and on his deathbed revealed his real name to his children. But the migration must have been very early in the fifteenth century to have produced two grandsons named Richard by the year 1478; and the vanity of the writer of the letter is such, that we can have no great confidence in his accuracy. Another theory is that the double name arose from an intermarriage. If so, it must have been very far back for the same reason. The northern origin is, however, perhaps supported by the fact that the name

Tyndale is not previously found in the county of Gloucester, while Hutchins and like names were common. In the village of Cam, two miles from Stinchcombe, there lived in 1414 a Walter Huchyns, and a family of this name flourished in the same place in the sixteenth and seventeenth centuries. One of them was Giles Huchyns (1510–69), who in 1539 acts as witness to a will along with a Tyndale of Stinchcombe. Then in Uley, three miles from Cam, there dwelt a John Huchyns (or Hychyns), who on May 12, 1517, climbed a ladder to the thatched roof of his house, was dashed to the ground by two rafters that slipped, and broke his neck. As far as date goes, this is the only Hutchins yet discovered who might have been the father of William, but his age is not given, and we do not know that either he or the Cam family used the name Tyndale. Still, the cloth trade was strong in Cam and Uley, and as William's brother John, the London merchant, seems to have dealt in this ware, it may yet turn out that our reformer sprang from one of these places.

It is tantalizing to think that all this uncertainty might have been spared us, and we might have been flooded with information, had John Smythe, the historian of the hundred of Berkeley, shown a little more perseverance. He tells us that records of the Tyndale family were then (about 1635) kept in a chest in the steeple of Stinchcombe church, which he " could never obtain to see." Maybe he did not try very hard: for he seems to have had little curiosity about William, and though he mentions the family frequently, never once tells the reader that it had given birth to the great translator.*

A word must be said upon the spelling of the name. For half a century the purists have been trying to persuade us to spell it *Tindale*, on the ground that it so appears in William's only autograph letter (1535), and also in his second and third New Testaments (1534–5). But it should be observed that the letter is in Latin, and the signature is therefore latinized,

---

* For the Tyndale family see *The Berkeley MSS.*, by John Smythe (ed. John Maclean), *Transactions of Bristol and Glos. Archaeol. Society*, 1877–8 (J. H. Cooke); *The Genealogist*, 1878 (B. W. Greenfield); *The Hockaday Abstracts* in the Gloucester public library; *Early Records of the Family Huchyns-Tyndale* (A. W. Hitchings, 1929; privately printed; a copy is in Gloucester public library).

as *W. Tindalus*; and since Latin is not fond of the letter *y* it would be natural enough to replace it with *i*. The evidence of the two New Testaments is cancelled out by that of his earlier books *Mammon* and *Obedience* (both 1528), which spell *Tyndale*. A more potent argument still is, that his brother Edward undoubtedly signs himself *Tyndale*; for two letters of his are extant, dated 1528 and 1544; and since that was the spelling used by the family in later years, there seems no good reason to change it. The fact is, there was no correct spelling of names, or indeed of other words, in those days. If we are to take the above evidence at its face value, one might suppose that on leaving England William normally spelt his name *Tyndale*, but that in the Low Countries, mixing often with men who spoke Latin and French, he came to prefer *Tindale*: but it matters not. He at least would not have cared how his name were spelt, so only that his work were fairly judged: for in small matters he carried the love of variety to the point of caprice. The second syllable of the name is often spelt by contemporaries *-dal*, *-dall*, or even *-dalle*, which proves that it was sounded short, as in the word *cymbal*.*

It will be seen that the Tyndale family was fairly well to do. Our translator's strong and simple style has sometimes been compared to Bunyan's; but the social conditions of the two were far apart. Bunyan was a travelling tinker; Tyndale belonged to the class of yeoman-farmers. His kinsfolk dwelt in some of the biggest houses in their villages, and they acquired to themselves no little property. In two cases we know the rents which they paid—nearly £11, and nearly £5, figures which must be multiplied by 15 or more to bring them to present value. And to this solid prosperity was added, what Bunyan never had, an education at the university.

* The *Answer to More* (1531) gives *Tindale* on the two title-pages, and mostly in the body of the book, but *Tyndale* also occurs. All his other books are either nameless or give *W. T.* only. *William* is spelt in three different ways in his headings and title-pages. The revolt against *Tyndale* was begun by Henry Bradshaw (*Bibliographer*, 1881). The name *Hutchins* is normally *Huchyns*, *Hochyns*, *Hewchyns*, etc., in the old records of the family, but is *Hychins*, etc., in Tyndale's *Mammon* and *Obedience* and in most of the entries of his degrees at Oxford.

Of his boyhood there is unhappily little to be said. Tyndale himself is very reticent in his writings, doubtless through fear of endangering his friends. We can imagine much: how he must have climbed the Cotswolds, and stood upon Stinchcombe hill, whence seven, or, as some even boasted, thirteen counties are to be seen; how he eyed with a boy's curiosity the gloomy and forbidding castle of Berkeley, dating back to Norman times, where so much good and evil had been planned and accomplished, and where Edward II had been murdered; how he roamed about the farms, making himself familiar with all the operations of country life: but we have certainty of nothing. He was plainly a sharp boy, taking in rapidly, and keeping in mind, what he saw and heard.

No doubt he had some schooling, though the educational standards of his instructors may not have been very high. In theory every parish incumbent had a duty to teach reading and writing to the youth of his flock, but many of them were far too ignorant to do this. Still, there must have been near by some little elementary school—ABC schools they were called—which he could attend; or perhaps he would walk over to some priest for private instruction. He might even have gone to a grammar-school; there was one within half a dozen miles, at Wotton-under-Edge, founded in 1384 by the dowager Lady Berkeley, and endowed so that the boys could be received free of charge; whose statutes, remarkable to say, ordain holidays of twelve weeks in the year, roughly corresponding to those of the English schoolboy of to-day: and it is not impossible that there were decent schools at Berkeley and at Dursley, perhaps in connection with the parish church. Still, the tender age at which he was sent to the university, makes it more likely that his instruction in grammar was reserved until he arrived at Magdalen hall.

Only one incident of his childhood has come down to us. In his book, *The Obedience of a Christian Man*, while defending the translation of scripture into English, he says, " Except my memory fail me, and that I have forgotten what I read when I was a child, thou shalt find in the English chronicle, how that king Athelstane caused the holy scripture to be translated into the tongue that then was in England, and how the prelates exhorted him thereto." Whether Tyndale remembered the name aright, has been debated; for such stories are commonly told not of Athelstane but of Alfred: but however that may be, we are thankful for this one and only glimpse of the sharp and studious little boy, fond of reading, retaining in his mind an historical fact, which was to lead him forward to his life's work.

And this brings us to the state of the church. Tyndale was a great reformer; what impression of religion is he likely to have received in his youthful days? The general state of the church at that time is well known to us. Great waves of indignation were beating up, had been beating up for years, which were shortly to sweep away the whole medieval system, destroy the dominance of priestcraft, and flood the church with the pure air of freedom. The explosion could not now be long delayed. Protest after protest had been made, both by clerks and by laymen, for hundreds of years, but in vain. Councils had been called for, had even been held, to reform the church, but all had broken on the unwillingness of popes and priests to surrender their privileges and monopolies. Before Tyndale came to full manhood, yet another council was summoned in 1512 by Julius II, but it was only a sop to appease the rebels, and it separated after a session of nearly five years with nothing accomplished. Meanwhile the evils grew. The exactions of the papal court were abhorrent to the clergy, those of the clergy were abhorrent to the laity. Priests, monks and nuns swarmed, large numbers living idle and useless lives. The ecclesiastical orders had amassed to themselves, in the name of God, enormous riches and a great proportion of the land, and on this they claimed to be exempt from taxation. They had other privileges too, being released from the jurisdiction of the secular courts of the realm, pleading benefit of clergy when charged, and thus getting off lightly for offences which would have been visited with heavy penalties if committed by a layman. Pluralism and non-residence were rife, and gigantic fortunes were built up by favoured ecclesiastics, while the poor people went unshepherded. An open scandal also was the unchastity of the clergy and of the monastic bodies. While claiming to be too pure for holy matrimony, they were at liberty to keep concubines, and in many parts of Europe could square the episcopal authorities by paying an annual tax. All this was alienating the respect of the people, and in 1515 the bishop of London demanded to have an important case withdrawn from the secular jury, on the ground that no clerk could now expect justice from a layman. Yet in this general decay of the Christian spirit the rites and ceremonies were carefully observed. Never were there more services, more holidays in honour of saints, never were relics and shrines more venerated, never were pilgrimages more splendid. The outward form was there, but the spirit was lacking. Religion was divorced from the life of holiness. In a word, the church was rotten, sunk in sloth and selfishness, forgetful of its high calling, false to the trust which it had received from God.

Of course not all churchmen were bad. There remained, as there ever remain even in the worst times, the faithful few, who kept the torch of righteousness alight, whose spirit was not frozen by the icy shell of the ecclesiastical system. But these were not sufficient in number, nor were they bold enough in temper, to turn away the sword of judgment. It has been said that in philosophy there is no problem of good; it is only evil which we feel to need explanation. So it is with the Christian church. A modest standard of goodness should be taken as a matter of course and cause no surprise; and if at any time her vices rather than her virtues strike the eye of the beholder, the day of vengeance cannot be far away.

In Gloucestershire Tyndale would see the church perhaps at its worst. The diocese of Worcester, to which the county belonged, forming one archdeaconry therein, was one of the most neglected of all. Since 1476 its chief pastors had been almost non-resident, rarely if ever visiting their cures, and from 1512 onwards it enjoyed three Italian bishops, who lived at ease in Rome, drawing meanwhile their stipends, and who never set foot in England at all. Yet the county was full of the externals of religion. It owned six great mitred abbeys, whose heads had seats in the House of Lords. The most venerated of these was Hailes, the chief place of pilgrimage, where the famous relic of the blood of Christ was kept, the sight of which was enough to ensure salvation, a relic whose genuineness had been vouched for by one who became pope, though later it was exposed as a fraud. The holiness of the county came to be summed up in a proverb: As sure as God is in Gloucester. Yet the ecclesiastics were, as we shall see later, sunk in an ignorance and superstition, which few dioceses can have equalled, much less surpassed.

There had indeed been in the county stirrings of revolt, which must have left some memories behind even up to Tyndale's day. Bristol, the second city of the kingdom, was, like all seaport towns, not unready for new things. Lollardism had been strong there. Wycliffe himself had held a living at Westbury-on-Trim, a few miles away, though it is doubtful whether he ever resided; and his famous disciple John Purvey had preached in the city. Nay, some faint whispers of reform hung about Berkeley Castle itself; for there in the latter years of the fourteenth century John Trevisa had been chaplain to the lord, and also vicar of the town church. Trevisa himself was never a thorough Wycliffite, but his sympathies lay that way, as did those of his master. He is even said by Caxton and by the preface to our 1611 bible to have himself translated the scriptures into English, but this is a mistake, and really refers to Purvey's version. Yet he certainly wrote a little work, still extant, called *The Dialogue between a Lord and a Clerk*, the two titles standing for his master and himself, which commends the rendering of holy writ into the tongue of the people. Indeed, in the castle itself there was to be seen a visible specimen of such a vernacular translation: for on the walls and the roof of the chapel were painted texts from the book of Revelation, both in Latin and in that Norman-French which had been until recently the language of the nobility; and traces of these inscriptions remain unto this day. The Lollard movement had been driven underground, and copies of the Wycliffe bibles could only circulate secretly, but some echoes of that great uprising must surely have reached the ears of the youthful Tyndale in the vale of Berkeley.

But before he is ready for his work, he must go to the university, and thither we must now follow him. Foxe's account is as follows:

" Brought up from a child in the university of Oxford, where he by long continuance grew up and increased, as well in the knowledge of tongues and other liberal arts, as especially in the knowledge of the scriptures, whereunto his mind was singularly addicted; insomuch that he, lying then in Magdalen hall, read privily to certain students and fellows of Magdalen college some parcel of divinity, instructing them in the knowledge and truth of the scriptures. His manners also and conversation, being correspondent to the same, were such, that all they that knew him reputed and esteemed him to be a man of most virtuous disposition and of life unspotted. Thus he in the university of Oxford increasing more and more in learning, and proceeding in degrees of the schools, spying his time, removed from thence to the university of Cambridge; where he, after he had likewise made his abode a certain space, being now farther ripened in the knowledge of God's word, leaving that university also, he resorted to one Master Welch, a knight of Gloucestershire, and was there school-master to his children."

Very meagre this is; but in dealing with Tyndale's career one grows to be thankful for small mercies. The dates of his degrees, however, have happily been recovered in recent years through the publication of the registers of Oxford university. There we learn that William Hychyns became bachelor of arts on July 4, 1512, and master of arts after the usual interval on July 2, 1515. Now as the whole arts course took seven years, we could state with some confidence that Tyndale went up to Oxford in 1508, provided that we could be sure that he began the course as soon as he arrived. But in 1508 he could not have been less than thirteen years old, an age which may seem to us absurdly young for a university, but which was nothing out of the common in those days, when the Magdalen college statutes laid down that their junior members, or demies, must be at least twelve years old on entry. Since Foxe describes him as a child, it seems better to suppose that he joined Magdalen hall at twelve or even younger, and that he at first attended the Magdalen grammar-school, until he was ready for the arts course. This was what the young demies of the college did, and it would be very natural for a boy at Magdalen hall, since that foundation adjoined the grammar-school, and had indeed some fifty years ago come into being as a home for outside students who wished to study grammar. For that reason it had originally been called Grammar hall, but by this time the new name was well-nigh established.

Of course if we push back Tyndale's birth beyond 1495, his entry at Magdalen hall will be correspondingly earlier. Have we the right to do this? The only argument in its favour is that it brings his ordination forward, and so leaves more scope for those varied preachings, in which he is said to have been engaged before leaving England. On the other hand, a lad so sharp and so earnest, going up to Oxford so young, would hardly defer his master's degree long beyond the earliest limit. Perhaps we shall not be far wrong, if we fix his birth in 1494 and his admission to Magdalen hall in 1506.

Magdalen hall drew its principals from its greater neighbour, and it obtained about this time one or two notable men. Stokesley held the office from 1502 to 1505, and was followed for the next two years by Longland, who became for many years bishop of Lincoln. Both these men Tyndale must surely have met in Oxford: certainly he met the latter: * both became bitter foes to the reformation. It may be added that Magdalen hall is now incorporated into Hertford college, and that a portrait of its great son hangs there in the dining-hall, a portrait originally owned by one of the principals, and bequeathed to the foundation in the seventeenth century.

But what would Tyndale learn at Oxford? The full master of arts course, which not more than about a sixth of the students completed—indeed only about a third even took the bachelor's degree—was supposed to consist of grammar, rhetoric and logic, the traditional *trivium*, descending from the

---

* In his *Practice of Prelates* he speaks of Wolsey exercising " that angel's wit of his, as my lord of Lincoln was wont to praise him " (II. 334).

dark ages, followed by the *quadrivium*, arithmetic, music, astronomy and geometry. These are high-sounding names, but the course was not in the least what these names denote to us; indeed, it seems doubtful whether by this date the *quadrivium* counted at all: for the universities throughout Europe were now at their lowest point. Into the question, what books were read, it is not worth while to enter, but two things may be said with confidence: first, a serious student would come out with a working knowledge of Latin; and secondly, the most important subject by far was logic, and everything else that was taught, was taught in a formal, logical way. For example, the Latin—included under rhetoric—was chiefly a matter of grammatical rules and definitions, and did not aim at revealing the spirit of the Romans by the wide reading of their authors. Great store was set upon the ability to dispute; there were disputations in the university schools, and there were private and unofficial disputations, especially in the evenings, in the colleges and halls. A successful student would come out of it with much sharpness and mental agility, but little spiritual fire or reverence for truth. The course was an education in names rather than in things, a mental gymnastic rather than a cultural training.

In the arts course there was no study of the bible. That was reserved for the theology course, taken after the master's degree. The instruction here was equally formal and artificial, dealing with words and texts rather than spiritual realities. The world was then in the grip of the scholastic theology, a theology which at its best lacked something of spontaneity and imagination, and now was hopelessly cut and dried. Scripture was not studied for its own sake, but for disputation; and this use of it was enormously facilitated by the medieval doctrine of a four-fold interpretation. A text was supposed to have four meanings, literal, allegorical, tropological and anagogical, the first of which was inferior to the other three. By a little manipulation you could make any text mean almost anything you pleased; and the most weird opinions could be bolstered up out of the bible. Of true religion there was little or nothing. " Theology," said

Erasmus in a fine sentence, " once venerable and full of majesty, has become almost dumb, poor and in rags."

Tyndale has left us some memories of his university career in a passage in the *Practice of Prelates* :—

" In the universities they have ordained that no man shall look on the scripture, until he be noselled in heathen learning eight or nine years, and armed with false principles, with which he is clean shut out of the understanding of the scripture: and at his first coming unto university he is sworn that he shall not defame the university, whatsoever he seeth; and when he taketh first degree, he is sworn that he shall hold none opinion condemned by the church; but what such opinions be, that he shall not know; and then, when they be admitted to study divinity, because the scripture is locked up with such false expositions and with false principles of natural philosophy, that they cannot enter in, they go about the outside, and dispute all their lives about words and vain opinions, pertaining as much unto the healing of a man's heel as health of his soul: provided yet alway, lest God give his singular grace unto any person, that none may preach except he be admitted of the bishops." *

The humanists indeed had long ago raised the flag of rebellion abroad, and the seed of better things had been planted in Oxford itself. It was ten years since Colet, fresh from his visit to Italy, had flabbergasted conventional Oxford by delivering lectures on St. Paul's epistles, though he had taken no degree in theology, and indeed was not even in deacon's orders; and had drawn large audiences, despite the fact, or rather because of the fact, that he threw contemptuously overboard the whole method of scholastic interpretation, and confined himself to the task of giving the historic background of the letters and expounding their spiritual truths; and among his hearers and loyal friends was a stranger named Erasmus. Even before that, Greek had been taught at Oxford by Grocyn and Linacre, a language which was bound to revolutionise the traditional teaching, and which deeply offended the conservatives, as

* II. 291. Elsewhere (*Obedience* I. 315) Tyndale says that he was once at the creating of doctors of divinity, where the subject of disputation was whether the widow has more merit than the virgin. His only other mentions of his Oxford days occur in II. 206, III. 179.

endangering the supremacy of the holy Latin tongue. But these great humanists had now left Oxford, having indeed lit a candle which should never be put out, but nevertheless leaving the bigots still with the reins of power in their hands.

Furious indeed were the contests between the old and the new ideas. In opposition to the Grecians, as the friends of the new learning were styled, the other party began to call themselves Trojans, and in Lent 1518 one of their number mounted the university pulpit, and delivered a violent attack upon liberal learning, calling its supporters devils and many other opprobrious names. Thomas More, who was then with the king at Abingdon, hearing of this, addressed a strong letter to the heads of the university, protesting against such a degradation of the pulpit, and begging them to restrain the offending faction in future. This may have happened after Tyndale left Oxford, but he was evidently familiar with such scenes, and has left us an account of them in his *Answer to More* :—

" Remember ye not how within this thirty years and far less, and yet dureth unto this day, the old barking curs, Duns' disciples and like draff, called Scotists [i.e. followers of Duns Scotus, the schoolman, the bête noire of the humanists and reformers], the children of darkness, raged in every pulpit against Greek, Latin and Hebrew, and what sorrow the schoolmasters, that taught the true Latin tongue, had with them, some beating the pulpit with their fists for madness, and roaring out with open and foaming mouth, that if there were but one Terence or Virgil in the world, and that same in their sleeves, and a fire before them, they would burn them therein, though it should cost them their lives; affirming that all good learning decayed and was utterly lost, since men gave them unto the Latin tongue."

Whether Tyndale himself took an active part in these conflicts, or was known as a leader of the Grecians, we cannot say. Perhaps not; for his early career gives us the impression of a man who was slowly finding his way, but not yet clear enough in his mind to be a leader. With this agree too Foxe's words, that he read the scripture privily with students and fellows of Magdalen college. There is no mention here of prominent leadership, of public lectures such as Colet had delivered. We see rather an independent mind, studying for itself, until it felt sure enough to step forward into the open.

For perhaps a dozen years Tyndale remained in Oxford, going home, we may presume, at the end of every June for the three months' long vacation. At whose expense did he go to the university? It is quite possible that his parents, solid middle-class people, were able to support him; or if not, some local patron may have taken him up, seeing the scholarly abilities of the boy. After taking his mastership he would be able to earn something by lecturing in the schools or perhaps by private coaching; and in fact he himself later mentions the name of one of his pupils, John Tisen, doubtless the man who appears in the university lists as taking the degree of bachelor of civil law in 1524.

From Oxford Tyndale passed to Cambridge. This cannot have been before 1516, for every master of arts was expected to lecture for a full year at least in the schools: and indeed it was probably later still; for Foxe's words—" a certain space " contrasted with the " long continuance " of his Oxford career—seem to imply that his Cambridge residence was much the shorter of the two. Why did he make the change? Foxe's quaint phrase " spying his time " gives us no help, and seems to mean little more than that all his movements were under providential direction. Some have thought that he found himself in suspicion and danger at Oxford from the heresy-hunts, which the bishop of Lincoln was instituting in his diocese; but these troubles seem not in these years to have touched Oxford itself, though we hear of them in Bucks, Lincolnshire and elsewhere. A much more likely reason is, that Cambridge was now a more profitable place of study. It had quite outstripped Oxford as a centre of the new learning. The great Erasmus had taught there from 1510 to 1514, and his influence was still felt. Besides, the whole atmosphere of the place was more tranquil, as Erasmus himself remarks. There was much opposition—in one college Erasmus' New Testament was altogether forbidden—but there were few of those furious outbursts of bigotry, which drew from More his letter to the university of Oxford. In 1518 Richard Croke, after studying several years on the continent and holding the professorship of Greek at Leipsic, had returned to Cambridge, and began to give public lectures on the Greek language. It may well have been these that helped to attract Tyndale thither.

Tyndale always turned his scholarship to religious ends, and at Cambridge he became, as Foxe says, " further ripened in the knowledge of God's word "; but it is not likely that he took any degree in divinity. There would indeed have been just time for him to gain the bachelorship; for the passage from Oxford to Cambridge would hardly in those days have been an insuperable obstacle; and indeed Foxe's first edition, as we shall see in the next chapter, ascribes to him some Cambridge degree of this kind. But the latter statement is very loose, and Foxe omits it in his second edition, presumably because he had found it to be untrue. During these years Tyndale's disgust at the teaching methods of the universities and at the scholastic theology must have been becoming more pronounced, and it is highly unlikely that he would enter upon a second course of study, which would seem to him a mere waste of time. Even if he began it, one cannot believe that he would finish it.

Where and when he was ordained, we cannot say. No record of any sort remains to enlighten us; but it must have been during the Oxford or Cambridge years. One thing at least may be said confidently. Our William Tyndale is certainly not the person of that name who was ordained in 1503 in London by letters dimissory, as priest to a nunnery in the diocese of Carlisle. The dates do not tally, and Tyndale was a common name in the border counties of the north. Nor again can he have been the William Tyndale who took the vows at the observant monastery at Greenwich in 1508, and whose father, in memory of the occasion, presented to the monastery a book, that is now in the library of St. Paul's cathedral in London. This theory, though still repeated by writers who ought to know better, cannot be reconciled with Foxe's account, and breaks down finally on the fact that Sir Thomas More, who condemns in the strongest terms those reformers—Luther and others—

who had broken their monastic vows, calling them again and again false friars, runaways from the cloister, and the like, never once uses those terms about Tyndale, but pointedly distinguishes him from that class.

Foxe has spoken of his spotless life and good repute at this period; Thomas More, bitter enemy though he is, tells the same story. Tyndale, writes More in 1529, " was, as men say, well known, before he went over the sea, for a man of right good living, studious and well learned in scripture, and in divers places in England was very well liked, and did great good with preaching." It is true that these words occur in a dialogue, and are put into the mouth of More's opponent, who has some sympathy with the reformers; but More would never thus have used them, if they had not expressed the common opinion. Besides, later in the dialogue he makes them his own; for, speaking in his own person, he says: " Tyndale was indeed, as ye said at the beginning, before his going, taken for a man of sober and honest living, and looked and preached holily," though he goes on to add that even then he smacked somewhat of heresy. Whence did More receive these reports? No doubt chiefly from Oxford and Cambridge; for he was closely in touch with both universities, and had many friends who could inform him. The double mention of preaching is of special interest; for this valuable work was now shamefully neglected, and Tyndale in his writings never fails to reproach the priests on this account. He himself in these years would seem to have concentrated upon it. But are we to include Oxford among the divers places in which he preached? Probably we should; More's words certainly gain greater point, if we so interpret them: for after Tyndale left Cambridge, there were only two places in England, Little Sodbury and London, in which he ever resided, and then only for a short time. All things considered, it is best to fix his ordination in the Oxford years, and to bring him to Cambridge about 1519. Some day his name may be recovered from one of the episcopal registers.*

* Halle says Tyndale was at Oxford when Luther began to write against the bishop of Rome, i.e. 1517–8.

Of his companions at Cambridge we have no certain knowledge. Very likely he met Latimer, Cranmer and Gardiner, who were all in residence, but the two former had not yet joined the reforming movement, and Latimer was even sharply hostile to it. There was, however, a group of younger men who had been touched by the new fire. There was Bilney ("little Bilney," as Latimer used to call him), who had been converted by the reading of Erasmus' Greek Testament on its first appearance in 1516, and thereafter, gentle and timid though he was, became a centre of evangelical truth, and later helped to open the eyes of Latimer. There was Robert Barnes, prior to the Augustinian monastery, and Coverdale, a member of the same house; and there was John Lambert, or Nicholson, who later became chaplain to the English merchants at Antwerp. With all these three men Tyndale was in touch on the continent; and two of them eventually perished at the stake.

Was there also at Cambridge an even dearer friend, John Frith, who became his best-loved disciple, and died heroically in the flames of Smithfield? It is not unlikely, though this view has found little acceptance. Frith, son of an innkeeper and scholar of Eton, took his bachelor's degree in January 1526, and therefore may well have overlapped with Tyndale, if the latter remained in Cambridge till the spring or summer of 1522. Where heart leaps to meet heart, a few months' acquaintance suffices to found a deep and enduring friendship. Cambridge is the only place in England where we know that they both resided, and if they did not meet here, we cannot say where it was. But wherever it may have been, Frith—says Foxe—received the seed of the gospel from his friend.*

Two notable events occurred at Cambridge which Tyndale may well have witnessed. One was the triumphal visit to the university of Wolsey in 1520, when he was entertained with the most lavish splendour, and was greeted with an oration, which for fulsome eulogy can never have been surpassed. The other was the burning of Luther's writings

* In Daye's folio Foxe says that the meeting place was London, but his narrative here is confused.

in the following year, only a few weeks after they had been burnt at Paul's Cross in London to the accompaniment of a sermon from bishop Fisher. We can imagine the intense interest, the scornful displeasure, with which Tyndale would watch both these proceedings. But he did not stay to see more of the great world; for after a sojourn of perhaps three years he left the university, and returned to Gloucestershire, to become tutor to the children of a country squire.*

* At the eleventh hour I find an entry in the Hereford register. On June 10, 1514, the bishop held an ordination at Whitborne, at which (1) " John Hychyns, Hereford diocese," was ordained acolite; (2) " William Hychyns, Hereford diocese," was ordained subdeacon " to the title of the priory of blessed Mary of Overy in Southwark, Winchester diocese." Two days later (June 12) " William Hychyns, subdeacon," was granted letters dimissory for the other sacred orders. Can this be Tyndale and his brother? The date fits, and the family may have dwelt over the Herefordshire border, which was about 15 miles from Stinchcombe. Perhaps the Southwark priory gave him a title, on the understanding that he should continue his course at Oxford. But I have searched the Winchester and Lincoln ordination registers in vain for his name, and previous investigators have searched those of Ely and Worcester. A search of the wills and other old records of the county of Hereford might throw light on the matter.

CHAPTER II

THIS may seem a strange step when we call to mind his after-career. What could possess an excellent scholar, of go-ahead temper and fighting spirit, of unblemished reputation, in the prime of life, endowed with talents of which the world stood in need, to bury himself in a remote village in order to teach little boys? One thing at least it makes plain to us: Tyndale had not yet discovered his life's work. No man in his senses would go from Cambridge to a Gloucestershire country house, if he wished to translate the New Testament. There he would lack books—which were too costly for a poor scholar to buy—and he would lack, what was almost as important in those days, the society of other learned men, with whom he could take counsel and resolve difficulties. Luther, indeed, was even now translating his New Testament in the lonely castle of the Wartburg, but then he had no choice in the matter; and he had to have large volumes sent thither by his friends: nor did he print his version until he had revised it at Wittenberg with the help of Melanchthon and other good scholars. Tyndale's retirement into the country proves up to the hilt the truth of his own statement, which some have doubted, that it was only in Gloucestershire that he formed the resolve to translate the New Testament.

Why then did he go? Perhaps we can read between the lines. He had passed through two universities, and had gained from them all the profit that he was ever likely to gain. He had been slowly feeling his way, acquiring the classical tongues, making himself master of scripture, learning a more spiritual religion than that in which he had been trained. These new truths he must have desired to make known to others, though he cannot yet have seen how far they would lead him. But a man must live. Was he to earn his bread lecturing as a master of arts at Oxford or Cambridge, carrying on the scholastic treadmill which he had learnt to despise? Or was he to play the priest, and perform a round of ceremonies in which he was ceasing to believe? Neither of these things did he desire to do. He was glad to preach, for in that office he could sound those deeper notes which were now ringing in his ears, though they had been too long silent in the church at large. If indeed some post had offered where he could teach Greek or otherwise promote the new learning, we can well believe that he would have accepted it. But such posts—rare at that time—are commonly won by favour as much as by merit, and Tyndale had a certain lonely independence of mind, which was not likely to commend him to the great ones of the earth. A tutorship in Gloucestershire would offer him a refuge and an honourable livelihood; he could teach his little pupils godliness and sound learning, and he would be free to preach as opportunity arose. No doubt the offer of the post came through his brother Edward, who must have been well known all over the county, and who in later years is found sitting on boards and commissions with William's new master, Sir John Walsh.

Little Sodbury Manor, which was now to be Tyndale's home, lies upon the slopes of the Cotswolds, a dozen miles or so south of the family headquarters at Stinchcombe. Its owner was a youngish man of some thirty or thirty-five years, who had been at the court of Henry VIII—he had acted as king's champion at his coronation—and who was now taking a leading place in the county, of which he was to be twice high sheriff. He had strengthened his position by his marriage with Anne Poyntz, daughter of a notable Gloucestershire family, and a distant kinswoman of that Thomas Poyntz who later befriended Tyndale in Antwerp. By her he had several children, and it was these whom Tyndale had now to teach. They were still very young; for at midsummer 1522, the latest date at which we can place Tyndale's arrival, the eldest boy, Maurice, cannot have been more than six or at most seven years old. He was not indeed so young as the little princess Mary, when at the early age of five she received two of the best scholars in Europe as her Latin tutors, but none the less Tyndale's teaching duties cannot have been very burdensome.

This little boy came to a singular end in a dreadful thunderstorm more than thirty years later, after he had himself succeeded to the estate. Sitting at dinner with his family, " a fiery sulphureous globe " came " rolling in at the parlour-door "—so runs the picturesque language of Atkyns, the old historian of Gloucestershire—and passed out through a window on the other side of the room. One child was killed outright, and the father and six others died within two months. But happily such terrible events do not cast their shadows before, and life at the ancient manor-house would go peacefully on its way. We must imagine Tyndale giving a few hours instruction a week to his young charge, teaching him the ABC and the elements of arithmetic, starting him on his Latin grammar, and—a rare thing in those days—telling him bible stories and giving him verses of scripture to learn by heart; taking him also perhaps for walks, rambling over the fields to the big village of Chipping Sodbury a mile distant, or climbing the steep hill against which the manor lies, up to the old Roman camp, where a part of the armies had encamped before the battle of Tewkesbury nearly forty years before, and whence one can look westward over the manor-house into the Welsh mountains, or northward can descry Stinchcombe hill, Nibley knoll and other places familiar to Tyndale's childhood.*

It is clear that with such light duties Tyndale would have a good deal of leisure. No doubt he spent much time in study, for he was ever a man to stick close to his book, and tradition says that his room was situated at the back of the house, looking against the hill. But he also was active in preaching, " specially," says Foxe, " about the town of Bristol, and also in the said town in the common place called

---

* Atkyns' remarkable story is confirmed by Maurice Walsh's will. He made it (he was a widower) on June 7, 1556, mentioning his nine children; added a codicil on June 21; added another codicil on July 18, saying that four daughters and one of his two elder sons were dead. The will was proved on Sept. 28, and the *third* son succeeded to the title and estate.

Saint Austin's green." This last, now called College green, was an open space in front of the Augustinian convent. Now Bristol was fifteen miles from Little Sodbury, and as Tyndale would probably go on foot, each preaching visit thither must have taken no little time. On this matter we would gladly know more, and particularly about the open-air preaching, but Foxe's meagre sentence is all the information we have.

The tender age of his pupils has led some to suppose that Tyndale was chaplain to Sir John Walsh rather than tutor to his children. This in itself would be likely enough: noblemen used in those days often to have resident chaplains, who would not only officiate in the private chapel, but make themselves useful in all sorts of ways. They would act as secretary, draw up documents, give, if need be, a little instruction to the children, perhaps accompany their masters to court; and it has been thought that Sir John, who was rapidly rising in the world, would not be ill pleased to attach to his household in this capacity a distinguished scholar from Cambridge. But if this was the case, why does not Foxe say so? He distinctly mentions teaching and preaching, but says no word of the ordinary work of a chaplain. The private chapel stood in the grounds of the manor a few yards from the building, and it also served the villagers as their parish church. It would certainly seem therefore that the chaplain would either be also incumbent of the parish, of which fact no whisper has reached us in Tyndale's case, or else would have no ecclesiastical duties to perform. We need not doubt that Tyndale preached in the church, as indeed he preached elsewhere in the county, nor that he helped his master in any way he could; but we have seen reason to believe that he was ill at ease in the routine duties of the priesthood, and if this be so, the position of tutor would be more to his taste than that of chaplain. The little chapel, dedicated to St. Adeline, stood until 1859, when, owing to its ruined state, it was pulled down, and rebuilt on the same plan, and partly with the same stones, in the centre of the village. But there still stands beside the great house a solitary arch, that formed part of the western porch of the old building. It is flanked by two noble and ancient yew trees, which must have been well known to Tyndale. Known to him also was the ancient pulpit that is still preserved in a farm house of the village.

We have now to see how it was that he took upon himself the task of translating the New Testament. This decisive turn to his life came not through his duties of preaching or teaching, but through private conversation with the guests at his master's dining-table. Of these conversations and the conflicts to which they led Foxe has left us a graphic account, obtained evidently from a first-hand authority who had it from Tyndale's own lips. This should be read in his first edition of 1563, where it stands in its original form, and not in the later editions, where Foxe has edited it, and combined it with reflections of his own, and with quotations from Tyndale's works. Foxe does not tell us the name of his informant, but he seems to be a Gloucestershire man, and there can be little doubt that Demaus is right in identifying him with Richard Webb, a native of Chipping Sodbury, who a few years afterwards, on the instructions of More, then lord chancellor, was apprehended in Bristol, and summoned to London for examination on the charge of selling heretical books, and who later still became servant to Latimer in his country vicarage in Wiltshire a few miles from Sodbury. In queen Elizabeth's reign he was living in London, and he was certainly known to Foxe; for he supplied him with information about events that had happened in his native town. If this be the man, he may well have been converted by Tyndale himself in 1522. To this highly interesting document we now turn.

" Master Tyndall," it runs, " being in good favour with his master, sat most commonly at his own table, which kept a good ordinary [liberal board], having resort to him many times divers great beneficed men, as abbots, deans, archdeacons, and other divers doctors and learned men. Amongst whom commonly was talk of learning, as well of Luther and Erasmus Roterodamus as of opinions in the scripture. The said Master Tyndall, being learned, and which had been a student of divinity in Cambridge, and had therein taken degree of school,* did many times therein show his mind and learning; wherein as those men and Tyndall did vary in opinions and judgments, then Master Tyndall would show them on the book the places, by open and manifest scripture: the which continued for a certain season . . . until . . . those great beneficed doctors waxed weary, and bare a secret grudge in their hearts against Master Tyndall."

Tyndale was ever a trenchant and formidable antagonist and no respecter of persons; and it is easy to imagine the disgust of the dignitaries at being confronted upon equal terms by this new comer, a whippersnapper from Cambridge, a mere tutor, whose proper place would be at the servants' table. His thorough mastery of the scripture, and his habit of producing the book to clench his arguments must have been very exasperating to men, who were none too sure that they could find their own way about it. However, before long they had opportunity to put a word in Sir John Walsh's ear, when the tutor was not present.

" So upon a time," the story proceeds, " some of those beneficed doctors had Master Welch and the lady his wife at a supper or banquet, there having among them talk at will without any gainsaying; and the supper or banquet being done, and Master Welch and the lady his wife come home, they called for Master Tyndall, and talked with him of such communication as had been, where they came from, and of their opinions. Master Tyndall thereunto made answer agreeable to the truth of God's word, and in reproving of their false opinions. The lady Welch, being a stout woman, and as Master Tyndall did report her to be wise—being there no more but they three, Master Welch, his wife and Master Tyndall:—Well, said she, there was such a doctor, he may dispend [spend] £200 by the year, another £100, and another £300; and what think ye, were it reason that we should believe you before them so great, learned and beneficed men? "

To arguments so solid and palpable as these there was no reply, and Tyndale held his peace, and thereafter spoke but

---

* This is unlikely, cf. page 18. But a countryman, knowing that Tyndale had come to Little Sodbury direct from Cambridge, might easily assume that he had gained his degrees there.

little on such matters, seeing that it would be vain.   But he found a more effective way to open the eyes of his employers. If the young scholar from Cambridge was scoffed at, he would call in an ally of world-wide fame, none less than the great Erasmus himself, the friend of the king of England and of the archbishop of Canterbury, whose Greek testament had received the approval of the pope.

" Then did he translate into English a book called, as I remember, *Enchiridion militis Christiani.*   The which being translated, he delivered to his master and lady; and after they had read that book, those great prelates were no more so often called to the house, nor when they came, had the cheer nor countenance as they were wont to have: the which they did well perceive, and that it was by the means and incensing of Master Tyndall, and at the last came no more there."

We are not to suppose that Sir John was rude to these high dignitaries, or cold-shouldered them from his table; but simply that he became more critical towards them: and they were displeased at finding themselves no longer taken at their own valuation, even more displeased doubtless that they were compelled on each visit to meet the heretic upstart, sitting there at the high table, secure in his master's favour.

This little book, the *Manual* (or *Pocket dagger*) *of the Christian Soldier,* had been written by Erasmus in 1502, at the request of a lady whose husband was a loose liver, and as an instrument to his conversion.   It describes the spiritual armour which the Christian knight should wear, the rules by which he should order his life.   There are indeed things in it which Tyndale afterwards came to reject, yet its whole trend was sharply hostile to the common dogmas and customs of the day.   Biblical quotations abound, the study of scripture is strongly counselled, and the New Testament is made the standard of judgment.   The book hung fire for a time, but then suddenly caught the interest of the world, and was reprinted again and again.   It was bitterly attacked by the priestly party, and so to the second edition in 1518 Erasmus added a long and spirited preface by way of reply.   It was doubtless this second edition that Tyndale rendered into English, and handed to his master and mistress.

But it was not the *Enchiridion* alone that worked the knight's conversion; something must also be ascribed to the character of Tyndale himself. He started with everything against him: he was young, a stranger, without influence, a paid dependent in the house; they were old acquaintance of his master, well settled in the countryside, wielders of ecclesiastical thunders: and yet he remained master of the field. A recent writer speaks of Tyndale as needlessly prickly and quarrelsome at Little Sodbury. Sir John Walsh clearly did not think so, and yet he would have had the greatest right to complain; for it was his table, hitherto theologically peaceful, which was made the arena of the disputes. It speaks well for the depth and simplicity of Tyndale's nature, and for the temper in which he conducted the debates, that he was able not only to hold his ground, but to gain his master's sympathy and support; which he retained until he left the village. All his life through he had a singular power of winning respect. Bigots might rage, men whose privileges he threatened might revile, but plain men of the world, who had no axe to grind, would often come to his aid.

The dignitaries might be checkmated at the manor dining-table, but they were not minded to suffer defeat. They railed upon their enemy in private, and when they assembled in the alehouse—"which is their preaching place," adds Tyndale scornfully—they denounced him as a heretic and embellished what he had said; but they had also a more powerful weapon still: they could inform against him to the authorities of the diocese. This weapon they now brought into play; and Tyndale found himself made a defendant before John Bell, chancellor and archdeacon, at a gathering of the clergy of Gloucestershire.

"After that," continues our document, "when there was a sitting of the bishop's commissary or chancellor, and warning was given to the priests to appear, Master Tyndall was also warned to be there. And whether he had knowledge by their threatening or that he did suspect that they would lay to his charge [*i.e.* whether they had openly threatened to report him, or he merely suspected that they might do so] it is not now perfectly in my mind: but thus he told me, that he doubted their examinations, so that he in his going thitherwards prayed in his mind heartily to God, to strengthen him to stand fast in the truth of his word. So he being there before them, they laid sore to his charge, saying he was an heretic in sophistry, an heretic in logic, an heretic in his divinity, and so continueth [and so on]. But they said unto him: You bear yourself boldly of the gentlemen here in this country, but you shall be otherwise talked with. Then Master Tyndall answered them: I am content that you bring me where you will into any country within England, giving me ten pounds a year to live with, so you bind me to nothing, but to teach children and preach. Then they had nothing more to say to him, and thus he departed, and went home to his master again."

Now it is plain that this accusation of heresy, followed by a threat of removal and by Tyndale's reply thereto, belongs to the scene before the chancellor; but Foxe in his second edition removes it thence, and makes it part of the private recriminations which Tyndale had afterwards to suffer in and around Little Sodbury. This deprives it of meaning. It must have been somebody in authority that threatened to have him moved from the county; no private person would have done this. Tyndale himself says that the chancellor threatened him grievously, and rated him like a dog, and this agrees with the words of Foxe's informant. The latter, however, couples together both the chancellor himself and Tyndale's accusers under the word " they," and fails to make plain—what we learn from Tyndale, and what indeed was the custom of the time—that the accusers remained throughout in the background. They had of course laid their information in private, but it was the chancellor himself who made its content known to Tyndale. Tyndale no doubt would maintain that he had said nothing which he could not justify out of the New Testament, and would demand to be confronted by his accusers. This would put the chancellor in a difficulty; and as he was loth to proceed to extremities, or to do anything to offend the powerful families of Walsh and Poyntz, he would think that the best medicine for this rebellious young man was a severe scolding, with threats of sterner measures to come. Tyndale's reply, that he was ready to live anywhere, provided that his duties were only teaching and preaching, gives us yet another glimpse into his unwillingness for the ordinary work of the priesthood, and strongly confirms the view given above, that he had come to Little Sodbury as tutor and not as chaplain.

When Tyndale had become famous, reports of this scene before the chancellor came to the ears of Thomas More. "Tyndale," he writes in 1529, "was taken for a man of sober and honest living, and looked and preached holily, saving that it sometimes savoured so shrewdly of heresy, that he was once or twice examined thereof. But yet, because he glossed these his words with a better sense, and said and swore that he meant no harm, folk were glad to take all for the best." More is not very accurate here: for no other examination than this is known; while as for the oath, Tyndale in his *Answer* denies point blank that he was even asked to make one: "He sware not," he retorts, "neither was there any man that required an oath from him." *

Tyndale had escaped the hands of his enemies, but the danger was only deferred. It was as certain as anything could well be, that unless he consented to muzzle himself, they would return to the attack, and no friends would be powerful enough to save him; indeed, they might but compromise themselves. Yet he could not bring himself to make terms with the ignorance and bigotry around him. Of his peril he received a warning from an old friend, a clergyman, living in the neighbourhood.

* John Bell (afterwards bishop of Worcester) became chancellor, or vicar-general, of the diocese, and also archdeacon of Gloucester, in 1518. He remained chancellor till August 17, 1526 (W. Thomas, *Survey of Worcester Cathedral*, p. 205; *L. & P.* III. 2178, IV. 1962; *Journal of Prior William More*, ed. E. S. Fegan, p. 11). Modern books wrongly say that Tyndale's chancellor was either Thomas Parker (who succeeded Bell in 1526) or William (Parker) of Malvern, abbot of Gloucester. Bell was active in the examination of the Steelyard Lutherans in the early months of 1526, and is then described as the "official," *i.e.* vicar-general, of Worcester.

" There dwelt not far off an old doctor, that had been archchancellor to a bishop, the which was of old familiar acquaintance with Master Tyndall, who also favoured him well : to whom Master Tyndall went, and opened his mind upon divers questions of the scriptures; for he durst boldly open unto him his mind. That ancient doctor said : Do you not know that the pope is the very antichrist, which the scripture speaketh of ? But beware what ye say, for if ye shall be perceived to be of that opinion, it will cost you your life : and said, I have been an officer of his, but I have given it up, and defy him and all his works."

But here the worthy doctor scarcely knew his man. His counsel might be excellent for them that could receive it, but it was of little use to our William, who was no trimmer, and who could never dissemble his thoughts for long.

The name of this ancient counsellor is unknown, but there is some likelihood that he was William Latimer, the humanist, the friend of Erasmus and More, who, after travelling in Italy, returned to Oxford about 1492, and was teaching there during part of Tyndale's period of residence. In 1523 he would be over sixty years of age, and we know that during the latter part of his life he held two livings in the north-east of Gloucestershire, Saintbury and Weston-sub-Edge.* It is true that they were some forty miles from Little Sodbury : still Tyndale may well have made a special journey to see him. Among his various preferments it is probable enough that he had held one which might be loosely described as an archchancellorship to a bishop, and his advice to his young friend tallies with what is known of his character—honest, kindly, scholarly, but lacking the high resolve and the heroic fires out of which apostles are made.

But if the hostility of the priests was likely to cut short Tyndale's sojourn in Gloucestershire, a plan was meanwhile maturing in his own brain which made it doubly desirable to depart. As he reflected on his experiences of the last few months, and on the deep offence that he had given, he saw that the root cause lay in ignorance of the scriptures. Neither clergy nor laity perceived what a wide gulf yawned

---

* Not Wotton-under-Edge, as some writers say.

between the religion of the day and that of the New Testament. The laity had no chance of knowing this, for they could not read the Latin bible; and the clergy were taught to wrest the text from its true meaning, in order to bolster up the current teaching. One thing alone could open the eyes of the people, and that was to read the scripture in English for themselves. What if he were to give them a translation? And thus it came about that William Tyndale began to discover his life's work; perhaps somewhat late in the day, for he was now at least twenty-eight years old.

That Tyndale does not over-state the ignorance of the clergy of the day, is proved by overwhelming evidence. It was one of the stock complaints of the middle ages. In 1222, for example, a visitation at Salisbury revealed the fact that five out of seventeen incumbents could not translate the words of consecration in the mass. Nearly three hundred years later Warham complains of the Canterbury monks, that when performing divine service they "are wholly ignorant of what they read." There was next to no inquiry into the learning or capacity of candidates for ordination. It sufficed that they could repeat certain prescribed formulas, and one very rarely hears of a man being rejected for lack of knowledge. In Gloucestershire the standard was assuredly not above the average: for there is extant a record of the visitation of its clergy, held by bishop Hooper in 1551. Out of 311 clerks examined 10 could not say the Lord's prayer; about 30 could not name its author or tell where it was written; 170 could not repeat the ten commandments; and although almost all could say the creed, two-thirds of them could not support its statements even fairly well out of the scriptures. Nor can the standard have been higher when Tyndale was at Little Sodbury: for the new learning had had less time to make its influence felt, and the clergy had not yet the vernacular bible from which to draw instruction.

In the last anecdote of our document we see our hero with his mind made up.

" Soon after, Master Tyndall happened to be in the company of a learned man, and in communing and disputing

with him drove him to that issue, that the learned man said:
We were better be without God's law than the pope's.
Master Tyndall, hearing that, answered him: I defy the
pope and all his laws; and said: If God spare my life, ere
many years I will cause a boy that driveth the plough shall
know more of the scripture than thou dost."

These famous words are an echo of those written in
1516 by Erasmus in the exhortation prefixed to his Greek
testament:

" I vehemently dissent from those who are unwilling that
the sacred scriptures, translated into the vulgar tongue,
should be read by private persons. Christ wishes his
mysteries to be published as widely as possible. I would
wish even all women to read the gospel and the epistles of
St Paul, and I wish that they were translated into all
languages of all Christian people, that they might be read
and known, not merely by the Scotch and the Irish, but
even by the Turks and the Saracens. I wish that the
husbandman may sing parts of them at his plow, that the
weaver may warble them at his shuttle, that the traveller
may with their narratives beguile the weariness of the way."

Erasmus himself was not master enough of any living
tongue to make a vernacular translation, but he prepared
the way thereto by giving to the modern world its first
Greek text of the New Testament, together with a Latin
version of his own. On the basis of this Greek text Luther
had in September 1522 published his German testament;
and Tyndale, possibly before the news of Luther's achievement had reached his ears, now determined to render the
same service to his native land.

But where was he to carry out the work? At Sodbury he
would not be safe long, neither could he command the helps
that he would need. But indeed could he hope to do it with
safety anywhere within the realm? For did not the constitution of Oxford, passed in 1408 against Lollardism, forbid
any man on his own authority to translate the scripture,
under pain of punishment as a heretic? There was only
one way to arm oneself against this stringent law; an
episcopal patron must be found to take the responsibility of
the enterprise. To what bishop should he apply? Fisher

he may possibly have met at Cambridge, where he was chancellor of the university; but his sermon at the burning of Luther's books in London, and his harsh treatment of the hapless Norman, who at Cambridge made a public protest against indulgences, were not such as to raise the hopes of any would-be translator. Longland, recently appointed bishop of Lincoln, had been known to Tyndale at Oxford; but to him too it was useless to apply, as his episcopal career had already proved. In this dilemma, however, he bethinks himself of the new bishop of London, Cuthbert Tonstall, a man still under fifty, an excellent scholar and a generous patron of scholars, liberal in outlook (so it was said), favoured by the king and commended by the great Erasmus; surely this man might be expected to welcome the prospect of an English testament. To him therefore he would go and tell him his desire, bringing with him also a proof of his competence, and would ask permission to reside as chaplain in his palace while he performed his task.

But let us hear Tyndale tell the story of these months himself. In the preface to his Pentateuch (1530), speaking of the hatred of the priests for the scripture, and of the false interpretations by which they throw dust in the eyes of the laity, he proceeds:—

" Which thing only moved me to translate the New Testament. Because I had perceived by experience, how that it was impossible to stablish the lay people in any truth, except the scripture were plainly laid before their eyes in their mother tongue, that they might see the process, order and meaning of the text. . . . And even in the bishop of London's house I intended to have done it. For when I was so turmoiled in the country where I was, that I could no longer there dwell (the process whereof were too long here to rehearse) I this wise thought in myself:—This I suffer because the priests of the country be unlearned, as (God it knoweth) there are a full ignorant sort, which have seen no more Latin than that they read in their portesses and missals [two service books], which yet many of them can scarcely read; . . . and therefore, because they are thus unlearned, thought I, when they come together to the alehouse, which is their preaching place, they affirm that my sayings are heresy; and besides that, they add to, of their own heads, things which I never spoke, as the manner is to prolong the tale to shorten the time withal, and accuse me secretly to the chancellor and other the bishop's officers. And indeed when I came before the chancellor, he threatened me grievously, and reviled me, and rated me as though I had been a dog, and laid to my charge whereof there could be none accuser brought forth, as their manner is not to bring forth the accuser; and yet all the priests of the country were that same day there. As I this thought, the bishop of London came to my remembrance; whom Erasmus (whose tongue maketh of little gnats great elephants, and lifteth up above the stars whosoever giveth him a little exhibition) praiseth exceedingly, among other, in his annotations on the New Testament, for his great learning. Then thought I, if I might come to this man's service, I were happy. And so I gat me to London."

But first he must obtain his master's leave to depart. " Sir," he said, " I perceive that I shall not be suffered to tarry long here in this country, nor you shall be able to keep me out of their hands; and what displeasure you might have thereby, is hard to know; for the which I should be right sorry." Sir John Walsh consented, and knowing the way of courts and the mind of bishops, gave him a letter of introduction to Sir Henry Guildford, the king's controller of the household, and till lately master of the horse, who might be able to smooth his way to the episcopal favour. With this, and with a speech of Isocrates which he himself has turned from Greek into English, he sets forth, bidding farewell to his master—not without regret, we may be sure; for his master has stood nobly by him. But he sees before him his guiding-star; he has found his life's work, to give the word of God to his countrymen; and to this all personal claims must yield. And so he sets out for the capital, turning his back upon his home county, which he was never more to behold, bidding farewell to his kinsfolk and old friends, and arrives in London about the month of July 1523.

LITTLE SODBURY MANOR 1875

CHAPTER III

TYNDALE arrived in London at a time of great political turmoil. It was the year of Henry VIII's fourth parliament, the only parliament which Wolsey suffered to be summoned between 1515 and the year of his own fall. Nor would this have been summoned had not hard necessity driven him on. The great minister, having dissipated his master's fortunes on two needless wars, had now embarked upon a still more wanton campaign, and he must screw money somehow or other out of an unwilling people. The parliament had met in April, and Wolsey had gone down in person to the House of Commons, and demanded a subsidy of £800,000, which was equivalent to a tax of four shillings in the pound on all property in the kingdom. The Commons resisted furiously, but Thomas More, their speaker, threw his influence on the side of Wolsey; and after bitter debates half the sum demanded was voted, but the payment was to be spread over two years. At the same time convocation, summoned by Wolsey's own writ, who thus overrode the authority of the archbishop of Canterbury, was forced to grant a heavy tax on every benefice in the country. Meanwhile the town was seething with excitement. Wolsey himself had become the best-hated man in the kingdom. His upstart origin, his fierce ambition and overweening pride, his enormous and ever-growing wealth, his more than oriental luxury, his insolence to the nobility, his intrusions upon the diocesan authority of the bishops, his unblushing pluralism and accumulation of pensions, his scandalous private life, his perpetual papal legacy, which, since it was wielded on the spot, made him a more bitter burden upon the people than any pope sitting in Rome had ever been, his unscrupulous foreign policy, which for years had made England the tool of other states and sacrificed English blood and treasure to promote papal interests and to smooth his own path to the papal chair—all these things had been kindling the fires of indignation and raising up enemies on every side. And now to these was added the engineering of a new war, where no English interests were involved, and the peremptory demand for unheard-of financial sacrifices, the like of which, said Thomas Cromwell, had never before been granted. Nevertheless on this occasion he weathered the storm; and having secured all the subsidy that he could extort from the Commons, he, after a decent interval, advised his master to dissolve parliament on August 13, a week or two, probably, after Tyndale's arrival in London.

All this might seem to have little to do with religion, but in fact the ecclesiastics were very much to the fore. To begin with, Wolsey was an archbishop and a cardinal, and derived much of his authority from his papal legacy; and the war that he was promoting was supposed to be for the benefit of the pope. Then, many of the chief offices of the state were held by clerks, and it was a bishop who delivered the king's speech to parliament. In the House of Lords also, the spiritual peers, though they no longer dominated the assembly, were about equal in numbers with their lay brethren, and wielded far greater power than they do to-day. Even in normal times the prelates had palaces in London, and were usually to be found there, bent upon business or pleasure, but now, with parliament and convocation in session, the higher clergy—bishops, chancellors, deans, canons, abbots—would be present in force. In a word, the church, no less than the state, was showing its full grandeur; and we can well imagine that the young Tyndale, who had likely never been in the capital before, drank it in with all his eyes and ears.

But the first thing to be done was to put his plan into execution. He therefore called on Sir Harry Guildford, and showed him his translation of Isocrates: for Guildford, though his life had been passed in kings' courts and in the field of battle, was something of a scholar, and had been a correspondent of Erasmus. The great man received him kindly, and promised to speak on his behalf to Tonstall. He fulfilled his promise, as he later informed Tyndale, and we may suppose that he obtained a not unfavourable reply; for he advised his client to write to the bishop and ask for an interview. Tyndale therefore wrote a letter, and took it in person to the episcopal palace in St. Paul's churchyard, and delivered it into the hand of a servant of the bishop, one William Hebblethwaite, whom he had himself known in past years—at Oxford or Cambridge, we may suppose. How long these negotiations took we are not told, but it seems that, for one reason or another, there was difficulty in obtaining the interview, and that several weeks elapsed before the summons came. It is likely that Tonstall was full of the duties of parliament and convocation, together with the business of the court and of his see, and was not disposed to put himself out for an unknown applicant from the country, whose business, if he had been informed of it by Guildford, had a rather suspicious look. However at last the summons came, and Tyndale presented himself at the palace. This would be about the month of September.

Tonstall was at this time a man of some forty-nine years of age. He had studied abroad, was acquainted with Greek and Hebrew, had mastered mathematics and the law, and had a year ago published a book on arithmetic, which was to become the standard work for a generation. He belonged to the circle of humanists, and had won the friendship and admiration of Erasmus, More and Warham, with the first of whom he had lodged, when in Brussels in 1516. Thomas More in his *Utopia* calls him "a man doubtless out of comparison," and to Erasmus he was one of the ornaments of the English court. "Our age," he writes, "does not possess a more learned, a better, or a kinder man. I seem not to be alive, now he is taken from me." The bishop's known friendship with such men as these, and his high repute as a scholar, might seem to Tyndale to favour his project: but there was another side to Tonstall. He had a rather smooth and accommodating nature, and was not the man to take up an unpopular cause, or to renounce the world for conscience' sake. In recent years he had been drawn more and more into the service of the crown. He had served as master of the rolls, and had been employed on diplomatic missions abroad. He was now keeper of the privy seal, and only lately he had delivered the king's speech at the opening of parliament before a splendid company. In such a man caution and worldly wisdom were more likely to rule than a glowing enthusiasm.

It may be that Tyndale did not make the best of himself at the interview. In a letter to Frith ten years later he describes himself as " evil favoured in this world, and without grace in the sight of men, speechless and rude, dull and slow witted." Such a man might well be ill at ease in the presence of a courtier and man of the world, and might even appear little better than a boor. But in truth the gulf between the two men was far deeper and wider than one of manner only. However brief the conversation, Tyndale's ruthless sincerity and directness, burning with zeal, ready to risk all so that he accomplish his task, must have grated on the bland and polite humanist. Here was a man of whom there was no saying what he might do, save that he would not be prudent, and would speak out instead of letting sleeping dogs lie. The state of affairs was delicate, and a false step might ruin a man's career, or even bring him to the block. Lutheranism was advancing daily in Germany, and it was proving none too easy to check the influx of heretical books into England. True, a bonfire had been made of them a couple of years ago at Paul's Cross, but still they came; and this year it was even reported that Cambridge university was seriously infected with the poison. Vernacular translations of the scriptures had always been suspect by the church, and any bishop who in these times threw the mantle of his patronage over such an enterprise, would be certain to win the hostility of his brethren, and would be made answerable for any harm that ensued. Luther's German testament had not yet been a year from the press, and already it was being attacked as false and as a breeder of heresy. Why should Tonstall, only just settled into his bishopric, compromise himself for the sake of a total stranger, who had no claim on him whatsoever? So the bishop must have felt deep down in his heart, as he listened to the story of his awkward guest; and because he felt thus, he made the great refusal, and turned his back upon the call of glory.

But let us hear Tyndale's own narrative.

" I gat me to London, and through the acquaintance of my master came to Sir Harry Guildford, the king's grace's controller, and brought him an oration of Isocrates, which I had translated out of Greek into English, and desired him to speak unto my lord of London for me: which he also did, as he showed me, and willed me to write a pistle to my lord, and to go to him myself; which I also did, and delivered my pistle to a servant of his own, one William Hebblethwaite, a man of mine old acquaintance. But God, which knoweth what is within hypocrites, saw that I was beguiled, and that that counsel was not the next way unto my purpose. And therefore he gat me no favour in my lord's sight. Whereupon my lord answered me, his house was full, he had more than he could well find [support], and advised me to seek in London, where he said I could not lack a service."

We are not to suppose that Tonstall was discourteous to his visitor; he was merely cool and reserved and evasive: and Tyndale felt instinctively that he was being put off with a pretext, and that the bishop could have helped him, if he would. It was a bitter disappointment, and Tyndale never forgot it. In his *Practice of Prelates* he speaks scornfully of Tonstall's cold and stiff manner, describing him as a " still Saturn, that so seldom speaketh, but walketh up and down all day musing, a ducking hypocrite made to dissemble." *

Such language has been held by one writer to betoken a lack of charity in Tyndale, but before consenting to this charge, we should at least try to enter into his feelings. The men of that day were by no means squeamish in their speech, and in the religious combat both parties freely bandied about the words hypocrite and pharisee, where we merely say that a man is inconsistent with his principles. To the eyes of the reformers the medieval system was a piece of hypocrisy; and if hypocrisy means to play a part, to make professions without

* George Constantine speaks of Tonstall's " stillness, soberness and subtlety " (*L. & P.*, 1539, II. p. 141).

acting on them, to carry out forms from which the living spirit has departed, it is hard to quarrel with the description. Besides, ought not Tonstall, on his own principles, to have bestirred himself in the matter of the translation? He was not asked to be the chief doer, only a helper. He was a bishop, and so pledged to make known the gospel to the simple of Christ's flock; he was a humanist, and so should have cared for the spread of knowledge. The work proposed was a good one, and it would be well performed, as the history of the English bible bears witness. To Tyndale, hazarding his life for the cause of God, this prudent dignitary, sitting aloft and secure, unwilling to risk anything at all, must have seemed like the men of Meroz, who came not to the help of the Lord against the mighty. Nor was this all: Tyndale was writing seven years later, when Tonstall had shown his full hand. He had not merely held back from the enterprise; he had become its bitter opponent. He had vilified the New Testament, burnt it at Paul's Cross, and filled his prisons to overflowing with its readers. At the interview he had been polite and non-committal, and perhaps had even thrown a crumb or two of half-commendation to his visitor, and yet all the time he kept these cruel weapons in the background ready for use. We can hardly wonder therefore that Tyndale branded him as a dissembler and a hypocrite. His judgment would have been even sterner, could he have foreseen that within a dozen years Tonstall would lend his name to the fourth edition of the Great Bible, and would permit a volume, whose New Testament was Tyndale's version almost unaltered, and whose Old Testament contained a big fraction of his doing, to go forth into the world, carrying upon its title page the words: " Overseen and perused, at the commandment of the king's highness, by the right reverend fathers in God, Cuthbert [Tonstall] bishop of Durham, and Nicolas [Heath] bishop of Rochester." Well had it been for Tonstall, had he plucked up his courage to share the dangers of the battle, instead of falling into line when all was easy, and when stouter souls had borne the burden and heat of the day.

Yet in fairness to the bishop one thing must be added.

Unlike pope Clement VII, who said that heretics themselves ought to be burnt instead of their writings, Tonstall, while eager enough to burn the books, seems to have desired to spare the men any punishment more severe than imprisonment. In his London episcopate, indeed, his powers of extreme action were gravely hampered by Wolsey's encroachments on the diocesan authority of the bishops; but thirty years later, in the dark days of the Marian terror, when nearly three hundred persons went to the stake within three years, it stands to Tonstall's credit that not one is known to have perished in his northern diocese of Durham. At that time, when pressed by his chancellor to examine further a preacher who had been brought before him, he replied: " Hitherto we have had a good report among our neighbours; I pray you, bring not this poor man's blood upon my head." Perhaps the cruel scenes which he had witnessed, and the memory of his own frailties, and of the shifts and turns to which he had been driven in holding his ground, had softened him. But let us at least pay him this tribute: inglorious as his behaviour to Tyndale was, there were more ruthless men than he; a reformer had less to fear from him than from Stokesley, Longland, Gardiner or Thomas More.

Some writers, however, have doubted whether Tyndale ever informed the bishop of his desire to translate the New Testament: for in his short account of the interview the exact nature of his request is not specified, and Tonstall's reply only mentions the chaplaincy, and not the translation. But the doubt is needless. Tyndale had shown his Isocrates to Guildford, and must therefore have spoken of his plan to him. What he did to the go-between, he would surely do to the chief party. In all likelihood Guildford himself had revealed it to Tonstall. Besides, it was only by getting the bishop's full consent that he could hope to ward off the prohibitions of the constitution of Oxford. To translate unbeknown in the palace would be of little use to him; the mere translating was illegal, let alone the printing; only active episcopal support could lend him any security.

Nevertheless the rebuff was a blessing in disguise, as Tyndale himself came to see. Had he entered the bishop's service, the disappointment would only have come later. His patron would have proved a broken reed, and when the storm began to rage, would have risked nothing to protect him. His New Testament would have been burnt, perhaps before publication instead of after, and Tyndale himself would have earned the martyr's crown several years earlier than he did, and with most of his work undone.

What was to be the next step? Tonstall had assured him that he could find work in London. This was true. Work of a kind would be easy for so able a man to obtain, if he were content to follow the old lines, and to give up his cherished project. But this he could not do. Where could he find a post that would enable him to translate the bible, and to work for the reform of the church? If the bishop of the diocese rebuffed him, would the lower clergy be more sympathetic, or if sympathetic, could they protect him against attack? Things looked black; and meanwhile he was a poor man, and must find some means of supporting himself. Happily he had already made a friend in the town, to whom he could turn. This was Humphrey Monmouth, a wealthy cloth merchant, dwelling in the parish of All Hallows Barking, whose mind for some years had been moving towards reform. He was a kindly and generous man, and of him Latimer relates a pleasing story, which he had heard at Cambridge from a common friend.

A great merchant in London had a very poor neighbour, whom he loved well, lent him money in need, and welcomed to his table at all times. About the time when dean Colet was in trouble for heresy [about 1512], " the rich man began to be a scripture-man," he began " to smell the gospel." The poor man, offended at what he now heard at the other's table, came no more to his house, borrowed no more money, and even accused him before the bishops. The rich man made many advances, but to no purpose; his friend would not speak to him, and when he met him in the street, turned out of the way. At length they chanced to meet in a lane so narrow, that they must perforce pass at close quarters. The poor man was minded to brush forward without speaking, but the rich man caught him by the hand, saying:— Neighbour, whence is this displeasure against me? What have I done to you? Tell me, and I will be ready to make amends. The poor man, overcome by this gentle and loving greeting, fell on his knees, and begged forgiveness, and they loved one another as well as ever they did afore.

Such was the man whom Tyndale had made his friend. While waiting for Tonstall's summons to the palace, he had preached a number of sermons in the church of St Dunstan-in-the-West, Fleet Street. Here Monmouth had heard him, and had afterwards happened to make his acquaintance. How Tyndale obtained this preaching engagement, we cannot tell. The then rector was Thomas Green, M.A., and Tyndale may have known him at Oxford or Cambridge. Or it has been suggested that the introduction, both to the rector and to Monmouth, may have been the work of Thomas Poyntz, who was a kinsman of Lady Walsh, and who later became Tyndale's host and stout supporter in Antwerp. Certainly Poyntz was buried at St Dunstan's forty years later, despite the fact that his family home was in Essex, and being a merchant and a member of the grocers' company, he was likely known to Monmouth. Nevertheless, attractive though this theory is at first sight, it cannot be reconciled with Monmouth's own account of his meeting with Tyndale. A rich man, who had been asked to interest himself in a poor stranger, might invite him to his house, or send him letters of commendation, but would hardly go three miles to hear him preach, in order to introduce himself. Besides, if Poyntz was Tyndale's earliest friend in London, and he had been requested by Lady Walsh to take him under his wing, why did Tyndale not turn to him in his extremity instead of to Monmouth? *

The meeting between Monmouth and Tyndale was an important one to both men. To Tyndale it meant the raising up of a helper in a day when he sorely needed one; to Monmouth it was the beginning of trials which, though a mere nothing compared to those which his friend was to endure, brought upon him suspicion, loss of fortune, and even imprisonment. For, four and a half years later, he was

* On the Poyntz family see *Incidents in the Lives of Thomas Poyntz and Richard Grafton* (J. A. Kingdon, 1895, privately printed).

arrested by order of the council on the charge of Lutheranism, examined by Sir Thomas More and others, and thrown into the Tower. There on May 19, 1528, in the presence of Tonstall, he signed a petition to Wolsey and the council, excusing himself upon the charge of heresy, protesting the ruin which was likely to overtake his business, and begging to be released. As the most important article against him was the succour that he had given to Tyndale, he describes at some length the occasion and the course of their friendship. To this invaluable document, still extant in the British Museum, we will now turn.

" They examined me . . . what exhibition [money] I did give to anybody beyond the sea. I said, None in three years past. . . . I told them, in four years past I did give unto a priest called Sir William Tyndal, otherwise called Hotchens. . . . Upon four years and a half past and more I heard the foresaid Sir William " (priests in those days were often addressed as Sir) " preach two or three sermons at St Dunstan's-in-the-West in London: and after that I chanced to meet with him, and with communication I examined what living he had. He said he had none at all, but he trusted to be with my lord of London in his service: and therefore I had the better fantasy to him. And afterward he went to my lord, and spake to him, as he told me, and my lord of London answered him that he had chaplains enough, and he said to him that he would have no more at that time. And so the priest came to me again, and besought me to help him, and so I took him into my house half a year; and there he lived like a good priest, as me thought. He studied most part of the day and of the night at his book, and he would eat but sodden meat by his good will, nor drink but small single beer. I never saw him wear linen about him in the space he was with me [i.e. but only woollen]. I did promise him £10 sterling to pray for my father and mother their souls and all Christian souls; I did pay it him when he made his exchange to Hamborow [Hamburg]. Afterwards he got of some other men £10 sterling more, the which he left with me; and within a year after, he sent for his £10 to me from Hamborow; and thither I sent it him by one Hans Collenbeke, as I remember is his name, a merchant of the Steelyard; and since I never sent him the value of one penny, nor never will."

Whether Tyndale preached any more sermons at St
Dunstan's, we know not; but it seems plain that he lived for
these six months at Monmouth's expense. It was a pleasing
habit of those times for rich men to offer hospitality to poor
scholars, nor was there any indignity in accepting it. It
had indeed its bad side, and Erasmus' begging letters to
noblemen and their friends sometimes grate upon us, but
when it was based on sympathy and esteem, and when the
scholar was in real need, the practice was nothing but good;
and we in these days, with our hard independence and unwillingness to owe anything to anybody, have lost, as well as
gained, something. In Tyndale's case all was noble. He
desired nothing for himself, he was giving up all for his
mission; Monmouth approved his project, and was able out
of his abundance to give him a refuge and a breathing space,
while he could consider what was next to do.

We may be sure that Tyndale kept his eyes and ears open
in Monmouth's house. His host was a man of the world.
He had a flourishing business, and big merchants would be at
his table. He had travelled to Rome and to Jerusalem, and
had received pardons from the pope. He was a religious
man, and was acquainted with prominent clergymen,
several of whom he had generously helped with exhibitions.
In this house Tyndale would have excellent opportunities
of hearing what was going on in the world, and of learning
the thoughts and opinions of men in general. Much also
he would see with his own eyes, as he went about the town:
the wealth and pride of the bishops and abbots, the grandeur
of the church rites, the poverty of the people, the interference
of ecclesiastics in secular matters, the crushing of the
simplicity of the gospel under a load of formalism. What
(he would ask himself) had he in common with this? Was
there any hope for him here? His New Testament was bound
to give offence; for it would strike at the abuses of the day;
it would be banned and destroyed, and he himself would
perish at the stake. With so strong a government, under a
single control, escape would be difficult; and the constitution of Oxford gave persecution the form of legalism. But
on the continent the prospect was better. The empire was a

unity in name only, and the single states were often powerful enough to defy the emperor's commands; what was forbidden in one part, could be done with impunity in another. Nay, the standard of revolt had already been openly raised by Luther, and though he was under the imperial ban, the new opinions were dominant in Saxony and one or two other districts. Abroad bibles might indeed be burnt in practice, but the mere translation seems not to have been a legal offence. Besides, an obscure Englishman, working away at a language that was not understood, would be likely to be unmolested. The art of printing also was far more advanced in Germany. Printers abounded; and they were exceedingly enterprising, and had already shown a healthy independence in publishing books that were forbidden or disapproved by the church. Of all this he would hear from German merchants of the Steelyard, which stood where Cannon Street station now lies, many of whom were strongly tinged with Lutheranism. From one of them he may even have obtained a copy of the new German testament.

And so the great decision was taken. Tyndale would forsake his land for the gospel's sake, and do his work overseas. No doubt he talked it over with his kind host, and with any others whom he felt that he could trust. A great difficulty was the need of money; he must live while the translation was making; he must have funds for travelling and for the purchase of books. But here his friends came to his aid, and smoothed his path. Monmouth gave him £10 on his departure; he had promised it to him before, to pray for the souls of his parents and of all other Christians. The stipulation may have been only a delicate way of putting money into his friend's pocket, but it is quite likely that Tyndale had not yet broken with masses for the dead, or at least that he was trying to give a new meaning to the customary rite. At any rate the money was only paid when he sailed, and when the need of it became urgent. The other £10 may have come from merchants, who thought the New Testament would prove a profitable article of trade in England. Besides ready money, he must also have received promises for the future; for when the printing began more than a year later, there were English merchants ready to guarantee the costs.

But Tyndale's own account of his London stay must be completed. After describing his rebuff in the palace he proceeds:—

"And so in London I abode almost a year, and marked the course of the world, and heard our praters (I would say our preachers) how they boasted themselves and their high authority, and beheld the pomp of our prelates, and how busied they were, as yet they are, to set peace and unity in the world . . . and saw things whereof I defer to speak at this time; and understood at the last, not only that there was no room in my lord of London's palace to translate the New Testament, but also that there was no place to do it in all England, as experience doth now openly declare."

On departing he would take with him his bibles and New Testaments in whatever tongues, but he left in the charge of his host the sermons which he had preached in St Dunstan's, and also a copy of the *Enchiridion* in English, in his own translation. Of the latter Monmouth possessed also a second copy, seemingly made for him by his servant, and he showed the book to several priests, who found no fault with it. At length he sent Tyndale's copy to the abbess of Denny in Cambridgeshire, who had desired to see it, and she seems not to have returned it; the other copy was given to a friar of Greenwich, who likewise had asked for it, and it was then seized by bishop Fisher. "I think my lord of Rochester hath it," writes Monmouth. The sermons, together with the letters written by Tyndale from Germany, and certain other Lutheran books, Monmouth burnt in his own house some two and a half years later, after the public burning of the English New Testament at Paul's Cross, and when Tyndale's name had become odious to the English authorities. "I did burn them," he says frankly, "for fear of the translator more than for any ill that I knew by them."

And so Tyndale went forth into exile, bidding a last farewell to his native land, the first of a long line of English reformers to seek refuge abroad. He was content to be without his country, that he might serve his country. He goes not for his own sake, but to safeguard the great work committed to his trust; and the wisdom of the step was abundantly proved by after events. He sails therefore for Hamburg in April or May 1524, some four years before the date of Monmouth's petition.

But we must hear the end of Monmouth. He was released from the Tower, but at the price of abjuring his opinions. Later he became alderman of the city of London, and then sheriff, and in the year 1537 he died, a few months after his friend. His will shows the strength of his sympathy for reform; for in it he speaks against the bishop of Rome, and leaves a sum of money, with the direction that during the months following his burial thirty sermons are to be preached in his parish church of All Hallows by the four reformers, Latimer, Barnes, Crome and Taylor, two of whom afterwards perished at the stake. This was an original variation on the customary trentals, or thirty masses for the soul of a dead man. The best way, Monmouth now thinks, to honour and help the dead is to serve their brethren, who are still struggling in the world.

CHAPTER IV

WE left Tyndale on the way to Hamburg. Within a year he sends from that city to London for the £10 which he had left in the keeping of his friend. This would be about April 1525. Where had he been in the meanwhile? One might naturally suppose that he remained at Hamburg, and so some modern writers maintain: but all ancient authority, whether friendly or hostile, asserts that he went to Wittenberg. He is even said to have had as companion at Wittenberg that William Roye who later assisted him with the printing of his New Testament.

Thus in 1528 Monmouth was charged with having helped " Sir Williams Hutchins, otherwise called Tyndall, and friar Roye, or either of them," to go " into Almayne [Germany] to Luther, there to study and learn his sect "; and this charge Monmouth does not deny in his petition. The following year Sir Thomas More, who had been one of the examiners of Monmouth, says in his *Dialogue* that " Tyndall, as soon as he gat him hence, got him to Luther straight," and that, while he translated the New Testament, " Hychens was with Luther in Wittenberg, . . . and the confederacy between Luther and him is a thing well known, and plainly confessed by such as have been taken and convicted here of heresy, coming from thence." Next, Cochlaeus, who in the autumn of 1525 came upon the trail of Tyndale and Roye in Cologne, whither they had brought the finished New Testament, describes them as " two apostates from England, who had learnt the German tongue at Wittenberg." Lastly, Foxe tells us that " on his first departing out of the realm, Tyndall took his journey into the further parts of Germany, as into Saxony, where he had conference with Luther and other learned men in those quarters." These four lines of testimony are somewhat vague, yet they agree upon the main point.

But we are told that Tyndale himself denies the visit to Wittenberg. If so, that settles the matter: but what does he say? To More's statement, quoted above, he replies: " When he saith Tyndall was confederate with Luther, that is not truth." He denies that he was confederate with Luther, not that he had visited him. Indeed all the probabilities are in favour of the visit. At Wittenberg the reformers were in control, and were backed by the elector of Saxony: there a man might work in peace and safety. At Hamburg he would be at the mercy of the papal party, who ruled the town and held back the triumph of the reformation for five more years. Hamburg was merely a trading centre; Wittenberg had an university, and offered all the helps that a scholar might need. There he would find books and libraries; there he could take counsel with Melanchthon professor of Greek, Aurogallus professor of Hebrew, Bugenhagen (Pomeranus) rector of the town church, and other learned men. Above all, there was Luther himself, no mean scholar, and one that had lately performed the very task which Tyndale had in his mind. That Luther was present in Wittenberg throughout this year, we know from the evidence of his own letters. Independent as Tyndale ever was, it would be strange if he did not desire to meet the great captain, who had braved the might of pope and emperor, and had successfully raised the standard of reform. Young men were flocking to Wittenberg; it was (so duke George of Saxony complained) " the common asylum of all apostates." Thither went in later years Tyndale's friends Barnes and Rogers; it is at least likely that he should go too.

But I am happy to be able to lay before the reader evidence —hitherto overlooked, though it has been in print for ninety-five years—which all but settles the matter. In the registers of the university of Wittenberg we read that *Guilhelmus Roy ex Londino*, William Roye of London, matriculated on June 10, 1525, more than a year after Tyndale's departure from England. So far, so good: but where is Tyndale's name?

One searches for it in vain; can he have resided in the town without matriculating? But stay! A year earlier a name meets our eyes, which at once awakens our interest. This is Matthias von Emersen of Hamburg, nephew to the widow Margaret von Emersen who entertained Tyndale five years later, when he visited that city. This young man matriculated on May 30, 1524; and in close neighbourhood to him, under date May 27, stands the name *Guillelmus Daltici ex Anglia*, William Daltici from England. Who is this?

It was Dr Reincke, the director of the Hamburg Staats-archiv, who suggested to me that William Tyndale lay here concealed. Indeed, it was he that brought to my notice the above entries in the matriculation lists: for up till then I had taken for granted that the Wittenberg registers had been thoroughly searched by the investigators of a hundred years ago. I felt at once that he was right; for the date exactly tallies with Monmouth's narrative: nevertheless for two days I could give no explanation of the name Daltici. I could not trace it as a place name, or a family name, or a Christian name. Its form seems not at home in English, or Latin, or in any other tongue that Tyndale was likely to use. But suddenly it flashed upon me that by reversing the two syllables of *Tindal* you get *Daltin*, which only differs from *Daltici* by one letter. The present register is but a copy of the original, and if the copyist misread the final letter, all becomes clear. In those perilous times it was common enough for men to disguise their names. Robert Barnes is entered in the Wittenberg register of 1533 as *Antonius Anglus*, though his real name was added in the margin by Melanchthon.

We must imagine, then, Tyndale staying a day or two in Hamburg with the Emersen family, who had likely been recommended to him by a merchant of the Steelyard, and then travelling with Matthias, either by horse or up the Elbe by boat, to Wittenberg. There he remained nine or ten months, probably till the end of the winter university term, and about April returned to Hamburg, to send for his money from England. By that time his New Testament must have been nearly completed. It was quick work, yet not so quick as Luther's, which in five months was ready for the printing. But Tyndale had to learn German, before he could avail himself of Luther's version and other German books of scholarship; and he was also less fortunate than Luther in having no one of his own race with whom to discuss questions of English idiom: for in the university lists no other English name appears during this year.* When sending to London for his £10, he no doubt wrote also to the merchants who had promised to bear the expense of the printing. It would be a month or more before he could receive the answers to his letters, and meanwhile he would lodge with the Emersen family.

But together with his letter to Monmouth, Tyndale sent what his London friend describes as "a little treatise": Monmouth burnt it eighteen months later along with his other Lutheran books and manuscripts. What was this? It has raised much discussion. Many have held it to be a work of Tyndale's own, and in particular an English translation of the gospels of Matthew and Mark, printed perhaps at Wittenberg, which is said to have been circulating in England before the complete New Testament appeared: but these reports, as we shall see, can be otherwise explained; and in any case Monmouth would hardly call the two gospels a treatise. There is a much simpler solution. Why may it not have been Bugenhagen's *Letter to the English*, the first greeting of the German reformers to England? This was printed in 1525, and was certainly a little treatise; for it contained only a dozen octavo pages. "We could not but rejoice, dear brethren," begins Bugenhagen, "when we heard that in England also the gospel of the glory of God has a good report. But we were also informed, that many have turned away from it" because of slanderous stories against us and our way of living. Know therefore, that whatsoever ye may have heard, and however simple minds may be puzzled and confused by the flood of controversy, we have only one doctrine: Christ is our righteousness.

---

* In the work of translation, said Luther, *unus vir nullus vir*, one man is no man. So Purvey says he had "many good fellows and cunning at the correction of his translation."

Such was the theme. It is true that we do not know the
month of its publication, but it cannot have been late in
the year; for three Latin and three German editions are
extant, all bearing date 1525, and Cochlaeus implies that
it preceded Luther's letter of September 1.* It is even
likely that Tyndale had a hand in the making thereof:
for according to Roye's little book of rhymes, of which we
shall hear more, the letter was written by request.
" Pomeran's epistle " he calls it; " Who by Christian men
required, According as he was desired, Did his part them [the
English] to instruct." Now this request can hardly have
been made by letter from England; for in that case it would
have been addressed to Luther or Melanchthon : it must have
come from some Englishman in Wittenberg, and we know of
none during the early months of 1525 save Tyndale. We may
suppose, then, that Tyndale sent either the printed Latin
copy, or else an English version in manuscript made by himself for the benefit of his friend : to whom it would be of
extreme interest.

There may also be traces of Tyndale's influence in
Luther's letter to Henry VIII, written at the persuasion of
the ex-king of Denmark, of which the first draft seems to
have been made in May, though it was not published till
September 1. Luther is excusing himself for his violent
onslaught against the king, and explains that he had been
misled by false information.

" I am told," he writes, " by trustworthy people, that the
little book against me [Henry VIII's treatise on the seven
sacraments, which won him his title of defender of the faith]
so far beneath the dignity of the king of England, was not
really written by you, as those crafty sophists dare affirm.
They surely do not know the danger of thus dishonouring
your royal name, and bringing into notice the monstrosity,
hated of both God and man, the cardinal of Eborack [York],
the destroyer of your majesty's kingdom."

This attack on Wolsey as the ruin of the kingdom reminds
us of Tyndale's language later on; and he may well have

* Otto Vogt (*Bugenhagen's Briefwechsel*, p. 583) places it under the
month February, on what grounds I know not.

been one of the trustworthy people spoken of: for the belief that the king was not the author of the pamphlet that went forth under his name, was widely held in England at the time.

Having received his packet from England, Tyndale travelled back to Wittenberg, and there was joined by Roye about the beginning of June, unless indeed he had met him at Hamburg, and returned in his company.* Roye was a friar observant of Greenwich. Several of the brethren of this convent were known to Monmouth, and no doubt it was Monmouth who sent him abroad to join Tyndale. He proved a troublesome companion, zealous indeed, but hot-headed, shallow and untrustworthy. Tyndale's account of him three years later, in the preface to his *Mammon*, is as follows:—

" While I abode [awaited] a faithful companion, which now hath taken another voyage upon him, to preach Christ where I supposed he was never yet preached (God, which put in his heart thither to go, send his spirit with him, comfort him, and bring his purpose to good effect), one William Roye, a man somewhat crafty when he cometh into new acquaintance, and before he be thorough known, and namely [especially] when all is spent, came unto me and offered his help. As long as he had no money, somewhat I could rule him ; but as soon as he had gotten him money, he became like himself again. Nevertheless I suffered all things till that was ended, which I could not do alone without one both to write, and to help me to compare the texts together. When that was ended, I took my leave, and bade him farewell for our two lives, and, as men say, a day longer."

Who this faithful companion was, whom Tyndale had appointed to follow him abroad, it is impossible to say. The description fits none of his known friends. But whoever he was, he was unable or unwilling to travel overseas, and Tyndale had to put up with Roye.

It may be that Tyndale had at first intended to print at Wittenberg, but this was too far inland for convenient transport to England. Hamburg might seem more favourable,

* It is likely that Tyndale was at Wittenberg at the time of Luther's marriage on June 13.

being a great seaport with constant communication with England, but printing here was in a backward state, and though there had been printers on and off for thirty or forty years, no permanent house had yet been established. It was clearly desirable to find some great centre, in easy touch with the ports and markets, where the art was flourishing and streams of books were being turned out. In the end Tyndale decided to make trial of Cologne, which was on the waterway of the Rhine and near to the great book-market of Frankfort. As Cochlaeus puts it, Cologne was chosen in preference to Wittenberg, because it was " nearer to England, more frequented by commerce, and more convenient for transport by boat."

The two companions arrived in Cologne about the month of August. The Rhine districts, like the rest of Germany, had been much disturbed through the peasants' war; but by midsummer the worst of the tumults had subsided. At Cologne a printer was found willing to undertake the work; and this is usually supposed to be Peter Quentel. The printing began, and all seemed to be going well, when an enemy interposed and put a stop to the enterprise. This was John Dobneck, commonly called Cochlaeus, a shallow and conceited man, a bitter foe to the reformation, who considered it his mission in life to attack Luther, and who flooded the world with his pamphlets. Lately he had been dean of St Mary's church in Frankfort, but was driven thence by a popular rising in April. Fleeing to Mainz, he was again dislodged from the same cause, and came to Cologne. Once more he found himself in danger; for here too the commons rose against the ecclesiastical authorities, and for a fortnight were in control of the city. By the end of June, however, the prince-archbishop had regained command, and restored order. Cochlaeus, though invited back to Frankfort, refused to return to so ungrateful a city, and he remained in Cologne almost a year; and while there, he happened upon the track of Tyndale and Roye.

How it came about, he has himself narrated in full. Indeed, he has left three accounts of his exploit, but the first two, written in 1533 and 1538, are very short, and it is only in the third, composed twenty-four years after the event, that he gives us the full story. It is of the highest interest. It occurs in a history of Luther, which he wrote three years after the reformer's death—bitterly hostile, as need hardly be said. He is describing in strong terms the impudence of Luther's letter to Henry VIII, and as an aggravation of his offence he brings in the story of the attempt to publish the English New Testament, an enterprise which he evidently ascribes to Luther's instigation :—

" Two English apostates, who had been some time at Wittenberg, not only sought to ruin (*subvertere*) their own merchants, who were secretly encouraging and supporting them in their exile, but even hoped that, whether the king would or not, all the people of England would shortly become Lutheran, by means of Luther's New Testament, which they had translated into the English tongue. They had come already [*i.e.* before September 1, when Luther wrote his letter], that they might through the printing-press multiply by many thousands the testament thus translated, and convey it thence secretly under cover of other merchandise to England. Such was their confidence of success, that at the first onset they asked the printers for an edition of six thousand. The printers however, fearing that if any mishap occurred, they would suffer very heavy loss, put only three thousand to press; and if these were happily sold, they could easily print afresh. Already Pomeranus had sent his letter to the saints in England, and Luther himself had also written to the king; and the Lutherans, believing that the New Testament would soon follow, were filled with such delight at the prospect, and so puffed up with vain confidence, that in their uncontrollable joy they made known the secret before its time."

Cochlaeus then goes on to relate how he himself was seeking to print some works of Rupert of Deutz, who four hundred years before had been abbot of the monastery on the other side of the Rhine. These were still in possession of the abbey, and the Lutherans were in process of printing them. To forestall this, Cochlaeus went to Peter Quentel, the chief printer in Cologne, and to Arnold Byrkman, the great bookseller, and begged them to publish the works, sharing the expense between them; and this they finally undertook to do, but only on condition that he himself did the editing of them.* It was while he was visiting the printing house on this errand, that Cochlaeus heard of the English New Testament.

" Having thus become more intimate and familiar with the Cologne printers, he heard them sometimes boast confidently in their cups, that, whether the king and cardinal of England would or no, the whole of England would soon be Lutheran. He heard also that two Englishmen were lurking there, learned and skilled in languages and fluent, whom however he never could see, nor speak with. He invited therefore some of the printers to his lodging, and when they were heated with wine, one of them in more private talk revealed to him the secret, by which England was to be brought over to the side of Luther. There were, he said, in the press three thousand copies of the Lutheran New Testament, translated into English, and the work had already advanced as far as the letter K in the order of the sheets (*quaterniones*) ; the expenses were being abundantly supplied by English merchants, who, when the work was printed, were going to convey it secretly into England, and would disseminate it unbeknown through the whole of the country, before the king or the cardinal could discover or prohibit it.

" Cochlaeus, though inwardly astonished and horrified, disguised his feelings under a show of admiration. But the next day, gloomily weighing with himself the greatness of the danger, he cast in mind how he might best checkmate that abominable plan. He went therefore secretly to Hermann Rinck, a senator of Cologne and a knight, who was a friend both to the emperor and to the king of England, and a counsellor, and he disclosed to him the whole thing, as he had heard it by the help of the wine. Rinck, in order to make the matter certain, sent another person to make an investigation in the house, where the work was being printed according to Cochlaeus' report. Understanding from him that the thing was even so, and that a great quantity of paper was lying there, he went to the senate, and obtained a prohibition on the printers against proceeding further with the work. The two English apostates, seizing the printed sheets, fled up the Rhine by ship to Worms,

* The books survive. The house of Byrkman bore the expense, Cochlaeus wrote some of the prefaces, but no printer's name is given.

where the people was under the full rage of Lutheranism, in order to complete the work there by another printer. Rinck however and Cochlaeus at once wrote letters to the king and the cardinal and the bishop of Rochester [Fisher], warning them to keep the strictest watch in all the ports of England, lest that most pernicious merchandise should be imported into the country."

When we read this account, we see what good reason Tyndale had for his complaints against Roye. It would be Roye who gossiped needlessly with the printers, throwing out defiance against king and cardinal, and pluming himself on a speedy triumph. It would be Roye who chattered to strangers about the sources of their income and the interest of the merchants in England. Tyndale, fierce and outspoken as he could be, was not the man to endanger a delicate enterprise by boasting and ostentation. The nature of the two men appears also in the treatment which they returned to the enemy who had defeated them. Tyndale never speaks of him at all, but Roye takes his revenge a couple of years later by devoting a stanza to Cochlaeus in his little book of rhymes:—" Cochlaye, A little praty foolish poad; But although his stature was small, Yet men say he lacketh no gall, More venomous than any toad," and therefore (he adds) sure to be in favour with Wolsey and the bishops, and to get a benefice before long. Cochlaeus himself, however, was far from gratified with the recompense which his exploit received. He complains bitterly of the ingratitude of the king. He had rendered him as great a service as Mordecai to Ahasuerus, he had saved the realm of England by disclosing a plot against its peace and welfare, he had written a private letter of warning to Henry, he had dedicated to him one volume, and presented to him another, of the works of Rupert of Deutz, and yet he received no letter at all of acknowledgment, and was allowed to languish in exile and misery without aid.

Of this Cologne edition only a single fragment remains. For a long time it was thought to have completely perished, or even never to have existed, but in 1834 a London bookseller discovered it bound up with a treatise of Oecolampadius, and sold it to Thomas Grenville, who bequeathed it with his splendid library to the British Museum. It is a quarto, and it contains only signatures *A* to *H* (viz. St Matthew i–xxii) instead of the *A* to *K* spoken of by Cochlaeus. The title page is lost, so that it bears no date nor place of printing, but internal evidence demonstrates that it was printed in Cologne. The ornamental *Y* with which the prologue opens, and several other letters, are found in books issued by Quentel about this time. Above all, the fragment contains a woodcut of St Matthew, dipping his pen into an inkpot held by an angel, which is identical with that found in Rupert of Deutz' commentary on the same gospel, published by Quentel for Cochlaeus in June 1526. But in the Deutz it has been slightly cut down, which proves decisively that the fragment is the earlier of the two books.*

Everything therefore points to Quentel as the printer. Nevertheless in recent years the bibliographers have been flirting with another candidate, Hiero Fuchs, also of Cologne, but of less renown. The sole ground of this reversal is that Fuchs is believed to have had Lutheran sympathies, while Quentel was more loyal to the papal cause. When it is asked, how then Quentel obtained the woodcut of St Matthew, the reply is made that the senate, finding that the translators were fled with the printed sheets, seized the type and the plates of Fuchs, and handed them over, or sold them, to his rival. But of this Cochlaeus says no word; he simply says that further printing was forbidden; and the natural meaning of his story certainly is that the drunken printers were employees of Quentel. The religious views of the two men need not be taken into account at all. Printers were business-men, not theologians, and would think twice before refusing a good offer from a customer who could pay. In 1525–6 Quentel printed three little books of Luther's making. In 1528 he printed Bugenhagen's low-German version of Luther's New Testament. In 1524 he had published

---

* The woodcut is used again, in its mutilated form, in two Latin bibles, printed by Quentel in 1527 and 1529, and in a German New Testament (Emser's version) of 1529, printed by Fuchs at the expense of Quentel.

another low-German version of the same book, but this time
Fuchs had done the printing. Quentel was fond of sending
his work to Fuchs and other smaller men, and it is possible
that he did this with Tyndale's New Testament: but that
is the utmost that can be conceded. Unless more direct and
pointed evidence can be discovered, the publisher, if not the
printer, of the Cologne fragment must be adjudged to be
Peter Quentel.*

Let us now turn to the fragment itself. It opens with a
prologue:—

> "I have here translated, brethren and sisters most
> dear and tenderly beloved in Christ, the New Testament
> for your spiritual edifying, consolation and solace,
> exhorting instantly and beseeching those that are
> better seen in the tongues than I, and that have higher
> gifts of grace to interpret the sense of the scripture and
> meaning of the spirit than I, to consider and ponder my
> labour, and that with the spirit of meekness. And if
> they perceive in any places that I have not attained the
> very sense of the tongue or meaning of the scripture,
> or have not given the right English word, that they put
> to their hands to amend it, remembering that so is their
> duty to do: for we have not received the gifts of God for
> ourselves only, or for to hide them, but for to bestow
> them unto the honouring of God and Christ, and
> edifying of the congregation, which is the body of Christ.
>
> "The causes that moved me to translate I thought
> better that other should imagine than that I should
> rehearse them. Moreover I supposed it superfluous:
> for who is so blind to ask why light should be showed to
> them that walk in darkness, where they cannot but
> stumble, and where to stumble is the danger of eternal
> damnation, or so despiteful that he would envy any man
> (I speak not his brother) so necessary a thing, or so
> bedlam mad to affirm that good is the natural cause of
> evil, and darkness to proceed out of light, and that
> lying should be grounded in truth and verity; and not
> rather clean contrary, that light destroyeth darkness,
> and verity reproveth all manner lying.
>
> "After it had pleased God to put in my mind, and

* See the lists of books in *Niederdeutsche Bibliographie* (C. Borchling
and B. Claussen, 1931).

also to give me grace, to translate this fore-rehearsed
New Testament into our English tongue, howsoever we
have done it, I supposed it very necessary to put you in
remembrance of certain points."

Then follows a long discourse upon law and gospel, nature
and grace, Old Testament and New. This is on the lines
of the introduction to Luther's New Testament, nearly half
of which is quoted almost verbatim, but Tyndale adds very
largely to it, so that in the end the borrowed matter amounts
only to about one eighth of the whole. In the portion
supplied by Tyndale himself occurs the famous sentence,
which so scandalized the favourers of the pope, and was held
up as a horrible example of Tyndale's depravity: " If I
live chaste [unmarried] I do it not . . . that I look for an
higher room in heaven than they shall have which live in
wedlock, or than a whore of the stews (if she repent); for
that were the pride of Lucifer; but truly to wait on the
evangelion, and to serve my brother withal." Yet this
passage is in full line with the New Testament. The critics
had forgotten the parable of the pharisee and the publican,
had forgotten the woman in the city who was a sinner; and
the fact that so decent and liberal a man as Tonstall was
horrified to think of a celibate saint equalling himself with a
penitent harlot, sheds a shining light on the formal and
unspiritual religion of the day.

After the prologue comes the table of the books. This is
given in Luther's order, with Hebrews, James, Jude and the
Revelation at the end. Then follows the woodcut of St
Matthew, and then the text itself. This is accompanied by
two sets of notes or glosses, on the outer and inner margins,
which borrow largely from Luther. Of the inner list, which
are merely references to parallel passages, nearly the whole,
190 out of 210, are Luther's; of the outer list—annotations
on the text, about 90 in number—more than half are
borrowed in substance, if not in language. The division
into the paragraphs is also as a rule the same. Thus it
will be seen that at first sight there was a good deal of
colour for the charge so frequently levelled against Tyndale,
that his New Testament was merely a translation of Luther's.

Here one thing must be firmly said. There is a legend, repeated by writer after writer, that the antagonism to Tyndale's New Testament was caused, not by the text itself, but by the biting and venomous glosses with which it was accompanied. Now certainly the prologue and glosses were violently denounced at the time, but so was the translation. But where are these biting glosses? I cannot find them in the Cologne fragment. Most of the notes merely explain or illustrate the text: *e.g.* " Racha is the hoarse sound in the throat, and betokeneth all signs of wrath " (Matthew v. 22): " No man should avenge himself, or seek reek, no, not by the law; but the ruler, which hath the sword, should do such things of himself, or when the neighbours of love warn him and require him " (Matthew v. 39). The only note with a touch of sharpness is that on Peter's confession in Matthew xvi, which, after urging to read Bede, Augustine and Jerome on binding and loosing, goes on :—

" Note how Jerome checketh the presumption of the pharisees of his time, which yet had not so monstrous interpretations as our new gods have feigned. Read Erasmus' annotations. . . . The evangelion, that joyful tidings, is now bitterer than the old law. Christ's burthen is heavier than the yoke of Moses, our condition and estate is ten times more grievous than was ever the Jews'."

In the prologue too there is only one sentence of the same kind : " of which things," writes Tyndale, " the belief of our papists, or of their father, whom they so magnify for his strong faith, hath none experience at all." This is mild compared to some of Erasmus' notes to his New Testament. The prologue and glosses are indeed Lutheran in tone, but they are not biting. Those who affirm that they are, are confounding the glosses of the New Testament with those of the Pentateuch, published four years later. These are certainly very much sharper : but by that time the New Testament had long ago been denounced as heretical, and committed to the flames. In fact, it was the very injustice with which his first noble work had been treated, that stung Tyndale into using more cutting language.

If Tyndale had published his New Testament without a

single note of any kind, his fate would have been exactly
the same.   It is quite a mistake to suppose that the hierarchy
would have approved of the circulation of the text by itself.
All through the middle ages, when there was any question
of vernacular translations—whether by Waldensians, or by
Wycliffites, or by whomsoever it might be—the cry was
always raised from the official church, that the " bare text "
of scripture was bound to mislead the people, that it needed
explaining if it were to be understood aright; and when in
1582 the papal party brought out the Rheims New Testament, they loaded it with marginal notes.   Tyndale
therefore, in putting glosses in the Cologne fragment, was
simply taking his enemies on their own ground.   They did
not indeed like his glosses; but they would not have been in
the least pacified, had he dispensed with them.

The warning of Cochlaeus was not the only one which
Henry VIII received.   Cochlaeus was no doubt greatly
excited by his discovery, and talked freely of it; and in a
few weeks the news had reached the ears of Edward Lee, the
king's almoner, afterwards archbishop of York, who had
been appointed ambassador to Spain, and was travelling
slowly thither through France.   On December 2 he wrote
from Bordeaux to the king:—

" I am certainly informed, as I passed in this country, that
an Englishman, your subject, at the solicitation and instance
of Luther, with whom he is, hath translated the New Testament into English, and within a few days intendeth to arrive
with the same imprinted in England.   I need not to
advertise your grace what infection and danger may ensue
hereby, if it be not withstanded.   This is the next way to
fulfil your realm with Lutherans.   For all Luther's perverse
opinions be grounded upon bare words of scripture, not well
taken nor understanded, which your grace hath opened in
sundry places of your royal book [against Luther].   All our
forefathers, governors of the church of England, hath with all
diligence forbad and eschewed publication of English bibles,
as appeareth in constitutions provincial of the church of
England [the constitution of Oxford].   Now sir, as God hath
endued your grace with Christian courage, to set forth the
standard against these Philistines, and to vanquish them, so
I doubt not but that he will assist your grace to prosecute

and perform the same, that is to undertread them, that they shall not now again lift up their heads, which they endeavour now by means of English bibles. They know what hurt such books hath done in your realm in times past. Hitherto, blessed be God, your realm is safe from infection of Luther's sect. . . . Blessed be God, your noble realm is yet unblotted. Wherefore, lest any danger might ensue if these books secretly should be brought in, I thought my duty to advertise your grace thereof, considering that it toucheth your high honour, and the wealth and integrity of the Christian faith within your realm; which cannot long endure, if these books may come in."

But we must now follow Tyndale and Roye to Worms. Here in 1521 Luther had so bravely faced the imperial diet, and in the last few months the town had gone over to the Lutheran cause. Close concealment therefore would not be so necessary; Roye's bragging and chattering would do less harm. All seems to have been plain sailing; a printer was engaged, and the first printed English New Testament saw the light of day. It meant no little labour for Tyndale and Roye; they would have to be constantly at the printing house; for the printers, being ignorant of English, would need much assistance and overlooking. The work would take several months. The printing of Luther's first testament—an edition, it is thought, of five thousand copies—took about four months, although two presses were working on it simultaneously, and for the last six or seven weeks a third was added. By this rate, if we suppose that Tyndale reached Worms late in September, the printing could hardly be finished before the end of February. And this tallies with the earliest notices of its presence in England. John Pykas, a baker of Colchester, charged with heresy, deposed on March 7, 1528 that "about a two years last past he bought in Colchester of a Lombard of London a New Testament in English, and paid for it four shillings"; and on April 28 of the same year John Tyball of Steeple Bumpstead in Essex confessed that "about two years ago" he showed the book to the curate of his village. Probably the first copies reached England about the end of March.

Of the printing at Worms we know nothing whatever,

save for a faint echo that reaches us several months later from the neighbouring city of Speyer. Here the imperial diet assembled in the summer of 1526, and was attended by the elector of Saxony, who took with him his secretary Spalatin, the friend of Luther. Spalatin kept a diary, and in it he describes a supper party given on August 11, at which one of the guests was the humanist Hermann von dem Busche, part-author of *The Letters of Obscure Men.*

" Buschius told us," he writes, " that at Worms six thousand copies of the New Testament have been printed in English. The work has been translated by an Englishman, staying there with two other Britons, who is so skilled in seven tongues, Hebrew, Greek, Latin, Italian, Spanish, English, French, that whichever he speaks, you would think it his native tongue. For the English (said Buschius), despite the opposition and unwillingness of the king, so long after the gospel, that they affirm that they will buy the New Testament, even if they must pay 100,000 pieces of money for it."

Buschius had evidently been recently at Worms and met Tyndale. Who the two Britons were, it is impossible to say. Roye can hardly be one; for according to Buschius the printing was finished, and by that time he and Tyndale would have parted. Probably they were newcomers from England, who had fled to the continent for their beliefs. One may well have been Thomas Hitton.

But though we know nothing of Tyndale's life at Worms, we have the book itself. It survives in two copies, one, imperfect at the beginning and the end, in St Paul's library, the other in the Baptist college at Bristol, complete save for the loss of its title-page. This last is the greatest treasure of all English printed bibles. Its existence has been known for two hundred years, but its value was not at first recognised. Lord Oxford gave 10 guineas for it in the first half of the eighteenth century, then it was sold for less than £1, and at length it came into the hands of a learned divine, a librarian at the British Museum, who bequeathed it to its present owners. That it was printed at Worms is undoubted; for its type and some of its watermarks and woodcuts are found in books issued by Peter Schoeffer of that city, son of the pioneer printer of Mainz; and to his press therefore it is confidently ascribed.

The Worms New Testament differs markedly from the Cologne fragment. It has indeed the same text, save for a few trifling corrections, but it is smaller in size, an octavo instead of a quarto. It lacks also the long prologue and the two sets of glosses. In a word, it gives merely the plain text of the scripture, save that a short epistle to the. reader is added at the end of the book. This is so beautiful that it must be quoted almost in full.

> " Give diligence, reader, I exhort thee, that thou come with a pure mind, and as the scripture saith, with a single eye, unto the words of health and of eternal life: by the which, if we repent and believe them, we are born anew, created afresh, and enjoy the fruits of the blood of Christ. . . . Mark the plain and manifest places of the scriptures, and in doubtful places see thou add no interpretation contrary to them; but, as Paul saith, let all be conformable and agreeing to the faith. Note the difference of the law and of the gospel. . . . Apply the gospel, that is to say the promises, unto the deserving of Christ and to the mercy of God and his truth, and so shalt thou not despair, but shalt feel God as a kind and a merciful father; and his spirit shall dwell in thee, and shall be strong in thee, and the promises shall be given thee at the last. . . .
>
> "Them that are learned Christianly I beseech— forasmuch as I am sure, and my conscience beareth me record, that of a pure intent, singly and faithfully I have interpreted it, as far forth as God gave me the gift of knowledge and understanding—that the rudeness of the work now at the first time offend them not; but that they consider how that I had no man to counterfeit [imitate], neither was holp with English of any that had interpreted the same or such like thing in the scripture beforetime. Moreover even very necessity and cumbrance (God is record) above strength, which I will not rehearse, lest we should seem to boast ourselves, caused that many things are lacking, which necessarily are required. Count it as a thing not having his full shape, but, as it were, born afore his time, even as a thing begun

rather than finished. In time to come, if God have
appointed us thereunto, we will give it his full shape,
and put out, if aught be added superfluously, and add
to, if aught be overseen through negligence, and will
enforce [take care] to bring to compendiousness that
which is now translated at the length, and to give light
where it is required, and to seek in certain places more
proper English, and with a table to expound the words
which are not commonly used, and show how the
scripture useth many words which are otherwise understood of the common people, and to help with a declaration [explanation] where one tongue taketh not another;
and will endeavour ourselves, as it were, to seethe it
better, and to make it more apt for the weak stomachs,
desiring them that are learned and able, to remember
their duty, and to help thereunto, and to bestow unto
the edifying of Christ's body (which is the congregation
of them that believe) those gifts which they have
received of God for the same purpose. The grace that
cometh of Christ be with them that love him. Pray for
us."

One might have thought that the simplicity and modesty of
this address would have softened the heart of even the
bitterest foe: but it was not so; they were soon after him
like a pack of hounds.

But how is the alteration in the form and content of the
book to be accounted for? The simplest explanation, and I
believe the true one, is that Tyndale, arriving at Worms
with the printed sheets, decided to abandon the quarto, and
to begin a new edition on another plan. It may be that
Schoeffer was unwilling to carry on another man's work,
or that he had no fount of type to match that of the Cologne
fragment. Still even so there was nothing to hinder him
from beginning the quarto afresh with other type. He can
hardly have disapproved of the prologue and glosses. Even if
he knew enough English to read them, German printers were
used to much stronger meat than this. No doubt it was
Tyndale who decided the matter. Having lost both time
and money at Cologne, it was plain wisdom to put in hand
only what was urgent, to print the text and get it off his
hands, before his enemies could attack him a second time,

or Roye could break out into some indiscretion. If this be the case, the six thousand copies of which Buschius speaks will all belong to the octavo, though it is just possible that he may be loosely including the three thousand copies of the Cologne fragment.

Simple as this view is, it has met with little favour from the experts, who maintain that there were *two* New Testaments circulating in England in 1526–7, one big, the other small, one with glosses, the other with a plain text. Assuming that the small one is likely to have had the plain text, we obtain a book like the Worms octavo; while the big one with glosses will resemble the Cologne quarto, if it had been completed. The traditional view therefore is that Tyndale completed the Cologne fragment at Worms, or perhaps began it afresh from the start, and that thus he issued two editions of the whole New Testament and not one.

Now if Tyndale really did this, he did a very surprising thing. Why should a man who had just had a severe setback, and to whom both time and money were of value, go out of his way to print two editions, when one would do? If he was so wedded to his glosses that he could not give them up, it was easy to print a quarto edition of six thousand copies on the lines of the Cologne fragment. But since he did elect to print an octavo, it is hard to believe that he should double his labours and expenses at a very critical time by setting up his book anew. Besides, it does not agree with his own words at the opening of his Pentateuch four years later:—" When I had translated the New Testament, I added a pistle unto the latter end, in which I desired them that were learned to amend, if aught were found amiss." The only New Testament here spoken of is the octavo, and yet the Cologne fragment contains the very same request in its prologue. Why too does Joye omit all mention of the quarto, when in his *Apology* of February 1535 he reproaches Tyndale with his slowness in revising his New Testament? Tyndale (he says) had promised a revision " at the end of his first translation," and he describes this first translation as one printed " about eight or nine years ago . . . in a mean [middling] great volume, without kalendar, concordances [references] in margin, and table at the end." This description exactly fits the Worms octavo.

What then is the evidence on the other side powerful enough to overweigh these improbabilities? In the first place we have certain general descriptions of the New Testaments circulating in England, which are thought to imply an edition with glosses. Thus when Tonstall on October 24, 1526, orders his archdeacons to call in copies of the offending book, he distinguishes them as " printed, some with glosses, some without glosses, as we have heard, *ut accepimus*." A month or two later Henry VIII, in the English preface to his reply to Luther, speaks of the New Testament as containing " certain prefaces and other pestilent glosses in the margins "; and Monmouth was charged in 1528 with aiding the translation and introduction of the New Testament, " as well with glosses as without glosses." * But these descriptions are very vague, and may be only a brief way of linking the Cologne fragment with the Worms octavo, both of which were entitled The New Testament. Neither Henry VIII nor bishop Nix, who was eighty years old and almost blind, is likely to have studied the books for himself; in fact, even Tonstall confesses that he is speaking partly from hearsay, though he at least must have had a testament of some kind in his house, since he preached against it a week later at Paul's Cross.

It so happens, however, that we can check Tonstall's words by a letter of his chaplain, Robert Ridley, uncle of Nicolas Ridley the martyr, written a few weeks later to the chaplain of archbishop Warham. The date is February 24, 1527, and the theme is the iniquity of the English New Testament " done by Mr William Hichyns, otherwise called Mr William Tyndale, and friar William Roy, manifest Lutherans, heretics and apostates." Ridley has examined Tonstall's copies of the translation, and he appeals to them throughout in support of his own statements. He distin-

---

* Cf. Nix on p. 120. So also More (*Works* 221):—" At the time of this translation Hychens was with Luther in Wittenberg, and set certain glosses in the margin, framed for the setting forth of the ungracious sect."

guishes two books only:—" the first print, with annotations
upon Matthew and Mark and the preface "; and " the
second print," which he describes as " the text of the
gospel," and to which also he attributes a preface. From
the preface to the first print he adduces several passages,
that are all found in the Cologne fragment, including that
of the penitent harlot; from the second print he alleges a
number of mistranslations in the gospels and epistles. Thus
his first print agrees with the Cologne fragment, save that it
includes Mark as well as Matthew; and his second print
agrees with the Worms octavo, save that he gives it a prologue instead of an epilogue. The last error is probably due
to memory; for he states that he has not the books before
him now, but that he is writing of what he remembers to
have read in them. At any rate Ridley appears to
know nothing of any complete New Testament with
glosses.

We now turn to what at first sight seems a far stronger
piece of evidence for the Worms quarto. This is the confession of Robert Necton, an active distributor of the New
Testament in London and the eastern counties, who was
thrown into jail by Tonstall in 1528. The month is not
given, but it is evidently May or June. Necton tells the
story of his traffic in these books, and distinguishes two sizes,
the " great " or " biggest " volume, which he began to buy
about December 1526, and sold at prices varying from 1/8
unbound to 2/8 bound, and the " small " volume, which he
bought after Easter 1528. Now it has usually been supposed
that Necton's " great volume " was the Worms quarto, and
" the small volume " the Worms octavo: but there was a
third rival now in the field. This was the pirate edition,
printed at Antwerp by Christopher van Endhoven in
autumn 1526, and described by Joye as a " small volume."
Necton's " small volume " is clearly Endhoven's reprint;
and this becomes a certainty, when we discover, from a piece
of evidence that has been strangely overlooked, that the
Antwerp merchant, Richard Herman, who supplied Necton's " great volume," was sending the Worms octavo to
England.

Only one difficulty now remains. What are we to make of
that translation of the first two gospels, which is said to have
been circulating in England before the New Testament?
When Robert Necton owns to having possessed first of all
" the chapters of Matthew," we are not surprised: for we see
at once a mention of our Cologne fragment. Nor are we
surprised, when Foxe tells us in Daye's folio that Tyndale,
" when he placed himself in Germany, did there first translate the gospel of St Matthew into English, and after the
whole New Testament." But what does Robert Ridley
mean by quoting from our Cologne fragment, and calling it
by the names of Matthew and Mark? And what means
John Tyball by confessing to Tonstall on April 28, 1528, that
about two years ago he had " the gospel of Matthew and
Mark in English " beside the New Testament? The solution
is perhaps not far to seek. When Cochlaeus sounded the
drunken printers, the New Testament had advanced as far
as the signature K, that is to say, up to about the middle
of Matthew xxvii. Two or three days more of labour
would bring it well into the second gospel. We have only to
suppose that the senate did not intervene at once, and all
becomes clear. Hermann Rinck would certainly move
cautiously in a matter that touched so prominent a citizen
as Quentel; the senate too may not have been at the
moment in session; or its members may have been divided,
and some may have asked why it was necessary to take
stronger measures against an English testament than
against a German. All these reasons would make for delay,
and meanwhile the printing would proceed. If the fragment had advanced to about the second chapter of St Mark
when it was cut short by authority, it could be described
with rough accuracy by the name either of one gospel or of
two.

Thus, despite one or two minor errors in our authorities,
the whole hangs together. We can bid a long farewell to
the Worms quarto, that faint and elusive phantom, which
pops up every now and again, but always slips from our
grasp. Tyndale only printed one New Testament at Worms,
the octavo edition of which two copies remain; but being

unwilling to lose his labour on the Cologne fragment, he decided to send this also to England, a little in advance of the complete book, as a herald of its coming.*

Note to p. 64. The sentence quoted as the only sharp thing in the prologue to the Cologne fragment does not (I now find) belong to it. Walter prints it as part of the prologue, but in fact it was added some years later, when the prologue was issued as a tract; cf. p. 203. Thus Tyndale's tone is even milder than I stated.

---

* The full evidence is given in Appendix C. The Worms octavo has been reprinted by G. Offor (1836), and, in facsimile, by F. Fry (1862). In Offor's book the spellings are not always trustworthy. The Cologne fragment has been printed in facsimile by Arber (1871) and A. W. Pollard (1926).

CHAPTER V

(1) *The Need.*

We have now to examine the translation itself: but before
we do so, one question demands attention. Was there need
for a new version? Were the churchmen of the day so
totally without the English bible as Tyndale makes out?
Or was he not rather magnifying his work by depicting the
prelates as much more hostile to the scripture than they
really were? To such questions, repeated by those who
desire to belittle the work of the reformers, it might be
enough to reply that a man would scarcely exile himself,
and suffer persecution and death, for a mere fantasy of his
imagination. But we will not be content with an answer
of this nature, true though it may be, but will look a little
deeper into the merits of the case. The chief facts are
undisputed.

Up to the time of the Norman conquest there seems to
have been no attempt to forbid the englishing of the bible.
The bishops were not, indeed, very zealous for translation,
and took no steps to supply an official version; but still
they put no hindrance in the way of pioneers. Portions of
the bible were rendered into Anglo-Saxon by Caedmon,
Bede, king Alfred and others. Not all of these were strictly
translations; some were adaptations in verse, and others
were paraphrases with the Anglo-Saxon word written under
its Latin fellow: which latter, although a great help to the
weak scholar, can hardly be called a rendering for the people.

But from about 1100 onwards opinion in the hierarchy
all over Europe began to harden against vernacular versions
of holy scripture. The real reason for this was the growing
corruption of the church, and the feeling, conscious or
unconscious, in the minds of the clergy, that many of the

ruling customs could not be made to square with the more spiritual standards of the New Testament. The matter was brought to a head by the rise of reforming companies, such as the Waldenses in the twelfth century, who not only appealed to the scripture themselves, but translated and circulated it, and from this vantage point attacked the abuses of the day. The official church, instead of admitting the justice of these attacks and putting right what was amiss, stood on her dignity, assumed an air of infallibility, and endeavoured to rob her critics of their strongest weapon by prohibiting vernacular scriptures. In the ensuing centuries it is possible to quote edict after edict from provincial councils, popes, kings, bishops, theologians, condemning the free reading of scripture by the laity. The forbiddal, indeed, was never complete; the church did not move as one man in the matter; in certain ages and in certain lands it was sometimes possible for zealots to slip through the meshes of discouragement and restriction. Nevertheless in the main the hierarchy was strongly hostile to the vernacular bible.

In England the position was complicated by the change of language at the Norman conquest. French was now installed as the speech of the upper classes, and Anglo-Saxon took a back seat; and for over two hundred and fifty years nothing was done in the way of a translation for the commons. Even when the enlightened bishop Grosseteste urges the study of the bible, he makes no efforts to provide an English translation for his flock. We hear indeed sometimes of French translations, but these were in the houses of the nobility and other privileged persons.

Then came the triumph of the English language over its foreign rival. This was complete by the middle of the fourteenth century, when English began to be used in the law courts and in parliament. Anglo-Saxon and French versions were now mere archaisms; if the people were to have the bible at all, it must be given them in the new English tongue, that was forming itself as the basis of our modern speech. What was done to meet the need? About 1330 Richard Rolle, hermit in Yorkshire, made a prose version

—exceedingly literal, with glosses—of the Psalter, and a version was made about the same time of the Apocalypse, which two scriptural books held for some reason a privileged position, and were considered less dangerous for general reading: but apart from this no part of the bible was translated until the time of John Wycliffe. Wycliffe and his disciples made two versions of the whole bible. The first, stiff and encumbered with Latinisms, appeared about 1382, shortly before the master's death; the second was a revision, made about 1396 by John Purvey, his ablest disciple. This was more free and easy in style, and is the first English version that can claim literary merit. These two editions were widely circulated by the Lollards, and despite burnings and persecution there are no less than a hundred and eighty manuscripts still extant, more than three-quarters of them belonging to Purvey's version.

But were no translations made by the other party, the supporters of the hierarchy? Thomas More, discussing the question in his attack upon Tyndale, says that there were; says that he has himself seen old pre-Wycliffe bibles in convents and in the houses of the nobility, and that the reading of these was permitted by the bishop to " such as he knew for good and catholic folk." What is to be said to this? It runs clean counter to the well-nigh universal tradition, that Wycliffe was the first to give the English scripture to the people. At first sight More's statement might seem to be confirmed by the discovery thirty or forty years ago of a small group of manuscripts, containing hitherto unknown fourteenth century versions of large parts of the New Testament. But these manuscripts, even if none of them sprang from the Lollard movement, had no circulation, and are so few in number, that they cannot claim to have been a people's bible, or a rival to the two great Wycliffite versions.*

* See *A fourteenth century English biblical version* (A. C. Paues, 1904). One of these translators performed his task with fear; for he says in his prologue: " Brother, I know well that I am hold by Christ's law to perform thine asking; but nevertheless we be now so far fallen away from Christ's law, that if I would answer to thine asking, I must in case underfonge [undergo] the death."

Others living in More's day seem to know nothing of any English bible approved by authority. Tyndale scoffs at the idea: " What may not Master More say by authority of his poetry? " he replies; "there is a lawful translation that no man knoweth : which is as much as no lawful translation. Why might not the bishops shew, which were that lawful translation, and let it be printed? " * Equally ignorant is a man of More's own party, Roger Edgeworth, who, preaching some twenty years later, says that a vernacular bible would be a good thing, " if we could get it well and truly translated, which will be very hard to be had." What then were the manuscripts which More saw in these great houses? There can be little doubt that they were really the Lollard versions. These were sometimes found in monasteries and noble mansions, usually with the omission of the prologue, which was considered heretical, though no such charge was brought against the translation itself. Thus the Sion convent at Isleworth received a copy by gift in 1517, the Charterhouse at Sheen had had one presented by Henry VI, the Dominicans at Cambridge owned one at the dissolution of the monasteries. Of these three houses the first was certainly visited by More, and very likely the others were also. Among the laity, Henry VI, Edward IV, Henry VII, duke Thomas of Gloucester, duke Humphrey of Gloucester are all said to have possessed copies.†

But the very success of the Lollard versions led to the passing of a new law, which completely changed the situation. In 1408 archbishop Arundel summoned his convocation to Oxford, the great centre and stronghold of Wycliffism, and here, among many laws against Lollardism, was passed the famous constitution, forbidding any man to translate the scripture without authority, or to read any translation made since the time of Wycliffe, or to be made in future, until it had been approved by the bishop, or, if

* So Barnes in 1531 : " Where is it? Why have we it not? If that [Tyndale's version] were not it, why do not you set the very true testament out? " (Daye's folio 283; Tyndale's *Works* III, 168.)

† The whole matter is carefully discussed in *The Lollard Bible* (Margaret Deanesly, 1920).

need be, by a provincial council. Offenders were to undergo the greater excommunication, and to be punished as heretics. Nothing could be clearer than this: from henceforth the hierarchy claimed the monopoly, took the whole business of translation under its control. How did they proceed? If they had really desired to give the people the bible, they would at once have issued an authorized version. But of this there is no shred of evidence, and meanwhile the cruel attacks upon the bible-reading Lollards continued. Then came the invention of printing, which should have acted as a spur to the bishops to bring out and to broadcast all the literary treasures which they possessed. They made no use of it: vernacular bibles were printed in other lands—not indeed by the hierarchy—and various religious books were printed in England, but no bible, not even a New Testament. Even if there had been an approved translation, as More imagined, of what avail were a few copies, lurking unseen in the houses of the great, and composed in half obsolete English? What was wanted was a version written in the common speech, and spread throughout the land, so that all might read: but this the bishops had never moved a finger to supply, and other men were overawed by the constitution of Oxford.

The spirit of the pre-reformation church is well illustrated by the preface to the Rheims New Testament of 1582, the first English version that appeared under papal auspices. The authors go out of their way to explain that vernacular scriptures are not " much requisite nor perchance wholly tolerable," and that they have often been " pernicious and much hurtful to many," but that this one is put out " upon special consideration of the present time, state and condition of our country," or, in other words, to counteract the effect of the protestant versions. Such a temper of mind will not give way until it is compelled. There needed a man to arise, and to do the deed in defiance of authority; and that man was William Tyndale.

But it is said: All this may be very true, but of what use is a book which the mass of the people are too poor to buy and too unlettered to read? Has not the effect of Tyndale's achievement been much over-praised? Now it is true that most of the people were unable to read, but still there were very many that could. Thomas More in his *Apology* says that " far more than four parts " out of every ten " could never read English yet," and so could not profit by an English bible. He was speaking roughly, of course, and no one would pin him down to this figure, but his proportion of literates is surprisingly high. Even if it was too high, even if we put the number of readers as low as one in twenty of the population, nevertheless the New Testament was worth translating for their sakes. Tyndale was not a man to despise the day of small things; he was willing, as we shall see, to offer his New Testament to the world, even if licence to read it were refused to all men except to the priests. As to the price, that seems to have varied, partly according to the size and binding of the book, and partly according to the amount of profit expected by the seller. For the Worms octavo we hear of prices, ranging from 4*s.* to 1*s.* 8*d.*; and the small pirate editions seem to have fetched about 1*s.* or less. Reduce these sums to modern values: you could get a testament for anything between 15*s.* and £3 10*s.*, just the sort of price which thousands of working men pay to-day for a bicycle or a wireless set.

If the people could neither buy nor read the New Testament, whence came the furious rage of the hierarchy against the book, the anxious consultations, the appeals to the king, the stern orders to all men to deliver it up, the prohibitions against printing, the public condemnations and burnings? This may show the bigotry of the rulers, but it also shows the effectiveness of the book. Cochlæus draws lurid pictures of the wide spread of Luther's New Testament in Germany, of its being read and discussed by tradesmen, labourers and even by women; and the same thing was true in England. We find it in the hands of men and women of the humblest classes, apprentices, tailors, founders, saddlers, weavers, bricklayers, servants, fishmongers, husbandmen. Sometimes two poor men would put their money together to buy a copy, sometimes groups would meet in the house of a fortunate possessor, and listen to his reading. At the outset it only touched a minority of the people: how could it do more, when the first edition numbered but six thousand, and three-quarters of these were likely destroyed within a couple of years of publication? Nevertheless in these small beginnings it was lighting a candle in the land, which has never been put out.

(2) *The Principles of the Work.*

But on what principles was Tyndale to make his translation? The answer is simple to us; it was not so then. First, what text should he use? In the middle ages there was no choice in the matter: the only text known was the Latin Vulgate, and the Lollard version had perforce been made from this. But now the Greek had been recovered, and had been given to the world by Erasmus in 1516. Luther had translated from the Greek, and Tyndale rightly decided to do the same. It is true that Erasmus' Greek text was not a very good one, being taken from late manuscripts, and in some places was inferior to the Vulgate; nevertheless on balance the gain far outweighed the loss. A translator will better catch the spirit of his author and enter into his meaning, if he meet him in his original dress and not through an interpreter: and whatever incidental blunders he may make, he is opening the road by which they will be most surely removed, as knowledge grows. Tyndale's instinct was a true one, as the whole course of English bible translation proves.

So much for the text; but what of the style? Here it is hard for us to put ourselves back into the frame of mind of the sixteenth century. Tyndale himself has settled the question for us, and we should never dream of reopening it. But in medieval days the intense veneration for the Latin text and the desire for verbal accuracy led men, in so far as they tolerated the idea of bible translation at all, to forge a special style for it, stilted and painfully literal, abounding with Latinisms; in extreme cases, indeed, hardly better than the word for word cribs, over which schoolboys make merry. This was the method followed by Richard Rolle and by the first Wycliffe version. Purvey's version was a great improvement, and has a genuine English ring; he aimed, as he says, at giving the sense rather than the words: but even here some of the old stiffness remains. Thus he renders:—

Luke xix. 17. For in little thing thou hast been true; thou shalt be having power on ten cities.
Hebrew iv. 13. All things be naked and open to his eyes, to whom a word to us.

The tradition was partly the same in Germany, but Luther boldly broke away from it. He was a German writing for his " dear Germans," as he called them, and he determined to give them a true, pure, living German translation. The very homeliness and raciness of the style made them feel at home with the contents of the gospel, and that has been one secret of its enormous popularity since the first day of publication; even its enemies have had to imitate it, in order to gain any hearing for their own versions. Tyndale followed the same example; he too threw overboard the stilted jargon of translation style. Whatever else his version might be, he would make it truly English, readily understandable by the people, and readable. If its contents are not foreign to the heart, neither should its sound be foreign to the ear. Better, he thinks, be a little inaccurate than be pompous and artificial. By this strong resolve he not only opened the gospel to the common people, but rendered a great service to our native tongue; for the bible became the people's book, and has spread its influence far and wide.

How strong the tradition of translation-English was, can best be seen by calling into comparison the Rheims version, published more than fifty years after Tyndale had pointed out the true path. It was made by good scholars, and is far from being without merit; many of its neat phrases have found a place in our king James' version: but its great vice is its stilted and peculiar English, due to an over-close imitation of the Latin text, from which it translates.

Thus it gives us many renderings like these:—

Mark xiv. 38.   The spirit indeed is prompt, but the flesh infirm.

Luke xxii. 42.   Father, if thou wilt, transfer this chalice from me.

Romans vi. 23.   For the stipends of sin, death.

And here is its rendering of Psalm xxiii:—

(1) Our Lord ruleth me, and nothing shall be wanting to me.   (2) In place of pasture there he hath placed me; upon the water of refection he hath brought me up.   (3) He hath converted my soul; he hath conducted me upon the paths of justice for his name.   (4) For although I shall walk in the midst of the shadow of death, I will not fear evils, because thou art with me: thy rod and thy staff they have comforted me.   (5) Thou hast prepared in my sight a table against them that trouble me: thou hast fatted my head with oil, and my chalice inebriating, how goodly it is. (6) And thy mercy shall follow me all the days of my life, and that I may dwell in the house of our Lord in longitude of days.

Compare this version, reader, not only with that in the Book of Common Prayer, but with the still finer one in our king James' bible, and then ask yourself, whether Tyndale does not deserve our gratitude for launching his vessel under the fair flag of pure English.

(3) *Scholarship and Accuracy.*

Tyndale then sets to work upon Erasmus' Greek text, of which three editions had already appeared.   What other aids did he have?   First, the Latin Vulgate, which would be as familiar to him as king James' Bible is to the Christian scholar of to-day; then, Erasmus' Latin translation and notes, accompanying his Greek text; and lastly, Luther's German version, of which the third edition appeared in 1524.   The Wycliffe bible he did not use, as we shall see presently.

Now it is plain that a man with three good versions in

front of him could very well make a translation from these alone, without any knowledge of Greek. Coverdale ten years later produced the first complete English bible on this method, only he had five versions to work upon instead of three. At one time it used to be said that Tyndale had done the same, despite his own claim to have translated from the Greek, and despite the many places in his works where he discusses the meaning of Greek words: and even now some critics will allow him nothing more than a smattering of the Greek tongue, and charge him with slavishly following either Erasmus or Luther; though which of the two it is, they cannot agree among themselves.

Happily the question is settled by an examination of the translation itself, and the answer is decisively in Tyndale's favour. A man working wholly or mainly from versions soon gives himself away. He will either stick predominantly to one version, and only differ from it for some urgent cause, or else he will try to select between the authorities, as best he can. In the first case the matter is clear from the very start; and in the second he will frequently fall into blunders, which a man with any knowledge of the original would avoid. With Tyndale, the more you read, the more certain you become that his basis is the Greek. A few verses might leave you in doubt, but the cumulative effect of chapter after chapter becomes overwhelming. Hundreds of little points come in to swell the stream of evidence, all moving in the one direction. There is really no shadow of doubt about the matter, as anyone will agree who has worked carefully through the book.

Of course this does not mean that Tyndale's Greek scholarship was equal to that of a modern professor. The knowledge of the language was only just being recovered, and it was some way behind even the standard of our Authorized Version. Tyndale makes blunders, but so do his three forerunners. Not one of them is accurate, when compared with our Revised Version. By the level of his own day Tyndale was a good Greek scholar, fully as good as Erasmus or Luther. He has, too, plenty of confidence in himself. When his authorities disagree, he selects boldly between them, and what is more, he usually comes down on the right side. In some scores of passages he gives a rendering which, although rejected by the Authorized Version, has been reinstated by the Revisers.

But the reader will desire to test the matter for himself; and therefore we now give a short list of places—out of some dozens that might be chosen—where Tyndale breaks away from his three guides and strikes out for himself. Such renderings are a decisive proof of his scholarship and independence: for they can only have been derived from the Greek. The versions of the three are given in brackets, and whenever Tyndale agrees (in sense) with the Authorized or Revised Version, the fact is stated at the end.

Matthew xxvii. 65.
Take watchmen (ye have a guard)—R.V. Margin.
Mark i. 24.
He cried saying, *Let me alone (Ah! or Stop!)*—A.V.
Mark xii. 7.
But the tenants said *within (among)* themselves.
Luke ii. 8.
And there were in the same region shepherds *abiding in the field*—A.V., R.V.
Watching (Vulgate, Erasmus); *In the field by the folds* (Luther).
Luke ii. 51.
His mother kept all these *things (sayings)* in her heart —R.V.M.
John xiv. 1.
Let not your heart be troubled; *believe in God, and believe (ye believe in God, believe also)* in me—R.V.M.
Acts i. 4.
To wait for the promise of the Father, *whereof (which, said he)* ye have heard of me.
The *said he* is not in the Greek.
Acts xxvii. 27.
As we *were carried (sailed)* in Adria—A.V., R.V.
Galatians i. 7.
I marvel that ye are so soon turned . . . unto another gospel, which is *nothing else but that (not another; but that)* there be some which trouble you.
This very interesting interpretation has become popular

in the last hundred years, but I cannot trace it earlier than Tyndale.

Galatians vi. 14.

The cross of our Lord Jesus Christ, *whereby* (*by whom*) the world is crucified as touching me—R.V.

Colossians i. 27.

The glorious riches of this mystery among the Gentiles, *which riches* (*which mystery*) is Christ in you.

Colossians ii. 4.

Beguile you with *enticing words*—A.V.

Loftiness of words (Vulgate); *Probability of words* (Erasmus); *Reasonable words* (Luther).

Hebrews x. 20.

By the new and living way, which he hath prepared for us, through the vail, that is to say *by his flesh* (*his flesh*).

Here the flesh is the *way*; the others (also A.V. and R.V.) make it the *vail*.

Hebrews xi. 8.

By faith *Abraham when he was called* (*he who received the name of Abraham*)—A.V., R.V.

II Peter ii. 8.

For he being *righteous* and dwelling among them, *in seeing and hearing* vexed his righteous soul—A.V., R.V.

Righteous in eyes and ears—(Vulgate, Erasmus); *They vexed*—(Vulgate, Luther).*

The attempt has sometimes been made to prove Tyndale's dependence upon one or other of his rivals by drawing up lists of passages where he follows their renderings. This does not carry us very far. Agreements may proceed from a common standpoint and a common method rather than a slavish imitation. That Tyndale should favour the Vulgate less than he favours Erasmus or Luther, is what we should expect from the circumstances. To Luther Tyndale was akin in two ways. Both men used living tongues of Germanic stock, and both were writing for the common people, whereas Erasmus wrote for scholars in a dead tongue and a prosaic style. Thus we find Luther and Tyndale both giving the familiar equivalents of the Jewish

---

* For an error, in which Tyndale stands alone, see Luke viii. 16:— " No man lighteth a candle and putteth it under *the table*." I cannot account for this.

feasts, Easter and Whitsun instead of Pasch and Pentecost. This common standpoint accounts for many agreements between the two translators.

On the other hand Tyndale sticks closer to the Greek text than Luther, and often refuses to follow him in those free and bold renderings which are so striking and pleasing a feature of the German version, *e.g.* where Paul addresses Agrippa as " *dear* king Agrippa." He prefers to find an idiomatic rendering of a more literal kind, and thus ranks himself by the side of Erasmus. On the whole it may be said that the cases where Tyndale sides with Erasmus from a more careful following of the Greek balance, and rather more than balance, his agreements with Luther from other causes. But whatever be decided on this point, it must again be strongly asserted that such agreements, with whichever party, are not proof of dependence, or of ignorance of the Greek tongue, but they proceed from the free and unfettered choice of a well-equipped scholar.*

To drive the point home, it may be well to quote the verdict of Westcott, the greatest scholar who has ever given a careful scrutiny to Tyndale's translation. The New Testament, says he, is " the complete proof of Tyndale's independence. . . . It is impossible to read a single chapter without gaining the assurance that Tyndale rendered the Greek directly. . . . He deals with the text as one who passed a scholar's judgment upon every fragment of the work, unbiased by any predecessor." If he uses the help of the other three versions, he does so " as a master and not as a disciple. . . . Style and interpretation are his own." Nor is Westcott the only good scholar to speak thus. Broadly it may be said that the more eminent the scholar, the more favourable his verdict upon Tyndale. It is the second and third-rate men, the men who are content to take a verdict according to their prepossessions, or who, in their zeal for tabulating details, fail to seize the salient points, or to view the facts as a whole, who would rob Tyndale of his due

* Cf. *The truth about the so-called Luther's testament in English* (L. F. Gruber, 1917): J. L. Cheney in *Anglia* VI (1883); B. F. Westcott's *English Bible*.

honour, and make him little more than a pale shadow of
Erasmus or Luther.

By what has already been said, it will have been perceived
that Tyndale's method of translation is somewhat loose.
In many respects, indeed, he is stricter than Luther, but as
a set-off to this he has a number of peculiarities of his own
which we must now consider, and by which his style is easily
recognized.

To begin with, he is very free in his treatment of connecting
particles, such as *therefore, but, and.*　The two Latin versions
are pedantically exact here;　Luther is rather easygoing;
but Tyndale has a waywardness all his own.　Often he
omits them altogether, no doubt mainly because the English
language has no great liking for them;　and indeed his own
style is in this respect very terse and bare.

As a rule there is little or no loss by this proceeding, but
sometimes the sense is impaired.　Thus he gives us:—

John xviii. 40.
Then cried they all again saying:—Not him but Barabbas.
Barabbas (Now Barabbas—A.V.) was a robber.
Acts iii. 6.
Silver and gold have I none;　*such (but such)* as I have
give I thee.

Occasionally indeed he will even alter the particle as in
John vii. 1.

After that, Jesus went about in Galilee, *and (for he)* would
not go about in Jewry.

This cavalier treatment of the particles is certainly a
defect, as Tyndale himself acknowledged in part: for he
amended many of the places in the second edition.

Beside this he has a number of little tricks of his own.
Thus he always writes (so had Purvey sometimes) *resurrection from death (the dead*—A.V.);　he always writes *father
and mother* (so often had Purvey) instead of *parents* or *elders*;
he frequently replaces *when* by the slightly sharper *as soon
as*;　he is fond of reversing phrases like *sold and bought, earth
and heaven, ink and pen,* and of inserting *both* or *either* before
phrases like *men and women, ox or sheep.*　Then he often

uses a more roundabout form of the imperative, writing
"*See that ye (be ye)* doers of the word" (James i. 22); and he
will change a present tense when the meaning looks towards
the future, *e.g.*: "Ye *shall have (have)* the poor always with
you, but me ye *shall not have (have not)* always." He has a
way too in questions of writing *what* for *who*: e.g.: "The
Jews sent priests . . . to ask him, What art thou?" (John
i. 19). This last peculiarity is not uncommon in old
English, and sometimes appears in the Authorized Version,
but there is no other bible translator that uses it nearly so
frequently as Tyndale.

Now these little waywardnesses (for so they are in the
light of the fierce accuracy of the Revised Version) do not
proceed from ignorance. A few are due to haste, and a
number are corrected in the second edition, but in the
main they spring out of his translating methods, and illustrate his habit of mind. He just throws them in when he
chooses, or when he thinks they give greater clearness or a
nobler sound to the sentence. The first thing with him is
to render the meaning of the sacred text into pure and
direct English. The world was panting for the gospel,
and he gave it as speedily as might be. For pedantic
exactness he cared not at all. Little errors, that made no
difference to the sense, could easily be set right later, if it
was worth while. In essential truth and accuracy Tyndale's version need fear no comparison with those of his
three rivals, while as a piece of literature it outshines them
all, save that of Luther alone.

(4) *The Charge of Wilful Mistranslation.*

But a far more damaging attack has been made upon
Tyndale than that of ignorance. He has been accused of
wilful perversion of the text to suit the ends of his party.
Tonstall and More set the ball rolling, but it has been carried
forward by a long line of eminent writers, ending with
Gairdner, Gasquet and others in our own time. First-class
scholars of the New Testament indeed do not join in the
outcry, but still the charge is repeated at second hand, and

it is high time that the full facts were set out before the general reader.

The chief prosecutor is Thomas More, and the others do but echo his accusation. It is first stated in his *Dialogue* of 1529, and when Tyndale had replied to it in his *Answer*, More returns to the attack in the second book of his *Confutation*. Tyndale's testament, he says in his *Dialogue*, is not the New Testament at all; " for so had Tyndale, after Luther's counsel, corrupted and changed it from the good and wholesome doctrine of Christ to the devilish heresies of their own, that it was a clean contrary thing." It is a false copper groat, silvered over to look true. It is as full of errors as the sea is full of water, and no good Christian should marvel or complain at its burning. In the *Confutation* he describes it as " a false English translation, . . . newly forged by Tyndale, so altered and changed in matters of great weight, maliciously to set forth against Christ's true doctrines Tyndale's antichristian heresies, that it was not worthy to be called Christ's testament, but either Tyndale's own testament or the testament of his master antichrist."

Now on what is this sweeping accusation grounded? Chiefly on the translation of half a dozen words. The first is *ecclesia* or *church*; which Tyndale always renders *congregation*. For this there was much to be said, if accuracy was the only thing aimed at. The Greek word *ecclesia*, which was taken over into Latin, means any assembly that is properly summoned or constituted. In the New Testament itself it is once used for the assembly of the pagan citizens of Ephesus, who cried out " Great is Diana of the Ephesians." The Greek translators of the Old Testament often use it to denote the assembly of the chosen people of Israel, and when the New Testament writers desired a word for the society of Christians, who were called out of the world through Christ, and who met together as one communion, they chose *ecclesia*. If Tyndale wished to find a broad and neutral word, that would give, as near as might be, the flavour of the original, it is hard to see what better he could find than *congregation*, especially as Jerome had sometimes used it (*congregatio*) in his Old Testament to signify the

Jewish ecclesia. The word *church* (*kuriake* in the Greek), on the other hand, was Christian from the start; it seems to have been first used for the Lord's house, and then came to mean the Lord's people that met in the house.

But there was more to be said than that. The word *church* had become debased in the long course of years. In practice it was largely employed to mean, not the Lord's people, but the officers of the Lord's people, and when thus used, it exalted the priesthood and dishonoured the laity. Thomas More, indeed, angrily denies this, and maintains that there is no preacher so ignorant but that he will include the laity under the term church; which may be true enough as far as definition goes, but facts have a way of outrunning definitions. An easy illustration is at hand. Turn up, reader, in your dictionary the word *churchman*. You will find that in the middle ages this invariably meant a priest or monk, and that its first use in the modern sense of church-member occurs only a century and a half after the reformation. Tyndale then wished to guard his readers from being misled by current usage. " Inasmuch," he says, " as the clergy . . . had appropriate unto themselves the term, that of right is common unto all the whole congregation of them that believe in Christ, . . . therefore in the translation of the New Testament, where I found this word *ecclesia*, I interpreted it by this word *congregation*."

On the point of accuracy, then, Tyndale has a strong case: nevertheless More charges him with perpetrating an unheard-of heretical novelty. But here he lays himself open to a damaging retort: Erasmus also had rendered the word by *congregatio*—not indeed throughout the New Testament, but in about one-tenth of the passages—and More had lauded his friend's book up to the skies. " How happeth it," asks Tyndale, " that Master More hath not contended in like wise against his darling Erasmus all this long while? " To this More replies that *ecclesia* is a Greek word, and that if Erasmus wished to find a Latin equivalent, there was nothing better than *congregatio*—a lame reply indeed; for if twelve hundred years of church use had not made *ecclesia* a Latin word, then neither are *honour* or *confession* English words. But he evidently feels that this argument does not go to the root of the matter, for in his previous paragraph he has exposed his whole hand: " I have not contended with Erasmus my darling, because I found no such malicious intent with Erasmus my darling, as I find with Tyndale. . . . I cannot take him for my darling, that the devil taketh for his darling." There we have the truth. All the pages of learned discussion of the word *church* might have been spared. The question is removed from the field of scholarship; it is prejudged from the start. To More Tyndale is a heretic, and therefore his translation must be wrong.

Why then has Tyndale's rendering *congregation* failed to hold its place in our English bible? for even the Geneva (Calvinistic) version abandoned it. The chief reason is its clumsiness. The English tongue loves short and pointed words. The long-winded *congregation*, of foreign extraction to boot, could hardly hope to oust the single-syllabled *church*, with its centuries of usage behind it. Men felt that it was better to purge the familiar word of its false associations, and this has been successfully accomplished. Luther was in this matter happier placed than Tyndale; he had a genuine German word *gemeine* at hand as a substitute for *kirche*, and this word has been retained in his German bible. Perhaps Tyndale might have been more fortunate if he had tried *fellowship*, but with *congregation* he could hardly hope to succeed. If More had attacked Tyndale on grounds of style or euphony, he would have had a good case; but when he alleges malicious mistranslation, he has no case at all.

The next word is *senior*, which Tyndale uses for the Greek word *presbyter* in places where *elder* stands in our English bible: *e.g.* " the priests and seniors of the Jews "; " he sent to Ephesus and called the seniors of the congregation." Senior! retorts More; what is that? It is no English word, but French or Latin. Tyndale admits the justice of the rebuke. " Of a truth," he says, " *senior* is no very good English, though *senior* and *junior* be used in the universities; but there came no better in my mind at the time. Howbeit I spied my fault since, long ere Master More told it me, and have mended it in all the works which I since made, and call it an *elder*." To this More replies with a scoff: Of course, he says, you do not wish to be thought to have learnt anything from me. Nevertheless Tyndale's words are true, as anyone may see by reading his *Obedience*, published before More's *Dialogue*, where he throughout uses *elder*, only twice giving *senior* as an alternative.

But this criticism of *senior* as bad English is only a piece of by-play with More; his dislike of *elder* is quite as strong, or even stronger. The true rendering, he says, should be *priest*. Why, Tyndale himself uses the word *priest* to denote the officers of the Jewish church; it is only the Christian ministers whom he robs of their true title: an evident token of his malice.

This argument shows More at his very worst. He had read his Greek testament for years, and he knew quite well that Tyndale translates the word *presbyter* in the same way (*senior*), whether it is used of Jewish or of Christian ministers. Whenever he gives the title *priest* to the Jewish ministers, it is to render a totally different Greek word, *hiereus*, which is applied to the sacrificing priests of the tribe of Levi; and whenever this word is used in the New Testament of Christians (four or five times only, and then of the whole society, and not of the ministers alone) he again renders by *priests*. In both cases he is perfectly fair; the word *hiereus* becomes *priest*, the word *presbyter* becomes *senior*. More was well aware of this, and yet he is willing to mislead his unscholarly readers into a belief that Tyndale is loading the scales.

That Tyndale's rendering of *senior* or *elder* is correct, is so certain that one is almost ashamed to state it. From Homer downwards the word denotes a superior age, and it was of course applied to Jewish or Christian officers, because such were normally men of fairly advanced years. Our king James' bible agrees with Tyndale, so does the Revised Version. Even More's own heroes, Jerome and Erasmus, leave him in the lurch: for they render the word by *senior* or *presbyter*, and never by the proper word for priest (*sacerdos*), which they regularly give to the Jewish levitical priests. When Tyndale raises this point, and asks how it is that Jerome and the apostles never call the Christian ministers *priests* (*sacerdos* or *hiereus*), More, instead of grappling with the question, slides out of it, saying that he has never spoken with these old writers, and therefore has been unable to ask them.

Tyndale's next offence is his use of *repentance* in place of *penance*. According to More, John the baptist said to the people: " Do penance, for the kingdom of heaven is at hand," and he accuses Tyndale of maliciously bringing in the word *repent* in order to banish all penance from the bible. But what does the Greek word mean? It means a change of mind, and exactly corresponds to the old English word *forthink*, which was used sometimes by the Wycliffe versions, and which might well have been revived by Tyndale. The phrase *do penance* is doubly wrong. First, it directs attention to external acts rather than to the change of heart; and secondly, the acts in question, punishments imposed on the sinner by a priest after ear-confession, had no necessary connection with the wrong that had been committed. In many cases they were valueless, and in some even harmful. Tyndale's rendering is perfectly correct, and has been followed by our chief English versions.

In this point too he gains countenance from Jerome and Erasmus, but of this More says no word at all. The Vulgate once in five times, and Erasmus twice in three times render *be penitent* or *come to a better mind*; and even when they translate *do penitence*, it is more than doubtful whether the Latin word *penitentia* was intended to include the formal penance, enjoined by a priest.*

The next word is *knowledge* [*i.e.* acknowledge] and its cognates, in place of *confess* and *confession*. To hear More's horrified protests, one would imagine that Tyndale had banished the word *confess* altogether from the New Testament; but this is not so. He retains it in well above half the passages, fourteen out of twenty-three. More's only serious argument is that the word *confess* implies a more willing opening of the heart than *knowledge*. Perhaps this may have been true of the origin of the words: but even if so, the

---

* Erasmus' note on Matthew iii. 2 shows that his interpretation is that of Tyndale.

sixteenth century writers, including More himself, do not observe the distinction, but treat them as practical synonyms; and in any case a differing shade of meaning offers a very slender ground for a charge of heretical mistranslation. The only just criticism of Tyndale here is that of giving two English renderings of the same Greek word; but as we shall see presently, that is a criticism which would have left him altogether unmoved.

Then we come to *favour* used instead of *grace*. More says that Tyndale " commonly " changes *grace* into *favour*. This is misleading. He retains the traditional word in a hundred passages or more, even introducing it once or twice where the Vulgate renders otherwise, and only twenty times does he replace it by *favour*, and in two of these he interprets it of human favour and not of God's grace. More objects to *favour* as being a wider term than *grace* and capable of an evil sense, but Tyndale replies justly that *grace* also can have an ungodly savour to it. In truth the two words correspond well enough, and the only solid reason against *favour* would be on the score of sound. It is a longer word—always a handicap in the English speech—and it is less pleasing to the ear, expressing less vividly the gentle flow of the loving kindness of God. Tyndale himself abandons it in his second edition except in five places; and no subsequent translator has attempted to revive it.

It is during this discussion that More makes his hit at Tyndale's university degree. " In the universities," said Tyndale, illustrating the uses of the word *grace*, " many ungracious graces there be gotten." " He should have made it more plain," replies More, " and better perceived, if he had said :—As for example, when his own grace was there granted to be made master of arts." Truly not a very *gracious* retort upon a scholar so well equipped as our reformer.

Tyndale's last, and perhaps crowning, offence is to cast out the word *charity* (Latin *caritas*) and to replace it by *love*, except in one passage where he renders by the adverb *charitably*. Charity, says More, means not every kind of love, but a good love, a Christian love; to which Tyndale replies that if love has more than one meaning, so also has charity. The Greek word, he argues, is a general and neutral word, and should therefore be rendered by the broad word *love*. He appeals also to common usage: in practice we speak of our *love* to God, not of our *charity* to God. Finally, he claims the advantage for *love*, on the ground that you can use it, like the Greek word, as a verb as well as a noun, but *charity* is only a noun, and you cannot say " *charity* God," or " *charity* your neighbour "; but this strong argument More waves aside as a " pretty point of juggling." Here too Tyndale can claim some support from Jerome and Erasmus, the former of whom occasionally, and the latter in more than a score of passages, render by *dilectio* or *love* instead of by *caritas*. The Revised Version also agrees with him completely, and the Authorized Version three times out of four. Thomas More himself quite lets the cat out of the bag by rendering *love* on several occasions: *e.g.* he quotes: " Faith that worketh by *love* " (Gal. v. 6), and " Faith and *love* in Christ Jesus " (II Timothy i. 13). The fact is, More's attack is simply based on conservatism, and is on a par with the outbreak of horror that was raised against the Revised Version for replacing *charity* by *love* in the famous hymn of I Corinthians xiii :—with this difference, however, that in that case the Revisers' offence was not made the basis of a charge of heresy, or turned into a token of a malicious mind.

To these six words More adds yet another in his *Confutation*, and his treatment here is equally illuminating. This is *idolon* or *idol*, which Tyndale sometimes renders by *image*. This, says More, is a deliberate perversion, designed to strike at the cult of image-worship; he wishes to make out that *idol* and *image* have the same meaning, whereas in fact an idol has the devil behind it, and an image has God. Now if Tyndale had this desire, he was not very thorough in putting it into action; for he retains *idol* in nineteen places out of thirty-four. However, no doubt he desired to draw attention to the fact that the Greek word *idol* is really a general word meaning *image*, and is applied in secular writers to pictures, busts, phantoms, ideas and the like.

The gentile Christians, who read St Paul's letters, would have this secular background in mind, and would know that the ecclesiastical sense of *idol*, meaning an image of a god, was only a special sense. The English readers, however, of More's day were without this knowledge, and Tyndale was quite entitled to jog their interest and their understandings, and by varying his translation to put them as far as possible in the position of the first readers. His action might properly be criticised on the grounds of convenience; for there was already another Greek word, *eikon*, which was normally (and by Tyndale himself) rendered *image*: but such a plea would have little weight with Tyndale, who rejoiced in variety of renderings.

Once again Tyndale can plead in his favour the example of Jerome and Erasmus, for they too vary their rendering of this word. Jerome once out of four times, and Erasmus in every place but two, translate by *simulacrum*, a general word meaning likeness or image.

As regards then the charge of wilful mistranslation, Tyndale remains complete master of the field. Here and there he is open to criticism on the score of convenience or euphony, but there is no dishonour. The dishonour rather rests upon the head of his assailant, who vilifies him for deeds which he had completely overlooked when committed by his friend Erasmus. But More has travelled far in the last ten or twelve years. Once upon a time Erasmus' New Testament had been bitterly attacked, as containing new and dangerous, even heretical, renderings, not sanctioned by the usage of the church. Then More came vigorously to his friend's aid, and swept the bigots confidently and contemptuously out of the way.* Now the position is reversed. It is More that now wields the big stick of authority, and wishes to suppress awkward questions. No longer does he stand in the open air, discussing the points on their merits, but he starts with a thesis, that must by hook or crook be established; and in his heart he knows that this is the case:

* Cf. More's defence of Erasmus' use of *sermo* for *verbum* in John i. 1 against the attacks of Lee.

for once or twice his learned reasonings on the meanings and derivations of words drop away from him, and he makes the frank avowal that it is not so much the renderings themselves to which he objects; in another translator they might have passed muster, but not in Tyndale, who has an evil purpose and a heretic mind, and who made his translation at Wittenberg with Luther. The man who can reason thus is ceasing to follow truth wholeheartedly for its own sake. Words and things should be appraised in their own right, even if they are spoken and done by the devil in hell.*

In a letter written three years before his death, Tyndale says:—" I call God to record, against the day we shall appear before our Lord Jesus to give a reckoning of our doings, that I never altered one syllable of God's word against my conscience, nor would do this day, if all that is in the earth, whether it be honour, pleasure, or riches, might be given me." The words ring true: and they are borne out by an examination of his New Testament.

(5) *Style.*

So far we have been dealing chiefly with the accuracy of the version; we now pass to its English style. Whether for good or for bad, Tyndale has stamped his own style upon our English bible, and given a standard for later translators to imitate. He was not indeed the first in the field, for the Wycliffite translators had preceded him. He must have known of their work and had doubtless seen manuscripts of it, but there is no reason to suppose that he owned one. Written copies of the bible, or even of the New Testament, would be expensive, and Tyndale would have no need of

---

* Why did not More translate the New Testament himself? He would have done it well, as the biblical extracts in his English works prove. But he preferred to carp at the honest work of another. J. Gairdner (*Lollardy and the Reformation*) charges Tyndale with wilful misrendering also in John v. 39 : " *Search* (imperative) the scriptures ": but this was the usual interpretation of the time, and is taken by Emser, More, the Rheims version, the medieval commentators, and most of the ancient fathers.

one himself, being able to understand the Vulgate. That he did not use these versions in making his own translation, we know from his own positive statement in the epilogue to his New Testament:—" I had no man to counterfeit [copy], neither was holp with English of any that had interpreted the same, or such like thing, in the scripture beforetime ": and this he confirms in the prologue to his second edition, where he says that he translated of his " own pregnant wits at the beginning without an ensample."

Nevertheless in recent years several writers have given him the lie, and have claimed to prove by a comparison of the texts, that he had Purvey's version in front of him. But they only succeed in this by lowering their standards of proof. They bring forward likenesses of the most trivial kind, such as must often occur independently to two different translators. Of what use is it to quote, as proof of Tyndale's indebtedness, " A ring on his hand and shoes on his feet " (Luke xv. 22), or " Love thy neighbour as thyself " (Romans xiii. 9)? These two phrases can hardly be rendered in any other way. Samuel McComb gives a list of sixty passages from Romans, James, and the epistles of Peter, to prove Tyndale's knowledge of Purvey. Now it so happens that forty-seven of these are also to be found in the fragmentary medieval versions edited by Miss Paues. In thirty-eight places out of forty-seven the Paues version, in one at least, and usually in both, of its two forms, agrees with Purvey and Tyndale. Of the nine disagreements four are due to the Paues translator misunderstanding his Latin text, and the other five are utterly valueless for the purpose, e.g. *take* for *receive*, *righteous* for *just*.

The only agreements worth considering are the striking ones; and there are singularly few of these, and when they do occur, they can be otherwise explained than by borrowing. Sometimes both writers are influenced by the Vulgate; for example:

Matthew iv. 5. *Pinnacle* of the temple. (*Pinnaculum*— Vulgate).
Matthew vii. 6. Lest they tread them under their feet,

and *the other* (*the hounds*—Purvey) turn again and alto rent you.

That the treading was done by the swine and the tearing by the dogs, was a common medieval interpretation; and many copies of the Vulgate actually inserted the word *canes*, dogs.

Luke xi. 39. Full of *ravening* (*raven*—Purvey) and wickedness. (*Rapina*—Vulgate.)

I Corinthians xii. 31. And yet shew I unto you a *more excellent way* (*excellentiorem viam*).

At other times the phrase, common to Tyndale and Purvey, is one that was already current in the middle ages, before Purvey began to write. Thus we have:

Matthew vii. 3. The *mote* and the *beam*.
John xiv. 16. He shall give you another *Comforter*.

Lastly, some likenesses are due merely to chance, to the independent choice of the same phrase. One would expect to find a number of these cases. Such probably are:

Matthew vii. 14. The *strait* gate, the *narrow* way.
Matthew xii. 18. My *darling* (*beloved*—A.V.).
Tyndale alters this in his second edition to *beloved*.
Acts xxv. 13. Agrippa and Bernice came unto Cæsarea to *welcome* (*salute*—A.V.) Festus.
In the second edition Tyndale gives *salute*.
I Corinthians xiii. 1. *Sounding brass . . . tinckling cymbal* (*brass sownyng . . . cymbal tinckling*—Purvey).
II Corinthians v. 5. The *earnest* of the spirit.

If Tyndale borrows from Purvey, what are we to say of those few passages where he gives a rendering markedly inferior to that of his model? Are we to believe that with open eyes he preferred the worse part to the better? Here are some examples, Tyndale's rendering being given in brackets.

Matthew xxiv. 41. The one shall be *taken* (*received*) and the other *left* (*shall be refused*).
Mark x. 14. *Of such is* (*unto such belongeth*) the kingdom of God.

Tyndale's second edition agrees with Purvey. Why not the first, if he knew it?

Luke xxiii. 25. He betook [= delivered] Jesus *to their will* (*to do with him what they would*).

Acts iii. 19. Times of *refreshing* (*comfort*).

Tyndale's second edition agrees with Purvey.

Rom. vi. 23. For the *wages* (*reward*) of sin is death.

In discussing his use of the word *senior*, Tyndale, as we have seen, states that no better rendering came into his mind at the time. How could he have said that, if Purvey, with his translation *elder men*, lay before him upon the table? *

It is of course likely, that the wide currency of the Wycliffite versions had helped to establish in common usage a number of phrases, which Tyndale put into his book. It is even possible that he had in earlier years looked into manuscript copies of those versions, and carried in his head a few renderings, which influenced his choice when he came to translate. But that is the extent of his indebtedness. If he had really had his forerunner's work in front of him, the agreements must have been far more striking than they are.

Upon one thing Tyndale is resolved: whatever the reader of his translation may suffer, he shall not suffer monotony. He varies his renderings constantly, and for no other reason than that he likes change for its own sake; he seems to have felt that it enlivens the mind, and keeps the reader from sinking into a rut. The translators of our king James' version deliberately varied their renderings, in order to enrich the language with words that might otherwise perish, but Tyndale goes far beyond them; his little finger is thicker than their loins. No translator of the first rank who ever lived can have approached him in this; Luther, in many ways so bold, is here by comparison a pedant. Tyndale stands at the extreme pole from our Revised Version, which makes it a settled principle to render the same Greek by the same English word.

* The first Lollard version, mostly in the Old Testament and some times in the New, gives *elders*. Purvey has *elders* three or four times in the Old Testament.

Thus for the phrase *it came to pass* he gives us five renderings, adding also *happened, chanced, fortuned,* and *followed.* The word *lo* is turned in five other ways, viz. *behold, mark, see, look,* and *take heed.* A *parable* is also called a *similitude;* *throne* becomes *seat; blessed* becomes *happy.* All this is harmless enough; for the varying renderings usually occur in different passages, and so do not clash: and some of them indeed are seldom used. But Tyndale thinks nothing of changing the translation in the same passage, or even in the same verse or sentence. Thus the *field* in which the tares were sown, before long becomes a *close;* the wicked *husbandmen* become *tenants;* the *lake of fire* becomes the *pond of fire;* the refrain *scribes and pharisees, hypocrites* of Matthew xxiii. becomes *scribes and pharisees, dissemblers.* When he varies an important word in the very same phrase, there is certainly a real loss; *e.g.*:—

Matthew xxiv. 34. This generation shall not *pass*, till all be fulfilled. Heaven and earth shall *perish*, but my words shall *abide.*
But in the parallel passage in Mark xiii. 31 he has: Heaven and earth shall *pass*, but my words shall *not pass.*
John iv. 24. God is a spirit, and they that *worship* him must *honour* him in spirit and *verity.*
In the second edition Tyndale has *worship* and *truth.*
Revelation vi. 2. Went forth *conquering* and for to *overcome.*

The two crowning examples of his waywardness are perhaps:—

Romans xiii. 7. Give to every man therefore his duty; tribute to whom tribute *belongeth*, custom to whom custom *is due*, fear to whom fear *belongeth*; honour to whom honour *pertaineth.*
Revelation xxi. 13. *On the east part* three gates, and *on the north side* three gates, and *towards the south* three gates, and *from the west* three gates.

This is wanton; he seems to be trying to show us what he can do when he has a mind; and even those of us who feel that the Revised Version carries its rigid rule

too far, must own that Tyndale goes astray in the opposite
direction.

We have seen that Tyndale desires to be easily understanded of the people. This affects his choice of words. He
does not worry about anachronisms or slight inaccuracies.
Thus he gives:—

Matthew xxvi. 30. And when they had *said grace* (*sung
an hymn*—A.V.) they went out unto the mount Olivet.

Matthew xxvii. 54. Mark xv. 39. *Petty* or *Under
Captain* (*Centurion*).

In his second edition he alters in both places to
centurion.

Luke ii. 3. Every man went into his own *shire town*
(*city*).

Tyndale's second edition has *city*.

John xii. 42. Lest they should be *excommunicate* (*put out
of the synagogue*).

Acts iv. 13. When they saw the boldness of Peter and
John, and knew that they were unlearned men and *lay
people* (*ignorant men*).

I Corinthians i. 14. I thank God that I *christened* (*baptised*)
none of you.

Revelation xviii. 12. Of pearls and *raynes* (*fine linen*) and
purple.

Raynes was a choice linen made at Rennes in Brittany.

But these homely and popular touches would have been
of little avail, had they not been borne along upon the stream
of a style that was equal to its task. It is here that his
greatness as a translator lies. He chooses the simplest
Anglo-Saxon words, and sets them out with a noble directness.
He has no conceits, he never aims at grandeur; but he
seldom fails to strike home. His own nature, deep but
simple, makes him an ideal interpreter of the gospel message,
and to that natural endowment is added a thorough mastery
of the English tongue. He is proud to be an Englishman,
and in all his books uses his mother tongue in preference to
the customary Latin. Therein he stands in contrast with
Thomas More, who, master of English though he was, chose
to write his *Utopia* in the learned language.

Occasionally indeed Tyndale falls below his principles,

being deflected into a Latinism through long familiarity
with the Vulgate. Thus he renders in John xii. 26: "If any
man *minister unto* (*serve*) me, let him follow me, and where
I am, there shall also my *minister* (*servant*) be." It is to be
wished also that he had always given us, as indeed he does
once or twice: "*Truly*, I say unto you"; and so saved our
English version from the rather pompous *verily*. But in his
day *verity* and *verily* were in constant use, whereas now they
are merely archaisms.

In many passages his version agrees almost word for word
with our Authorized Version. Such are, of course, as a
rule the simpler passages, either of straightforward narrative
or where the thought moves easily on from one point to
another. With the more complex and difficult passages,
the theological and argumentative parts of the epistles, he
is not so successful, but he is not singular in this respect.
His habit of bringing out the meaning, either by a paraphrase or by the repetition of a noun, sometimes makes for
clumsiness; but even here the general effect is noble, as
if we saw a man grappling with an intractable material,
that needs time for its mastery, preparing the first plan out
of which perfection might grow.

He has a wonderful power of finding an apt and telling
phrase, and his rhythm is matchless. Many of the most
familiar quotations of our New Testament come from his
pen. Thus he is the author of:

Matthew xx. 12. Born the burden and heat of the day.
Born the charge of the day and the heat. (Purvey.)
Matthew xxii. 10. The wedding was furnished with
guests.
The bridal was fulfilled with men sitting at the meat.
(Purvey.)
Luke i. 78. Through the tender mercy of our Lord,
wherewith has visited us the dayspring from on high.
By the *inwardness* [the first Lollard version has *entrails*]
of the mercy of our God, in which he springing up from on
high hath visited us. (Purvey.)
Tyndale's second edition agrees exactly with our prayer-
book and bible version.
Luke xii. 19. Take thine ease, eat, drink and be merry.

Rest thou, eat, drink and make feast. (Purvey.)
Luke xxiii. 41. But this man hath done nothing amiss.
But this man did nothing of evil. (Purvey.)
Here Tyndale, like Luther (*ungeschickt*), exactly hits the mark. The Latin versions render *evil*.
Acts v. 24. They doubted of them whereunto this would grow.
They doubted of them what was done. (Purvey.)
Acts ix. 15. For he is a chosen vessel unto me.
For this is to me a vessel of choosing. (Purvey.)
Acts xvii. 28. For in him we live, move and have our being.
For in him we live and move and be. (Purvey.)
Romans xi. 25. Wise in your own conceits.
Wise to yourselves. (Purvey.)
I Corinthians iv. 11. We . . . are buffeted with fists, and have no certain dwelling place.
We . . . be smitten with buffets, and we be unstable. (Purvey.)
Colossians iii. 22. Not with eyeservice, as men pleasers, but in singleness of heart, fearing God.
Not serving with the eye as pleasing to men, but in simpleness of heart, dreading the Lord. (Purvey.)
Hebrews xii. 2. Looking unto Jesus, the author and finisher of our faith, which for the joy that was set before him abode the cross, and despised the shame, and is set down on the right hand of the throne of God.
Beholding into the maker of faith and the perfect ender Jesus, which when joy was purposed to him, he suffered the cross and despised confusion, and sitteth on the right hand of the seat of God. (Purvey.)
II Peter i. 19. Until the day dawn and the daystar arise in your hearts.
Till the day begin to give light, and the daystar spring up in your hearts. (Purvey.)

There are in Tyndale's version a number of archaisms, and no doubt there would be more, but for the powerful influence of his language upon the development of English speech. A few of his words have dropped out, and others are no longer used in the same meaning. Thus he always writes *health* for *salvation*, and occasionally uses *grudge* for *be angry*, *arede* for *prophecy*, *unghostly* for *profane*, *appose* for *question.* But on the whole there is wonderfully little that cannot be easily understood to-day.

Some of his renderings sound quaint to our ears. Thus he gives us:—

Matthew xxv. 35. I was harbourless, and ye lodged me.

Mark xiv. 51. Clothed in linen upon the bare.

This rendering might well have been preserved by our Authorized Version.

Luke ii. 13. A multitude of heavenly soldiers lauding God.

Luke xxii. 25. They that bear rule over them are called gracious lords.

John xvii. 12. None of them is lost but that lost child.

I Corinthians iv. 9. For we are made a *gazing stock* unto the world.

The translators of the Authorized Version were at fault in casting out this striking word in favour of *spectacle*.

II Corinthians iv. 8. We are troubled on every side, yet are we not without shift.

I Timothy iii. 16. And without *nay* (*controversy*) great is the mystery of godliness.

This rendering also might have been kept.

I Timothy vi. 4. *Wasteth his brains* (*doting*) about questions and strife of words.

Revelation vi. 8. I looked, and behold a *green* (*pale*) horse.

It only remains to put before the reader two longer specimens of the version, so that he judge its merits for himself in consecutive passages. The changes made by Tyndale in his second edition (1534) are given in the margin of the page.

Luke xvi. 19–31.

 ᵃ bysse

There was a certain rich man, which was clothed in purple and fine ᵃ*raynes*, and fared deliciously every day. (20) And there was a certain beggar, named Lazarus, which lay at his gate full of sores, (21) desiring to be refreshed with the crumbs which fell from the rich man's board.   Nevertheless the dogs came and licked his sores.   (22) And it fortuned that the beggar died, and was carried by the angels into Abraham's bosom.   The rich man also died, and was buried *b in hell.* (23) *When he lift up his eyes, as he was in torments, he* saw Abraham afar off, and Lazarus in his bosom.   (24) And *c cried* and said: father Abraham, have mercy on me, and send Lazarus that he may dip the tip of his finger in water, and cool my tongue, for I am tormented in this flame.   (25) *d Abraham* said unto him: Son, remember, that thou in thy life time receivedst thy pleasure and contrary wise Lazarus pain.   Now therefore is he comforted, and thou art punished.   (26) Beyond all this between you and us there is a great space set, so that they which would go from hence to you, cannot: neither *e from thence come hither.*   (27) *f And* he said: I pray thee therefore, father, send him to my father's house;   (28) for I have five brethren: for to warn them, lest they also come into this place of torment.   (29) Abraham said unto him: they have Moses and the prophets, let them hear them.   (30) And he said: nay, father Abraham, but *g if one from the dead came unto them,* they would repent.   (31) He said unto him: If they hear not Moses and the prophets neither will they believe, though one rose from death again.

b and being in hell in torments he lift up his eyes and

c he cried

d But Abraham

e may come from thence to us

f Then

g if one came unto them from the dead

Hebrews i.

God in time past diversly and many ways spake unto the fathers by prophets: (2) but in these last days he hath spoken unto us by his son, whom he hath made heir of all things, by whom also he made the world: (3) which son being the brightness of his glory, and very image of his substance, bearing up all things with the word of his power, hath in his own person purged our sins, and is sitten on the right hand of the majesty on high, (4) and is

more excellent than the angels, in as much as
he hath by inheritance obtained an excellenter
name than have they. (5) For unto which of
the angels said he at any time: Thou art my
son, this day begat I thee? And again:
will be his father, and he shall be my son
(6) And again when he bringeth in the first
a into   begotten son ^a *in* the world, he saith: And
all the angels of God shall worship him. (7)
b of   And ^b *unto* the angels he saith: He maketh his
angels spirits, and his ministers flames of fire
(8) But unto the son he saith: God thy seat
shall be for ever and ever; the sceptre of thy
kingdom is a right sceptre; (9) thou hast
loved righteousness and hated iniquity: where-
c God which is   fore ^c *hath God, which is thy God,* anointed thee
thy God hath   with the oil of gladness above thy fellows
(10) And thou, Lord, in the beginning hast
laid the foundation of the earth, and the
heavens are the works of thy hands. (11) They
shall perish, but thou shalt endure. They all
shall wax old as doth a garment: (12) and as a
vesture shalt thou change them, and they shall
d always   be changed: but thou art ^d *the same,* and thy
years shall not fail. (13) Unto which of the
angels said he at any time: Sit on my right
hand till I make thine enemies thy foot stool?
e ministering   (14) Are they not all ^e *spirits to do service, sent for*
spirits sent   to minister for their sakes, which shall be heirs
f salvation   of ^f *health* ?

Of Tyndale's work, as it appears in the second edition, it
has been calculated that ninety per cent. stands unaltered
in our Authorized Version, and seventy-five per cent. in
the Revised; and the rate is even higher, if changes due to
obsolete words and to improved Greek text are taken into
account. His translation has been the foundation, and his
method has been made the norm. Later translators have
entered into his spirit. His errors have been removed, his
obscurities made light, and his imperfect renderings replaced
by better; and the process of improvement is not yet ended.
This is what he would have wished. He had no false pride.

From his first New Testament to his death he calls upon
any man that would to correct his version, or to make
another himself, so only that he do it with a finer knowledge
and skill.   He would not have cared greatly that for a long
season his name was well-nigh forgotten by his own countrymen; for his work and his spirit have lived on, and will still
live.   He did not labour in vain; and if he has been mis-
judged, or even vilified, some amends have been made in
the last hundred years, and we in our day can repay still
more of the debt of honour.

CHAPTER VI

THE BATTLE BEGINS: 1526–8

AFTER the publication of the New Testament, Tyndale remained at Worms for more than a year, possibly even for two years; but, as we have seen, he got rid of Roye, as soon as he could dispense with his services. Roye stayed a few weeks longer in Worms, and then proceeded about the month of April to Strassburg.

" After we were departed [parted]," writes Tyndale in his preface to *Mammon*, " he went and gat him new friends, which thing to do he passeth all that ever I yet knew. And there when he had stored him of money, he gat him to Argentine [Strassburg]. . . . A year after that, and now twelve months before the printing of this work [May 8, 1528], came one Jerome, a brother of Greenwich also [*i.e.* as well as Roye], through Worms to Argentine, saying that he intended to be Christ's disciple another while, and to keep (as nigh as God would give him grace) the profession of his baptism, and to get his living with his hands, and to live no longer idly and of the sweat and labour of those captives, which they had taught not to believe in Christ, but in cut shoes and russet coats [the apparel of monks]. Which Jerome with all diligence I warned of Roye's boldness, and exhorted him to beware of him, and to walk quietly, and with all patience and long suffering, according as we have Christ and his apostles for an ensample: which thing he also promised me. Nevertheless when he was come to Argentine, William Roye (whose tongue is able not only to make fools stark mad, but also to deceive the wisest, that is at the first sight and acquaintance) gat him to him, and set him a-work to make rhymes, while he himself translated a dialogue out of Latin into English, in whose prologue he promiseth more a great deal than I fear me he will ever pay."

This meeting with Jerome in the spring of 1527 is the one piece of knowledge that we possess of Tyndale's life at

Worms, except for what we can glean from Buschius' statement already quoted. Jerome, who bore the surname of Barlow, had no doubt come abroad in search of his fellow-friar Roye. Of their doings at Strassburg we shall hear more later.

To Tyndale Worms was not merely a safe place of refuge; it was also the post of duty. He must stay there to super-intend the sale and distribution of his New Testaments, and it is likely that he made it his headquarters until the bulk of the books was off his hands. We should dearly like to know how they were transported to England. Probably some were shipped down the Rhine, though this might be a risky business, since Cologne was hostile to the reformation, and its rulers, spurred on by Cochlaeus, might be on the watch. Many no doubt were taken to the great spring and autumn fairs at Frankfort, then the centre of the bookselling trade, whither resorted merchants from all the countries of Europe; and in fact, as we shall learn later, Tyndale himself is reported to have been seen in this city. Some might be sent overland to Antwerp. Great caution and secrecy would be necessary, particularly when embarking the books for England; and no doubt they were usually disguised in some way, or packed under other merchandise.

Meanwhile in England Wolsey had been endeavouring to check the growth of Lutheranism. At Cambridge Robert Barnes fell into trouble over a sermon which he had preached at Christmas 1525, and was haled to London before the cardinal, his friend Coverdale accompanying him to assist with his defence. He was offered the choice between re-canting and burning, and after some hesitation he chose the former. On February 11, 1526 he bore a faggot at Paul's Cross along with four German merchants of the Steelyard. A high scaffold was erected, upon which Wolsey sat in all his splendour with thirty-six bishops, abbots and priors, and Fisher preached the sermon. The five victims then marched to a fire which had been kindled, and cast in each his faggot, while great basketfuls of Lutheran books were committed to the flames. On Barnes' arrest Cambridge had been searched for prohibited books by officers from London, but with no great results; for the owners received timely warning, and were able to conceal them. The Steelyard too was visited on the cardinal's behalf by Sir Thomas More at the end of January. The merchants young and old were compelled to take an oath in disclaimer of Lutheranism, and eight or ten of the leaders had to appear before Wolsey at Westminster. The rooms were ransacked by Sir Thomas, who succeeded in collecting a number of German testaments and Pentateuchs, and other foreign books. All this might seem very well. But a far more dangerous enemy was now at hand.

The first copies of the New Testament reached England about the month of March. At first the book would circulate quietly and cautiously, being sold in small numbers to safe persons, who were eager for reform. There were many such especially in London and the eastern counties, successors of the old Lollards, men often in a humble station, who treasured manuscript copies of the scripture, and would meet together in their houses to read and to pray. In 1517 in the diocese of London thirty-five persons were forced to abjure their opinions, and in 1521 Longland, the bishop of Lincoln, arrested some hundreds of Lollards. Among such the printed New Testament would find a ready welcome.

The first buyers would not know who the author was, for Tyndale's name was not upon the title-page, nor indeed is it likely that the name of place or printer was given. Monmouth would know, being in the secret, and it is probable (though the opposite view is usually held) that Wolsey would know; for it is hard to believe that Cochlæus and Rinck, in warning the king, would omit to tell him the names of the two Englishmen who were printing it. And in fact when we first find a name attached to it, in Ridley's letter of February 1527, it is ascribed, after the manner of Cochlæus, to both Tyndale and Roye, although the two fellow-workers had long since parted. It was only by degrees that the knowledge sickered through into the general mind, that the real maker of the book was Tyndale, and that Roye had been only an assistant.

As the summer proceeded, the circulation of the New Testament became wide enough to force itself upon the notice of the bishops, and it became necessary for them to decide how they were to act. They therefore held a conclave to consider the matter. Unhappily we have no account of their deliberations save that given us in *Rede me, and be not wroth,* the scurrilous poem of Roye and Jerome; still this account is no doubt true in its main facts. Jerome would have heard the story in his monastery of Greenwich, and would bring it with him to Germany in the spring of 1527.

The poem contains a violent attack on Wolsey, who is styled the mastiff cur bred in Ipswich town, worse than Nero or Herod, an execrable murderer, the devil's darling, a butcherly bishop, the prophet of Satan, a painted pastor, and so on; and who is charged in particular with " burning God's word, the holy testament," which last phrase is repeated again and again as a refrain.* Then the tale is told. The New Testament had been translated into English, " Wherein the authors with meekness, Utterly avoiding conviciousness, Demeaned them so discreetly," that no fault could be found with their work. It reached England through " good Christian men," who " with pure affect with cost did him thither convey." There it was betrayed, like its master Christ, the part of Judas being played by the " holy bishop of St Asse [Asaph], A post of Satan's jurisdiction, Whom they call Dr Standish." As soon as he heard that the gospel was come to England, " Immediately he did him [the gospel] trap, And to the man in the red cap, He brought him with strong hand; Before whose proud consistory, Bringing in false testimony, The gospel he did there accuse." He said: " Pleaseth your honourable grace, Here is chanced a piteous case, And to the church a great lack. The gospel in our English tongue, Of laymen to be

* Here is a stanza : O miserable monster, most malicious,
　　　　　　　　　Father of perversity, patron of hell,
　　　　　　　　　O terrible tyrant, to God and man odious,
　　　　　　　　　Advocate of antichrist, to Christ rebel,
　　　　　　　　　To thee I speak, O caitiff cardinal so cruel,
　　　　　　　　　Causeless charging by thy cursed commandment
　　　　　　　　　To brenne God's word the holy testament.

read and sung, Is now hither come to remain: Which many heretics shall make, Except your grace some way take, By your authority him to restrain." But Wolsey was lukewarm: "He spake the words of Pilate, Saying, I find no fault therein." However he asked the opinions of the bishops assembled. "Then answered bishop Caiaphas, That a great part better it was, The gospel to be condemned. . . . The cardinal then incontinent Against the gospel gave judgment, Saying to burn he deserved. Whereto all the bishops cried, Answering: it cannot be denied, He is worthy so to be served." Caiaphas stands for Tonstall, as is proved by the marginal note: *Hoc est London episcopus*, this is the bishop of London. The description of Wolsey's part in the matter fits exactly his known character; he had many vices, but he had no zeal for persecution, and during the last eight years of his power, when the grip of his papal legacy was thoroughly fastened upon the land, not a single person seems to have been burnt in England on the charge of heresy.

This episcopal conclave is alluded to in the preface to the English edition of Henry VIII's reply to Luther, printed about February 1527. Speaking of the peril from the New Testament the king says: "We . . . with the deliberate advice of the most reverend fathers of the spirituality, have determined the said and untrue translations to be burned, with further sharp correction and punishment against the keepers and readers of the same." The date however cannot be ascertained. Probably it was late in August: for on September 3 John Sadler of London writes to Antwerp to Richard Herman, the importer of the book, that the news in England was, that the English New Testament should be put down and burnt. It is, however, possible that there was more than one meeting of the bishops.

The great centre of distribution was of course London, and so Tonstall was more concerned than any of his brethren. On October 25 he summoned the booksellers of the town to a chapel in the palace of the bishop of Norwich, near Charing Cross, and warned them against importing Lutheran books, whether Latin or English. He had done this two years before, and his second attempt was no more successful than the first. He also issued on October 24 an injunction to his archdeacons.

" Certain children of iniquity," he writes, " maintainers of Luther's sect, blinded by extreme wickedness, declining from the way of truth and the orthodox faith, have with crafty trickery translated the holy gospel of God into our vulgar English tongue, intermingling certain articles of heretical depravity and pernicious erroneous opinions, pestilent, scandalous, and seductive of simple minds, and have endeavoured by their nefarious and crooked interpretations to profane the hitherto undefiled majesty of holy scripture, and cunningly and perversely to abuse the most sacred word of God, and the right sense of the same. Of which translation many books, containing the pestilent and pernicious poison in the vulgar tongue, have been dispersed in great numbers throughout our diocese; which truly, unless it be speedily foreseen, will without doubt infect and contaminate the flock committed to us, with the pestilent poison and the deadly disease of heretical depravity, to the grievous peril of the souls committed to us and the most grievous offence of the divine majesty " ;

and he orders the archdeacons within thirty days to call in all copies of the offending work, whether with or without glosses, under pain of excommunication and suspicion of heresy. Next, on November 3, archbishop Warham follows with a like order to the suffragan bishops of his province, framed in almost exactly the same words. He seems to have been content to borrow Tonstall's document, and to adapt it to his own needs.

The burning took place at Paul's Cross, the usual scene of such spectacular demonstrations, and the sermon was preached by Tonstall himself. Monmouth was present. " When," he says, " I heard my lord of London preach at Paul's Cross, that Sir William Tyndale had translated the New Testament into English, and was naughtily translated, that was the first time that ever I suspected or knew any evil by him." That Tonstall actually named Tyndale as the translator is highly probable, but not quite certain; for Monmouth, who was in the secret of the authorship,

may have supplied the name himself. If Tonstall did name
him, he doubtless linked Roye also with him, as his chaplain
Ridley did four months later. One of the testaments committed to the flames was in all likelihood Monmouth's
own: for he says that he handed it to the father confessor
of Sion, and that it afterwards passed to the bishop of London.
In his sermon Tonstall branded the new version as *doctrinam
peregrinam*,* strange doctrine, and denounced its falsity,
professing to have found two thousand errors in it. At
least this is the number given by Cochlæus; Roye and
Jerome put it at three thousand.

Here is the account of the burning as given in the poem;
it forms part of a conversation between two servants of a
priest, named Jeffrey and Watkin:—

> *Jeffrey* : They set not by the gospel a fly.
> Didst thou not hear what villany
> They did unto the gospel?
>
> *Watkin* : Why? did they against him conspire?
>
> *Jeffrey* : By my troth they set him afire
> Openly in London city.
>
> *Watkin* : Who caused it so to be done?
>
> *Jeffrey* : In sooth the bishop of London,
> With the cardinal's authority;
> Which at Paul's Cross earnestly
> Denounced it to be heresy,
> That the gospel should come to light;
> Calling them heretics execrable,
> Which caused the gospel venerable
> To come unto laymen's sight.
> He declared there in his furiousness,
> That he found errors, more and less,
> Above three thousand in the translation.
> Howbeit when all came to pass,
> I daresay unable he was
> Of one error to make probation.
> Alas, he said: Masters and friends,
> Consider well now in your minds
> These heretics diligently;
> They say that common women
> Shall as soon come unto heaven,
> As those that live perfectly.
>
> *Watkin* : And was that their very saying?
>
> *Jeffrey* : After this wise without feigning
> In a certain prologue they write,

---

* So says Tyndale himself (*Practice of Prelates*, II. 337).

That a whore or an open sinner,
By means of Christ our redeemer,
Whom God to repent doth incite,
Shall sooner come to salvation
By merits of Christ's passion
Than an outward holy liver.

Watkin : They did there none other thing show
Than is rehearsed in Matthew
In the one and twenty chapter.

Jeffrey : For all that, he said in his sermon,
Rather than the gospel should be common,
Bringing people into error,
He would gladly suffer martyrdom
To uphold the devil's freedom,
Of whom he is a confessor.

The exact date of the burning is unknown, and some have placed it before Tonstall's injunction to his archdeacons; but a careful examination of the evidence enables us with some confidence to fix it a few days afterwards. For on November 21 cardinal Campeggio writes from Rome to Wolsey, saying that he has lately heard with pleasure of the burning of the " sacred codex of the bible, perverted in the vernacular tongue, and brought into the realm by perfidious followers of the abominable Lutheran sect; than which assuredly no holocaust could be more pleasing to Almighty God." Now couriers went very frequently between London and Rome. On November 7 Campeggio had written to Wolsey in answer to a letter dated October 18, twenty days before; and on November 9 pope Clement VII had written to Henry VIII, seemingly in reply to his letter of October 23, written seventeen days before. Neither of these letters mentions the burning; and yet it would have been of great interest to the papal court, and would have been communicated almost as soon as it happened. If we may take seventeen days as the minimum period required for the journey to Rome, we obtain November 4 as the latest possible date of the burning. But these spectacles seem usually to have been held on a Sunday; at least that was the day selected for the burning of Lutheran books in May 1521 and February 1526. Now in this year November 4 was a Sunday; but as this date barely leaves time for the news to reach

Campeggio, it is probable that we should fix the burning a week earlier, on Sunday October 28.*

Meanwhile Tyndale was adding to his offences. At some time in the latter part of the year 1526 he issued his *Introduction to the Epistle to the Romans*, of which only one copy exists as a separate work, in the Bodleian library at Oxford. It bears no name, nor date, nor place, but was without doubt printed by Schoeffer of Worms.† It is attacked by Robert Ridley in his letter of February 1527, and is there ascribed to Tyndale and Roye. The little book is a summary of the epistle, and of the doctrine of faith and works therein contained. It is in the main a translation of Luther's preface, which appeared in his New Testament of 1522, and which in the following year was turned into Latin by Justus Jonas; and Westcott has shown that Tyndale used both the German and the Latin editions. The ground plan is Luther's and most of the wording also; but Tyndale expands it, and adds whole paragraphs of his own, amounting to perhaps one quarter of the whole. This is followed, "to fill up the leaf withal," by a little dialogue between the sinner and his God, which is taken from Luther's treatise on the Lord's prayer.

The spectacular burning of a few copies was not likely to check the inflow of a book that found a ready market, and in a few weeks another edition was in the field. This was a pirate reprint, made at Antwerp, and from Joye's *Apology* we gather that it was sextodecimo in size. The first copies must have been in England by mid-November; for by the 21st of that month John Hackett, the English ambassador to the Low Countries, had received instructions from Wolsey to discover the printers or sellers, and to take action against them. In a few days he is able to send copies of the book, fresh from the printing house, and to report that the printer,

---

* Cf. Tyndale's *Practice of Prelates*, II. 296; "St. Peter's vicar shall have word in fifteen or sixteen days from the uttermost part of Christendom."

† The border of the title-page appears also in Hätzer and Denck's *Alle Propheten* (April 13, 1527,'8vo., Schoeffer). This point seems not hitherto to have been observed. A facsimile is in Fry's *The First New Testament* (1862).

Christopher van Endhoven, has been arrested at his suit: but the lords of Antwerp are unwilling to punish him or to destroy the books. On January 12 he is so much disgusted at the delay that he proposes to buy up the testaments himself, and to send them to England to be burnt; but in the end the obstacles were overcome, and within the next few days all the suspected books that could be found (he seems to mean others as well as the New Testament) were seized and burnt in Antwerp and Bergen-op-Zoom. In one case, however, his prey escaped him. He had hoped to intercept a cargo of books, bought by Scotch merchants and embarked upon Scotch ships, which were lying in harbour in Zeeland, and were bound for St Andrews and Edinburgh: but they had sailed the day before his coming. From Joye's account it would appear that this first pirate edition numbered two or three thousand; and if Hackett was even half as thorough as he believed, some hundreds of these must have been destroyed. It is to this that Ridley refers, when he writes on February 24 that " many hundreds " of New Testaments have been " burnt beyond the sea."

But where profit is to be made, men are not easily intimidated. On May 21 Hackett hears that " some new printers " of Antwerp are bringing English testaments to the Bergen market. Hastening thither to take punishment, he finds twenty-four copies in possession of one man. These may be the German prints: for he learns that at Frankfort at the last (April) fair " more than two thousand such like English books " were for sale. He therefore requires the deputy of the English nation to read out to the Englishmen in Bergen the king's letter to Luther, and to order them to deliver up all books of this nature.

Meanwhile Warham had been putting into action elsewhere the plan, which Hackett had before conceived, of buying up books to destroy them. To the cool observer this will not seem a very wise proceeding, for it would only encourage the printers to print more: still it was at least better than burning the readers. On May 26, 1527 the archbishop wrote a letter to his suffragans, asking them each to bear a share of the cost which he had thus incurred, amounting to £62 9s. 4d. The reply of one of the bishops, Nix of Norwich, is extant, and from his letter, written on June 14, we learn that in exchange for this sum the archbishop had got into his hands " all the books of the New Testament translated into English and printed beyond the sea, as well those with the glosses joined unto them as the other without the glosses." Nix sends ten marks, or £6 13s. 4d., offering to give more if necessary, and congratulates the archbishop on doing " a gracious and a blessed deed," for which God would highly reward him. These testaments seem to be the books printed at Cologne and Worms, and they were very likely bought by an emissary of the archbishop at the recent Frankfort fair. If we put the average price at 1s. 4d., the total number purchased will be about one thousand.

All this while the bible readers themselves were not greatly molested. Maybe the authorities thought that their first measures of suppression would be effective, or else they could not lay their hands on the chief distributors in England, and so could not trace the sales : but for one reason or another the buyers of the book were left in peace, and its influence spread quietly for many months. Cambridge was still a great centre of Lutheranism, but Oxford now was not far behind; for the group of young Cambridge men (John Frith among them), whom Wolsey in 1525 had imported as canons of his newly founded college, had a strong zeal for reform, and the new ideas, so the warden of New College complained, were infecting " the most towardly young men in the university." At both places Tyndale's New Testament found many readers; but it had an even more powerful influence in London and the eastern counties, upon the less educated Lollards, who could not read the Latin bible.

This happy state however did not last long. In November 1527 Bilney of Cambridge was arrested, and brought to trial in London; and although he recanted and carried a faggot, it has been thought that from the revelations made at his trial Wolsey obtained the clue to the distribution of the New Testament. At all events early in 1528 a vigorous search for the book, and a cruel attack upon its readers was instituted, particularly in Tonstall's diocese and in the university of Oxford. At the latter place Thomas Garrett, a priest from London, who had within the last few months brought three hundred and fifty suspected books into the university, was arrested in the month of February, and sent to London to Wolsey. Many of his supporters, including Frith and other canons of Cardinal's college, were thrown into prison, where they remained several months, and where three of them died in August. In the end the ringleaders were compelled to abjure, and to carry a faggot in procession at Oxford, and the rest cast a book into a fire kindled at Carfax. Frith, however, seems to have escaped this fate; for after the death of his three comrades he had been released by Wolsey's command, on condition that he should not travel more than ten miles out of Oxford. But after witnessing the humiliating fate of his brethren, he thought it better to retire over seas, probably about the month of December 1528.

In February also Tonstall commenced his great drive against the Lollards and Lutherans of his diocese, which then took in the county of Essex as well as London, and he carried it on until midsummer. He made a visitation of the whole city, and by March 15 his own prisons were so full that he had to commit a fresh suspect to the Fleet. It is from the depositions of these prisoners that we gain most of our information about the circulation of the first New Testament. As a rule they were of humble position, blacksmiths, bakers, weavers, servants, husbandmen and the like, but a few (Monmouth for example) were of higher rank; and clerks were in trouble as well as laymen. Usually they abjured, and were put to punishment. An interesting confession is that made at Colchester on April 4 by a clothmaker named Boswell, who states that on the Friday after Ash Wednesday last [*i.e.* on February 28] he was in the Colchester hall, London, with cloth to sell, when " one John Tyndale of London, merchant, dwelling about the well with the two buckets towards Austin Friars, chanced to come in." Boswell asked him to buy some cloth, but he refused, on the ground that he should be unable to sell

it again: nor (said John Tyndale) did he see any remedy
for the present evil state, unless the commons arose and
complained to the king, because the people were not half
set to work. This John Tyndale must have been our
William's brother, and we can safely hazard the guess that
his conversation with Boswell turned upon other matters,
beside the price of cloth and the unemployment of the
people. Boswell was sent up to Wolsey for examination,
since he had "named a person in London," but whether
the cardinal took any action against John Tyndale, we know
not.

About this time the rulers of England were still further
infuriated by the arrival of two little books, published at
Strassburg by Roye and Jerome. The first was the *Dialogue
of the Father and the Son*, translated from the Latin by Roye.
The text of this still exists,* and is harmless enough, but
Roye's prologue has been lost. The other book was of a
very different kind. It was the poem, *Rede me and be not
wroth*, of which we have already heard; and it displeased
Tyndale mightily.

" Paul saith," he writes in his preface to *Mammon*, " the
servant of the Lord must not strive, but be peaceable unto
all men, and ready to teach, and one that can suffer the evil
with meekness, and that can inform [instruct] them that
resist, if God at any time will give them repentance for to
know the truth. It becometh not then the Lord's servant
to use railing rhymes, but God's word; which is the right
weapon to slay sin, vice and all iniquity."

Tyndale was offended, as well he might be, by the
frivolous and abusive tone of the book, and not the less so,
because it was fathered upon himself. "In the beginning,"
writes More in his *Dialogue*, it was " reckoned to be made
by Tyndale, and whether it be so or not, we be not yet
very sure." It was to guard against this false opinion that
in his *Mammon* Tyndale spoke out so strongly against Roye,
and began from that time forward to put his name to his
works. He might also with justice have complained,

---

* The original sheets were re-issued in 1550, under title, *The True
Belief in Christ and his Sacraments.*

though he did not in fact do so, that the authors speak as
if Roye had had an equal share with himself in the making
of the New Testament. The poem was not only harming
his reputation: it was also adding to his dangers: for in
the summer of 1528 Wolsey, stung no doubt by the furious
railing against himself, endeavoured to have Tyndale and
Roye seized, and brought to England for punishment.

But where was Tyndale now? We left him at Worms in
April 1527, when Barlow passed through the city on the
way to Strassburg. It has generally been supposed that he
removed later in the year to Marburg, and stayed there,
with a few intervals of absence, for three years. The ground
for this belief lay in the title-pages and colophons of his next
four books. *Mammon* and *Obedience* appeared in 1528,
and the Pentateuch and *Practice of Prelates* in 1530, all professing to have been printed by Hans Lufft at Marlborow,
or Marborch, in Hesse. It is true that Hans Lufft, famous
as one of Luther's printers in Wittenberg, was not known
to have had a branch press at Marburg, but still the thing
was not impossible, and no one was able to establish a better
title for any other town.

Nevertheless the bibliographers have been uneasy, and for
some time have suspected a Dutch origin for the books,
and now at length they claim to be able to name the man.
A careful examination of type, woodcuts, ornaments and the
like proves that this whole series of Lufft-Marburg books,
whether written by Tyndale, Frith or others, really proceeded from a printer named John Hoochstraten. This
man was printing at Antwerp under his own name in
1525–6, then for four years 1526–30 he vanishes, just the
very years in which the first Lufft-Marburg group is produced.
Then from 1531 to early 1535 his name reappears first in
Lübeck, and then in Malmö, where he becomes technical
assistant to Pedersen, the translator of the Danish bible;
then from 1535 to 1540, during the reign of the second
Lufft-Marburg group, he vanishes again; and finally he is
found once more at Antwerp printing under his own name
in 1540–3. It all fits together beautifully, and according
to Miss Kronenberg, who has been the chief unraveller of

the mystery, there is no shadow of doubt about the identification. To print Lutheran books was a dangerous matter, as Endhoven had discovered; it might mean imprisonment, a heavy fine, loss of stock, banishment or even worse: and many printers therefore issued such books without name. Hoochstraten preferred to protect himself by a false name, and indeed he used two or three other pseudonyms besides that of Hans Lufft.*

But granting him to be the printer, where did he print the books? In all likelihood at Antwerp. He was certainly printing there before and afterwards, and his family seems to have belonged to the town. Also we learn from Foxe that an Englishman, Michael Lobley, fell into trouble in London in 1531 for buying in Antwerp three of these Lufft-Marburg books, two by Tyndale and one by Frith: which looks as if they had been printed there; for Antwerp was not a great book fair like Frankfort. Pedersen too, who later employed Hoochstraten in the north, was residing in Antwerp in 1529–31, and may have formed his acquaintance there. Lastly, though Tyndale's movements after he left Worms are mysterious, and he must have frequently changed his place of abode, still the only town with which his name is constantly linked is Antwerp, and it was certainly the most convenient for printing for the English market.

Must we then abandon the sojourn at Marburg altogether, since its chief prop is withdrawn? We cannot speak decisively, but it is likely that he visited the place. He would sometimes go to Frankfort for the fairs, and Marburg was within easy reach of that city. It was a safe place too, safer perhaps than Worms, since its prince, the landgrave Philip, had wholeheartedly embraced the reformation; and it was also attractive to a scholar, for in May 1527 Philip had founded an university, and had drawn to it

---

* Cf. M. E. Kronenberg's articles in *Het Boek*, 1919, and *Transactions of the Bibliographical Society*, Vol. IX., 1928. Miss Kronenberg, who is completing the *Nederlandsche Bibliographie*, has kindly given me information about the printing of some of Tyndale's first editions. These printers of reformation books in the Low Countries deserve our gratitude. Under a still more stringent edict of October, 1531 they might be branded with a red hot iron, and lose an eye or a hand at the discretion of the judge.

as professors not only Francis Lambert, the French reformer, but Buschius, Tyndale's old acquaintance of Worms. Among the first names on the list of students are those of three Scotsmen, one of whom was Patrick Hamilton, the brave young nobleman, who, after a short stay at Marburg, returned home in the autumn of the year, to die gloriously in the flames at St Andrews in February 1528. If Tyndale visited Marburg in 1527, he might meet Hamilton, and it is some slight support of this, that his young disciple Frith, who crossed the sea in the following year, translated Hamilton's *Patrick's Places* from Latin into English, and speaks with great admiration of the young martyr. Hoochstraten may perhaps have derived the name Marburg for his title-page from the fact that Tyndale had recently been staying there; for he never uses it, until he prints the *Mammon* for Tyndale. If so, the book may have been written at Marburg, and brought to Antwerp for printing.

This work must now be considered. Its full title is *The Parable of the Wicked Mammon*, and it is the first of Tyndale's writings to bear his name. The colophon gives the date May 8, 1528,* but it seems to have been written before the tidings of the February persecutions had reached the continent. It shows, however, strong resentment at the vilification and burning of the New Testament. The preface is headed "William Tyndale, otherwise called Hychins, to the reader," and is full of interest. Parts have already been quoted. It begins :—

"Grace and peace, with all manner of spiritual feeling and living, worthy of the kindness of Christ, be with the reader and with all that thirst the will of God. Amen. The cause why I set my name before this little treatise, and have not rather done it in the New Testament, is that then I followed the counsel of Christ, which exhorteth men to do their good deeds secretly, and to be content with the conscience of welldoing, and that God seeth us; and patiently to abide the reward of the last day, which Christ hath purchased for us : and now would I fain have done likewise, but am compelled otherwise to do."

* Daye's folio gives May 8, 1527, an impossible date, which has caused much confusion.

Tyndale then describes his association with Roye and Jerome, and sharply condemns them for putting out foolish, railing rhymes instead of fighting with the sword of the word of God.

" Let it not offend thee that some walk inordinately; let not the wickedness of Judas cause thee to despise the doctrine of his fellows. No man ought to think that Stephen was a false preacher, because that Nicolas, which was chosen fellow with him to minister unto the widows, fell after into great heresies, as histories make mention. Good and evil go always together; one cannot be known without the other."

He then turns from his offending comrades to the great enemy against whom he is fighting. Antichrist, he says, is not an outward thing, as our fathers thought; he is a spiritual thing. He is ever present; he was in the Old Testament and in the New Testament; he is here now, and he will endure till the world's end.

" But his nature is (when he is uttered [exposed], and overcome by the word of God) to go out of the play for a season, and to disguise himself, and then to come in again with a new name and new raiment. . . . There is a difference in the names between a pope, a cardinal, a bishop, and so forth, and to say a scribe, a pharisee, a senior, and so forth; but the thing is all one. . . . We had spied out antichrist long ago, if we had looked in the doctrine of Christ and his apostles; where because the beast seeth himself now to be sought for, he roareth, and seeketh new holes to hide himself in, and changeth himself into a thousand fashions, with all manner wiliness, falsehood, subtlety and craft. Because that his excommunications are come to light, he maketh it treason unto the king to be acquainted with Christ. . . . The old antichrists brought Christ unto Pilate, saying: By our law he ought to die; and when Pilate bade them judge him after their law, they answered: It is not lawful for us to kill any man. . . . They do all things of a good zeal, they say; they love you so well, that they had rather burn you than that you should have fellowship with Christ. . . . They would divide you from Christ and his holy testament, and join you to the pope, to believe in his testament and promises.

" Some men will ask peradventure, why I took the labour

to make this work, inasmuch as they will burn it, seeing they
burnt the gospel? I answer: In burning the New Testament they did none other thing than I looked for; no more
shall they do, if they burn me also, if it be God's will it shall
so be. Nevertheless in translating the New Testament I
did my duty, and so do I now, and will do as much more as
God hath ordained me to do. And as I offered that to all
men to correct it, whosoever could, even so do I this. Whosoever therefore readeth this, compare it unto the scripture.
If God's word bear record unto it, and thou also feelest in
thine heart that it is so, be of good comfort and give God
thanks. If God's word condemn it, then hold it accursed,
and so do all other doctrines, as Paul counselleth his Galatians.
Believe not every spirit suddenly, but judge them by the word
of God, which is the trial of all doctrine, and lasteth for
ever. Amen."

The treatise itself, starting from the parable of the unjust
steward, grows into an exposition upon the doctrine of
justification by faith. This doctrine was a corner-stone of
the reformation, and in a sharper or milder form is enshrined
in all the confessions begotten thereby; and it seems that
Tyndale put out the book as an aid to the proper understanding of the New Testament. It is not, however, entirely
his own. Large sections of the early part are taken word for
word from a sermon on the parable of the unjust steward,
preached by Luther in 1522 and soon afterwards printed.
Much of the remainder is written in Luther's spirit. The
boldness of the following passage, for instance, is worthy of
the great German:

" Christ is thine, and all his deeds are thy deeds. Christ
is in thee, and thou in him, knit together inseparably.
Neither canst thou be damned, except Christ be damned
with thee: neither can Christ be saved, except thou be
saved with him." *

The argument is ably sustained, and the tone is noble.
Good works, says Tyndale, can only proceed out of a good
heart. From fear or from conformity a man may do acts

---

* Cf. Luther's *Werke* (Weimar edition) 10 (3), p. 283. Tyndale takes
over almost the whole sermon. Of pp. 49–70 in Vol. I of his *Works*
about half is Luther's, making about one sixth of the whole treatise.

of goodness, but that is not true goodness in the sight of God. But let once the heart be touched by the fire of faith in Christ, and good deeds will follow as naturally as healthy fruit springs from a healthy tree. The book shows little order or arrangement, and the interpretation of biblical texts may not always commend itself: but on the whole Tyndale makes out a strong case. Nor is he content with theologizing. One of the most attractive features of the book is its strong practical tone, its interest in the common man.

" How many are there," he asks, " of the same sort [*i.e.* of orthodox belief], which thou canst not make believe that a thousand things are sin, which God damneth for sin all the scripture throughout: as to buy as good cheap as he can, and to sell as dear as he can; to raise the market of corn and victuals for his own vantage, without the respect of his neighbour, or of the poor, or of the commonwealth, and such like."

Here too we first meet in Tyndale the doctrine, that the man who denies help to his neighbour is a thief.

" Christ is Lord over all; and every Christian is heir annexed with Christ, and therefore lord over all; and every-one lord of whatsoever another hath. If thy brother or neighbour therefore need, and thou have to help him, and yet shewest not mercy, but withdrawest thy hands from him, then robbest thou him of his own, and art a thief."

How simple and touching too is the following passage upon the hiring of professional prayers:—

" If thou give me £1000 to pray for thee, I am no more bound than I was before. Man's imagination can make the commandment of God neither greater nor smaller, neither can to the law of God either add or minish. God's command-ment is as great as himself. I am bound to love the Turk with all my might and power—yea, and above my power— even from the ground of my heart, after the ensample that Christ loved me; neither to spare goods, body or life, to win him to Christ. And what can I do more for thee, if thou gavest me all the world? Where I see need, there can I not but pray, if God's spirit be in me."

Below the colophon Tyndale adds, as an afterthought, a remarkable apology for the errors of printing :—

" Be not offended, most dear reader, that divers things are overseen through negligence in this little treatise. For verily the chance was such, that I marvel that it is so well as it is. Moreover it becometh the book even so to come as a mourner and in vile apparel to wait on his master; which sheweth himself now again, not in honour and glory, as between Moses and Elias; but in rebuke and shame, as between two murderers, to try his true friends, and to prove whether there be any faith on the earth."

We may suppose that at the time of printing the perils besetting Tyndale were specially severe, and that the work had to be done hastily.

It need hardly be said that the treatise was violently attacked. It figures in list after list of prohibited books. Sir Thomas More calls it a "very *mammona iniquitatis*, a very treasury and wellspring of wickedness," " the wicked book of *Mammon*," " a book by which many have been beguiled and brought into many wicked heresies." By Warham it was denounced as " containing many detestable errors and damnable opinions," and his council of divines drew up a list of twenty-nine heresies to be found within its pages.

The *Mammon* had not been long in the country, and perhaps it had not yet come to the ears of Wolsey, when he determined to strike directly at the ringleaders of the English Lutherans abroad. On June 18 he instructed Hackett to demand from the regent of the Low Countries the delivery of three heretics, who appear to have been Tyndale, Roye, and the English merchant Richard Herman, who was a citizen of Antwerp. The regent and her council replied that even the emperor himself could not send a heretic into another land without examination. They would, however, arrest the three men and their books, and try them; and if found guilty, they would either send them to England, or punish them on the spot. On July 14 Hackett reports that the regent has had a diligent search made, but that two of the offenders could not be discovered.

He himself, however, has had Herman arrested and thrown into prison. The charges against him were that he had supported the English heretics in Antwerp, taken their books to England and sold them, and thus fomented rebellion against the king.

At the end of August Wolsey sends over a certain John West, a friar observant of Greenwich, and therefore acquainted with Roye and Jerome, to aid in the search. He writes on September 2 to Hackett from the convent of his order in Antwerp. After saying that he hopes to be able to arrest Constantine, a priest, newly fled from England, and to get possession of certain compromising letters seized in Herman's house, he proceeds to the main object of his mission:

" I have spoken with Francis Byrkman, bookbinder of this town, and he hath showed me that Pety * Gueliem Roye and one Jerome Burlowe, both friars of our religion, and Hucthyns otherwise called Tyndale, hath made this book that was last made against the king's highness and my lord cardinal [*i.e. Rede me*], and . . . that one John Schott, a printer of Strassburg, printed them, and that there is yet another whole pipe of them at Frankfort; and he desired me to write him a letter . . . whether he shall buy them or not: and if he buyeth them, he intended to send Roye with the other two to Cologne to receive there the money for the books, and then I and Mr Herman Ryng of Cologne shall take them there."

Hackett's answer has not been preserved; but about the middle of September West and another observant friar, named Flegh, set out for Cologne with a guide. West had been supplied with money by Hackett, and he intended on reaching Cologne to change his monastic dress. From Cologne he proceeded to Frankfort for the fair, where he joined forces with Hermann Rinck, who also, on Wolsey's instructions, was occupied in the same business. It is from

* Roye's father was known in Antwerp as Petit, cf. p. 133. He is likely the William Roye, native of Brabant, who received letters of denization in England in 1512.

Rinck's letter of October 4, written to Wolsey from Cologne, that we learn how they fared :—

I received, he says, on September 21 your letter of August 5, asking me to " buy up everywhere books printed in English and to seize Roye and Hutchins. But they and their accomplices have not been seen at Frankfort since Easter [April 12] and the fair next to Lent, nor is it known whither they have gone, and whether they are alive or dead. John Schott, citizen of Strassburg and their printer, says he knows not whither they have vanished." Their books are crammed with heresy, offensive to your grace, and make the king odious to all Christians. " Three weeks ago, before receiving your grace's letter, I learnt that those very books had been pawned to the Jews at Frankfort for a certain sum of money, and I was on my own account taking measures to get hold of them as soon as possible. The printer John Schott, beside the interest that must be paid to the Jews, demanded both a recompense for his labour and the cost of the paper, and said that he would sell them to the person who would offer the most money." I therefore spared no labour nor expense, and using the letters which you sent me from England, and also the imperial privileges which I possess, I by gifts gained over the consuls of Frankfort and some of the senators and judges, and obtained leave to collect all those books wherever they could be found. They were in three or four places, and now, I hope, I hold them all except two copies, which I have given to West to take to you. " Unless I had learned of the matter and had interposed, the books were to have been bound and concealed in paper covers, packed in ten bundles, covered with flax, and at a suitable opportunity craftily and without suspicion transported across the sea to Scotland and England, there to be sold merely as blank paper : but I think very few or none have been taken across or sold." The printer himself has been forbidden by the consuls to print any more from the copper types, and he has taken an oath to obey and also to send me the original written copy. " I will make the most strenuous efforts to arrest the aforesaid Roy and Hutchins, and all other enemies and rebels against the king's grace and yours, and to find out where they live."

Rinck then offers to obtain for the king from the emperor

fresh privileges in the matter of the extradition of English fugitives, who may be charged with rebellion or heresy.

"William Roye, William Tyntaell, Jerome Barlow, Alexander Barckley and their adherents, formerly observants of the Franciscan order, but now apostates, together with George Constans [Constantine] and many others, ought to be arrested, punished and handed over for their Lutheran heresy." At Frankfort, using my papal and imperial mandates, I compelled Schott to swear before the consuls how many of these books he has printed in English, German and French. "He confessed on oath that in the English tongue he had only printed hitherto a thousand books of six sheets (*quaterniones*) and a thousand of nine sheets,* and this at the order of Roy and Hutchins, who, having no money, could not pay for the printed books, much less have them printed in other languages. I have therefore bought almost the whole, and have them in my house at Cologne. . . . Will your grace inform me what you wish to be done with the books thus purchased?"

These highly interesting letters show how much the English authorities were in the dark about the movements of Tyndale. He is throughout spoken of as if he were hand in glove with Roye, though he had parted from him two and a half years ago. He is even said to have gone to Strassburg, and to be the part author of the two little books which were seized at Frankfort, though he himself had denied the fact in his *Mammon*. The letter of Rinck throws a light upon Roye's character. Without money or influence he was nevertheless able to print two thousand books, which speaks volumes for the glibness of tongue and the persuasive powers, with which Tyndale credits him.

Meanwhile Hackett was in trouble over Richard Herman. He had had him thrown into prison, but it was not easy to find evidence against him. For three months there was no hearing, and then the case was deferred two or three times, that further inquiries might be made; for Herman demanded the names of the Lutherans and rebels, whom

---

* This description agrees with the extant copies of the *Dialogue* and *Rede me*.

he was accused of harbouring, and the dates and the manner of the support which he had given. Hackett writes letter after letter to Wolsey, begging to be supplied with proofs, but receives no answer at all. At length on January 22 the prosecution produced some names: the defendant had supported certain heretics and rebels, of whom " the one was named Willem Tandeloo, and the other was the son of Petit Roy, being a runaway monk of the observant order." The court, however, was not satisfied with this, but demanded more details as to times and places and methods; and as these were not forthcoming by February 5, an order was made that Herman be set at liberty.*

Things therefore were not going very well for the persecutors. Nevertheless West, now back in his monastery at Greenwich, does not give up hope. In December 1528 he tries to trace Roye, whom he hears to have recently been in England on a visit to his mother at Westminster, but the head of the monastery puts obstacles in his way. He plans also a further attempt in the Netherlands, and believes that by using greater secrecy and by obtaining a dispensation from his monastic habit, he may succeed in entrapping the Lutherans. Early in February he requests an interview with Wolsey in order, among other things, to show him where Tyndale and Jerome Barlowe are, and how they are to be taken. His plan seems to have been approved; for a week or two later, as the time of the Frankfort market drew near, he asks Wolsey to prepare a letter to the bishop of Mainz, in whose diocese Frankfort lay, calling for the delivery of " William Roye and William Hutchyns, otherwise Tendalle, traitors and heretics," and also a bill of payment for the £63 4s., which was still owing to Rinck for his purchase of the books in the autumn: † which books were in Rinck's house in Cologne. But here our information ceases. If West went, he failed again;

---

* Cf. *Antwerpsch Archievenblad*, VII., 166.

† If Rinck bought 1500 books, that works out at 10*d.* each; if he bought 1750, at 8½*d.* But no doubt he added to the bill his bribes and other expenses.

for he was back in England in June, hot upon the track of Roye and a red-headed companion (whom he believes to be Jerome Barlow) in the eastern counties. In this pursuit also he failed; and here we may take our leave of Roye, who vanishes from our story; and not from our story only: for nothing further is known of him, save that he is said by both More and Foxe to have perished in 1531 at the stake in Portugal. Flighty and untrustworthy as he may have been, he had enough courage to stand the fire, and his heroic death may well be permitted to cover and atone for some of the vagaries of his life.

At the very time when Richard Herman was making his earliest appearance before his judges in Antwerp, and when Rinck and West were hunting for Lutherans in the Rhineland, Tyndale was putting through the press of Hoochstraten the last pages of the long and powerful work of controversy, called *The Obedience of a Christian Man*. Our earliest copies are dated October 2, 1528, and Foxe gives it the same date in Daye's folio. The book was certainly written after *Mammon*, for it refers to it more than once, and it also reached England later, according to the testimony of Thomas More. Yet this date is not without difficulty. Tyndale himself, who was usually accurate in such matters, says at the end of the *Practice of Prelates*, that he " sent forth " his *Obedience* " well towards three years agone "; but the *Practice* was in England by mid-November 1530 at latest. He may have been thinking of the date when he finished the writing of the book, rather than of that when it issued from the press; but it would certainly be easier, if we could suppose that there was an earlier edition, which came out in the summer shortly after *Mammon*, and which has totally disappeared.

The book is Tyndale's answer to the charge, brought against the reformers, of teaching disobedience to princes, and of stirring up rebellion. This had become a burning question, particularly since the peasants' war of 1524–5 in Germany, which was laid by his enemies at Luther's door. But beside this Tyndale desires to say a word of encouragement to the bible readers, who were the victims of persecution in England. This he does in a long and striking preface:—

" Let it not make thee despair, neither yet discourage thee, O reader, that it is forbidden thee in pain of life and goods, or that it is made breaking of the king's peace, or treason unto his highness, to read the word of thy soul's health; but much rather be bold in the Lord, and comfort thy soul . . . . Christ is with us unto the world's end. Let his little flock be bold therefore: for if God be on our side, what matter maketh it who be against us, be they bishops, cardinals, popes, or whatsoever names they will? . . . If God promise riches, the way thereto is poverty. Whom he loveth, him he chasteneth; whom he exalteth, he casteth down; whom he saveth, he damneth first. He bringeth no man to heaven, except he send him to hell first. If he promise life, he slayeth first; when he buildeth, he casteth all down first. He is no patcher; he cannot build on another man's foundation. . . . We are called, not to dispute, as the pope's disciples do, but to die with Christ, that we may live with him, and to suffer with him, that we may reign with him. . . . Tribulation for righteousness is not a blessing only, but also a gift, that God giveth unto none save his special friends. . . . Let thy care be to prepare thyself with all thy strength, for to walk which way he will have thee, and to believe that he will go with thee and assist thee, and strengthen thee against all tyrants, and deliver thee out of all tribulation. But what way or by what means he will do it, that commit unto him and his godly pleasure and wisdom, and cast that care upon him. . . . If any man clean against his heart, but overcome with the weakness of the flesh, for fear of persecution have denied, as Peter did, or have delivered his book [i.e. surrendered his New Testament to the bishops] or put it away secretly, let him, if he repent, come again, and take better hold, and not despair." Through such failures we learn to trust not in ourselves but in God, whose work alone can endure in the fire of tribulation.

They tell you that scripture ought not to be in the mother tongue, but that is only because they fear the light, and desire to lead you blindfold and in captivity.

The Old Testament was in the mother tongue; yet those ages were in twilight, while we walk in the noonday: did Christ come to make the world more blind? At that rate he is not the light of the world, but its darkness. They say that scripture needs a pure and quiet mind, and that laymen are too cumbered with worldly business to understand it. This weapon strikes themselves: for who is so tangled with worldly matters as the prelates? They say that laymen would interpret it each after his own way. Why then do the curates not teach the people the right way? The scripture would be a basis for such teaching and a test of it. At present their lives and their preaching are so contrary, that the people do not believe them, even when they preach truth. " But alas, the curates themselves, for the most part, wot no more what the New or Old Testament meaneth than do the Turks; neither know they of any more than that they read at mass, matins and evensong, which yet they understand not; neither care they but even to mumble up so much every day, as the pie and popinjay speak, they wot not what, to fill their bellies withal. If they will not let the layman have the word of God in his mother tongue, yet let the priests have it; which for a great part of them do understand no Latin at all, but sing and say and patter all day, with the lips only, that which the heart understandeth not."

They say our tongue is too rude. It is not so. Greek and Hebrew go more easily into English than into Latin. Has not God made the English tongue as well as others? They suffer you to read in English of Robin Hood, Bevis of Hampton, Hercules, Troilus, and a thousand ribald or filthy tales. It is only the scripture that is forbidden. It is therefore clearer than the sun, that this forbiddal is not " for love of your souls, which they care for as the fox doth for the geese."

They say we need doctors to interpret scripture, it is so hard. That is to measure the meteyard by the cloth. There are errors even in Origen and Augustine; how can we test them save by the scripture? As to our preachers, they brawl like scolds, one quoting Aquinas, another Duns Scotus, another Bonaventura, and twisting the scriptural texts to suit themselves, and to prove all kinds of scholastic subtleties thereby.

We do not wish to abolish teaching and to make every man his own master; but if the curates will not teach the gospel, the layman must have the scripture, and read it for himself, taking God for his teacher.

A thousand more reasons might be given, as you may see them in the writings of Erasmus. "But I hope that these are sufficient unto them that thirst the truth. God for his mercy and truth shall well open them more, yea, and other secrets of his godly wisdom, if they be diligent to cry unto him; which grace grant God. Amen."

The theme of the book is announced in a short prologue :—

The prelates tell the kings that we are teaching the people to rise against their princes. It would hardly be wonderful, if we were ready to fight for God's word with the sword: for we are not all perfect, and we have been taught as babes to kill Turk and Jew, and to burn heretics for the pope's cause. Nevertheless it is not so. Here not we, but our enemies are guilty. "It is the bloody doctrine of the pope which causeth disobedience, rebellion and insurrection"; for he sets up his own sovereignty against that of kings, emperors or parents. Our teaching is that of Christ, to obey the civil powers, and to leave all vengeance to God, who will act in his season.

All rulers, whether parents, husbands, masters, landlords, wield an authority from God, and must be obeyed. At the head of all stands the king, who has no superior; he "is in this world without law, and may at his lust do right or wrong, and shall give accounts but to God only." Subjects that rise against their prince, rebel against God. If he is cruel and downtreads them, they must bear it in patience, and leave all punishment to God, who has set him in his place. Yet though kings are supreme, they may not rule as they list. They are servants of their people, and must treat every man, no matter how humble, as a brother. The prince must keep the law of Christ, order the realm justly, and only use the sword for the restraint and punishment of evil doers. He must permit no class to be exempt from his authority. At present we see the pope and the hierarchy claiming independence of the secular powers, setting up a law of their own, refusing to pay taxes or to share the burdens of the commonwealth, stirring up king against king, instigating subjects to rebel: and kings are content to suffer this. " They are but shadows, vain names and things idle, having nothing to do in the world, but when our holy father needeth their help." Let kings do their duty to the people, and rule their own kingdom; let them put the priests to their own proper work, strip them of their worldly honours and riches, and set good laymen in the chief offices of state. " Is it not a shame above all shames, and a monstrous thing, that no man should be found able to govern a worldly kingdom save bishops and prelates, that have forsaken the world, and are taken out of the world, and appointed to preach the kingdom of God? " Let the king rule in fact as well as in name, and decide his own matters. When men are charged with heresy, let him no longer accept the verdict of the priests. If he is asked to use the sword, let him judge the case himself, and by his own law and the law of Christ; for the hierarchy should not be judges in their own cause. " The emperor and kings are nothing nowadays but even hangmen unto the pope and bishops, to kill whomsoever they condemn without any more ado; as Pilate was unto the scribes and pharisees and the high bishops, to hang Christ." What then is the duty of the Christian in this terror? He must disobey ungodly commands, but he must never resist by force. If the king, at the bidding of the bishops, makes bible-reading a treason against the state, and punishes it with prison and the fire, the true believer will stand firm, and suffer every penalty for Christ's sake.

Such is the main theme; but the book ranges over a wide field. It contains a long and very able discussion of the four senses of scripture, and lays down the thesis—a novelty in those times but self-evident to-day—that the plain historical meaning of the text is the all-important one; that this alone can be used for the purposes of proof, though allegorical interpretations may be useful by way of illustration. It contains also an attack upon the sermon, preached by Fisher at the burning of Luther's books in 1521. This gives Tyndale the opportunity of making a neat retort. The bishop had used a " goodly argument," that Luther, since he had burnt the pope's books—that is, the decretals— would burn the pope himself also, if he had him in his power.

"A like argument," replies Tyndale, "which I suppose to be rather true, I make: Rochester and his holy brethren have burnt Christ's testament; an evident sign verily that they would have burnt Christ himself also, if they had had him."

The tone of the work is much sharper than anything that he had yet written. The persecution of his friends in England is having its effect on his mind. Fiercely and with unsparing zeal he strikes at the manifold evils and vices of the church. At times his denunciation attains an extraordinary power of terse and vivid eloquence. Amos himself gives us nothing more forcible than the following attack upon the greed and idleness of the clergy. As a piece of English it is magnificent.

"The spirituality increaseth daily. More prelates, more priests, more monks, friars, canons, nuns, and more heretics (I would say heremites) with like draff. Set before thee the increase of St Francis' disciples in so few years. Reckon how many thousands, yea, how many twenty thousands, not disciples only, but whole cloisters, are sprung out of hell of them in so little a space. Pattering of prayers increaseth daily. Their service, as they call it, waxeth longer and longer, and the labour of their lips greater; new saints, new services, new feasts and new holidays. What take all these away? Sin? Nay; for we see the contrary by experience, and that sin groweth as they grow. But they take away first God's word, with faith, hope, peace, unity, love and concord; then house and land, rent and fee, tower and town, goods and cattle, and the very meat out of men's mouths. All these live by purgatory. When other weep for their friends, they sing merrily; when other lose their friends, they get friends. The pope with all his pardons is grounded on purgatory. Priests, monks, canons, friars, with all other swarms of hypocrites, do but empty purgatory and fill hell. Every mass, they say, delivereth one soul out of purgatory. If that were true, yea, if ten masses were enough for one soul, yet were the parish priests and curates of every parish sufficient to scour purgatory: all the other costly workmen might be well spared."

Yet Tyndale is no mere destroyer. He desires to purge and to build. Through all his denunciation there runs the lofty enthusiasm of the prophet, who sees the temple of God defiled by wicked men, and would restore it to its glory and holiness. He loves his country, and grieves for the common people, misgoverned and robbed of their rights. In his advice to landlords he touches one of the burning questions of the day, the enclosure of common lands:—

> " Let Christian landlords be content with their rent and old customs; not raising the rent or fines, and bringing up new customs to oppress their tenants, neither letting two or three tenantries unto one man. Let them not take in their commons, neither make parks nor pastures of whole parishes: for God gave the earth to man to inherit, and not unto sheep and wild deer. Be as fathers unto your tenants; yea, be unto them as Christ was unto us, and shew unto them all love and kindness. Whatsoever business is among them, be not partial, favouring one more than another. The complaints, quarrels and strife that are among them, count diseases of sick people; and as a merciful physician heal them with wisdom and good counsel. Be pitiful and tender-hearted unto them, and let not one of thy tenants tear out another's throat; but judge their causes indifferently, and compel them to make their ditches, hedges, gates and ways. For even for such causes were ye made landlords; and for such causes paid men rent at the beginning."

In his teaching concerning the secular rulers Tyndale returns to the New Testament. " Let every soul," says St Paul, " be subject unto the higher powers; for there is no power but of God: the powers that be are ordained of God. Whosoever therefore resisteth the power, resisteth the ordinance of God." " Submit yourselves," wrote St Peter, " to every ordinance of man for the Lord's sake, whether it be to the king as supreme, or unto governors." In the New Testament the Christian is commanded to disobey rulers for conscience' sake, but there is no word concerning force or rebellion, no, not even in the book of Revelation, in the cruel days of the terror. This doctrine

was also common in the middle ages, only then it was usually
linked with, and limited by, obedience to the papacy;
there were two despots, a spiritual and a temporal, and
these were ever wrangling for the mastery. Now, however,
the spiritual tyranny was being broken, and in Tyndale's
theory a return was made to the old order of things. Nevertheless in fifteen hundred years of Christianity the problem
had changed somewhat. In the modern state the professing
believers were in a majority, or at least were numerous
enough to bring pressure upon the ruling powers. Force
therefore might be an effective weapon in purging a state
of evil governors. In New Testament times the Christians
were so few in number that any appeal to the sword would
have been worse than useless. Tyndale's solution therefore
was only a halting place; sooner or later the time would
come when Christians would ask themselves whether, if a
king might use the sword to restrain evil men, the people
also might not use the sword to rid themselves of a wicked
king, who was misruling them in the name of God. But
such questions were rarely asked in the sixteenth century.
In the circumstances of the moment Tyndale's advice was
sound. The evangelicals, whom he has specially in mind,
were too weak and insignificant to count in comparison
with the lordships of the world. Politically they were
powerless. Any change of government would only have
meant a change of masters; the time was not yet come for
the people to rule themselves. Prudence alone, not to speak
of principle, demanded that the only weapons used by the
little band of reformers should be those of the spirit.

In respect of this book, with its exaltation of the royal
power, Tyndale has been termed one of the fathers of the
reformation settlement in England. This is hardly just.
Certainly Henry VIII followed a portion of his advice. He
confined the clergy to their proper sphere, stopped their
intrusion into secular affairs, made them amenable to the
civil law, and stripped the church of much of the wealth
that was strangling its soul. There was nothing here with
which to quarrel; all countries of the west have since
trodden this path, and there will be no return. But when

the king ministered the spoils to the greed of laymen, he could claim no countenance from Tyndale, who, if he had lived to see it, would have reprobated it as strongly as Latimer or Rogers. Tyndale's teaching was that moneys, now misused by the church, should (a decent living for the clergy being first provided) be applied to the good of Christ's people, to the relief of the poor, and the welfare of the whole realm. Again, when the king demanded a supremacy in spiritual things, he could not appeal to Tyndale for support. According to the *Obedience*, princes must govern by the law of God, and if they command anything contrary to that law, their Christian subjects not only may, but must disobey, though they may not rebel. To Thomas More this passive resistance seemed so shocking that he charged Tyndale with inculcating disloyalty and insurrection against the king. There is certainly nothing servile in Tyndale's own behaviour towards princes. He addresses them as directly and forcibly as he does bishops; he shows a noble independence, a manly dignity, which is in refreshing contrast to the fulsome compliments, the overstrained humilities of Coverdale, Cranmer, Erasmus, More, and most of the men of that age.

Nevertheless it is not surprising that Henry was pleased with the book; for the human mind has a wonderful power of taking what pleases it and overlooking the rest. His first knowledge of it seems to have come from Anne Boleyn, who possessed a copy and lent it to Mrs Gainford, a fair young gentlewoman in her service. In the same service also was a Mr George Zouch, who was a suitor for the young maid of honour. One day in sport he plucked the book away from her, and beginning to read was so charmed with it, that he refused to return it, despite her tears. It happened, however, that Dr Sampson, dean of the king's chapel, observed him reading it at service time, and calling the young man, he seized the book and delivered it to the cardinal: for Wolsey had warned him to keep a watch for unsuitable books, lest they come to the king's reading. When Anne Boleyn asked her maid for the book, the young woman fell on her knees and confessed the truth.

" The Lady Anne shewed herself not sorry, nor angry with either of the two. But, said she, well, it shall be the dearest book that ever the dean or cardinal took away. The noble woman goes to the king, and upon her knees she desireth the king's help for her book. Upon the king's token the book was restored. And now bringing the book to him, she besought his grace most tenderly to read it. The king did so, and delighted in the book. For, saith he, this is a book for me and all kings to read."

Such is the story told in a manuscript, that was in the possession of Foxe, and later was printed by Strype. Its main facts are corroborated by a history of Anne Boleyn, compiled late in the sixteenth century by George Wyatt, the grandson of that Thomas Wyatt the poet, who was charged with being one of the queen's paramours. In this second version— a less detailed and accurate one—the book is not named, but is described as dealing with the " controversies concerning religion, and specially of the authority of the pope and his clergy, and of their doings against kings and states." Anne Boleyn had read the book, marking with her nail such places as the king ought to read. Her maid, finding it lying in a window, began to read it, when her suitor came in and took it from her. As she was called away to her mistress, he walked out reading it, and met one of the cardinal's gentlemen, who borrowed it and gave it to Wolsey. Anne, hearing of this, went at once to inform the king, and told him of the places that she had marked. Scarcely had she left the chamber, when Wolsey entered with the book in his hand, intending to complain of it, and to use it as a lever against Anne. But the king's mind was already hardening against the cardinal, and finding the marks which Anne had made, he read the book, and the reading hastened the cardinal's ruin.

But though Henry VIII might deem the *Obedience* to be a book for all kings to read, this did not save it from condemnation. Thomas More calls it a " holy book of disobedience," a book " whereby we were taught to disobey Christ's holy catholic church." Warham and his divines discovered thirty heresies therein, and it was denounced in royal proclamations. Nevertheless it did not lack readers, and indeed became the most popular of all Tyndale's books, save the translations of the bible. When a Lutheran was seized and brought before the bishops, not the least damaging article of accusation against him was to have been found in possession of *The Obedience of a Christian Man*.

CHAPTER VII

ALL this time Tyndale had not been idle in the field of bible translation. Having completed his New Testament, it was to be expected that he should take in hand the Old, as Luther had done, whose Pentateuch appeared in the following year. Tyndale was not quite so speedy; first he must learn Hebrew. He can hardly have known the language when he left England; for Jews had been banished from the country since the reign of Edward I, and there was as yet no professor of Hebrew at Oxford or at Cambridge. Some Hebrew grammar, published abroad, might indeed have crossed the sea, and found its way into his hands, but more likely he only began the study of the language when his work on the New Testament was over. The university of Wittenberg boasted a professor of Hebrew, and good teachers could be found at Hamburg, Worms and Marburg. Tyndale must have begun the actual translating by the early part of 1527; for on May 23 of that year Hackett writes to Wolsey from Bergen after his seizure of the New Testament: " I am informed that there be some Englishmen, Luther his disciples, that begins in Dutchland [Germany] to translate the bible into English." This can only refer to Tyndale, who was still at Worms: for the next Englishman to take the field as bible-translator, George Joye, was not yet come oversea. Now Tyndale was a good scholar, and would make rapid progress. When Buschius met him about the summer of 1526, he pronounced, doubtless with some exaggeration, that he spoke Hebrew and six other tongues with the mastery of a native. Despite Tyndale's uncertain and dangerous way of life, despite his diversion into controversial writing in the year 1528, despite the necessity which lay upon him of personally

145

overlooking the printing of his books, still one would expect him to have his Pentateuch ready in a couple of years after he had mastered the elements of the language.

And so indeed it came to pass, if we may trust the well-known story added by Foxe to the second edition (1570) of his great work.

" At what time Tyndale had translated the fifth book of Moses called Deuteronomy, minding to print the same at Hamborough, he sailed thereward [from Antwerp] : where by the way, upon the coast of Holland, he suffered ship-wreck, by the which he lost all his books, writings and copies, and so was compelled to begin all again anew, to his hindrance and doubling of his labours. Thus having lost by that ship both money, his copies and time, he came in another ship to Hamborough, where at his appointment Master Coverdale tarried for him, and helped him in the translating the whole five books of Moses, from Easter [March 28] till December, in the house of a worshipful widow, Mistress Margaret van Emmerson, Anno 1529, a great sweating sickness being the same time in the town. So having dispatched his business at Hamborough, he returned afterward to Antwerp again."

This story has caused much shaking of heads among the wiseacres, and many have brushed it aside as a fable : yet it bears the stamp of truth. Foxe was often careless and inaccurate, but he would be a hardy liar indeed if he added the names of the persons, the marks of time, and the other graphic little details, in order to give an air of likelihood to an invention. What are the grounds for suspecting the story? They are supposed to be three. Firstly, Hamburg had then no printer, and so Tyndale would not have gone thither to print his Pentateuch : and when the book came to be printed in January 1530, the place is given as Marburg, which, even if a pseudonym, can hardly stand for Hamburg. Secondly, nowhere else do we find any trace of a meeting between Tyndale and Coverdale on the continent, still less of their working together upon the bible; for Coverdale's scholarship was poor, and he could not have given much assistance to the translating. Thirdly, and most important of all, Tyndale is proved by other evidence to have been in

Antwerp at the middle of the period during which Foxe places him in Hamburg.

The third point, if established, will almost settle the matter; so we will take it at once. It is based upon a story related in Halle's *Chronicle*, a story so charming that it must be given in full. After describing the so-called women's peace of Cambrai, which was signed on August 5, 1529, and of which the English negotiators were Tonstall, More, Hackett and another, Halle goes on to tell of certain business transacted by Tonstall in Antwerp, seemingly on his homeward journey to England.

" Here is to be remembered, that at this present time William Tyndale had newly translated and imprinted the New Testament in English, and the bishop of London, not pleased with the translation thereof, debated with himself, how he might compass and devise to destroy that false and erroneous translation, as he said. And so it happened that one Augustine Packington, a mercer and merchant of London and of a great honesty, the same time was in Antwerp, where the bishop then was : and this Packington was a man that highly favoured William Tyndale, but to the bishop utterly showed himself to the contrary. The bishop, desirous to have his purpose brought to pass, communed of the New Testaments, and how gladly he would buy them. Packington then, hearing that he wished for, said unto the bishop : My lord, if it be your pleasure, I can in this matter do more, I dare say, than most of the merchants of England that are here; for I know the Dutchmen and strangers that have bought them of Tyndale, and have them here to sell; so that if it be your lordship's pleasure to pay for them, (for otherwise I cannot come by them, but I must disburse money for them) I will then assure you to have every book of them, that is imprinted and is here unsold. The bishop, thinking that he had God by the toe, when indeed he had (as after he thought) the devil by the fist, said : Gentle Master Packington, do your diligence and get them, and with all my heart I will pay for them, whatsoever they cost you; for the books are erroneous and naughtes, and I intend surely to destroy them all, and to burn them at Paul's Cross. Augustine Packington came to William Tyndale and said : William, I know thou art a poor man, and hast a heap of New Testaments and books by thee, for the which thou hast both endangered thy friends and beggared thyself; and I have now gotten thee a merchant, which with ready money shall dispatch thee of all that thou hast, if you think it so profitable for yourself. Who is the merchant? said Tyndale. The bishop of London, said Packington. O, that is because he will burn them, said Tyndale. Yea marry, quoth Packington. I am the gladder, said Tyndale; for these two benefits shall come thereof: I shall get money of him for these books, to bring myself out of debt, and the whole world shall cry out upon the burning of God's word. And the overplus of the money, that shall remain to me, shall make me more studious to correct the said New Testament, and so newly to imprint the same once again; and I trust the second will much better like you than ever did the first. And so forward went the bargain: the bishop had the books, Packington had the thanks, and Tyndale had the money.

" Afterward when more New Testaments were imprinted, they came thick and threefold into England. The bishop of London, hearing that still there were so many New Testaments abroad, sent for Augustine Packington and said unto him: Sir, how cometh this, that there are so many New Testaments abroad, and you promised and assured me that you had bought all? Then said Packington: I promise you, I bought all that then was to be had; but I perceive they have made more since, and it will never be better, as long as they have the letters and stamps; therefore it were best for your lordship to buy the stamps too, and then are you sure. The bishop smiled at him and said: Well, Packington, well; and so ended this matter.

" Shortly after, it fortuned one George Constantine to be apprehended by Sir Thomas More, which then was lord chancellor of England, of suspicion of certain heresies. And this Constantine being with More, after divers examinations of divers things, among other Master More said in this wise to Constantine: Constantine, I would have thee plain with me in one thing that I will ask of thee, and I promise thee I will show thee favour in all the other things, whereof thou art accused to me. There is beyond the sea Tyndale, Joye, and a great many more of you. I know they cannot live without help: some sendeth them money and succoureth them; and thyself, being one of them, hadst part thereof, and therefore knowest from whence it came; I pray thee, who be they that thus help them? My lord, quoth Constantine, will you that I shall tell you the truth?

Yea, I pray thee, quoth my lord. Marry I will, quoth
Constantine. Truly, quoth he, it is the bishop of London
that hath holpen us; for he hath bestowed among us a
great deal of money in New Testaments to burn them, and
that hath, and yet is, our only succour and comfort. Now
by my troth, quoth More, I think even the same, and I
said so much to the bishop, when he went about to buy
them."

This is a delightful tale, but it has lost nothing in the
telling; it bears all the marks of embellishment. It does
not even agree with itself. At first Packington tells the
bishop that the books are in the hands of Dutch merchants
and strangers, who have bought them of Tyndale and are
ready to sell, and that for cash every copy in Antwerp can
be secured. But when the purchase is narrated, there is
no mention of merchants; Packington goes direct to
Tyndale himself, who appears to have this " heap of New
Testaments and books " under his own hand, and who takes
the money for them. Nor is it at all likely that Tyndale
had many testaments of his own edition remaining; for
the Worms octavo must have been sold out in three and a
half years, and if there were testaments to be bought in
Antwerp, they would be the pirate editions of the Dutch
printers, over which Tyndale had no control. One cannot
believe also that Tyndale would have sold his New Testaments for burning, not even to get himself out of debt, if
he was really in debt; and as for the revision, which was to
be hastened and forwarded by the overplus of the sale
money, this was not carried out till five years later: for
Tyndale's second edition is dated November 1534.

Are we then to dismiss the whole story as a mere variant
on Warham's purchase of New Testaments two years
before? This would be an excess of scepticism. The main
fact of the purchase by Tonstall of testaments in Antwerp
may be accepted. His campaign against the bible readers
in 1528 had failed; the books were still coming in, and he
would be disposed to try any measure that offered hope of
success. No doubt he discussed the problem with More
and Hackett at Cambrai, and it is likely enough that

Hackett suggested the new plan; for he had himself been contemplating it in January 1527, as we have seen. Tonstall did not, indeed, spend long on his homeward journey, for he was still at Cambrai on August 11, and was at Woodstock on August 24, but he may have found time for a hasty visit to Antwerp, or if not, he may have instructed Hackett to act for him, or else may have met Packington later in London. The books purchased would be not New Testaments only; no doubt Tyndale's *Mammon* and *Obedience*, and Frith's *Antichrist* were also destined for destruction.

We pass now to Coverdale. In 1527 he was still at Cambridge; in the spring of the following year he was preaching in the eastern counties. Then he vanishes completely for seven years, until the publication, somewhere on the continent,* of his bible in October 1535. It is generally assumed that he left England in 1528, as so many others did, and spent most of these seven years abroad. Why may he not have been in Hamburg in 1529? His friend Barnes sought refuge there a couple of years later: why may not he have done the same? † At any rate, until some other city can produce a better title to have harboured him in 1529, Foxe's story holds the field.

Tyndale must have met Coverdale at Cambridge, and it is likely enough that, having completed his Pentateuch, and hearing that Coverdale was thinking of leaving England, he should desire him as an assistant for the rest of the work, and should make an appointment to meet him at Hamburg. Coverdale, though ignorant of Greek and Hebrew, was no fool, as his English bible testifies: and he could give very valuable help in the way of comparing the versions and correcting the copies. When he came to publish his own bible, he speaks in high terms of Tyndale, though without naming him, and in a way that almost implies that he had in recent years met or corresponded with him. In his

---

* Perhaps at Cologne; cf. *Transactions of the Bibliographical Society,* Dec. 1935. It was not he, but John Coverdale, who took a degree at Cambridge in 1531.

† Barnes may have been in Hamburg in 1529–30. He left England for Antwerp late in 1528. Nothing is known of him till we find him in Bugenhagen's house at Wittenberg in the summer of 1530.

preface, after saying that he was at first loth to meddle with
the task, thinking himself too weak for the office of translator, he proceeds :—" Notwithstanding, when I considered
how great pity it was that we should want it so long, and
called to my remembrance the adversity of them, which
were not only of ripe knowledge, but would also with all
their hearts have performed that they began, if they had not
had impediment: considering (I say) that by reason of
their adversity it could not so soon have been brought to an
end, as our most prosperous nation would fain have had it, . . .
I was the more bold to take it in hand; " and he begs the
reader to overlook the " rudeness " of his work, but trusts
that " God shall . . . send it thee in a better shape by
the ministration of other that began it before." Finally,
Coverdale was living in London from 1559 to 1568, being
incumbent of a city church for three of those years, and he
must surely have met Foxe, who seems to have been mostly
in London during this period.

There remains then only the question of printing in
Hamburg. Now it is true that Hamburg was not a great
printing centre like Antwerp or Cologne: but there had
been printers there. In 1522–3 a number of reformation
books had been turned out by the so-called " heretic press,"
which was probably owned by a Dutch printer, and in
1526 one or two books had appeared under the name of
Wickradt. But more important still, George Richolff the
younger, of the famous printing house of Lübeck, had
recently settled in the town, and his first Hamburg books
appeared in the year 1528. There seems no reason why
Tyndale should not have designed to print his Pentateuch
with Richolff. If not, he may have taken with him from
Antwerp a printing press, which was lost in the shipwreck,
or he may have intended to print in some place in the
neighbourhood of Hamburg, perhaps at Lübeck, only
thirty-five miles away, which was the great centre of printing
for north Germany, and whence the books could easily be
taken to Hamburg for shipment to England.*

* The books of these Hamburg printers are given in Borchling and
Claussen, *Niederdeutsche Bibliographie*.

Foxe therefore can beat off the attacks that have been made upon his story, but he can do more than that: he can carry the war into the enemy's camp. His mention of the sweating sickness is confirmed by history. This disease, called upon the continent the English sweat, usually confined its ravages to our island, but on this, the fourth of its five visitations, it spread over the whole of northern and central Europe. After raging in England for more than a year, it found a footing in Hamburg in June or July 1529, where within a month it had swept away no fewer than a thousand persons.

But the most decisive proof of the truth of Foxe's story is still to come. The study of the unpublished documents of Hamburg has revealed much concerning the family von Emersen. It was one of the great Lutheran families of the town. Matthias von Emersen, a senator, died in 1522, having taken for his second wife a sister of Marquard Schuldorp, the reformer of Schleswig-Holstein. His younger brother John married a lady named Margaret, and when he died at some date before May 8, 1523, he left her with six children, seemingly in no very good circumstances. In 1526, braving the stern forbiddal of the senate, she sent two of her sons to Wittenberg university, whither also, as we have seen, her nephew, Matthias the younger, had gone two years before. This young man became later secretary of the Steelyard in London, where he died. His aunt Margaret was still alive in 1541; for in that year she entered into an agreement, by which she resigned her house, situated " auf dem Huxter," to Christopher Kellinghusen, a forbear of the notable Kellinghusen family, which still flourishes in the town. This will be the house in which she entertained Tyndale and Coverdale in 1529.*

The year 1528 was an anxious and dangerous one for Tyndale. He was in some difficulty over the printing of his *Mammon* in April; at the end of June the regent began

---

* I owe this information, much of which is not to be found in printed books, to the director and the staff of the Hamburg Staats-archiv. Every student of Tyndale will be grateful to Mr Reincke and his colleagues (one of whom bears the name Kellinghusen) for the trouble they have taken in clearing up this important point.

to search for him in the Low Countries; in September Rinck and West were on his track in Antwerp, Cologne and Frankfort; in January 1529 his name was mentioned in open court as a heretic and a rebel, and early in February a fresh hunt was being planned. Antwerp was becoming too hot a place to be comfortable. To attempt to print his Pentateuch there would endanger both himself and his printer; he must seek a safer abode for the time being. His mind turns to Hamburg far away in the north, where he had loyal friends, and where the good cause was triumphing. In July 1528 his old acquaintance Bugenhagen had been invited to come and organize the reformed church: early in October he arrived and began his work, and by the end of February the rulers of the town had finally established the reformation. At Hamburg Tyndale would be out of peril, and he could print his Pentateuch with young Richolff. The design was frustrated by the shipwreck, and six or seven months had to be given to the retranslation in the house of Margaret von Emersen. When that was ended, the danger in Antwerp had abated: the matter of the divorce had become urgent, Wolsey had fallen, parliament was just assembled; and the rulers of England were not likely to molest him for a while. He therefore decided to return to Antwerp, and to print once more with Hoochstraten.

From this time onward Antwerp becomes his headquarters. We never hear of him elsewhere, though no doubt he retired from the town at seasons of special peril. At Antwerp he was in easy touch with England. He could transport his books, welcome the refugees, follow the course of the conflict. No one would blame him, had he withdrawn into Germany, and settled down in safety, as some of his friends did. Coverdale became schoolmaster on the upper Rhine, Barnes found useful employment in Hamburg and Wittenberg, Rogers looked after a parish in Saxony. These men were glad to return to England, when they could; but meanwhile they had found a second home abroad. But Tyndale chose to remain at the post of danger. He had no certain dwelling-place, but he hovered ever on the bounds of the narrow sea, that separated him from his native land.

England was his true home; for England he was working in his exile; his heart was across the water.

Of the first edition of Tyndale's Pentateuch some half-dozen copies remain. The book presents some very curious features, which have never been properly cleared up. To begin with, it is not in the same type throughout. Whereas Genesis and Numbers are in the familiar black letter of the period, the other three books give the Roman letter. In the three latter books also catchwords are used, but not in the two former. Nevertheless it is clear that all five books issued from the same printing house: for the title-pages of all have the same woodcut border, and there are other points of likeness.

Next we observe that each book has its own set of signatures, and that on the colophon of Genesis (the others have no colophons) appears the only mark of date in the whole volume: Printed by me Hans Lufft, in Marborow in the land of Hesse, January 17, 1530. Each book therefore might have been circulated by itself; and in fact this was the case: for in the Bodleian library at Oxford there is extant a copy of Genesis alone, and lists of prohibited books, of date 1530 or 1531, have come down to us, mentioning the five books severally. Thus in November 1531 one of the charges on which Bayfield was condemned by Stokesley, was of bringing into the realm a great number of Lutheran books, among which were " a prologue to the fifth book of Moses called Deuteronomy; the first book of Moses called Genesis; a prologue to the third book of Moses called Leviticus; a prologue to the fourth book of Moses called Numbers; a prologue to the second book of Moses called Exodus." Now these are the titles of the five sections of Tyndale's Pentateuch. They are described in the same way and in the same order in certain statutes of convocation of about the same year, and also—but this time in their normal order—in a proclamation made at Paul's Cross in Advent 1531. Lastly, in a list in Tonstall's register two books only are mentioned, " the chapters of Moses called Genesis, the chapters of Moses called Deuteronomy." *

* For these four descriptions see Foxe IV. 685; Wilkins' *Concilia* III. 717; *L. & P. V.*, p. 768; Foxe, IV., 676.

Another singular thing is that the book of Exodus alone has illustrations, being adorned in chapters 25–30 with eleven woodcuts, one of which depicts Aaron in his high-priestly robes, and the rest show the ornaments of the tabernacle. These woodcuts had been used by Vostermann, the Antwerp printer, in two editions of the Dutch bible, both of them dated 1528; * but there the rest of the Pentateuch also—the historical parts at least—had been illustrated. When he reprinted his bible in 1532, he used a new set of woodcuts, but that might be accounted for by the smaller page and type of the new volume.

But though the five books stand apart from one another in these ways, they were clearly intended to form a whole. The book of Genesis contains not only the special prologue, which all the other books have, but also a more general preface. The prologues of the later books too refer once or twice to those of the earlier, as if they were regarded as part of one volume. Luther had made the Pentateuch the first instalment of his Old Testament. It would be natural for Tyndale to follow this example, and we know that the five books were bound together in the end.

Now what is intended by the date, January 17, 1530, in the colophon of Genesis? Is it our modern reckoning, or is it the old style, under which the year was calculated as beginning on March 25? Some writers decide for the latter, and therefore date the book on what we call January 17, 1531. But this is most unlikely. We know no reason why Tyndale should wait a year before bringing out his Pentateuch; so far as we know, he printed no other work in the first half of the year 1530. There was every reason for speed, lest some fresh mishap should overtake him, and his labour be wasted. We have also evidence that part at least of the Pentateuch was in England by the early summer of 1530; for a *Public Instrument*, put out by Warham and a meeting of divines on May 24, denounces " the translation of scripture corrupted by William Tyndale, as well in the Old Testament as in the New," and the king's

---

* They appear also in Quentel's two Latin bibles of 1527 and 1529.

proclamation of June speaks of both these translations as being " now in print." *

With this point settled, how are we to explain the puzzling features of the book? The following theory seems to meet the facts. Tyndale, having lost a year through the shipwreck, and being always in some peril in Antwerp, asked Hoochstraten to set two presses to work simultaneously. If one of these used black letter and the other Roman, the division of the books in type would be fairly explained: for Genesis is the longest of the books, and Leviticus the shortest. And here we must take into account the very singular order in which the books appear in the English lists. Out of four such lists only one names them in the usual order; twice the order is Deuteronomy, Genesis, Leviticus, Numbers, Exodus; and once Genesis and Deuteronomy are alone named. It certainly looks from this as if Deuteronomy and Genesis entered England first, and Exodus came at the end. But why should Deuteronomy have been printed before Exodus? Perhaps because it was a special favourite with Tyndale; for he calls it in his prologue " a book worthy to be read day and night, the most excellent of all Moses' books ": or possibly because, when the printing of Genesis began, Hoochstraten had not succeeded in finding a suitable set of woodcuts, with which to illustrate the tabernacle in Exodus. But however this may be, one thing seems certain: all five books were in England by about midsummer, before Tyndale began his next work, the *Practice of Prelates*.

The special prologues illustrate the doctrines in the several books. There is an able treatment of the lawfulness and use of vows in the prologue to Numbers, and ceremonies are discussed in that to Leviticus. The two following passages may be quoted:—

" If any man ask me, seeing that faith justifieth me: Why I work, I answer: Love compelleth me. For as long as my soul feeleth what love God hath shewed me in Christ, I cannot but love God again and his will and

* Cf. Wilkins *Concilia*, III., 727, Pollard 163 (a like proclamation in Wilkins 740).

commandments, and of love work them, nor can they seem hard unto me. I think not myself better for my working, nor seek heaven nor a higher place in heaven because of it. For a Christian worketh to make his weak brother perfecter, and not to seek an higher place in heaven. I compare not myself unto him that worketh not. No, he that worketh not to-day, shall have grace to turn and to work to-morrow; and in the mean season I pity him, and pray for him. If I had wrought the will of God these thousand years, and another had wrought the will of the devil as long, and this day turn, and be as well willing to suffer with Christ as I, he hath this day overtaken me, and is as far come as I, and shall have as much reward as I : and I envy him not, but rejoice most of all, as of lost treasure found. For if I be of God, I have these thousand years suffered to win him, for to come and praise the name of God with me. These thousand years I have prayed, sorrowed, longed, sighed, and sought for that which I have this day found; and therefore rejoice with all my might, and praise God for his grace and mercy." (Prologue to Exodus.)

" If thou wilt vow pilgrimage, thou must put salt thereto . . . if it shall be accepted. If thou vow to go and visit the poor, or to hear God's word, or whatsoever edifieth thy soul unto love, . . . it is well done, and a sacrifice that savoureth well. Ye will haply say that ye will go to this or that place, because God hath chosen one place more than another, and will hear your petition more in one place than another. . . . If it were wisdom, how could we excuse the death of Stephen, which died for that article, that God dwelleth not in temples made with hands? We that believe in God are the temple of God, saith Paul. . . . If thou believe in Christ, and hast the promises which God hath made thee in thine heart, then go on pilgrimage unto thine own heart, and there pray, and God will hear thee for his mercy and truth's sake, and for his Son Christ's sake, and not for a few stones' sake. What careth God for the temple? The very beasts, in that they have life in them, be much better than an heap of stones couched together." (Prologue to Numbers.)

From the general preface to the Pentateuch we have already quoted largely in narrating Tyndale's life in Little

Sodbury and in London: but some sentences from the beginning and the end must be given, in order to show his deep feeling of resentment at the treatment meted out to his New Testament. After describing the hostile welcome the book had received from the hierarchy, who, so far from responding to his invitation to amend it, had merely forbidden it under various excuses, he proceeds:—

" And as for my translation, in which they affirm unto the lay people (as I have heard say) to be I wot not how many thousand heresies, so that it cannot be mended or correct, they have yet taken so great pain to examine it . . . that they might with as little labour (as I suppose) have translated the most part of the bible. For they which in times past were wont to look on no more scripture than they found in their Duns [Scotus] or such like devilish doctrine, have yet now so narrowly looked on my translation, that there is not so much as one *i* therein, if it lack a tittle over his head, but they have noted it, and number it unto the ignorant people for an heresy. . . . Under what manner therefore should I now submit this book to be corrected and amended of them which can suffer nothing to be well? Or what protestation should I make in such a matter unto our prelates, those stubborn Nimrods, which so mightily fight against God, and resist his Holy Spirit," . . . and which have seduced the princes and rulers to torment such as tell them the truth, and to burn the word of their soul's health, and slay whosoever believeth thereon? " Notwithstanding yet I submit this book, and all other that I have either made or translated, or shall in time to come (if it be God's will that I shall further labour in his harvest), unto all them that submit themselves unto the word of God, to be corrected of them; yea, and moreover to be disallowed and also burnt, if it seem worthy, when they have examined it with the Hebrew, so that they first put forth of their own translating another that is more correct."

Here once more we mark Tyndale's admirable modesty. He has no thought for himself or his own repute. Anybody may correct, or supersede, or even destroy his version, so only that they do it with a greater knowledge of the original tongues, and put forth a text that is more worthy.

The version itself will be discussed in the next chapter. Here it only remains to say a word about the marginal notes with which the text is adorned. These are 108 in number; all come from Tyndale himself; not a single one is borrowed from Luther: and yet, as Westcott remarks, their boldness and vigour remind one of the great German reformer. Many of them merely explain or illustrate the text:—*e.g.* Houses are flat in those countries (Deut. xxii. 8); but others are strongly controversial, and attack sharply the misdeeds of the pope and the hierarchy. These are the biting glosses, which—according to the legend—were the cause of the condemnation and the burning of the New Testament three and a half years before. Here are a few examples:—

Exodus xxxii. 28 (where three thousand were slain after worshipping the golden calf). The pope's bull slayeth more than Aaron's calf, even one hundred thousand for one hair of them.
Numbers xi. 29 (where Moses says: Would God that all the Lord's people could prophesy, and that the Lord would put his spirit upon them). The pope would that none of the Lord's people could prophesy, and that none had his spirit.
Numbers xviii. 24 (where the Levites are to have no property save the tithes). Ours will have tithe, and lands, and rents, and kingdoms, and empire and all.
Deuteronomy vi. 6 (where God commands Israel to keep his words in their heart). It is heresy with us for a layman to look on God's word or to read it.
Deuteronomy xxiii. 18 (where an whore is not to be brought into the house of God). The pope will take tribute of them yet, and bishops and abbots desire no better tenants.

Everyone will agree that notes of this kind are out of place in an edition of the scriptures. Not that they were untrue: the evils which they attacked really existed, and were condoned, or actively supported, by the pope and the hierarchy. Nevertheless it is better to permit the bible to make its own appeal, and to rebuke the vices of the time in its own way. But no one who fairly considers Tyndale's situation will severely blame him for such glosses, or for the growing sharpness of his language, which we have already observed in his *Obedience*. The reformation had begun with a just protest of Luther against indulgences, couched in language that was at first not only moderate, but might almost be called servile. What answer did this receive from the vicar of Christ? He not only refused to remedy the evils, but he branded the young monk as a rebel and a heretic, excommunicated him, and demanded his body from the secular powers for trial and punishment. Almost by a miracle Luther escaped the fire; but not all his followers were so fortunate. In 1523 the first two Lutheran martyrs perished at Brussels, and in December 1524, just when Tyndale himself was at Wittenberg, the news arrived of the brutal murder in north-west Germany of Henry of Zutphen, a young man who not so long ago had been sitting at Luther's feet: and so the tale went on. Meanwhile the German testament came out, was denounced as a foul thing, and committed to the flames. All this did not promise very well for Tyndale; but he hoped for the best, and sent his New Testament to England in a spirit of moderation. What followed? His noble work was greeted with contempt and reviling. Not a voice was raised in its favour; bigots and humanists alike denounced it. The books were destroyed, the readers were thrown into prison and forced to abjure, and the author himself was hunted upon the continent, and had to keep in hiding. So far indeed no one in England had been put to death, but the respite would not be for long. The first twenty years of the century had seen many English martyrs. Only eleven years ago, in 1519, six men and one woman had perished in the same fire at Coventry. At any moment such scenes might be repeated, the news might come that a victim had been offered in sacrifice: and so it proved. Early in March 1530, within two months of the publication of Genesis, Tyndale's friend and ally, Thomas Hitton, went to the stake at Maidstone, condemned by the humanists, Warham and Fisher. Are men to be made of stone? Is it any wonder that those who were suffering under this cruel tyranny, upon which to-day we look back with the mild interest of historians, burst into cries of anger and denunciation? Harsh words are not so terrible to bear as exile, or the dungeon, or the sword, or the flame.

Meanwhile in England the circulation of the New Testament had been going on apace, and the maintainers of the old order were becoming more and more alarmed; what was worse, it was beginning to be rumoured that the king himself secretly favoured the spread of the book. In May 1530 bishop Nix of Norwich sends a message to Henry, begging him to kill the rumours by a proclamation; otherwise, he says, he himself cannot hope to check the growing Lutheranism of his diocese. In answer to such appeals as these Henry summoned to the palace of Westminster an assembly of bishops and divines—some thirty in number, twelve of whom came from either university—to discuss the whole question of Lutheran books. Warham, Tonstall, Gardiner, More, Hugh Latimer, William Latimer, John Bell (who browbeat Tyndale in old days), Crome, Sampson, all these were present, and a leading part in the deliberations was taken by Thomas More. On May 24 the conclave put out a *Public Instrument*, pronouncing against the free circulation of Old or New Testament, and condemning long lists of propositions, selected from Tyndale's *Mammon* and *Obedience*, Frith's *Antichrist*, and other works. The lists were perhaps supplied by More, who had recently read the books. From Latimer's letter to the king, written six months later, we learn that three or four of the divines had favoured an English bible, but were overborne by the majority. Latimer himself would be one, his namesake William might be another, and Crome a third.*

The king acted upon the advice of his divines. On May 25 he entered the Star Chamber, and in the presence of the lords spiritual and temporal made his will known to the justices of the realm who were there assembled; and this will he embodied in a proclamation printed in the month of June. In it he denounced the *Mammon* and the *Obedience*, and other " blasphemous and pestiferous English books,"

---

* Cf. Tyndale, *Answer to More*, III. 168: " And what can you say to this, how that besides they [the bishops] have done their best to disannul all translating by parliament, they have disputed before the king's grace that it is perilous and not meet, and so concluded that it shall not be, under a pretence of deferring it of certain years: where Master More was their special orator, to feign lies for their purpose."

imported into the realm to pervert faith and to stir up sedition and disobedience. As to holy writ, he deems that it is not necessary for the commons to have it in the vulgar tongue; at present it would only do harm. But if his people forsake " all perverse, erroneous and seditious opinions, with the New Testament and the Old, corruptly translated into the English tongue, now being in print," he will in due course provide for the making of a translation by " great, learned and catholic persons." Meanwhile all books of scripture in English, and all other forbidden books, are to be surrendered within fifteen days to the ecclesiastical officers. The king's promise of a new translation was but lip-service; it was never fulfilled.*

In May also Tonstall made another of his spectacular demonstrations at Paul's Cross. He caused, says Halle, " all his New Testaments which he had bought, with many other books, to be brought into Paul's churchyard in London, and there openly burned." Tidings of the holocaust reached Campeggio in Augsburg, and on June 28 he writes to the king, wishing him joy of so worthy a deed, that added great glory to his name.

From all this it was clear that a fresh effort was to be made to crush Lutheranism in England; a sharper outbreak of persecution was at hand. Wolsey was removed, and the bishops could move more freely in their dioceses. Thomas More sat in the lord chancellor's seat, Stokesley was succeeding to the important bishopric of London, two men from whom the reformers could expect no mercy. In the Low Countries too a more stringent edict had been put forth by the emperor in October 1529, ordering all copies of the New Testament, in whatever language, to be surrendered for destruction, forbidding any further printing of such books, and condemning heretics to death—the men by the sword, the women by burying alive, the relapsed by the fire. The prospect looked ominous for Tyndale and his

---

* Halle overstates when he says the king *ordered* the bishops to make a translation. The king's instruction in the Star Chamber (says More, *Works* 351) bespeaks " his blessed disposition " and " the mildness of his benign nature."

friends; nevertheless there were some few rays of hope on the horizon, though they had not as yet fallen upon his eyes.

Of Tyndale's doings in the latter part of 1530 little is known, save that towards the end of the year he put out his *Practice of Prelates*, the fiercest of all his works. This was the last of his books published by Hoochstraten; no month is given in the colophon, only the year 1530. The title-page bears also a second heading: *Whether the king's grace may be separated from his queen, because she was his brother's wife ;* and though this question occupies only a few pages towards the end of the book, it was the main cause of his writing. The divorce of Catherine was now in the very forefront of things. The court of Wolsey and Campeggio, which was to have decided the matter, had adjourned more than a year ago; and Henry, seeing that the pope, though willing enough, dared not help him out of his difficulty, was engaged in securing verdicts from the universities of Europe in condemnation of his marriage with Catherine. Opinion upon the continent and in England was sharply divided; and a right decision was not only a matter of theological truth, but concerned the welfare of the realm. Tyndale feels that he ought to speak. He had thought long on the matter, he had searched the scripture, he had consulted learned men, but he could not find reasons for the divorce. " Wherefore," he says, " I could not but declare my mind, to discharge my conscience withal; which thing I had done long since, if I could have brought it to pass. Howbeit I had liefer now do it at the last than that any man should cast me in the teeth in time to come, when this old marriage were broken, and a new made, why I had not spoken rather [earlier]. Neither can the king's grace or any other man of right be discontent with me." Even " so vile a wretch " as himself may compare a fellow Christian's doings with the law of God.

The verdict which Tyndale pronounces at least shows his independence. The Lutheran divines in Germany held that, though the marriage with Catherine might have been invalid, it ought to stand, since it had been made. The English reformers, on the other hand, almost to a man, held it to be no marriage, and one that ought to be broken; and Latimer had worked vigorously for the divorce at Cambridge. Tyndale agrees with neither party: the marriage (he pronounces) was lawful, and cannot be set aside without great wrong.

But the plan of the divorce had come from Wolsey and from his henchman Longland, the bishop of Lincoln; it was thus, in Tyndale's eyes, part of the long and dark intrigues in which the ecclesiastics had engaged for hundreds of years. He therefore turns the book into an indictment of the hierarchy. " As for wickedness, whence it springeth," he writes at the end of his preface, " and who is the cause of all insurrection, and of the fall of princes, and the shortening of their days upon the earth, thou shalt see in the glass following, which I have set before thine eyes." Describing first the simplicity of the primitive church, he traces the beginnings of slackness and coldness in her rulers with the evils that followed thereon. " Then, while they that had the plough by the tail looked back, the plough went awry; faith waxed feeble and fainty; love waxed cold; the scripture waxed dark; Christ was no more seen. He was in the mount with Moses; and therefore the bishops would have a god upon the earth, whom they might see, and thereupon they began to dispute who should be greatest."

In this struggle the bishop of Rome gained the mastery, and finally claimed lordship not only over the church, but over all the earth. His slow ascent from lowliness to sovereignty is painted in the famous simile of the ivy tree. As the ivy springing up out of the ground creeps along it until it finds a great tree; and climbing little by little, at first seems glorious and beautiful, but then thrusts its roots into the bark, and mounting to the top and overgrowing the branches, it sucks out the moisture and stifles the vigour, and at length, as the tree decays, becomes itself the nest for all unclean birds of the night: " even so the bishop of Rome, now called pope, at the beginning crope along upon the earth, and every man trod upon him in this world. But as soon as there came a Christian emperor, he joined himself unto his feet and kissed them, and crope up a little " with begging and flatteries and superstitious teaching. Then fastening his roots in the heart of the emperor, he used his sword to subdue his fellow-bishops, and by their help in turn " clamb above the emperor . . . and made him stoop unto his feet and kiss them." Thus lording it over all Christendom, he has " put down the kingdom of Christ, and set up the kingdom of the devil, whose vicar he is," and made the church a lodging of all manner of wickedness.

So the accusation proceeds. The growing ambition and avarice of the prelates, their plotting and subtlety, their engineering of wars for their own ends, their selfishness and lust, their alternate flattery and brow-beating of the secular powers, all these things are forcibly described. At length the story comes down to modern times, and Wolsey is made the type of the un-Christian temper which had destroyed the purity of the church. His rise to supremacy is depicted in a striking passage :—

" When the king's grace came first to the right of the crown, and unto the governance of the realm, young and unexpert, Thomas Wolfsee, a man of lust and courage and bodily strength, to do and to suffer great things, and to endure in all manner of voluptuousness; expert and exercised in the course of the world, as he which had heard, read, and seen much policy, and had done many things himself, and had been of the secret counsel of weighty matters, as subtle as Sinon that betrayed Troy; utterly appointed to semble and dissemble, to have one thing in the heart and another in the mouth, being thereto as eloquent as subtle, and able to persuade what he lusted to them that were unexpert; so desirous and greedy of honour, that he cared not but for the next and most compendious way thereto, whether godly or ungodly; this wily wolf, I say, and raging sea, and shipwreck of all England, though he shewed himself pleasant and calm at the first (as whores do unto their lovers), came unto the king's grace, and waited upon him, and was no man so obsequious and serviceable, and in all games and sports the first and next at hand; and as a captain to courage other, and a gay finder out of new pastimes, to obtain favour withal.

" And ever as he grew in promotions and dignity, so gathered he unto him of the most subtle-witted, and of them that were drunk in the desire of honour, most like unto himself: and after they were sworn, he promoted them, and with great promises made them in falsehood faithful, and of them ever presented unto the king's grace, and put them into his service, saying: This is a man meet for your grace. And by these spies, if aught were done or spoken in the court against the cardinal, of that he had word within an hour or two; and then came the cardinal to court with all his magic, to persuade the contrary. If any in the court had spoken against the cardinal, and the same not great in the king's favour, the cardinal bade him walk a villain, and thrust him out of the court headlong. If he were in conceit with the king's grace, then he flattered, and persuaded, and corrupted some with gifts, and sent some ambassadors, and some he made captains. . . .

" And in like manner played he with the ladies and gentlewomen. Whosoever of them was great, with her was he familiar, and to her gave he gifts: yea, and where St Thomas of Canterbury was wont to come after, Thomas cardinal went oft before, preventing his prince, and perverted the order of that holy man. If any were subtle-witted, and meet for his purpose, her made he sworn to betray the queen likewise, and tell him what she said or did. I know one that departed the court for no other cause, than that she would no longer betray her mistress.*

" And, after the same example, he furnished the court with chaplains of his own sworn disciples, and children of his own bringing up, to be alway present, and to dispute of vanities, and to water whatsoever the cardinal had planted. . . .

" He promoted the bishop of Lincoln that now is, his most faithful friend and old companion, and made him confessor: to whom of whatsoever the king's grace shrove himself, think ye not that he spake so loud that the cardinal heard it? And not unright; for as God's creatures ought to obey God and serve his honour, so ought the pope's creatures to obey the pope, and serve his majesty.

* Perhaps one of the Poyntz family. Lady Walsh's aunt and niece were both in the service of Catherine.

" Finally, Thomas Wolfsee became what he would, even porter of heaven, so that no man could enter into promotion but through him."

Then follows the narrative of the early years of Henry VIII, of Wolsey's successful attempts to involve England in war for the sake of the papacy, of the shifts and turns of his policy, of his pressing for the divorce, and of his fall only a year ago. But here Tyndale makes a blunder. Far away from his native land, depending on such information as he can get from refugees, he cannot believe that Wolsey is fallen for ever, and that a beginning has been made towards breaking the tyranny of Rome in England. No, Wolsey's retirement to his northern diocese of York is but one of the familiar tricks of the hierarchy. He will soon be back in power, and meanwhile he has left More as lord chancellor, and Tonstall as bishop of Durham, to keep his old positions warm for him, and to carry on his policy. Tyndale was not the only Englishman who believed that Wolsey would recover his power, but he was completely mistaken. The great cardinal could do no more harm to his country; the teeth of the papacy were being drawn for ever.

As to the divorce itself, Tyndale condemns it on two grounds, theological and political. The theological involves a discussion on the reconciling of the text in Leviticus xviii., which forbids a marriage with a brother's wife, with that in Deuteronomy xxv., which orders the so-called Levirate marriage. Much ingenuity was spent on both sides in such endeavours; some gave the preference to Leviticus, others to Deuteronomy, and for neither conclusion could very satisfactory reasons be given. Tyndale takes rather a hesitating tone, but he solves the problem by saying that the Leviticus text only forbids such a marriage during the lifetime of the first husband: but he is led into an abstract discussion of the grounds of the prohibited degrees, which certainly does not show him at his best. He even puts forward the very singular idea that a wedding between a brother and a sister, though unnatural, was less unnatural than that between a man and his aunt, and that for very special reasons, where the peace and unity of states were concerned, it might perhaps be permitted. Such theories were not unknown at the time. Only the previous year Campeggio, the papal legate, had given his approval to a union between princess Mary and her half-brother the duke of Richmond, in order to avoid the need for the divorce: but it is strange indeed to find Tyndale of all people deserting the plain straightforward ground of natural law, in however tentative and theoretic a way. In this section, however, he seems rather uneasy, and less confident than is his wont. He ends with the following words: " Ye will haply say, my reasons be not good. They may be the sooner solved, and shall thereto make the contrary part better, and set it out, and make it appear to all men's sight, and stablish it; and so shall they do good every way."

He is on much stronger ground when he deals with the political risks of the divorce. It would throw into uncertainty the succession to the crown, and might lead to civil war, foreign invasion, murder of rivals; and he begs the king and the great lords to settle at once who is to be the next occupant of the throne, so as to spare the state these impending dangers. Look, he says, at our position in Europe; we have meddled in all matters, beggared ourselves in wars and intrigues for the supposed good of the church, " and have gotten nothing but rebuke and shame and hate among all nations, and a mock and a scorn thereto of them whom we have most holpen "; and if the succession is to be settled with the sword, it may cost the realm of England.

The book ends with an appeal to the king, to the lords, and to the people to do each his part in saving the realm. As for himself, he takes God to record that he has not spoken in hate of any person; for he too is a sinner and a grievous. But wickedness cannot go on unpunished for ever. Let the king cease to persecute Christ and his holy testament at the prelates' bidding; let him have mercy on his subjects. The reformers do not preach disobedience. If there is disobedience, it is due to the long tyranny of the pope and the bishops. " This is a sure conclusion: none obedience that is not of love, can long endure; and in your deeds [*i.e.* of the hierarchy] can no man see any cause of love:

and the knowledge of Christ, for whose sake only a man would love you, though ye were never so evil, ye persecute. Now then, if any disobedience rise, are ye not the cause of it yourselves? Say not but that ye be warned."

The *Practice of Prelates* is that work of Tyndale which we could most readily spare. Much of the indictment is true and just, and the fierceness and even savagery of tone can be excused in a man facing a dreadful power, which, like some grim ogre, is trampling on the truths he loves, devouring his friends, and imperilling his native land. Nevertheless, one could wish that Tyndale had never put his finger into this divorce controversy, where neither of the contending parties could claim to have clean hands. As a translator of scripture he was unrivalled: as a prophet of woe or a pamphleteer there were others who could take his place. Despite its force and a few passages of fine English, we should gladly exchange the *Practice of Prelates* for another Old Testament book from his pen.

The work was not likely to find favour in any quarter, and it soon found its way to the list of forbidden books. Thomas More censures it in the preface to his *Confutation*, but in less violent terms than usual; and Demaus acutely suggests that this may be because his censure is not without ground.

" Tyndale," he writes, " has weened to have made a special show of his high worldly wit, and that men should have seen therein that there was nothing done among princes, but that he was fully advertised of all the secrets, and that so far forth, that he knew the privy practice, made between the king's highness and the late lord cardinal and the reverend father Cuthbert, then bishop of London, and me, that it was wilily devised that the cardinal should leave the chancellorship to me, and the bishopric of Durham to my lord of London for a while, till he list himself to take them both again."

Such " frantic drifts," concludes More, can only have been " devised of his own imagination."

The book also gave great offence to the king's party, and provoked a speedy retort. On some day before December 4, as we learn from the reports of the imperial and the Milanese ambassadors in London, a placard was put out by authority and posted in conspicuous places, recounting the opinions of the universities in favour of the divorce, and attacking the *Practice of Prelates* by name. But of what use is this? asks Chapuys, the ambassador of the emperor. It only makes the people read the book more eagerly. However, more prudent counsels prevailed, and within a few days Chapuys reports that the placard has been withdrawn and destroyed, whether for this reason, or because the king fears that the author may reply. The divorce is treated, he adds, in a masterly and most complete manner. The Milanese ambassador says that there are three thousand copies in circulation, and that the author is one Tindaro or Tindal, an Englishman who has lived some time, and still lives, in Germany, and is reported to be a man *magnæ doctrinæ*, of great learning.

According to both ambassadors, it was for circulating this work that John Tyndale and other Lutheran merchants came into trouble. They were arrested about mid-November, and before the 27th had undergone their punishment. They were paraded through the streets of London, with copies of the offending book suspended from their necks, and pasteboard mitres upon their heads, bearing the inscription: " I have sinned against the commandments of the king," *peccasse contra mandata regis*; and having passed through the circuit of the main thoroughfares, they cast the book into a fire prepared for the purpose. Of this too Chapuys disapproves; for it only makes a hundred persons talk where one talked before.*

Happily we can check this account by the narrative of Foxe, which no doubt refers to the same event. In his *Acts and Monuments*, indeed, he only tells us that John Tyndale was abjured in 1530 for sending five marks to his brother William beyond the sea, and for receiving and keeping his

---

* Cf. *Spanish Calendar* November 27, December 4, December 17; *Venetian Calendar* December 16. Latimer, in his letter of December 1 on behalf of the English bible, speaks of " those persons, which of late were punished in London for keeping such books, as your grace had prohibited by proclamation."

letters: but a manuscript left by Foxe at his death, and
printed by Strype, gives us some very interesting details.
The other victims were a merchant, named Thomas Patmore, and a young man dwelling near London Bridge.
They were apprehended by the bishop of London, and
brought before the chancellor, Thomas More, and by him
put in ward. Then they went before the Star Chamber,
and were there charged with " receiving of Tyndale's testaments and divers other books, and delivering and scattering
the same " throughout the city of London. They confessed
to the charge, and judgment was pronounced: they were
to be " sent to the Counter of London [a prison in Cheap-
side], and there to remain until the next market day, and
then each of them to be set upon a horse, and their faces to
the horse's tail, and to have papers upon their heads, and . . .
upon their gowns and cloaks to be tacked or pinned thick
with the said New Testaments and other books. And at
the Standard in Chepe should be made a great fire, wherein
every one of them should throw their said books; and farther
to abide such fines, to be paid to the king, as should be
assessed upon them: which penance they observed. This
is extant to be seen in the records of the Star Chamber."
No mention is made of any fine on John Tyndale, but
Patmore appears to have paid to the king the very large
sum of £100.

We have heard from Chapuys how the royal proclamation,
attacking the *Practice of Prelates*, was withdrawn. That may
surprise us, but still more surprising is it when he goes on
to say, that he hears on the most trustworthy authority that
the king, afraid lest the priest Tyndale shall write more
boldly against him, and hoping to persuade him to retract
what he has already written, has invited him back to
England, and offered him several good appointments and
a seat in his council. This report is evidently embellished,
and we might rule out the whole thing as mere court gossip,
were it not in part confirmed by certain events which will
come before us later. Though the first feeling of Henry
over the *Practice of Prelates* was one of anger, there was then
a sudden change; and herein we trace the hand of Crom-

well. Cromwell conceived the plan of winning over the
author, and employing his powerful pen on the side of the
king instead of against him; and he persuaded his royal
master to put the matter to the test. To us who know our
William, the project will not appear very hopeful: but
Cromwell did not know him. He was accustomed to deal
with timeservers, place hunters and sycophants; and, like
a great minister of later days, he probably thought that
every man has his price.*

* A letter is extant from Thomas Jermyn to Cromwell, dated Monday
the 19th, which says:—"I have sent to Mr. Tyndall . . . and my servant
in his house delivered the king's letter to himself, so that he cannot deny
the receipt thereof." The editor of *L. & P.* places this in June 1531,
and refers it to William Tyndale. This seems unlikely. May it not be
John Tyndale, and the date December 1530? The king's letter might be
a demand to John to reveal the whereabouts of William.

WILLIAM TYNDALE
(from Beza's Vrais Pourtraits, 1581)

Facing p. 173

CHAPTER VIII

THE OLD TESTAMENT

In translating the Old Testament Tyndale had to meet much the same problems as he had mastered in the New. He had first to learn Hebrew, but this, though not so easy as it is to-day, would be well within the powers of so able a scholar as he was. Once again he found three versions at hand to help him, first, Jerome's Vulgate, second, the German of Luther, and thirdly, the Greek translation, made about 200–100 B.C. in Egypt, and commonly called the Septuagint. Some writers have doubted whether he used this last, but the evidence is too strong to be resisted; and it would be surprising if in his wrestlings with the many obscurities of the Hebrew text he had failed to consult this ancient version, two editions of which had been printed by the year 1520. Then, he would have at his disposal the old commentators, and the writings of Hebraists of his own time; and finally, he might perhaps gain some assistance from the Rabbis of the Jewish communities on the continent, who had inherited the traditional interpretations of their church.

Of the Old Testament Tyndale put forth three parts during his lifetime, and under his own name or initials. The first was the Pentateuch, which came out in 1530, a second edition of Genesis being published in 1534; then came Jonah about May 1531; and lastly, when issuing his revised New Testament in November 1534, he added at the end of the volume a translation of those passages in the Old Testament that were read as epistles in the liturgy of the church. But beside these, there is a strong tradition that he composed, and left behind at his death, a version of the later historical books, Joshua to II Chronicles, and that this was included by his disciple Rogers in the so-called

Matthew's bible of 1537. It will be our business later to consider whether this tradition is trustworthy. Now we will take those portions which are without dispute his handiwork.

Tyndale's Old Testament translations have not escaped the attacks that have been showered upon his New. If his knowledge of Greek has been held to be doubtful, it has been doubly easy to make a plausible case for his ignorance of Hebrew, a tongue which fifty years before was known to hardly a single Christian in Europe, and of which the first professor in an English university was only appointed in 1524. Despite the emphatic verdict of Westcott in favour of his Hebrew scholarship, some writers have said that his Old Testament translations are little more than a borrowing from the Latin and German versions, especially the latter.

This opinion is not borne out by an examination of the text. Imperfect as Tyndale's knowledge of Hebrew was in comparison with the advanced standards of to-day, he was a good scholar for his own time; and he has no need to be ashamed of his work. He is still a loose translator; but then so are the others. The Vulgate, which in the New Testament errs on the side of literalism, is here very easy-going,* and the Septuagint is even more free. If then Tyndale is loose in small points, he is in good company; while in catching the genius of the language and mastering its idioms he fully holds his own with his three competitors.

Here too, as in the New Testament, a number of Tyndale's renderings are followed by the Revised Version in preference to those of the Authorized. We find again the old boldness in selecting between his authorities, and once more he gives the decisive proof of independence by deserting his three guides every now and then, and striking out for himself. He is not indeed always right when he does this; in some hard places all the four versions are wrong; but as a rule he has a good deal to say for himself, and his

---

* The Old Testament is Jerome's own work; the New Testament is his revision, often perfunctory, of the old Latin version.

renderings testify to his sound knowledge of Hebrew. Here are some examples, the renderings of his three rivals being given in the brackets:—

Genesis vi. 3. My spirit shall not alway *strive with* (*abide in* or *rule among*) man—A.V., R.V.

Genesis xviii. 25. Should not *the judge* of all the world *do according to right?* A.V., R.V.

The others have the second person: *thou who judgest*; and the Vulgate and Luther also mistranslate the last words, rendering: *thou wilt not make this judgment.*

Genesis xli. 16. God shall give Pharaoh answer of *peace* (*prosperity*)—A.V., R.V.

Genesis xli. 43. And they cried before him: *Abrech.*

Tyndale simply sets down this obscure Hebrew word. The others omit it, or render: *Bow the knee* (so A.V., R.V.).

Exodus v. 3. Lest *he smyte us either with pestilence* (*there befall us pestilence*) or with sword—A.V., R.V.

Exodus xxxiv. 18. In the time *appointed* in the month of *Abib*—R.V.

The other three omit *appointed*, and the Greek and Latin versions also give *the month of the new corn* instead of *Abib.*

Numbers xiii. 19. Whether they dwell in *tents or walled* (*walled or unwalled*) towns—A.V., R.V.

Numbers xxv. 3. Israel *coupled himself* (*was initiated* or *submitted*) unto Baal-Peor—A.V., R.V.

Deuteronomy i. 33. To *search* you *out* (*choose, measure* or *show*) a place to pitch your tents in—A.V., R.V.

Deuteronomy iii. 17. Under the *springs* (*mountain* or *Ashdoth*) of Pisgah—R.V.M.

Deuteronomy xxiv. 14. Thou shalt not *defraud an hired servant that is* (*keep back the hire of a man*) needy and poor—A.V., R.V.

Isaiah lviii. 1. Cry *with the throat* (*aloud*) and spare not—R.V.M.

Tyndale translates the Hebrew literally.

Jonah i. 4. But the Lord *hurled* (*sent*, or *awaked*) a great wind into the sea—R.V.M.

This graphic word, expressing the violence and suddenness of the storm, is watered down by the other versions, and also by the Authorized and Revised Versions.

Having illustrated Tyndale's knowledge of Hebrew, we

can now turn to the English style. We find it to bear the strongest likeness to that of his New Testament. His disregard for the particles, indeed, is not so prominent, for the simple reason that Hebrew is far more vague and easygoing in this respect than Greek; but otherwise his old habits are there. Whenever he has a mind, he uses *as soon as* for *when*, *what* for *who*, *see that ye do this* for *do ye this*. He is again ready to invert the order of two nouns, or to insert *both* or *either* when they are linked by *and* or *or*. He is fond too of bringing out the meaning of an obscure sentence either by a paraphrase or by the repetition of a noun: for example, in Numbers xxi. 26 he gives: " Heshbon was the city of Sihon king of the Amorites, which *Sihon* had fought." Above all, his love of variety is as strong and unbridled as ever. Thus the *covenant* between God and his people is also described as a *testament, appointment,* or *bond*; and in one passage of four verses (Lev. xxvi. 42–5) all four renderings occur together. When a human covenant is in question, *promise* or *agreement* may be used. The phrase *it came to pass* is usually omitted (the other three versions do the same), but when it is retained, it receives four out of the five renderings which we found in the New Testament. The *cities of refuge* seem not to be so named in Tyndale's version, but they are termed instead *privileged towns, free cities, cities of franchise* and *franchised cities*. The *avenger of blood* becomes also the *executer*, or the *justice* (or *judge*) of blood. Joseph's *coat of many colours* becomes a few verses later his *gay coat*; *unleavened bread* turns in the next verse into *sweet bread*; and within three verses the furniture of the tabernacle is described as the *ornaments, ordinances, apparel,* and *vessels*: and so on. Clearly our William has not changed his nature during the four years that have passed since his first New Testament.

In the New Testament Tyndale had coined one or two words and phrases. He gave us *shewbread* (from Luther's *Schaubrot*), *tendermercies* and *longsuffering*; he seems too to have been the first to give a theological meaning to *atonement*. But the Pentateuch gives him more scope for such activities: special words had to be found for the Jewish rites and observances: for these stand at the very heart of the book, and are described with minute accuracy. In some cases, indeed, there were renderings already well established in the English speech: thus Tyndale made no attempt to oust the time-honoured *tabernacle*. But where there was no satisfactory English equivalent, he did not hesitate to try his hand at invention: and not without success, for it is he that has given to our language the words *passover, scapegoat* and *mercy seat*. The last was formed after the pattern of Luther's *Gnadenstuhl*, and Tyndale had already gone half-way towards it by his use of *mercy stool* in the prologue to the Cologne fragment, and by his rendering *seat of mercy* in Romans iii. 25.

Tyndale's Pentateuch contains many more rare and archaic words than does his New Testament: but this is mainly due to the subjects dealt with. The book abounds with curious facts and out-of-the-way allusions, and the modern editor of his translation has compiled quite a long glossary of words that need interpretation to-day. The primitive and remote society described also gives Tyndale plenty of scope for those simple and quaint renderings, which are so pleasing to the modern reader. Such are:—

Genesis iii. 4. Then said the serpent unto the woman: *Tush, ye shall not* (*ye shall not surely*—A.V.) die.

Genesis xii. 19. But now lo, there is the wife, take her, and *be walking* (*go thy way*).

Genesis xxx. 29. Thou knowest what service I have done thee, and *in what taking* (*how*) thy cattle have been under me.

Genesis xxxix. 2. And the Lord was with Joseph, and he was a *lucky fellow* (*prosperous man*).

Exodus xv. 4. His *jolly* (*chosen*) captains are drowned in the Red Sea.

Jolly here means valiant.

Exodus xv. 26. For I am the Lord *thy surgeon* (*that healeth thee*).

Leviticus xiii. 45. And the leper, in whom the plague is, shall have his clothes rent and his head bare and *his mouth muffled* (*he shall put a covering upon his upper lip*).

Numbers xi. 4. And the *rascal people* (*mixed multitude*) that was among them fell alusting.

Deuteronomy xxi. 11. Seest among the captives a beautiful woman and hast a *fantasy* (*desire*) unto her.

Deuteronomy xxxiv. 7. And yet his eyes were not dim, nor his *cheeks* (*natural force*) abated.

The Vulgate renders: his *teeth* had not fallen out.

But to judge of the version aright, we must see it in the large; and therefore a longer passage will now be given. Here will be found the same noble simplicity, the same strength of rhythm, which we have admired in the New Testament.

Exodus xxxiii. 12–23

(12) And Moses said unto the Lord: See, thou saidest unto me: Lead this people forth, but thou shewest me not whom thou wilt send with me; and hast said moreover: I know thee by name, and thou hast also found grace in my sight. (13) Now therefore, if I have found favour in thy sight, then shew me thy way, and let me know thee, that I may find grace in thy sight. And look on this also, how that this nation is thy people. (14) And he said: My presence * shall go with thee, and I will give thee rest. (15) And he said: If thy presence go not with me, carry us not hence; (16) for how shall it be known now, that both I and thy people have found favour in thy sight, but in that thou goest with us; that both I and thy people have a preeminence before all the people that are upon the face of the earth. (17) And the Lord said unto Moses: I will do this also that thou hast said, for thou hast found grace in my sight, and I know thee by name. (18) And he said: I beseech thee, shew me thy glory. (19) And he said: I will make all my good go before thee, and I will be called in this name Jehovah before thee, and will shew mercy to whom I shew mercy, and will have compassion on whom I have compassion. (20) And he said furthermore: Thou mayst not see my face, for there shall no man see me and live. (21) And the Lord said: Behold, there is a place by me, and thou shalt stand upon a rock; (22) and while my glory goeth forth, I will put thee in a clift of the rock, and will put mine hand upon thee, while I pass by.

---

* One of those fine touches, of which Tyndale held the secret. The previous versions have: My *face* (*facies, angesicht*) shall go with thee.

(23) And then I will take away mine hand, and thou shalt see my back parts: but my face shall not be seen.*

Having now gained some notion of Tyndale's Old Testament translation, we can turn to consider that version of the remaining historical books, which finds a place in Matthew's bible, and of which Tyndale is said to have been the author. This bible was printed in July 1537, nine months after his death, and upon its title-page stood the name Thomas Matthew. That Matthew was none other than Rogers, is stated by Foxe and Bale, and it was certainly believed during his own lifetime; for in his condemnation in 1555 he is described as "John Rogers priest, alias called Matthew." The book was printed at Antwerp at the expense of Grafton and Whitchurch, two members of the grocers' company. In the New Testament and the Pentateuch Tyndale's version is used with trifling revision, but the rest of the Old Testament and the Apocrypha are derived from Coverdale's bible of 1535, save only the books Joshua to II Chronicles, which come from an unknown source.

Had Rogers been the author, he would hardly have stopped at II Chronicles, but would have completed the Old Testament. But more than this—we have one good witness, who states positively that Tyndale translated these books, though he does not go on to say that they were included in Matthew's bible. This is Halle's *Chronicle* of 1548; and Halle was not only known to Grafton, but made him his executor; and Grafton it was that edited and printed the *Chronicle* after its author's death. Halle's words are as follows:—"This man translated the New Testament into English, and first put it in print, and likewise he translated the five books of Moses, Joshua, Judges,

---

* Tyndale's Pentateuch was reprinted by J. I. Mombert in 1884, and a facsimile of his Jonas was issued in 1863 by Francis Fry. See also *The Sources of Tyndale's Version of the Pentateuch* (J. R. Slater, Chicago, 1906); *Journal of Theological Studies*, Oct. 1935 (J. F. Mozley). Slater overstates Tyndale's dependence on Luther. Moreover his comparison of the two is often untrustworthy, because he uses a German bible of 1583, whereas Tyndale used Luther's first Pentateuch of 1523, which differs in many places.

Ruth, the books of the Kings [*i.e.* Samuel and Kings] and the books of Paralipomenon [Chronicles], Nehemiah or the first of Esdras, the prophet Jonas, and no more of the holy scripture." It is true that Halle gives Tyndale two more books, Ezra and Nehemiah, than appear from this unnamed source in Matthew's bible; but these two books were often—and indeed by Halle himself—reckoned as one, and he may have understood his informant to be speaking inclusively instead of exclusively; or it is possible that these two books were left by Tyndale in a rough draft only, and were considered by Rogers too imperfect to put into his bible.

That Tyndale had some part in Matthew's bible, we have a faint record in the pages of the book itself, where he figures under his initials, as indeed do all the chief doers save Coverdale. The fictitious Thomas Matthew has his full name on the title-page and at the end of the dedication to the king. The initials J.R. for John Rogers are placed at the bottom of one of the prefaces, R.G. and E.W. for the two publishers appear on the title-page of the prophets, and at the end of Malachi stands W.T.

Thus the direct evidence hangs together and makes a story that is very probable in itself. Indeed, if Tyndale was not the author, it is not easy to see why Rogers should have brought out the book at all. All its contents, except these books from a nameless source, were already accessible to the public in the Tyndale and Coverdale translations. Piety to a deceased master, and a desire to rescue his unpublished work from oblivion, would account excellently well for the publication. Rogers himself in the remaining seventeen years of his life never put his hand to the work of translation, and if a third person was the author, he would naturally have published his work himself, preferably also in a complete form, instead of handing a fragment to Rogers.

But the question is completely set at rest by an examination of the version itself: and as it is much more inaccessible than the rest of Tyndale's translations, having never been reprinted in modern times, it will be well to treat the matter somewhat thoroughly. The version of Joshua to II Chronicles strongly resembles that of the Pentateuch, and bears all the marks of Tyndale's mind and style, marks that should be familiar to the reader by now. To begin with there is the same sound scholarship, the same strong and independent judgment. He translates direct from the Hebrew, and is found siding now with one version and now with another. Not a few of his renderings are more accurate than the Authorized Version, and in agreement either with the Revised Version or its margin, or with good scholars of to-day. Once more too we find him sometimes throwing over his three predecessors, and giving renderings which can only have been derived from the original. Here are some examples; the renderings of the three are placed in the brackets.

Joshua v. 1. To the *seaward* (*westward*).
Joshua ix. 21. And *they were made* (*but let them be*) hewers of wood and drawers of water—R.V.
Judges i. 14. *She counselled him* (*he counselled her*) to ask of her father a field—A.V., R.V.
Ruth iii. 11. For all the *gates* (*town* or *tribe*) of my people knoweth that thou art a woman of virtue.
I Samuel xxviii. 13. I see *a god* (*gods*) ascending up out of the earth—R.V.
The Greek and Latin versions give also a past tense: *I saw*.
II Samuel xiv. 17. I pray God that the word of my lord the king may be *immutable* (*as a sacrifice*).
A.V. and R.V. have *comfortable*.
II Samuel xxii. 17. Plucked me out of *mighty* (*many*) waters—R.V.M.
I Kings xxii. 34. And a certain man drew a bow *ignorantly*, and smote the king of Israel between *the ribs of his harness* (*lung and stomach*)—A.V., R.V.
For *ignorantly* the Septuagint gives *with good aim*, and Luther *hard*.
II Kings iv. 35. And then the lad *neesed* (*yawned* or *snorted*) seven times—A.V., R.V.
II Kings xii. 4. All the silver that is dedicate and brought to the house of the Lord *in current money* (*according to the assessment* or *by the passers by*)—R.V.

II Kings xxii. 9. Thy servants have *poured out* (*melted* or *gathered*) the silver—R.V.M. [= R.V. *emptied out*].

II Kings xxv. 24. Fear not ye *the servants* (*to serve*) the Chaldeans—R.V.

II Chronicles xxii. 10. Athaliah arose and *spake with* (*destroyed*) all the seed of the kingdom. Tyndale prefers to follow the Hebrew, despite the fact that it makes no very good sense.

II Chronicles xxviii. 20. Came upon and besieged him *but prevailed not against him* (*and he could not resist him*)—R.V.M.

So far we seem to trace Tyndale's hand. The author of these disputed books is a sound scholar, always using his own judgment, and on the whole he keeps rather closer to his Hebrew text than does any of his three forerunners. Next we observe that he carries on from Tyndale's Pentateuch certain renderings, which were by no means a matter of course. Thus *elon* is rendered *oak*, though some translators (and also A.V.) took it to mean *plain*; *toph*, a musical instrument, becomes *timbrel*, whereas Coverdale nearly always gives *tabret*; for *Ashdoth-Pisgah* the translator gives Tyndale's *springs of Pisgah*, and not *mountains* (or *waters*) *of Pisgah*; the garment worn by ministrants is again called an *ephod* and not, as with Coverdale, an *overbody coat*. Again, the striking renderings *observe dismal days* (*observe times*—A.V.) and *pluck up your hearts* (*be of good courage*) occur in both sections: and it would be easy to add to this list. The repetition of such renderings certainly points to Tyndale as the maker of these books.*

But the strongest proof is still to come. A rendering of a difficult phrase, or a rendering that is in any way remarkable in itself, might be imitated by a disciple, who, mistrusting his own competence for the work of translation, thought it safer to follow Tyndale. But in these unnamed books we find also all the little peculiarities, the unusual habits, the tricks and inconsistencies, which we have learnt

---

* A dozen such examples of varying strength have been noticed by two or three different scholars; cf. Westcott (1905), p. 176. Apart from this, no one has hitherto made any serious comparison of these books with Tyndale's Pentateuch.

to know in Tyndale's New Testament and Pentateuch. No one would dream of imitating these, or could succeed if he tried. Thus we find once more the roundabout imperative, the needless inversion of two nouns, the use of *what* for *who*, and *as soon as* for *when*, the repetition of nouns to make the meaning clearer, and so on. These devices are not constantly used, but only when he has a mind.

Above all, the extravagant love of variation is here. Thus a *covenant* between God and man is frequently rendered by *appointment* and *testament*, and in other connections it becomes a *bond, league* or *confederation*. The phrase *it came to pass*, when not omitted, is rendered also by *chanced, fortuned* and *happened*. And there are plenty of new examples of this love of change. In Judges x. 12-14 the word *deliver* is also translated *help* and *save*; in I Kings ix. a *talent* of gold becomes later a *hundredweight* of gold; in II Chronicles xii. 6-7 the same word receives three renderings, *humble themselves, submit themselves*, and *meek themselves*.

But it is needless to multiply instances of what can be found on every page. It will be enough to add one more, of a very striking kind. With the well-known formula, summing up the reigns of the kings of Israel and Judah, our excellent translator has a regular field day, and thoroughly enjoys himself. In our sober bible of king James it runs: Now the rest of the acts of X and his might, etc., are they not written in the book of the chronicles of the kings of Israel? And X slept with his fathers, and was buried . . . And Y his son reigned in his stead. Tyndale, however, finds many opportunities of introducing variety. *Rest* can become *remnant*; *acts* are also *deeds*, and once the word is omitted altogether. The *book of the chronicles* becomes also *book of the histories, book of the stories, chronicle book, book of the deeds* (or *acts*) *done in the days*, or simply *stories*. *Slept* can become *was laid to rest* (or *sleep*), *laid him to rest* (or *sleep*), or *fell on sleep*; and *stead* is sometimes *room*. He can hardly have twice given the formula in exactly the same way. No one but Tyndale could rise to these heights of waywardness.

Thus the case is abundantly clear. It is not enough to

say, as some writers do, that there is no reason to doubt the tradition ascribing these books to Tyndale. There is overwhelming reason to accept it. All the lines of proof support one another; and there is not a shadow of evidence on the other side. And when we examine the version as literature, our conviction is only strengthened, if that be possible. There are the same bold touches, the same quaint turns of phrase, which, though sometimes rather free of the Hebrew, always awake our interest and pleasure. Thus he gives us:—

Judges iv. 15. But the Lord *trounced* (*discomfited*—A.V.) Sisera.

Judges ix. 53. A woman cast a piece of a millstone upon his head, and alto brake his *brainpan* (*skull*).

Judges xiii. 5. The lad shall be an *abstainer* (*Nazarite*). This rendering is also found in Tyndale's Pentateuch, and it is to be wished that later translators had followed him. Its meaning is clear to the simplest.

I Samuel vi. 6. When he [God] had *played his pageants with them* (*wrought wonderfully among them*).

I Samuel x. 24. All the people shouted and said: God *lend the king life* (*save the king*).

I Samuel xx. 12. When I have *groped my father's mind* (*sounded my father*).

II Samuel vi. 20. Oh how glorious was the king of Israel to-day, which *stripped* (*uncovered*) himself before the eyes of the maidens of his servants, as *a light brained fellow is wont to strip himself* (*one of the vain fellows shamelessly uncovereth himself*).

II Samuel xi. 20. If *he begin to fume* (*the king's wrath arise*).

II Samuel xiii. 28. (Absalom to his young men) *Be bold therefore and play the lusty bloods* (*be courageous and be valiant*).

I Kings xvii. 24. Now I know that thou art *God's man* (*a man of God*). Tyndale uses the same phrase in the Pentateuch.

I Kings xx. 17. The *sheriffs of the shires* (*princes of the provinces*). A verse or two before Tyndale renders the same phrase *governors of the shires*.

II Kings iv. 28. Did I not say *that thou shouldst not bring me in a fool's paradise* (*Do not deceive me*).

II Kings ix. 20. For he driveth *as he were mad* (*furiously*).

II Kings ix. 30. Jezebel . . *starched her eyes* (*painted her face*) and tired her head.

II Kings xix. 9. Tirhakah, king of the *black mores* (*Ethiopia*).

II Kings xix. 27. *How thou settest up thy bristles* (*thy rage*) against me.

Or if we test the version in the large, our conclusion is the same. There is the same firm hand, the same simple and direct style, the same wonderful rhythm, the same noble dignity that rises with its theme. All bears the stamp of Tyndale; and there can be no more fitting way of ending this chapter than by setting a familiar passage before the reader.

II Samuel xviii. 19–33

(19) Then said Ahimaaz the son of Sadock: Let me run,
I pray thee, and bear the king tidings, how that the Lord
hath judged him quit of the hands of all his enemies.
(20) And Joab said unto him: Thou art no man to bear
tidings to-day; thou shalt bear tidings another time: but
to-day thou shalt bear none, because the king's son is dead.
(21) Then said Joab to Chusi: Go and tell the king what
thou hast seen. And Chusi bowed himself unto Joab and
ran. (22) Then said Ahimaaz the son of Sadock again to
Joab: Come what come will, let me run, I pray thee,
after Chusi. And Joab said: Wherefore shouldest thou
run, my son? for and thou run, thou gettest no reward.
(23) Well, come what will, let me run. And he said unto
him: Run. Then Ahimaaz ran by the plain and overran
Chusi. (24) And David sat between the two gates. And
the watchman went up to the roof over the gate unto the
wall, and lift up his eyes and saw: and behold there came
a man running alone. (25) And the watchman called and
told the king. And the king said: If he come alone, there
is tidings in his mouth. And he came and drew nigh.
(26) And the watchman saw another man running, and
called unto the porter and said: Behold, there cometh
another running alone. And the king answered: He is
also a tidings-bringer. (27) And the watchman said:
Methinketh the running of the foremost is like the running
of Ahimaaz the son of Sadock. And the king said: He is
a good man and cometh with good tidings. (28) And

Ahimaaz called and said to the king: Good tidings; and bowed himself to the earth upon his face before the king, and said: Blessed be the Lord thy God, which hath shut up all the men that lift up their hands against my lord the king. (29) And the king said: Is the lad Absalom safe? And Ahimaaz answered: I saw a great ado, when the king's servant Joab sent me thy servant; but I wot not what it was. (30) And the king said: Turn, and stand here. And he turned and stood. (31) And behold, Chusi came and said: Tidings, my lord the king; the Lord hath quitted thee this day out of the hands of all that rose against thee. (32) And the king said to Chusi: Is the lad Absalom safe? And Chusi answered: The enemies of my lord the king, and all that rise against thee to have [? harm] thee, be as thy lad is. (33) And the king was moved, and went up to a chamber over the gate, and wept; and as he went, thus he said: My son Absalom, my son, my son, my son, Absalom: would to God I had died for thee, Absalom, my son, my son.*

* Let the reader compare Coverdale's rendering of this passage. Tyndale's rhythm is much stronger; his style marches.

CHAPTER IX

THE agent employed to persuade Tyndale back to England, and to win him over to the king's cause, was Stephen Vaughan, a merchant adventurer of Antwerp. He had been in Cromwell's service, and owed his rise largely to his master's assistance. Like so many of the merchants of the day, he was sympathetic towards reform, and in 1529 had found himself under suspicion of heresy with the governor of the English house. Recently he had been appointed king's factor in the Netherlands, and now he was entrusted with the delicate matter of approaching Tyndale. Happily some of his letters have been preserved, otherwise our knowledge of Tyndale's doings in 1531 would be meagre indeed. He probably received his instructions by word of mouth, when he left England at the end of November 1530, and in his letter of January 26, written from Bergen to the king, he tells how he has fared.

I have been much desirous, he says, " to attain the knowledge of such things as your majesty commanded me to learn and practise in these parts," but my endeavours have been repeatedly brought to nought, whereat I am right sorry. " Of late I have written three sundry letters unto William Tyndale, and the same sent for the more surety to three sundry places, to Frankforde, Hanboroughe and Marleborughe, I then not assured in which of the same he was." As I had " heard say in England, that he would, upon the promise of your majesty and of your most gracious safe conduct, be content to repair and come into England," I made him the offer, using certain other persuasions to move him, and above all promising him that " whatsoever surety he would reasonably desire for his safe coming in and going out of your realm, my friends [*i.e.* Cromwell] should labour to have the same granted by your majesty." I had great

187

hopes of success, but " the bruit and fame of such things as, since my writing to him, hath chanced within your realm," has led him not only to refuse, but to suspect a trap to bring him into peril. Were he but in your gracious presence, he would soon perceive how needless are his fears: for you are ever so benign and merciful to your subjects, who, " knowledging their offences," humbly ask your pardon. In reply to my offer he sent me a " letter written with his own hand," and also " the copy of another letter of his, answering some other person, whom your majesty perhaps had commanded to persuade by like means: . . . which letters, like as together I received from the party, so send I herewith enclosed to your highness." I informed you in a previous letter that Tyndale's answer to my lord chancellor's book is finished. I have searched for a copy to send to your majesty, and indeed I was doing so, even before the treasurer of your household gave me the instruction, but I have failed to find one; nor can I even discover whether it be yet printed: but as soon as it is, I will send it without fail.

From this letter it is evident that in Henry's eyes Tyndale was an offender, who stood in need of pardon; but it is equally evident that he was esteemed to be a man of power. Great interest is taken in his doings; news of his completing a new book finds its way to England, while it is still in manuscript, and every effort is made to secure a copy when it should be printed. It was felt that he was a man worth winning over, and the plan was to bring him to England under such a safe-conduct, as was a year later offered to, and accepted by, Robert Barnes. The policy of using Lutheranism as an ally no doubt originated with Cromwell, but the king was quite agreeable, if it would serve his turn.

Of this letter to the king, and of Tyndale's answer to himself, Vaughan sends a copy to Cromwell, but he adds also a note for his master's private eye. " Sir," he begins, " here see you my rudeness and inability to be a writer to so great a prince "; and he desires him to present his letter to Henry at a suitable moment, and to excuse its faults. Then he proceeds: " It is unlikely to get Tyndale into England, when he daily heareth so many things from thence which feareth him. After his book, answering my lord chancellor's book, be put forth, I think he will write no more. The man is of a greater knowledge than the king's highness doth take him for; which well appeareth by his works. Would God he were in England!"

It is to be wished that Vaughan had told us from what place Tyndale had replied to his letter, but very likely he did not know himself. Tyndale may even have been in Antwerp all the time; at all events a good deal was known about him in that city. There Vaughan learns of the new book against More; there too he is informed that it will likely be his last book; there too he must have received the advice to write to Frankfort, Hamburg and Marburg, as places which Tyndale was known, or believed, to have visited in recent years; and all that he heard of Tyndale's character and talents impressed him favourably.

But what were the things, happening within the realm, the news of which frightened Tyndale, and impelled him to reject Vaughan's offer? This can hardly refer to the ignominy inflicted on his brother John, for that had occurred before Vaughan left England: but John's punishment was only a part of the more stringent persecution which was now breaking out against the reformers. Stokesley had become bishop of London in November, and was exerting himself with all the vigour of a new broom, and Thomas More, the chancellor, was nothing loth to play his part. The ecclesiastics, being compelled during these early months of 1531 to suffer so many humiliations at the king's hands, to pay him an enormous fine to escape the penalty of premunire, to accept him as " head of the church, so far as the law of Christ allows," were eager to avenge themselves on their theological opponents. Many things would reach Tyndale's ears, the memory of which has since perished; but we know quite enough to estimate the situation.

In February the house of convocation even turned its indignation against the body of a dead man. This was William Tracey, squire of Toddington in Gloucestershire, an old acquaintance of Tyndale, described by him as " a learned man, and better seen in the works of St Austin twenty years before he died, than ever I knew doctor in

England." In his will, which was dated October 5, 1530, and had a wide circulation, he proclaimed his belief in salvation through Christ alone, rejected all other mediators between God and man, and stated that he would bestow no part of his goods for the buying of prayers for his soul. Horrified at these Lutheran sentiments, the assembled fathers condemned the will as scandalous, impious and heretical, and threatened to have the body of its author exhumed, and cast out of consecrated ground. After the lapse of a year the sentence was carried out, and the body burnt into the bargain; but it is satisfactory to know that Thomas Parker, the chancellor of Worcester, executor of this wanton outrage, did not escape scot free, but was mulcted in the very heavy sum of £300.

Early in March Latimer, Crome and Bilney were in trouble before the same august assembly. The former got off for the time being, and Crome recanted; but for Bilney it was the beginning of the end, and he went to the stake a few months later. The next victim was John Nicholson or Lambert, who had been for a year and more chaplain to the English house in Antwerp. There, according to Foxe, he was accused by one Barlow, probably our old friend Jerome Barlow, and Thomas More found means to have him sent to England.* At the end of March he was examined before convocation. How he fared, we know not; but if he escaped punishment, it cannot have been for long, for he was in prison when Warham died sixteen months later. Worse still was the news from the north, where three humble persons, two men and a woman, went to the stake at York in the month of March.

Such happenings would speedily reach the ears of Tyndale. In the spring, indeed, he had a particularly trustworthy channel of information; for John Frith paid a short visit to England during Lent. What he learnt was well calculated to alarm him. Nor would he be reassured by promises of safe-conduct. Safe-conducts had been broken before at the instigation of the hierarchy, and might be again. Huss had

---

* More says (*Works* 405) that the author of *Rede me* [Barlow] " is graciously turned again to God."

been burnt at Constance despite a safe-conduct; Luther was not far from the same fate at Worms; and when Barnes came to England at the end of the year, no less a person than Thomas More desired to see his safe-conduct set aside. Had Tyndale, " the captain of our English heretics," as More called him, ventured to England, he would hardly have left the realm alive.*

In the ensuing weeks Vaughan continues his inquiries, and imparts the result of them in a letter to Cromwell from Antwerp on March 25.

" So it is that, as I lately advertised you by my letters [not preserved] that I have obtained a copy [in manuscript] of the third part of Tyndale's book against my lord chancellor's book; which is so rudely scribbled that I am constrained to write it again, and am writing of it as busily as I can. When that part is written, I intend to labour to obtain the other part, which I will jointly write in a fair book, and send unto the king's highness. It containeth, with all the three parts, as I am informed, three quires of paper thoroughly written. Sir, he hath made in the beginning of the same a pistle to the king's highness, as I am informed, which as yet is not come unto his hands. I would gladly have your advice, whether it be best that I shall put it to his book, as he putteth it, or otherwise. I am in doubt whether the king's highness will be pleased to receive any such epistle from him or not; I pray you let me have herein your advice, as soon as is possible. I promise you, he maketh my lord chancellor such an answer, as I am loth to praise or dispraise. No work that ever he made is written in so gentle a style. Sir,

---

* More's words about Barnes are these (*Confutation* 343) : " Yet hath he so demeaned himself, since his coming hither, that he had clearly broken and forfeited his safe conduct, and lawfully might be burned for his heresies, if we would lay his heresies and his demeanour, since his coming hither, both twain to his charge. But let him go this once; for God shall find his time full well." This tallies with the account of Foxe and Frith. Foxe says (V., 419) that More " would fain have entrapped " Barnes, but the king and Cromwell protected him. Frith says: " It was plainly told him that you [More] had conspired his death, and that notwithstanding his safe-conduct you were minded to murder him," and therefore Barnes had to keep close in London. More's excuse that Barnes had forfeited his safe-conduct was common form on these occasions. Frith retorts that he himself had read Barnes' safe-conduct [*i.e.* in Antwerp], and the only condition on it was that he must arrive before Christmas: which he did. (Daye's folio 155; cf. *L. & P.*, V., 593, 737).

this work will he not put in print, till he know how the king's
highness will accept and take it.   If he hear that his grace
take it well, it may then peradventure be a mean to bring
him into England.   Howbeit, whether he come or not come
into England, he will make no more works after this.   He
would no doubt come into England, and submit him to the
king's highness, if he had any sure hope of his gracious favour.
I can little or nothing profit with him by my letters, for so
much as the man hath me greatly suspected.   Howbeit I
have stayed the impression [printing] of this book hitherto,
and will hereafter do as much as I can.''

It appears from this letter that Vaughan had got into touch
with one of the English refugees in Antwerp, who knew something of Tyndale and his proceedings.   This may have been
George Joye, to whom Vaughan went for information on a
like occasion a couple of years later.   His informant, indeed,
seems not to have been very accurate in his reports.   No
epistle to the king was included in the book when it was
printed some three months afterwards, and if Tyndale ever
intended to add this, he must have altered his mind.   Nor
can we believe that he really undertook to hold the book up
at the king's pleasure, or to write no more in the future.*
No doubt what he had really said was that he would wait a
little, to see whether the king would reverse his policy and
permit the free circulation of scripture, and if only that boon
were granted, he was well content to lay down his pen.
Vaughan and his informant, as is the manner of go-betweens
and peacemakers all the world over, stretched Tyndale's
words to their utmost limit, to produce as favourable an
impression as possible.   Vaughan, indeed, is determined to
wear rose-coloured spectacles: for whatever may be said of
Tyndale's *Answer to More*, it is certainly not written in his
most gentle style.

When three weeks had passed, Vaughan had completed his
fair copy, and on April 18 he sends it with a letter to the king.

" The matter therein contained," he says, " for the
modest order thereof in regard of his former writing, will

* The report, however, went round the court. " This is his last
book," says More (*Works,* 505).

somewhat better like you than some other of his works, which he hath with less advisement, more rashness, and ruder spirit put forth before this time. This part, which your grace receives now, is but a third or fourth part of his whole work; but comprehendeth in effect the substance and pith of the other parts; where he particularly answereth to every chapter of my lord's book, with such grounds as he hath laid in his first part, though he use in it a larger circumstance. The second part I have in like wise obtained, which I will in like wise write, and send unto your grace, with all convenient speed and celerity."

But Vaughan has a still more interesting thing to communicate to the king. All unexpected, he has had an interview with Tyndale himself. This is his description:—

" The day before the date hereof I spake with Tyndale without the town of Antwerp, and by this means. He sent a certain person to seek me, whom he had advised to say that a certain friend of mine, unknown to the messenger, was very desirous to speak with me; praying me to take pains to go unto him, to such place as he should bring me. Then I to the messenger, ' What is your friend, and where is he? ' ' His name I know not,' said he; ' but if it be your pleasure to go where he is, I will be glad thither to bring you.' Thus, doubtful what this matter meant, I concluded to go with him, and followed him till he brought me without the gates of Antwerp, into a field lying nigh unto the same; where was abiding me this said Tyndale. At our meeting, ' Do you not know me? ' said this Tyndale. ' I do not well remember you,' said I to him. ' My name,' said he, ' is Tyndale.' ' But Tyndale! ' said I, ' fortunate be our meeting.' Then Tyndale, ' Sir, I have been exceeding desirous to speak with you.' ' And I with you; what is your mind? ' ' Sir,' said he, ' I am informed that the king's grace taketh great displeasure with me for putting forth of certain books, which I lately made in these parts; but specially for the book named *The Practice of Prelates ;* whereof I have no little marvel, considering that in it I did but warn his grace of the subtle demeanour of the clergy of his realm towards his person, and of the shameful abusions by them practised, not a little threatening the displeasure of his grace and weal of his realm : in which doing I showed and declared the heart of a true subject, which sought the safeguard of his royal person and weal of his commons, to the intent that his grace, thereof warned, might in due time prepare his remedies against their subtle dreams. If for my pains therein taken, if for my poverty, if for mine exile out of my natural country, and bitter absence from my friends, if for my hunger, my thirst, my cold, the great danger wherewith I am everywhere encompassed, and finally if for innumerable other hard and sharp fightings which I endure, not yet feeling their asperity by reason I hoped with my labours to do honour to God, true service to my prince, and pleasure to his commons; how is it that his grace, this considering, may either by himself think, or by the persuasions of others be brought to think, that in this doing I should not show a pure mind, a true and incorrupt zeal and affection to his grace? Was there in me any such mind, when I warned his grace to beware of his cardinal, whose iniquity he shortly after approved [*i.e.* proved] according to my writing? Doth this deserve hatred? Again, may his grace, being a Christian prince, be so unkind to God, which hath commanded his word to be spread throughout the world, to give more faith to the wicked persuasions of men, which, presuming above God's wisdom, and contrary to that which Christ expressly commandeth in his testament, dare say that it is not lawful for the people to have the same in a tongue that they understand, because the purity thereof should open men's eyes to see their wickedness? Is there more danger in the king's subjects than in the subjects of all other princes, which in every of their tongues have the same, under privilege of their sovereigns? As I now am, very death were more pleasant to me than life, considering man's nature to be such as can bear no truth.'

" Thus, after a long conversation had between us, for my part making answer as my wit would serve me, which were too long to write, I assayed him with gentle persuasions, to know whether he would come into England; ascertaining him that means should be made, if he thereto were minded, without his peril or danger, that he might so do; and that what surety he would devise for the same purpose, should, by labour of friends, be obtained of your majesty. But to this he answered, that he neither would nor durst come into England, albeit your grace would promise him never so much the surety; fearing lest, as he hath before written, your promise made should shortly be broken, by the persuasion of the clergy, which would affirm that promises made with heretics ought not to be kept.

" After this, he told me how he had finished a work against

my lord chancellor's book, and would not put it in print till such time as your grace had seen it; because he apperceiveth your displeasure towards him, for hasty putting forth of his other work, and because it should appear that he is not of so obstinate mind, as he thinks he is reported unto your grace. This is the substance of his conversation had with me, which, as he spake, I have written to your grace word for word, as near as I could by any possible means bring to remembrance. My trust therefore is, that your grace will not but take my labours in the best part, I thought necessary to be written unto your grace. After these words, he then, being something fearful of me, lest I would have pursued him, and drawing also towards night, he took his leave of me, and departed from the town, and I toward the town, saying I should shortly, peradventure, see him again, or if not, hear from him. Howbeit I suppose he afterward returned to the town by another way; for there is no likelihood that he should lodge without the town. Hasty to pursue him I was not, because I had some likelihood to speak shortly again with him; and in pursuing him I might perchance have failed of my purpose, and put myself in danger.

" To declare to your majesty what, in my poor judgment, I think of the man, I ascertain [assure] your grace, I have not communed with a man——"

But here our copy of Vaughan's despatch breaks off; and it has been thought that Henry, in an outburst of fury at the commendations upon Tyndale, tore the paper across, even as king Jehoiakim cut and burnt the roll of Jeremiah. This may be so; for, as we shall see, the king was much displeased with Vaughan's letter. He had indeed, despite his wrath at *The Practice of Prelates*, suffered his minister to persuade him, that Tyndale be invited to return; but it was to be as a penitent and a prodigal, to whom he could use the prerogative of mercy. He had no mind to treat him as a hero, as a great man unjustly persecuted, as more orthodox than the bishops of the realm. Yet here was Vaughan, the chosen emissary of the crown, going over to the camp of the very man, whom it was his duty to bring to reason.

The reply to the above letter was penned by Cromwell, and from the number of erasures and corrections it is clear that it gave him a great deal of trouble. Some writers are of opinion that the first version was not bitter enough for the king, and that it was he who insisted on the rewriting; but I cannot say that on the whole I find the corrected version sharper than the first, and as the first version was somewhat clumsy, the changes are more likely due to a wish to improve the style. The letter is not dated, but it was written before the middle of May, for it reached Vaughan at Bergen on May 18.

It runs thus:—

" I have received your letters, dated at Antwerp the 18th day of April, with also that part of Tyndale's book inclosed in leather, which ye with your letters directed to the king's highness." These I took to the court, and presented to the king, who answered that he would read them at his leisure. On my next visit to court he called for me, and communicated to me the contents of both letter and book. I could see that he is pleased with your pains and trouble, " yet his highness nothing liked the said book, being filled with seditions, slanderous lies, and fantastical opinions, shewing therein neither learning nor truth." I could see also " that he thought that ye bare much affection towards the said Tyndale; whom in his manners and knowledge in worldly things ye undoubtedly in your letters do much allow and commend; whose works, being replete with so abominable slanders and lies, imagined only and feigned to infect the people, doth declare him both to lack grace, virtue, learning, discretion, and all other good qualities, nothing else pretending in all his works, but to seduce, deceive and sow sedition among the people of this realm. The king's highness therefore hath commanded me to advertise you, that ye should desist and leave any further to persuade or attempt the said Tyndale to come into this realm; alleging that he, perceiving the malicious, perverse, uncharitable, and indurate mind of the said Tyndale, is in manner without hope of reconciliation in him, and is very joyous to have his realm destitute of such a person, than that he should return into the same, there to manifest his errors and seditious opinions, which, being out of the realm, by his most uncharitable, venomous and pestilent books, crafty and false persuasions he hath partly done already. For his highness right prudently considereth, if he were present, by all likelihood he would shortly (which God defend) do as much as in him were to infect and corrupt the whole realm, to the great inquieta-

tion and hurt of the commonwealth of the same. Wherefore, Stephen, I heartily pray you, in all your doing, pro-
viding, and writing to the king's highness, ye do justly,
truly and unfeignedly, without dissimulation shew yourself
his true, loving and obedient subject; bearing no manner
favor, love or affection to the said Tyndale, nor to his works,
in any manner of wise, but utterly to contemn and abhor the
same." Otherwise you will anger the king, check your own
advancement, and disappoint the hopes of myself and your
other friends.

"As touching Frith, mentioned in your said letter" [a lost
one], the king hears good reports of his learning, and
laments that he should misuse it in furthering "the venomous
and pestiferous works, erroneous and seditious opinions of
the said Tyndale and other." He hopes however that he is
not "so far as yet inrooted" in such evil doctrines, but that
he may be recalled to the right way; and he instructs you
to speak with Frith, if you are able, and to urge him to
"leave his wilful opinions, and like a good Christian to
return unto his native country, where he assuredly shall find
the king's highness most merciful, and benignly, upon his
conversion, disposed to accept him to his grace and mercy.
Wherefore eftsoons I exhort you, for the love of God, not
only utterly to forsake, leave and withdraw your affection
from the said Tyndale and all his sort," but also to endeavour
to win over Frith and other heretical persons in those
parts. So you will win merit with God, and thanks from
the king.

Thus wrote Cromwell at the bidding of his master, but
he was unwilling to take this as the final word. No doubt
he knew that Henry had not read the book himself, but was
trusting to the opinions of others, and he believed that the
king's second-hand indignation, however keen, was likely to
give way before an accomplished fact, promising credit or
advantage to himself. He therefore added to the fair copy
a postscript of his own, largely cancelling the strong instructions just given, and hinting that Vaughan should still work
for the reconcilement of Tyndale. This we only learn from
Vaughan's reply, written to the king on May 20 from
Bergen.

I received (he says) two days ago your instructions, sent by
Cromwell. . . . As to Frith, I will do my utmost, as soon as

I meet him, to persuade him to return. "Howbeit I am informed that he is very lately married in Holland, and there dwelleth, but in what place I cannot tell. This marriage may by chance hinder my persuasions. I suppose him to have been thereunto driven through poverty, which is to be pitied, his qualities considered.

"I have again been in hand to persuade Tyndale; and to draw him the rather to favour my persuasions, and not to think the same feigned, I showed him a clause contained in Master Cromwell's letter, containing these words following:— 'And notwithstanding other the premises in this my letter contained, if it were possible, by good and wholesome exhortations, to reconcile and convert the said Tyndale from the train and affection which he now is in, and to excerpt and take away the opinions and fantasies sorely rooted in him, I doubt not but the king's highness would be much joyous of his conversion and amendment; and so being converted, if then he would return into this realm, undoubtedly the king's royal majesty is so inclined to mercy, pity, and compassion, that he refuseth none which he seeth to submit themselves to the obedience and good order of the world.'

"In these words I thought to be such sweetness and virtue as were able to pierce the hardest heart of the world; and as I thought, so it came to pass. For after sight thereof I perceived the man to be exceedingly altered, and moved to take the same very near unto his heart, in such wise that water stood in his eyes, and answered, 'What gracious words are these! *I assure you,' said he, 'if it would stand with the king's most gracious pleasure to grant only a bare text of the scripture to be put forth among his people, like as is put forth among the subjects of the emperor in these parts, and of other Christian princes, be it of the translation of what person soever shall please his majesty, I shall immediately make faithful promise never to write more, nor abide two days in these parts after the same; but immediately to repair into his realm, and there most humbly submit myself at the feet of his royal majesty, offering my body to suffer what pain or torture, yea, what death his grace will, so this be obtained. And till that time, I will abide the asperity of all chances, whatsoever shall come, and endure my life in as many pains as it is able to bear and suffer.* And as concerning my reconciliation, his grace may be assured that, whatsoever I have said or written in all my life against the honour of God's word, and so proved, the same shall I before his majesty and all the world utterly renounce and forsake, and with most humble and meek mind embrace the truth, abhorring all error, sooner at the most gracious and benign request of his royal majesty, of whose wisdom, prudence, and learning I hear so great praise and commendation, than of any other creature living. But if those things which I have written be true, and stand with God's word, why should his majesty, having so excellent gift of knowledge in the scriptures, move me to do anything against my conscience?' with many other words which were too long to write.

"Finally, I have some good hope in the man, and would not doubt to bring him to some good point, were it that some thing now and then might proceed from your majesty towards me, whereby the man might take the better comfort of my persuasions. I advertised the same Tyndale that he should not put forth the same book, till your most gracious pleasure were known: whereunto he answered, mine advertisement came too late; for he feared lest one that had his copy, would put it very shortly in print, which he would let [*i.e.* prevent] if he could; if not, there is no remedy. I shall stay it as much as I can. As yet it is not come forth, nor will not in a while, by that I perceive."

The passage between the asterisks gives us the key to Tyndale's life, and bespeaks his greatness of soul. He desired his countrymen to have the scripture in their mother tongue. From this aim he never wavered; for this he had been content to become an exile, and to live in constant peril; for this he now held stubbornly out, refusing pardons and promotions, which he could have had for the asking, if only he would submit. Nor was he seeking his own glory: he was willing that another man's translation should be licensed, and not his own; and if that were but done, he would accept any personal suffering, however unjust. His courage and steadfastness have not gone without their reward, though he did not live to see it, and indeed was willing to forgo it. The fight was being won by his labours and sacrifices, and his own translation was to be selected as the foundation of the English bible.

After this interview Vaughan's hopes of persuading Tyndale must have waned, yet he did not abate his efforts.

Within a month he met him again, for the third and last time, but once more in vain. Writing to Cromwell from Antwerp on June 19, he speaks first of Luther's book against the emperor and of Melanchthon's *Augsburg Confession*, both newly come out, and then proceeds:—

" I would gladly send such things to his highness; but I am informed he looketh not upon them himself, but committeth them to others. I am sorry he so doth, because I know his high judgment in learning to be such, as might safely without danger approve men's opinions by reading thereof. . . . I was never more desirous to speak with you than now, wherefore I pray you help me to come home. I have spoken with Tyndale, and showed him, as you wrote me the king's royal pleasure was, but I find him always singing one note. You wrote that the answer, which he made to the chancellor, was unclerkly done: and so seem all his works to eloquent men, because he useth so rude and simple style, nothing seeking any vain praise and commendation. If the king's royal pleasure had been to have looked thereupon, he should then have better judged it than upon the sight of another man. The prophets Esay [by Joye, May 10, from the Vulgate] and Jonas [by Tyndale] are put forth in the English tongue, and passeth any man's power to stop them from coming forth."

Here Vaughan's endeavours to win Tyndale cease. Within a few weeks he is in England, and he does not return to the Low Countries until the autumn.

We must now say a word about the two books from Tyndale's pen of which Vaughan has made mention. The first is the *Answer to More*, which, though completed by the month of January, was not printed until about July. The contents of this famous work of controversy will be discussed in the next chapter: but where was it printed? George Joye, writing three years later in his *Apology*, says that Frith first wrote it for Tyndale, and then saw it through the press at Amsterdam. Now Joye is not a careful writer, but still this tallies with Vaughan's report to the king on May 20, that Frith was in Holland, and with Tyndale's statement to Vaughan on May 19, that " one that had his copy " would very shortly print it, and that it was most likely too late to stop him. On the other hand, the book itself shows no marks of a Dutch origin, and the bibliographers with one consent ascribe it to Antwerp. We must suppose therefore that Frith, who was expected back in Antwerp at the end of June, arrived with the manuscript still unprinted, and put it through the press in that city, together with his own *Purgatory*, which was directed against Fisher, More and John Rastell.*

Concerning Jonas there are no doubts. This proceeded from the press of Martin de Keyser, otherwise called Empereur, who henceforth became Tyndale's usual printer. It came out before the *Answer*, in May or early June, but it was likely written later. It consists of an English version of Jonah's prophecy, preceded by a prologue with the signature W. T. For many years the book was completely lost, and although the prologue was well known, having been reprinted in three or four bibles of the sixteenth century, some scholars had come to doubt whether Tyndale had ever translated the text. In 1861, however, Lord Arthur Hervey, afterwards bishop of Bath and Wells, discovered a copy bound up with several other rare tracts, which had been in the ownership of his family for more than two hundred years. The volume is now in the British Museum.

The prophecy of Jonah was very popular in that day, especially on the reformers' side, and many translations of it were put out. Luther himself had rendered it into German in 1526, several years before he took in hand the rest of the prophets. It was considered a tract meet for the times. The contrast between the pious Jews and the sinful Ninevites, the slow awaking of Jonah's mind from its disobedience, the free forgiveness offered to the citizens and their humble acceptance—all these things had their counterparts in the then world. These lessons Tyndale applies in his prologue : let the reader, he begs, come to the book not as a poetic fable, which has to be allegorized, but as a true picture of God's dealing with the soul, " an ernest penny given of God " that

---

* Cf. *L. & P.*, V., 311. The above-named two books belong to the same press. So does Barnes' *Supplication* (Nov. 1531). Barnes was at Wittenberg till the beginning of September; then he went to Lübeck via Magdeburg, and so to Antwerp. Miss Kronenberg tells me that she ascribes the three books to Symon Cock of Antwerp.

he will help us. Here the gospel of grace is to be found. With this key we can unlock every part of the scripture; thus instructed, we can feed anywhere: otherwise all is dark and closed. Come then, he concludes, in lowliness of mind; take the free gift of God, and when thou hast it, sing his praises and help thy brethren.

With Jonas finished, Tyndale must have turned without delay to his next work, the *Exposition of the First Epistle of St John*, which appeared in September 1531 from the press of Martin de Keyser. In Jonas he had returned for a moment to the translation of the bible, but here he deserts it again, not indeed for controversy, but for exposition. Why did he do this? Because he felt that the vernacular scripture was only one weapon, albeit the most powerful weapon, in the cleansing and reformation of the church; with the scripture should go also the light by which to interpret it, the key to the unlocking of its mysteries. Our Rabbins and great clerks, he says in his prologue, cannot find their way in the scripture. A hundred doctors have a hundred interpretations, and the right understanding they persecute. They say that the letter killeth, that the scripture makes heretics. It cannot do this for those who have the profession of their baptism written upon their hearts, who have embraced the free love of God in Christ, to whom the gospel is the inner light of the soul, and not a matter of external ordinances.

" Therefore are they faithful servants of Christ, and faithful ministers and dispensers of his doctrine, and true hearted toward their brethren, which have given themselves up into the hand of God, and put themselves in jeopardy of all persecution, their very life despised, and have translated the scripture purely and with good conscience, submitting themselves, and desiring them that can to amend their translation, or, if it please them, to translate it themselves after their best manner; yea, and let them sew to their glosses, as many as they think they can make cleave thereto, and then put other men's translation out of the way.

" Howbeit, though God hath so wrought with them that a great part is translated; yet, as it is not enough that the father and the mother have both begotten the child and brought it into this world, except they care for it and bring it up, till it can help itself; even so it is not enough to have translated, though it were the whole scripture, into the vulgar and common tongue, except we also brought again the light to understand it by, and expel that dark cloud which the hypocrites have spread over the face of the scripture, to blind the right sense and true meaning thereof. And therefore are there divers introductions ordained for you, to teach you the profession of your baptism, the only light of the scripture; one upon the epistle of Paul to the Romans, and another called the *Pathway into the Scripture.** And for the same cause have I taken in hand to interpret this epistle of St John the evangelist, to edify the layman, and to teach him how to read the scripture, and what to seek therein; and that he may have to answer the hypocrites, and to stop their mouths withal."

The text of the epistle given here differs somewhat from that in the printed New Testament, and Tyndale seems to have translated it afresh from the Greek. The exposition is not one of his most striking works. He keeps fairly close to his text, and it may be that this, together with the division of the book into short sections, acts as a bar upon the freedom of his expression. At all events he rarely gets into his stride. Nevertheless there are many fine thoughts, and it will be well to put a short extract before the reader, which shows us his recoil from the legalisms of the dominant religion.

On iv. 12. (No man hath at any time seen God. If we love one another, God dwelleth in us, and his love is perfect in us.)

"Though we cannot see God, yet if we love one another, we be sure that he abideth in us, and that his love is perfect in us; that is, that we love him un-feignedly. For to love God truly, and to give him thanks, is only to love our neighbour for his sake; for upon his person thou canst bestow no benefit. And forasmuch as we never saw God, let us make no image of him, nor do him any image-service after our own imagination; but let us go to the scripture, that hath

* This is the earliest notice of the *Pathway*, which was an enlarged edition of the prologue to the Cologne fragment.

seen him, and there wete what fashion he is of, and what service he will be served with. Blind reason saith, God is a carved post, and will be served with a candle: but scripture saith, God is love, and will be served with love. If thou love thy neighbour, then art thou the image of God thyself; and he dwelleth in the living temple of thine heart. And thy loving of thy neighbour for his sake is his service and worship in the spirit, and a candle that burneth before him in thine heart, and casteth out the light of good works before the world, and draweth all to God, and maketh his enemies leave their evil, and come and worship him also."

It need hardly be said that this exposition and the prologue to Jonas earned the bitter condemnation of the friends of the pope. Jonas figures on the list of forbidden books proclaimed at Paul's Cross in Advent 1531, and Thomas More, writing a month later in the preface to his *Confutation*, says that "Jonas was never so swallowed up with the whale, as by the delight of that book a man's soul may be so swallowed up by the devil, that he shall never have the grace to get out again." Of the exposition he says: "Then have we from Tyndale the first epistle of St John, in such wise expounded, that I daresay that blessed apostle, rather than his holy words were in such a sense believed of all Christian people, had liefer his epistle had never been put in writing." But in More's eyes Tyndale could do nothing right; his blame has become a matter of form. With each new book that comes out he simply seeks new words to express his loathing and horror. Tyndale is a heretic, and therefore his most harmless writings, such as the prologue to Jonas, must be full of poison.

Meanwhile in England the persecution was gathering strength, and before the end of the year it had issued in three more martyrdoms. In August Bilney perished in the flames at Norwich. In the autumn was arrested Richard Bayfield, a graduate of Cambridge and formerly a monk of Bury St Edmunds, who, after abjuring before Tonstall in 1528, had fled oversea. There, says Foxe, he was "beneficial to Master Tyndale and Master Frith, for he brought substance with him, and was their own hand, and sold all their works and the works of the Germans, both in France and England." Three times he conveyed great loads of books across the seas. At midsummer 1530 he landed on the east coast, and took them to London by way of Colchester; in November he unshipped them at St Katherine's docks, but they were seized by Sir Thomas More; and about Easter 1531 he landed in Norfolk, and brought them to London. Here he was betrayed to the authorities, and burnt at Smithfield on December 4. The third victim was a leather-seller named Tewkesbury, who had been converted by Tyndale's New Testament and *Mammon*, had abjured and carried a faggot in May 1529, and now in the autumn of 1531 was arrested, sentenced by Stokesley in More's house at Chelsea, and burnt at Smithfield late in December. On all this the king looked unmoved. He had won his own battle against the hierarchy, and in exchange he was quite willing to give them a free hand in the burning of Lutherans, and thus to prove himself a good catholic.

There was also another reformer in peril this autumn, but happily for himself he escaped the toils, though not without showing a weakness which, as Demaus says, contrasted strongly with the steadfastness denoted by his name. This was George Constantine or Constans, of whom we have already heard, who had fled to the Low Countries in 1528, and was searched for by West and Rinck in the autumn of that year. He then became active in the circulation of forbidden books, and may even have taken some part in the writing of them: but returning to England, he was arrested, and put in irons in the house of Sir Thomas More. There he confessed matters which the chancellor was very anxious to learn. He disclosed the names of certain of his associates, including Robert Necton, who was thereupon seized and committed to Newgate prison; and he enabled More to seize a cargo of books, by showing him " the shipman's name that had them, and the marks of the fardels." Among those against whom he laid information was Stephen Vaughan. What fate was destined for him, we know not; for he succeeded in slipping from the shackles of his captor, and fleeing across the seas, reached Antwerp on December 6.

We must now return to Vaughan, who after his sojourn in England was despatched in October once more to the Low Countries, but no longer as an instrument for persuading Tyndale. This plan had been abandoned; instead the new ambassador to the imperial court, Sir Thomas Elyot, was instructed to take means to apprehend him forcibly, and to send him to England for punishment. Vaughan has no more to do with Tyndale, but yet his letters to his patron during the next three months are of great value in illustrating the struggles and sufferings of the reformers, and the sharp examinations practised upon them by Sir Thomas More. On November 14 he writes two letters to Cromwell:—

"I am informed that George Constantine hath of late declared certain things against me before my lord chancellor. If it be true, I pray you let me know what things they be. Be you hereof assured, he can declare nothing against me, that is truth, to hurt me. Peradventure he hath declared that I spake with Tyndale. If so he have done, what hath he herein declared, that I myself have not signified to the king's highness? Peradventure he hath also declared that I labored Tyndale, upon the king's safe conduct, to come into England. This also I have signified to his highness. What other thing soever he have declared against me, being true, I care not for it; if otherwise, *veritas liberabit*,"

i.e. the truth will free him from the imputation. Vehemently he protests his loyalty to the king, a loyalty too firm to be shaken by any bribes, threats or terrors.

Together with the letters he sends two new books for delivery to the king. The first is already familiar to us; it is Tyndale's exposition upon the first epistle of John. The second is a book by Barnes; " such a piece of work as I yet have not seen one like unto it; I think he shall seal it with his blood ": and he urges his patron to procure " that Dr Barnes might declare the opinions of his book before the king's majesty and the world," so that it could be seen whether there was any case for their toleration. Such an open examination before virtuous, learned and fair judges would remove men's doubts and bring the truth to light; but " when men be secretly examined, the world murmureth, and hath thereby cause to deem wrongfully." Probably it was in answer to this appeal from Vaughan, that Barnes was invited to England under a safe-conduct. He reached London before December 21, and he seems to have received some kind of public hearing, and to have been given a counsellor to assist him. He failed, however, to satisfy his judges, and before January 22 he had left England in peace and safety.

These letters appear to have been crossed by one from Cromwell, informing Vaughan that Constantine had been taken, and was likely to accuse him of Lutheranism, and earnestly warning him to be more careful and circumspect. In his reply, written on December 9, three days after Constantine's arrival in Antwerp, Vaughan rebuts the charge, and bursts out into a noble and indignant protest against the folly and cruelty of the persecution.

" If Constantine have accused me to be of the Lutheran sect, a fautor and setter forth of erroneous and suspect works, I do not thereat marvel, for two causes specially. Once is, for that my lord chancellor, in his examination of the said George and of all other men, as I am credibly informed, being brought before him for cases of heresy, doth deeply inquire to know what may be said of me; and in the examination thereof sheweth evident and clear desire in his countenance and haviour to hear something of me, whereby an occasion of evil might be fastened against me; which no doubt shall soon be espied in the patient whom he examineth, who apperceiving his desire in that behalf, and trusting, by accusing of me, to scape and avoid his present danger, of pure frailty and weakness spareth not to accuse the innocent. The other is, for that George, besides the imminent peril and danger wherein he was, abiding prisoner in my lord's house, was vehemently stirred and provoked, what with the remembrance of his poor wife, remaining here desperate, bewashed with continual tears and pinched with hourly sorrow, sighs and mourning . . . likely to be brought into an extreme danger of poverty "; and therefore he chose " to accuse whom they had longed for, rather than to be tied by the leg with a cold and heavy iron like a beast— as appeareth by the shift he made to undo the same, and scape such tortures and punishments. Will not these perils, fears, punishments, make a son forget the father which gat him, and the mother that bare him and fed him with her breasts? If they will, who should wonder though he would accuse me, a thousand times less dear unto him than either father or mother, to rid him out of the same?

"Would God it might please the king's majesty to look unto these kinds of punishments; which in my poor opinion threateneth a more hurt to his realm than those, that be his ministers to execute the same tortures and punishments, do think or conject; and by this reason only. It shall constrain his subjects in great number to forsake his realm, and to inhabit strange regions and countries, where they shall not practise a little hurt to the same. Yea, and whereas they think that tortures, punishments and death shall be a mean to rid the realm of erroneous opinions, and bring men in such fear that they shall not once be so hardy to speak or look; be you assured, and let the king's grace be thereof advertised of my mouth, that his highness shall duly approve [discover] that in the end it shall cause the sect to wax greater, and those errors to be more plenteously sowed in his realm than ever afore. For who have so mightily sowed those errors, as those persons which for fear of tortures and death have fled his realm? Shall they not, by driving men out of his realm, make the rout and company greater in strange countries, and shall not many do more than one or two? Shall not four write where one wrote afore? Counsel you the king's highness, as his true subject, to look upon this matter, and no more to trust to other men's policies, which threateneth in mine opinion the weal of his realm; and let me no longer be blamed nor suspected for my true saying. That I write, I know to be true, and daily do see the experience of that I now write, which, between you and me, I have often said and written, though peradventure you have little regarded it. But tarry awhile, and you shall be learned by experience. I see it begin already."

I write not thus because, as they suppose, I belong to the sect and desire them to go unpunished. Nay, truly; but I would have evildoers charitably punished, and if possible, won over thereby. "And let his majesty be further assured that he shall with no policy, nor with no threatenings of tortures and punishments, take away the opinions of his people, till his grace shall fatherly and lovingly reform the clergy of his realm. For there springeth the opinion. From thence riseth the grudge of his people; out of that take and find men occasions to complain." As for me, "let all men know, whatsoever the world babble of me, that I am neither Lutheran nor yet Tyndalin"; they and their like are not my gods, nor do I put my trust in the learning of any earthly creature. I have the holy scripture, given to me by Christ's church, and that is a learning sufficient for me, infallible and taught by Christ. . . . From my loyalty to my prince none can corrupt me. I do my duty without thought of reward. If I were venal, like some others, maybe I should find more favour. But "God hath eyes to see, and his reward prepared, and will prepare a living for me, wheresoever I be come, no less than he doth for those his creatures which neither sow nor mow. I am unkindly handled to have such sharp inquisitions made of me in mine absence; I am unkindly handled for my service. Such stripes and bitter rewards would faint and make weak the hearts of some men towards their prince; but I am the stronger, because I know my truth. . . .

"I hear everywhere how diligently my lord chancellor inquireth, of all those he examineth in cases of heresy, for me—what are my manners, my opinions, my conversation, my faith"; and others too are deputed to make like inquisitions. Why take they so great pains? What think they to hear? I am a man, as they are; a sinner too. This they might know without this painstaking. I see that I must depart out of this country. Here I am suspected above all men. Would that I might come to England, and live in a corner of the realm for the residue of my short time, far from these dangerous occupations. "My policies have been here divers; my conversation among men like unto theirs; among Christians I have been a Christian, among Jews like to them, among Lutherans a Lutheran also. What can I here do without such policy?" . . . I am grieved also to hear that I am likely to lose your friendship and patronage, and that you have been excusing yourself to the king for me, telling him you are sorry that you ever commended me to his service. So at least it is reported to me from the mouth of my lord chancellor. If it be so, my heart will still never turn away from you, whatever my body may suffer. I speak this not feignedly, in hope to win your favour, or gaping for your gifts; for I need them not, and am well able to get my living. . . . "George Constantine came to Antwerp after his breaking from my lord chancellor, the 6th day of December. With him nor with none other such will I meddle or have to do, considering that I am beaten with mine own labours."

This outspoken and generous letter seems to have evoked

no answer from England, perhaps because in their hearts the
king and his minister agreed with it, but considered it
advisable to humour the hierarchy for a time. But Vaughan
feels deeply on the matter, and he returns to the attack in his
letter of December 30.

" I hear of divers, as well men as women, of the Lutheran
sect, whose persons nor names I know not nor will know, to
be fled out of England for fear of punishment, and that
lately, bringing with them all that ever they can make: so
that by this means it is likely that new Tyndales shall spring,
or worse than he. I am unwise thus to write, being so
unkindly entreated in England in examinations," where any
evildisposed person, trusting to save himself, is able to lie
and spit out his venom against me. " I am utterly determined from henceforth never to intermeddle, or to have
communication with any one of them; but shall rather give
place to some other man, which peradventure shall have
better luck than I hitherto have had; whom they go about
thus unkindly to threaten, beat, rend, and tear for my
service." Why do they long to bring me into jeopardy?
I never offended them. If my examiners' opinions and
behaviour were as closely scrutinized as mine, would they
be found innocent? Nay, more guilty than mine. " I
would they all, which so greedily examine, did know, I am
no heretic, nor for them all will be made one. I neither
have so corrupt a mind, so evil a conscience, nor so little
understanding, as it seemeth they would I had, which seek
ways to destroy the innocent. I pray God amend them.
If in any part of this my writing I have erred or offended, I
ask thereof pardon; my passion is so great, I cannot resist."

Here Vaughan passes from the scene, and we must needs
pay him our tribute of respect and gratitude. He was not
indeed formed in heroic mould; for he thought overmuch
of his own perils; he was unwilling to burn his boats, or to
sacrifice his prosperity for the sake of truth. Yet he risked
something by his bold speech on behalf of Tyndale, and we
cannot forget it. His letters help us to understand the rapid
spread of Lutheranism, and its backing by men of business.
Such men might not be theologians, but they ardently
desired one thing, which the reformation secured for them,
and that was to be delivered from the inquisitions and
tyrannies of the priests.

To the priests themselves, however, Vaughan was but a pawn in the great contest. They were willing enough to entrap him, but they were flying at higher game than he. Lutheranism in England would never be crushed while its ringleaders lived in safety beyond the seas: and the chief of these was William Tyndale. We have seen how More cross-questioned his prisoners concerning Vaughan: how much more searching enquiries must have been made into the habits and doings of Tyndale. That in fact this was so, we learn from a remarkable passage in Foxe:—

"In the registers of London it appeareth manifest, how that the bishops and Sir Thomas More, having any poor man under coram [*i.e.* called to account] to be examined before them, namely [specially] such as had been at Antwerp, most studiously would search and examine all things belonging to Tyndale, where and with whom he hosted, whereabouts stood the house, what was his stature, in what apparel he went, what resort he had, etc. All which things when they had diligently learned, as may appear by the examination of Simon Smith and others, then began they to work their feats."

Unhappily these registers have not been preserved. Simon Smith was a graduate of Cambridge and a fellow of his college, and had likely been known to Tyndale. He became a Lutheran, married a wife, and fled with her overseas. On their return they were called to examination in London, she being with child, were compelled to abjure, underwent penance, and were sentenced to perpetual imprisonment. This was in 1531. That such inquiries were being made about him in England, would certainly come to the ears of Tyndale. His caution and secrecy in making himself known to Vaughan had the best of reasons. He was a marked man. Danger was ever around him; at any moment his foes might strike him down.*

* For Simon Smith see J. A. Venn, *Biographical History of Gonville and Caius College*, I., 24. It was doubtless from such inquiries as these that More describes Tyndale to Erasmus in 1533 as *hereticus nostras, qui et nusquam et ubique exsulat*, the heretic of our land who is in exile both nowhere and everywhere (Erasmus, *Epistolae*, Leyden 1706, column 1856).

CHAPTER X

TYNDALE's controversy with More is one of the most famous literary battles in history. The greatness of the combatants and the importance of the issues alike make it memorable. It was started from More's side, but he was not drawn into the fray of his own prompting: he waited to be invited. The call came from his old friend the bishop of London. Tonstall had, as we have seen, tried in vain to stem the tide of Lutheran books. He had issued injunctions, browbeaten booksellers, burnt the books themselves: but still they came flooding into the country. He now bethinks him of another expedient. If the thunders of the law have failed, let the still voice of reason be tried; let the books be answered. For this purpose no champion was better equipped than Sir Thomas More. He was no ecclesiastical backwoodsman, no rude zealot, but a scholar and humanist, who had for years been a friend of the new learning. He had sat at the feet of Colet, and was the familiar of Erasmus. He had also a certain lively delicacy of mind that was all his own, and his *Utopia* had earned him a great reputation abroad. Added to that, he was a master of the English tongue, and his graces of style would be likely to commend the cause to his countrymen. He might not be a profound theologian, but even on this field he was no novice, and his devotion and abilities would speedily make good what he lacked of knowledge. If anybody could vanquish the Lutherans with words, it would be Thomas More.

And so on March 7, 1528, about the time that he launched his great campaign against the bible-readers, Tonstall wrote an official letter in Latin to his friend, a letter that can still be read in the episcopal register. He says:—

> There are certain " sons of iniquity," who by translating Lutheran books and printing them in great number

are trying to infect the land with heresy, and there is
much fear lest the catholic faith perish utterly, unless good
and learned men meet the danger by quickly putting
forth sound books in the vernacular on the catholic
side. Now you can play the Demosthenes both in
English and Latin, and at every assembly you are wont
to be the keenest champion of the truth. You cannot
better bestow your leisure hours, if any you have, than
in writing an English work, to shew to simpleminded
people " the crafty malignity of these impious heretics."
Our illustrious king has set you a glorious example by
his defence of the sacraments against Luther, thereby
winning the immortal name of defender of the church.
And that you may not fight blindfold, in ignorance of
your opponents, I send to you their mad follies in
English, and also some of Luther's books [*i.e.* in Latin] ;
from these you will learn the habits of these serpents,
where they lurk, by what shifts and turns they seek to
escape when grasped, and what they hope to achieve.
Go forward then to this holy work; succour the church,
and win for yourself an immortal name, and eternal
glory in heaven: and to this end I give you license
to keep and to read books of that nature.

In the last sentence we see the reformation struggle in
miniature: the great Sir Thomas More may not read
Lutheran books, except by licence from his bishop. A small
thing perhaps, if it had stood alone, but a symbol of the
general state of the church. How long were good and
sincere men to be treated as children, and kept in leading-
strings? Were the gifts which God had given them for ever
to be held and used only at the pleasure of a class of men,
who not only had the common frailties of our humanity,
but had grown to have a personal interest in the upholding
of abuses and the silencing of criticism? Thomas More
might not resent this for himself, but there were thousands
that did; and when once the cry of freedom from priestcraft was raised in trumpet tones by Luther and Tyndale
and a host of others all over Europe, there could be only
one answer; the combat could end only in one way.
Now it should be observed that Tyndale's name is not
mentioned at all in the letter; nevertheless we cannot

doubt that his New Testament and *Introduction to Romans*, the only two works that he had as yet published, were in the parcel of books sent by the bishop to his friend. In fact, More himself in his *Dialogue* speaks of having a New Testament " with the places ready noted," that had been lent to him by licence; and this is evidently Tonstall's own copy, in which the bishop—according to the letter of Robert Ridley, his chaplain—had marked the alleged errors and mistranslations. However More had not long to wait for fresh proofs of Tyndale's activity; for while he was writing his book, the *Mammon* and the *Obedience* arrived from Antwerp, and it was speedily borne in upon his mind that Tyndale was the ablest and the most dangerous of the English reformers, and that in him he had a foeman worthy of his steel. From that time onwards it is not too much to say that the main work of More's life was to confute Tyndale. During the next five or six years he puts forth a thousand and more folio pages, in which Tyndale is the chief target of attack. He affects to despise him, he boasts repeatedly that he has driven him from the field, but he returns to him again and again.

Once summoned to the work by his bishop, Sir Thomas sets to with a will, and within a year he has compiled a volume of more than a hundred and fifty pages, which he publishes in June 1529. It is entitled: *A dialogue of Sir Thomas More knight . . . wherein be treated divers matters, as of the veneration and worship of images and relics, praying to saints and going on pilgrimage, with many other things touching the pestilent sect of Luther and Tyndale, by the tone begun in Saxony, and by the tother labored to be brought into England.*

In casting his argument into a dialogue, More chose a form that not only provided more lively reading than a straightforward treatise, but also made it easy for him to put his enemy's case in a way that suited himself. Every reader of Plato must have been sometimes irritated to see the antagonist of Socrates, after being dislodged from some impossible position, suddenly lower his flag and surrender, when all the time there was a much stronger argument waiting to be employed. So it is here. The " messenger,"

who carries on the discussion with More, and who, though
not himself a Lutheran, acts as the spokesman of that party,
and protests that they are being harshly treated, marshals
his case quite well for a while, but he is fighting with one
hand tied behind his back. He never presses his points
home, or brings out all the weapons in his armoury. The
reader feels always sure, that when the debate has proceeded
some time, and when More has (as if to show his fairness)
given away one or two points of little importance, he will
produce a trump card, and the messenger will collapse at
once, leaving the great Thomas bestriding the field.

The book, although dull in parts, contains much of the
charm of the real More. He is still the artist and the man
of letters, and whatever we may think of the reasoning, he
has given us a book worth reading in its own right. It is
not overlong; he has not yet sunk to the hack-work of
controversy; he is not yet become the mere grinder out of
arguments, the overwhelmer of the enemy with sheer length
and strength of words.

In the title of the *Dialogue* Luther's name stands before
Tyndale's, and the last of its four books is directed against
the great German reformer; nevertheless the chief antagonist
throughout is Tyndale. The work ranges over the greater
part of the controversy, but three matters stand out pre-
eminently. The first is the cult of the saints, the second
the bible, and the third the nature of the church. It is here
that More makes his grand attack on Tyndale's New Testament. Here too he puts forward his singular scheme for an
episcopal licence of bible-reading. He starts by laying down
the healthy principle, that the abuse of a thing does not
take away its proper use. To translate the scripture into
English therefore is good; no man will take harm from it
but by his own pride; he himself would not withhold the
profit which one good devout layman might gain from
reading, though a hundred heretics were hurt. But More
is faced by the hard fact that the bishops have none of this
healthy confidence, but are saying and doing just the
opposite. So he speedily throws his principle overboard,
and proposes a compromise. Let the bishops translate

and print the bible, keeping all copies in their own hands. Let each of them buy as many as will suffice to serve his whole diocese; the cost to each would be only £10 or a little more. Let him then dole out the books to good men, whom he could trust to read them wisely, and reclaim them on their death. One man would be permitted to read the synoptists, but not the gospel of John, one the Acts, not the Apocalypse, one the Ephesians, but not the Romans. The bishop would treat his flock (More makes no bones about the simile) as a father his children, who withholds a knife from one, and grants it to another. Nothing could show more plainly than this timid compromise that there were two Mores, More the humanist, and More the meek follower of church authority. Here we see the two sides of his nature seeking an uneasy balance, and producing a scheme which not only is altogether unworkable, but which, under a faint air of liberality, would, if it were workable, rob most laymen of the scripture in their own tongue.

The great defect of the *Dialogue* is its refusal to grapple with, or even wholeheartedly to condemn, the gross moral scandals of the church of the day. More skirts round such matters so far as he can, and the most that he permits himself is a little mild and theoretic regret. I will not talk with you, he tells the messenger, about the vices of the clergy, nor about the living of any man, except indeed (this touch is typical of More) of heretics, who are throughout all Christendom " damned and defamed already by their own obstinate malice." There are many bad clerks, but our English ones are no worse than those beyond the sea. We paint their misdeeds in the blackest colours. I trust there are more good than bad; but anyhow they are no wickeder than we laymen, in fact better. We ought to look on our own faults first. May God amend us all! The truth is, there are too many unfit persons ordained. If I were pope, we should not have " such a rabble." And there More leaves the matter. It is most unfortunate indeed, but still not a thing to burn into the heart of every Christian man, whether clerk or layman, and drive him on to work for a remedy.

But More is not merely unwilling to act, or even to speak, himself; he is determined to muzzle and to crush into impotence those that do. He gives a whole-hearted verdict for the persecution and burning of Lutherans, and of other rebels against the dominant church. Heretics, he says, " be kept but for the fire, first here and after in hell." They must be " oppressed and overwhelmed in the beginning "; their burning is " lawful, necessary and well done." Nothing could be clearer than this, and no doubt his Lutheran opponents marked the words well, and found it ominous when the news arrived that the author had been made chancellor of England. Wolsey, easygoing and busy with great matters of state, had been content often to wink at Lutherans and their doings; there would be less winking now, when a theological zealot sat in the seat of secular power.*

Of Tyndale himself, and indeed of all the reformers, More draws a picture that is far from flattering. He is a dissembler, waiting his time, and then casting off his " visor of hypocrisy." He is " so puffed up with the poison of pride, malice and envy, that it is more than marvel that the skin can hold together. For he hath not only sucked out the most poison that he could find through all Luther's books, or take of him by mouth, and all that Luther hath spat out in these books, but hath also in many things far passed his master, running forth so mad for malice, that he fareth as though he heard not his own voice." He has wilfully mistranslated the scripture, and deceived blind unlearned people by teaching what he knows to be false. His life is of likelihood as evil as his teaching; worse it cannot be. He is a beast who teaches vice, a forewalker of antichrist, a devil's limb, and so on.

* And so it proved. More " imprisoned and punished a great number," says Halle. More himself gives us the names of several whom he had arrested, Webb, Lobley, Constantine, Necton, Phillips, Segar Nicolson, and an unnamed clerk in the *Debellation*. Tewkesbury and Baynham were both lodged in his house. It is clear that he worked wholehcartedly with Stokesley in what he called " God's great cause " : and to the last this great judge pleads vehemently against the abolition of the cruelly unjust system of trial *ex officio*, without accusers or open witnesses. Some of More's Lutheran prisoners were released by his successor (Erasmus, *Epistolae*, col. 1809).

Having thus been singled out before the whole world as the leader of the English Lutherans, the falsifier of scripture, the hater of all goodness, and the reckless destroyer of the hard-won gains of the past, Tyndale could not refuse the challenge, and after he had seen his Pentateuch and his *Practice of Prelates* through the press, into the latter of which he threw a few sentences against More, he was at leisure to devote himself to his formal defence. This was ready by January 1531, but was not printed until the month of July. It bears this title:—*An Answer unto Sir Thomas More's Dialogue, made by Willyam Tindale. First he declareth what the church is, and giveth a reason of certain words which Master More rebuketh in the translation of the New Testament.*

After that he answereth particularly unto every chapter which seemeth to have any appearance of truth through all his four books. Awake thou that sleepest and stand up from death, and Christ shall give thee light. Ephesians v.

" Of all wretches," wrote More in his *Dialogue*, " worst shall he walk that, forcing [caring] little of the faith of Christ's church, cometh to the scripture of God, to look and try therein whether the church believe aright or not." Tyndale's reply shows him to be one of these worst wretches: for throughout he appeals to scripture as a test not only of the doctrine, but of the practice of the church of his day. Judge for yourself, he says to the reader; do not be deceived by fine spun theories; take the facts as they are. " Judge whether the pope with his be the church, whether their authority be above the scripture, whether all they teach without scripture be equal with the scripture, whether they *have* erred, and not only whether they *can*." To ask whether the church can err, if by the church you mean " the pope and his generation, is as hard a question as to ask whether he which hath both his eyes out be blind or no, or whether it be possible for him that hath one leg shorter than another to halt."

The book therefore is strong just where More's was weakest. It insists on trying the present church by its fruits. With all his might Tyndale strikes at the wickedness and formalism of the day: but however fierce his language, he makes it plain (though More never gives him the credit for this) that he desires to purge and not to destroy. Confession, orders, celibacy, fasting, holy days, and other external ceremonies might become, as indeed they once were, aids to the life of holiness: but then they must be employed in a free and spiritual way, and not usurp a place to which they are not entitled. Now they are become in part engines of priestly tyranny, and in part blinds hiding from the people the deeper goods of love, mercy and purity. Herein, as always, Tyndale shows himself to be a true Englishman. He keeps close to mother earth; he is plain and practical. Deeds mean more to him than words.

Towards his antagonist Tyndale shows no little bitterness. He had in no way meddled with More, and indeed had not hitherto even mentioned his name; and we cannot wonder that he resented the unwarranted attack that had been made upon his honesty, and indeed upon his general virtue. Besides, since writing the *Dialogue*, More had added to his offences by taking a leading part in the council of May 1530, which condemned Tyndale's works root and branch, and recommended that they be destroyed. Nor was this all. The man who was now vilifying an excellent piece of scholarship, and calling for the severe punishment and burning of the reformers, had himself only a few years ago been known as a liberal, a humanist, a smiter of bigots. How was this change of front to be accounted for? The answer seemed clear. More had sold his early convictions for wealth and power; he saw that a reputation for liberalism would hinder his rise. " But verily," writes Tyndale, " I think that as Judas betrayed not Christ for any love that he had unto the highpriests, scribes and pharisees, but only to come by that wherefore he thirsted: even so Master More (as there are tokens evident) wrote not these books for any affection that he bare unto the spirituality, or unto the opinions which he so barely defendeth, but to obtain only that which he was an hungred for "; and later in the book his motive is defined as " to get honour, promotion, dignity, and money, by help of our mitred monsters."

This is the earliest statement of a charge that is repeated more than once by Tyndale during the next two or three years, and which appears in its sharpest and most offensive form in the exposition of the sermon on the mount, composed when the controversy between the two men had waxed still fiercer:

" Covetousness," he there writes, " maketh many, whom the truth pleaseth at the beginning, to cast it up again, and to be afterward the most cruel enemies thereof, after the ensample of Simon Magus; yea, and after the ensample of Sir Thomas More, knight, which knew the truth, and for covetousness forsook it again. . . . Covetousness blinded the eyes of that gleering fox more and more, and hardened his heart against the truth, with the confidence of his painted poetry, babbling eloquence, and juggling arguments of subtle sophistry, grounded on his unwritten verities, as true and as authentic as his story of *Utopia*."

But on this point Tyndale does his enemy a serious injustice. More might be unfair and cruel to the Lutherans, but he was not venal, as his after-history proved. Nevertheless the accusation was not trumped up by Tyndale, it did not spring out of nothing. We can easily see how the belief arose in the minds of men far away from England, and bitterly aggrieved at the persecution directed against them. For the last dozen years More had been rising in the world. He had entered the service of the king, become speaker of the House of Commons, received the dignity of knighthood, been loaded with gifts, praises and dignities. Meanwhile he had been lending his services to crush the reformers. He had come to the king's aid in his controversy with Luther, he had at Wolsey's request searched the Steelyard and thrown several merchants into jail, he had been one of those who examined Tyndale's friend, Monmouth. So far he had been playing the part of a second: but now with his *Dialogue* and its companion-volume the *Supplication of Souls* (a defence of purgatory against Simon Fish) he had stepped to the front, and shouldered the whole weight of the battle, disowning his liberal past. What followed? Within four months of the earlier of these works he received the chancellorship of England, an office that would certainly not have been bestowed upon a Lutheran, and one which no layman had held for hundreds of years. Plainly a reward for the loan of his pen, said the reformers; a clear proof of venality. In the same way More and his friends read the worst meaning into Luther's marriage, seeing in it only a token of lechery and of the hollowness of his religious professions. Both charges were baseless; but they were certain to be made at a time when feeling ran so high. Suspicions and half-beliefs of this kind, when repeated from mouth to mouth, soon grow into certainties; and when in the summer of 1532 the news reached Antwerp, as it probably would, that the clergy had collected the big sum of £4000 or £5000, to present to More on his resignation from the chancellorship in gratitude for his championship of the church, this—even though More refused the gift, saying that he would sooner throw it into the Thames— would be likely to confirm rather than to allay the suspicions, since it at least proved the eagerness of the bishops to reward their defender with money.*

The style of Tyndale's *Answer* matches the content. It is plain and workmanlike, terse, direct, and vigorous. It lacks the gracefulness of More's *Dialogue*, but it is more robust, and moves forward more quickly and surely, though there is, as usual, some repetition. There is no fine writing or straining after artistic effect, yet every now and then we happen upon some outburst of noble eloquence. Thus in answering the question, how are we to know what the scripture is, unless we have an infallible church to tell us, Tyndale says:—

" Who taught the eagles to spy out their prey? Even so the children of God spy out their father; and Christ's elect spy out their lord, and trace out the paths of his feet and. follow; yea, though he go upon the plain and liquid water, which will receive no step, and yet

* Cf. Latimer's letter to the king: " There be some that, for fear of losing of their worldly worship and honour, will not leave off their opinion, which rashly—and that to please men withal, by whom they had great promotion—they took upon them to defend by writing." (December 1, 1530.)

there they find out his foot: his elect know him, but
the world knoweth him not."

To this glorious passage More replies with a scoff:—
I suppose, then, that Augustine was only a chicken, since he
took his knowledge of scripture from the church.

A few pages later the same point is simply and nobly
treated:

> " And hereby ye see that it is a plain and an evident
> conclusion, as bright as the sun's shining, that the truth
> of God's word dependeth not of the truth of the con-
> gregation. And therefore, when thou art asked, why
> thou believest that thou shalt be saved through Christ,
> and of such like principles of our faith; answer, Thou
> wottest and feelest that it is true. And when he asketh,
> how thou knowest that it is true; answer, Because it is
> written in thine heart. And if he ask who wrote it;
> answer, The Spirit of God. And if he ask how thou
> camest first by it; tell him whether by reading in books,
> or hearing it preached, as by an outward instrument,
> but that inwardly thou wast taught by the Spirit of
> God. And if he ask, whether thou believest it not
> because it is written in books, or because the priests so
> preach; answer, No, not now; but only because it is
> written in thine heart; and because the Spirit of God
> so preacheth, and so testifieth unto thy soul: and say,
> though at the beginning thou wast moved by reading
> or preaching, yet now thou believest it not therefore
> any longer; but only because thou hast heard it of the
> Spirit of God, and read it written in thine heart."

Very powerful too is the following passage:—

> " And upon that Master More concludeth his first
> book, that whatsoever the church—that is to wit, the
> pope and his brood—say, it is God's word, though it be
> not written, nor confirmed with miracle, nor yet good
> living; yea, and though they say to-day this, and to-
> morrow the contrary, all is good enough and God's
> word; yea, and though one pope condemn another
> (nine or ten popes a-row with all their works) for
> heretics, as it is to see in the stories, yet all is right, and
> none error. And thus good night and good rest!
> Christ is brought asleep, and laid in his grave; and the

door sealed to; and the men of arms about the grave to keep him down with pole-axes. For that is the surest argument to help at need, and to be rid of these babbling heretics, that so bark at the holy spirituality with the scripture, being thereto wretches of no reputation, neither cardinals, nor bishops, nor yet great beneficed men; yea, and without tot quots and pluralities, having no hold but the very scripture, whereunto they cleave as burs, so fast that they cannot be pulled away, save with very singeing them off."

Tyndale's defence must have reached More by the late summer of 1531, and although immersed in the duties of his high office, he lost no time in preparing his reply, and in the early months of 1532 he produced the first three books of a portentous work, called *the Confutation of Tyndale*. This was completed a year later by the publication of six more books, making nine in all, of which, however, the last but one was directed against Barnes' recent volume. Of this fresh attack Tyndale took no notice, and retired from the controversy: but More was drawn into the fray again by a combatant on his own side, a lawyer named Saintgerman, who, taking a mediating position, blamed sharply the conduct of the clergy towards the Lutherans. For answer More published his *Apology* about Easter 1533, defending the clergy, and indeed himself too, against these and other like charges, and devoting a good deal of attention to Tyndale, Frith and the rest of the brethren, as he mockingly called them; and he and Saintgerman carried on this debate until the end of the year. Meanwhile Tyndale held his peace, save that in April 1533 he—in all likelihood—put out without name a little book on the Lord's supper, to aid Frith in his controversy against More: and to this More wrote a reply six months later.

The *Confutation* is eloquent proof of the devastating effects of controversial zeal on More's mind and style. The *Dialogue*, though tiresome in parts, had retained much of the real man. You walk in a garden, not quite so fresh and fragrant as of yore, but still with flowers in bloom and the tokens of order and loving care. The *Confutation* is a vast expanse of arid waste, with hardly a single oasis to relieve the misery of the traveller. Its gigantic length alone is almost fatal to it. A critic friendly to More has calculated that his treatment is to that of Tyndale in the ratio of twenty to one, rising in places to forty to one. He seems to have felt that the whole faith would fall to the ground, if he omitted to rebut a single argument, which Tyndale not only had used, but might possibly use. The work did not escape censure on this account in More's own day, and in his *Apology*, a little hurt by this criticism, he retorts that certain friends of his have read it through three times: but such stout souls cannot have been many in number. There are things which flesh and blood will not bear; and it is strange that More's common sense and literary judgment did not teach him that this length of wind was simply damaging his own cause.

Worse still, his temper suffers. He begins to nag and to scold. He harps on the same themes, in season, out of season, like a woman with a grievance. His especial king Charles' head is the marriage of a monk with a nun, as typified by Luther's marriage with Catharine von Bora. That he puts this down to lechery, is hardly surprising; though in remembrance of his own youthful unchastity and his unconquerable desire for wedlock, he might have been a little more tender to the frailties (if frailties they were) of a brother man. What is surprising, is the tastelessness with which he uses this weapon. The subject may be free will, or the invisible church, or the vernacular scripture; but whatever it is, Luther's marriage will not be far away. There must be hundreds of allusions to it, and he describes it in the coarsest terms. The only result is to nauseate the reader, and to make him wonder whether these interminable repetitions do not betoken a secret doubt in the author's mind of the value of the argument used.

If More in his *Dialogue* drew an unflattering picture of Tyndale, he here lays on the colours even more thickly. It is true Tyndale had not been backward in returning railing for railing. Quite apart from the false charge of covetousness, which More was entitled to resent, Tyndale had poured the vials of his wrath on his adversary and the party to which he belonged. He can be fierce, bitter, even savage. Thus the bishops are foul monsters, who crush the gospel and persecute its followers to the death. More himself is their willing helper, working for the kingdom of antichrist, serving the devil's church; he is fleshly-minded, and thinks of God as of his cardinal [Wolsey], to whom he is nothing inferior in lying, feigning, and bearing two faces in one hood; he is a sophist who distorts facts, a poet without shame, a natural son of Satan. But these epithets, strong as they are, pale before those which are now heaped on him by his antagonist. In his *Apology* More pleads that, even if he uses hard words of the Lutherans, he cannot match them in railing; but he very much under-estimates his powers in this direction. He owns a rich and lurid eloquence, which gives an astonishing variety of effects. Tyndale has a devilish, proud, dispitious heart; has the devil's mark on his forehead; is a hell hound in the kennel of the devil; a drowsy drudge drinking deep in the devil's dregs; an abominable beast; a new Judas; an idolater and devil worshipper, worse than a Mahometan; a serpent lurking in his dark den; a publican and a paynim, worse than Sodom and Gomorrah; a Lucifer cast out from heaven; if he endures pain, it is, as the devil does, to injure the truth; he will burn in hell, with those whom he has misled to keep him company. This last prophecy, several times repeated, is one that Tyndale had spared to his opponent.

Once again More accuses his enemy of dishonesty in translating the New Testament; taxes him with self-seeking in the matter, and that he desires his followers to fight and " to die in the quarrel for the defence of his glory." He also returns upon Tyndale's head the charge of covetousness. He is greedy of money, and with his friends he milks the factors of the English merchants beyond the sea, and brings them into trouble. He once sent an evangelical brother, Sir Thomas Bolde, to London to preach, and to steal an evangelical book out of a poor friar's library, and bring it to him to Germany; and though his purse was full of gold at the time, he only doled out one small coin for the expenses of the journey. To this story we need pay no heed. It contradicts all that we know of Tyndale; and More's informants so often misled him, not without his own willingness, that little trust can be placed on their statements, even if we had them at first hand.*

In fairness to our two disputants, it should be said that such revilings were common enough at the time. It was not only the theologians who indulged in them. The politicians, the scholars, indeed the champions of all causes, fought with the gloves off, and were by no means indisposed to put the worst face upon the proceedings of the other side. Nevertheless in this contest Tyndale must be adjudged to be the less faulty. His words are the less violent, and he certainly had the more excuse for his violence. Like many good scholars, he had a spice of sharpness in his nature; he was keen, downright, easily roused. More was of gentler mould: *suavis*, sweet, charming, agreeable, is the epithet applied to him on all hands by his friends. In such a character anger and fierceness are more blamable than in fiery souls. Besides, the position of the two men must be taken into account; Tyndale was down, More was up. The reformers were struggling desperately for the right to live at all; More was fighting for the retention of a monopoly, and for the extinction of his enemies. Everything was in his favour; he had the big battalions, the whole weight of custom, the sympathy of the great ones of the earth, and, humanly speaking, he seemed sure of victory. If bitterness is ever pardonable, it is when men are faced by such odds as these.

Nothing shows more clearly what was at stake for the reformers than the language used once again by More in favour of persecution. In the *Dialogue* he had spoken plainly enough: here he outdoes himself. " It is enough," he writes, " for good Christian men . . . to abhor and burn up his [Tyndale's] books, and the likers of them with them." But he soon waxes fiercer than this: " If the prelates had taken as good heed in time as they should have done, there should peradventure at length fewer have been burned

---

* *Works* 639. A Thomas Bolte was rector of St Mary Axe, London, from 1550 to 1556, when he died.

thereby; but there should have been more burned by a great many than there have been within this seven year last past. The lack whereof, I fear me, will make more burned within this seven year next coming, than else should have needed to have been burned in seven score. . . . If the zeal of God were among men that should be, such railing ribalds [as Luther, Tyndale and the rest], that so mock with holy scripture, should at every such exposition have an hot iron thrust through their blasphemous tongues." Of Bayfield, Baynham, and other of Tyndale's friends, who have perished at the stake, he says: " Tyndale's books and their own malice maketh them heretics; and for heretics, as they be, the clergy doth denounce them; and, as they be well worthy, the temporality doth burn them; and after the fire of Smithfield hell doth receive them, where the wretches burn for ever." These are fearful words. Is it any wonder that More is described by Tyndale as " the most cruel enemy " of the truth? We cannot fairly judge the reformers, unless we see what they had to meet, what their dangers, what their sufferings, what the prospects of complete extermination by ruthless foes.*

But this is not all. Tyndale, fierce though his words may be, attacks great potentates and strong institutions, which might at any moment get him into their power and break him. More does not disdain to drag the little men into his net, and death is not permitted to pay off any scores, rather it adds to the bill against them. It would have been impossible for Tyndale to pen the heartless description of the death of Thomas Hitton, which appears in the preface to the *Confutation*. Hitton was an obscure clerk, who had fled oversea, and having paid a visit to England, was seized in Kent on his way to the coast, condemned by Warham and Fisher, and burnt at Maidstone early in March 1530. Now Thomas More in his *Dialogue* had taunted Tyndale with the weakness of the English Lutherans, in that they recanted when threatened with the fire: a taunt not without truth, but by no means befitting

* More, *Works* 443, 492, 500, 621.

the mouth of one, whose friends were of set purpose using the fire as a weapon to extort such recantations. This taunt Tyndale countered by adducing the case of Hitton, a man whom he evidently greatly respected, for he mentions his martyrdom in four different books of the years 1530 and 1531. More's answer was as follows:—

" Now to the intent that ye may somewhat see what good Christian faith Sir Thomas Hitton was of, this new saint of Tyndale's canonization, in whose burning Tyndale so gaily glorieth, . . . I shall somewhat shew you what wholesome heresies this holy martyr held. First ye shall understand that he was a priest, and falling to Luther's sect, and after that to the sect of friar Huskin and Zwinglius, cast off matins and mass and all divine service, and so became an apostle, sent to and fro between our English heretics beyond the sea and such as were here at home.

" Now happed it so, that after he had visited here his holy congregations in divers corners and lusks lanes, and comforted them in the Lord to stand stiff with the devil in their errors and heresies, as he was going back again at Gravesend, God, considering the great labor that he had taken already, and determining to bring his business to his welldeserved end, gave him suddenly such a favor and so great a grace in the visage, that every man that beheld him took him for a thief. For whereas there had been certain linen clothes pilfered away, that were hanging on an hedge, and Sir Thomas Hitton was walking not far off suspiciously in the meditation of his heresies, the people, doubting that the beggarly knave had stolen the clouts, fell in question with him, and searched him, and so found they certain letters secretly conveyed in his coat, written from evangelical brethren here unto the evangelical heretics beyond the sea. And upon those letters founden, he was with his letters brought before the most reverend father in God the archbishop of Canterbury, and afterward as well by his lordship as by the reverend father the bishop of Rochester examined, and after for his abominable heresies delivered to the secular hands and burned. . . .

" And so was he, after much favor shewed him, and much labor charitably taken for the saving of him, delivered in conclusion for his obstinacy to the secular hands, and burned up in his false faith and heresies, whereof he learned the great part of Tyndale's holy books; and now the spirit of error and lying hath taken his wretched soul with him straight from the short fire to the fire eternal.

"And this is lo Sir Thomas Hitton, the devil's stinking martyr, of whose burning Tyndale maketh boast."

More's friends had done this unhappy man to death. He might at least have let him be.*

There was indeed a nobler side to More; but he never showed it to the reformers. It is passing strange that a man so finely-natured, sitting at home wealthy and secure, with his family around him, enjoying high office, honoured and petted by the great, not expecting at that time any reversal of fortune, should never have permitted a single shoot of compassion to cross his mind for men who, however wrong he might think them, were at least making great sacrifices for their beliefs, had given up home and country, were living in exile and poverty, hunted from place to place, and dogged by the hounds of death. One would like to think that when a few years later he himself sat in the Tower, with his fate all but sealed, wondering miserably whether he should not recant, if put to the torture—an ordeal happily spared to him—that then he looked back with regret on his cruel words against men who for conscience' sake had undergone fiery trials equal to anything that might lie before him. Yet in the day of his prosperity there was no sign of any such relenting. Even in his later books of controversy his language is the same: a Lutheran

* Charles Lamb's comment on the above passage is worth quoting (*Works* I., 203, ed. E. V. Lucas): "The same hatred in kind, which he [Sir Thomas Browne] professed against our great spiritual enemy, was in downright earnest cultivated and defended by More against that portentous phenomenon in those times, a heretic. . . . His account of poor Hitton . . . is penned with a wit and malice hyper-satanic. It is infinitely diverting in the midst of its diabolism, if it be not rather what Coleridge calls, Too wicked for a smile, too foolish for a tear." The story of the clothes sounds like a fable. Foxe merely says that Hitton was arrested by Warham's bailiff, Thomas Swainesland, who suspected him to be a heretic. Foxe's kalendar places his death in March.

is worse than a murderer or other criminal; he must be stamped out; the land must be purged; the laws against heresy must be maintained in all their ruthless severity. That More was a persecutor is proved abundantly out of his own mouth, and if his theological enemies, having suffered through his zeal, sometimes painted him even in darker colours than he deserved, he himself had hardly the right to be surprised.

We can now turn from the manner of the combatants to their matter: but first one thing should be made clear. More complains frequently that Tyndale misquotes his words and misrehearses his arguments, while he on the other hand puts his enemy's case with scrupulous accuracy, often quoting it verbatim, and sometimes—so anxious is he to be fair—throwing it into a stronger form than Tyndale himself had given it. This would indeed be generous, if it were true; but when we examine the books themselves, this superior rectitude is hard to discover. At all events Tyndale did not notice it; for he often accuses More of misrepresenting him. The only substance in More's claim is that he quotes word for word much more largely than his opponent: but how far does that carry us? Any day you may hear in the law courts an advocate quoting documents with minute exactness, but endeavouring to build up a thoroughly unjust conclusion. There is such a thing as straining out the gnat and swallowing the camel. Again and again More ascribes to Tyndale views which he had never expressed, and which he certainly did not hold. Thus he charges him with teaching that a Christian need not obey any law made by man, that no oath or vow need be kept, that if a man has faith, he can sin as much as he likes, that friars may no more live without nuns than David without meat, that a sin after baptism, done with consent, can never be forgiven, and so on. None of these things had Tyndale said. They are an utter distortion of his words, and spring out of More's heated imagination. Not that Tyndale on his side is always blameless,* but on the whole he gives greater justice than he receives. When feelings run high,

* Cf. *Works* III., 236 (*Supper of the Lord*).

misunderstanding is easy. By taking a word in its worst
sense, or by carrying a phrase to what seems to you its
logical conclusion, or by saddling your enemy with the
misdeeds of his allies, you may easily be unfair to him.
All this is common enough: and the matter would be
scarcely worth raising, were it not that one or two recent
writers have taken More at his own valuation, and so done
an injustice to our reformer.

As a piece of reasoning the battle loses in interest because
of More's habit of bringing in a *deus ex machina*, a supernatural
ally, to give him victory. He has an ace of trumps in his
pocket all the time, which cannot fail to win the trick.
He is like the Homeric hero, who fights in the happy con-
sciousness that his god or goddess stands unseen behind
him, ready to dazzle or bemuse his enemy should things
go amiss. The two combatants may go on their way for
some time, capping one another with texts from scripture,
appealing to the fathers or to history, invoking the laws of
reason, and so on. So far they use the same weapons:
but then More will produce his supernatural ally, the
infallibility of the church. This he states in its most naked
form again and again. If the church could fall into any
damnable error, "all were quite at large." Even on a
trivial matter, such as the falsity of relics, he pleads that it
is unthinkable that God should suffer an erroneous belief
to endure. This becomes tiresome to the reader; nay,
worse than tiresome, it adds insult to injury. What!
he says to himself: have I ploughed through so many
weary pages, only to discover that the contest is a puppet
show, that the dice are loaded? Here again we see that
there were two Mores. More the humanist disports himself
on the field of scholarship and dialectics, and charges
Tyndale with belittling the faculty of reason: but More,
the disciplinarian, stands ever behind, ready to intervene
with a high hand.

It is in line with this that he often gives the impression
of stating a case, speaking to a brief, rather than of uttering
burning beliefs, that spring from the depths of his soul.
Whenever he does begin to feel, as in those parts of the

Apology where he defends himself against charges of covetousness, and cruelty, and wordiness, the reader awakes from his torpor, and is moved to real sympathy with him. He is hurt; he wishes to justify himself. We become conscious that we are dealing with flesh and blood: we have a living man before us, and not merely a subtle arguer, or powerful advocate.

It would be tedious to go at length into the course of the debate. Naturally enough there is a good deal of one-sided statement on both sides: and in dealing with some fundamental questions the reader may well feel that the two men see the reverse sides of the same shield. Many pages too could have been saved, had they always used words in the same sense. Yet, when we try to sum up the general results of the contest, it is impossible to deny that Tyndale drove a wedge into the position that More was trying to maintain, and established certain things which the Christian world has never since let go, and which have profoundly influenced even those parts of the church that still own obedience to the papal see.

He was certainly right in calling for a more spiritual type of Christianity than was customary in the middle ages. It was this demand that underlay the combat over faith and works. Are we to place the stress within or without? The medievalist put enormous value on bodily acts ordained by the church. Tell your sins to a priest, he said; go to this or that shrine; flagellate the body; say a psalm fifty times on end: by such means you win health to the soul. Yet these things have no moral value in themselves, and were frequently done with a lifeless, unwilling, or even downright sinful heart. A deeper type of churchmanship was needed. Approach from within, said Tyndale. The spirit of man is the candle of the Lord, or at least can become so, when kindled from above. Let a man once receive the gift of faith, and turn his whole being to Christ, and all else follows. Faith, hope, and love are three inseparable sisters, and cannot exist apart. To start from without is to rely upon what at best are crutches, and at worst fetters. A man may hobble along on crutches, but it is uphill and weary work: he is only cured when he can throw external aids aside. Then he walks and leaps, runs and dances.

Now this is in line with sound psychology. It implies that the mind is one, and that any division between its parts is unhealthy, and indeed in the long run impossible. It is striking to observe how unashamedly More splits up the mind. Again and again we find him treating faith as if it were merely a belief in dogmas. A man, he says, may have a good faith and live wickedly. No, says Tyndale: wicked deeds show that the heart is unfaithful. Unless you are hitting the mark with your deeds, the aim of your soul must be crooked. Your faith should influence every activity of your being.

With this inward approach external ceremonies become secondary. They are not abolished; but they are used in obedience to the spirit of the Christian man. Fastings, pilgrimages, ear-confession, sabbaths, holy-days and the like have no value in themselves, but are committed to the church and its members, to be used at discretion. "We be lords over the sabbath," says Tyndale; and we might change it to another day of the week, or make it more or less frequent, if that were for the benefit of the church of God. This bold claim shocks More very much. He is even more shocked at Tyndale's attacks on ear-confession, which to himself is a matter of life and death: "He that, after Tyndale's doctrine, repenteth without care of shrift, and dieth in a false heresy against his holy housel, such folk be finally reprobates, foreknown unto God before the world was wrought, that they would finally for impenitence fall utterly to nought." * To Tyndale it was a blasphemy to say that a man who repents in heart, could be cast away and judged as impenitent, merely because of the omission of an outward act, which had no connection whatever with any wrong that he might have done; yet such was the opinion of his great adversary. The conflict between the two men might almost be summed up in More's hair-shirt. If Tyndale had known of this, he would have regarded it as a mere treatment of symptoms, a timid, negative measure,

* *Works* 573.

which at best could do no more than distract a man from evil thoughts, but was powerless to liberate within him desires of active goodness. Let the soul once learn the true energies of her being, and she would rise with Christ into the spheres, and returning thence, touched with the divine fire, would burn with a brightness of her own, albeit ever renewed from above, and forgetting her trembling and benighted past, would kindle the earth with glory.

But what of the bible? Did not Tyndale teach a slavish reverence for the written word, and endeavour to base the Christian religion upon that alone? So it has been said; but the charge is untrue. What is true, is that he and his fellow-reformers recovered the bible, brought it to the forefront, and used it as a touchstone—indeed the chief touchstone—by which to try the beliefs and practices of the day. In this they were perfectly right: in no other sphere of history would a scholar refuse the appeal to the earliest documents. No doubt in their delight at recovering the book they sometimes used too sweeping language. But there was a good deal of excuse for this, when the other side made such extravagant claims for tradition. We find Thomas More actually maintaining that the order and ceremonies used at the mass have been handed down by word of mouth from the apostles, and are sacrosanct. Against such fantasies Tyndale rebelled: but his position is reasonable enough. Nothing, he said, ought to be considered to be of the essence of the Christian religion, unless it is found in the New Testament.

To this More replies that scripture needs interpretation; indeed, that the testimony of scripture cannot even be accepted at all until some one has decided it to be scripture. The living voice of the church came before the written word, and goes along with it, using it and interpreting it. This is excellent sense: and for a moment the reader wonders whether More is going to show real prophetic insight, and to build up an advantage over his adversary, by forecasting an ideal church, in which scripture is free and has its full authority, but is ever interpreted and reinterpreted by the generations, each man being permitted to offer his

gifts thereto. But More has no such visions; he is in fact
bringing the argument to quench, not to glorify the witness
of the book. In any case his words have no terrors for
Tyndale. For Tyndale does not deny that scripture is
approved and interpreted by the living voice; what he
says is, that the living voice is that of the church as a whole,
and not that of one man or one line of men. According
to More, scripture is committed to the pope or to the
hierarchy; according to Tyndale, it belongs to the whole
body of Christian men, guided by the spirit of God. In
practice, Tyndale's treatment of the bible is more liberal
than More's. Both men quote texts in the usual way of
their time; both have some strange exegesis: yet Tyndale
is the more venturesome. He is willing in a measure to
divide between the spiritual worth of divers parts, to doubt
the authorship of books, and so on. This shocks More very
much: yet we can see now that Tyndale was right. The
living voice of this fallible but God-inspired man spoke
more truly than the living voice of that infallible pontiff,
with whom More was so eager to sing in tune.

We pass now to the question of the church, on which many
pages are expended. Tyndale denied that the church of his
day was the true church of Christ; it had abandoned the
teaching of the gospel, and disowned its Lord. Where
then is the church? It is in the hearts of those men who are
truly redeemed. Who these are, can never be said with
complete certainty: for you can only judge a man by his
actions; and these, however good, may not spring from the
heart. Only God can know the names of his true churchmen. With this view More makes much skilful play. Of
what use, he says, is an invisible church? Members of any
society need to see, hear, touch each other. You cannot
convert a man to an invisible church; he will not know
whom to take for his teacher, or to whom to join himself in
worship. A church must have a body, and that body is
" the common known catholic church," containing both
good and bad.

More's logic is unassailable: but Tyndale did not really
deny this. He knew that the disciples of Christ must

meet together as a visible society, even if that society is never in fact fully redeemed: and he says this. If More had ever tried to understand the reformation, he would have seen (as in his heart he must have seen) that this emphasis on the invisible church was only a symptom of the scandals of the time. Men always begin to feed their spirits upon an ideal, when the real is hopelessly bad. The one chance of parrying and defeating Tyndale's onslaughts lay in removing the fearful evils which repelled men from the visible church, and made them call up a picture of a church disallowed of men, but known to God. Sarcasm, dialectics, verbal plays would not help More. A victory in the academy would be of no avail, if he lost the day on the field of action.

Thus we are brought back once more from words to deeds; and here this chapter may well close. As a reasoner More was fully equal to Tyndale. The great defect of his controversial books is that they skirt round the burning facts of the day. We see now why he accomplished so little for the church. Scholars sometimes express regret that the peaceful reform desired by Erasmus and the humanists gave place to the more violent reform of Luther and his allies, that the quiet voice of reason faded into silence before the loud cries of passion. The answer is clear. The victory went to those who were the more worthy of it. With all their mistakes, the reformers showed a grit and a driving force, a moral backbone, which was lacking in the humanists. They launched their boat upon the swirling waters; they risked their lives to purge the church; they lived dangerously and whole-heartedly, and they had their reward. They forced reform into the forefront of things, and at length even their theological enemies were driven to address themselves to the task.

If apt and well-aimed words could have reformed the church, Erasmus would have reformed it. None saw the need more clearly than he; his diatribes left no scandal unexposed; all classes fell under his lash. But his deeds were not correspondent with his words. He sat still, and let things take their course. He remained all the time on

familiar terms with popes, cardinals, bishops, kings, the very
men who could have purged the church, but refused to do
so. He poured upon them compliments, wrote flattering
letters, took gifts, received pensions. He writes anonym-
ously a skit on pope Julius II, recently dead, showing him
up as unfit for heaven. An outcry is raised. What does
he do? He as good as denies the authorship; and Thomas
More by an evasion helps to keep the thing dark. When
Luther comes to the front, Erasmus half-sympathizes, but
he scents danger. He will not oppose him, for he fears he
may be fighting against the Spirit of God; he will not
support him, for he has not the strength for martyrdom.
He will take the safe side, and follow the decision of pope
and emperor. The reformation advances, and he addresses
to its leaders some excellent advice: but he does nothing
himself. Not all men (he pleads) are called upon to
uphold the ark. He is a worm, a pigmy, a sheep able only
to bleat when the gospel is destroyed. It is not for him
to reform the court of Rome. Sometimes one must be
content to conceal the truth. It is not well to censure
popes or kings.

This is not the stuff out of which reformers are made.
They that would purge a church must throw their all into
the scale, their life and their death. Erasmus was a book-
man and an invalid, and we can sympathize with his weakness: but that sympathy must not make us unjust to those
sterner souls, who risked and gave all that they had, and who
rode the storm on which he feared to venture.

But what of More? He at least died for his beliefs. For
a piece of them certainly: but not for that reform of the
church which his admirers tell us that he so greatly desired.
For that end he neither died nor lived. He contented himself with pious hopes, and left it to the hierarchy to act.
Had he been determined, he could have struck stout blows
for the cause of a more moderate reform than Luther's.
Many opportunities came his way; a golden one was afforded
by Tonstall's letter of invitation. To this he might have
replied: I will be your spokesman, but only on two conditions; that I condemn in my book the faults of the church

and her leaders, as frankly and strongly as those of the Lutherans; and that you on your part undertake without delay to gather the bishops of England together, and to give them no rest, until they pledge themselves to a thorough cleansing of the heritage committed to their charge. I cannot be silent under these fearful scandals.

If More had taken the lead for reform, he might have failed; he might even have died as a heretic a year or two earlier than he did: but he would have died, while straining all his powers upon the mark. There would have been fewer of those picturesque scenes which so delight his friends, but there would have been more solid achievement. He would have found himself less frequently in situations where he was expected to do, and often did, things inconsistent with his deepest principles. He would have burned with a fiercer and steadier glow. As it was, balanced uneasily between pope and king, and at long last siding with pope, he was never wholly himself. There is always a touch of masterly inactivity about him. Had men waited for More and the humanists to reform the church, we should still be waiting to-day.

CHAPTER XI

HAVING failed to bring Tyndale to submission, Henry VIII determined to treat him as an enemy, and to gain possession of his person. He therefore instructed his ambassador to demand his delivery, not this time from the queen regent, as Wolsey had done three years before, but from the emperor himself, who was now in the Low Countries. Tyndale, he said, was hiding in the imperial dominions, and sending thence seditious books to England, and he should be extradited under the recent treaty of Cambrai. Happily for Tyndale the emperor and the king of England were not on the best of terms. The question of the divorce was now becoming acute, and Henry was at this very moment openly reproaching Charles with inciting the pope to recall the case for trial at Rome. It was not likely therefore that the emperor would go out of his way to do him a favour, and he replied somewhat bluntly, that he had as yet no proof that Tyndale had so offended, either by word or writing, as to justify so strong a measure. If the seditious books really existed (and proof could easily be given, if they did), he would comply with the king's desire: but otherwise he could not send him to England without violating the privileges of the English and other foreign nations in the Netherlands. He must himself first examine the case. The general opinion, however, was that Tyndale was only persecuted because of his attachment to the queen's cause.*

This demand appears to have been made between the months of August and November 1531. If in the former part of this period, it will have been presented by Hackett, the ambassador in the Netherlands, if in the latter, by Sir Thomas Elyot, the author of the *Governor*, who became

* *L. & P.*, V., 265, 354, appendix 15.

ambassador to the imperial court in the month of October.
Be this as it may, it was certainly Elyot to whom the next
steps were entrusted. Since Charles V refused to hand
over the offender, more private and unofficial methods were
to be tried. Tyndale was to be kidnapped and brought to
England. On March 14, 1532 Elyot writes to the duke of
Norfolk from Regensburg, whither he and Cranmer, not yet
archbishop, had travelled for the opening of the imperial
diet :—

" The king willeth me, by his grace's letters, to remain
at Brussels some space of time for the apprehension of Tyndale, which somewhat minisheth my hope of soon return [to
England]; considering that, like as he is in wit movable,
semblably so is his person uncertain to come by; and as far
as I can perceive, hearing of the king's diligence in the
apprehension of him, he withdraweth him into such places
where he thinketh to be farthest out of danger."

But though Elyot spent money freely in bribes, he was no
more successful in seizing Tyndale's person than West and
Rinck had been. By the month of June he was back in
England, having resigned his post, and in November he
writes discontentedly to Cromwell, complaining that his
embassy has landed him in debt, and begging to be re-
imbursed : " I gave many rewards," he says, " partly to the
emperor's servants to get knowledge, partly to such as by
whose means I trusted to apprehend Tyndale, according to
the king's commandment." Once more Tyndale had
escaped the toils and circumvented the plotting of his foes,
as he was always to do, until a traitor came to him in the
guise of a friend.

Of his doings in the year 1532 we are totally ignorant.
Doubtless he was mostly in Antwerp or the neighbourhood,
warily looking out from his hiding-places, and moving
whenever danger seemed to threaten. We cannot even
point to any book of his which certainly belongs to this year.
Only two come into question at all. The first is his exposition
of Tracy's will. Tracy's body was exhumed and burnt
about the month of March, and Frith had written his
exposition on the will, before he sailed for England in July.

Tyndale may have written his at the same time; but he did not publish it. It was discovered after his arrest in May 1535, bound together with Frith's (the latter in Frith's own handwriting), and the two were published together in the same year, perhaps by Rogers, from the press of Hoochstraten. To us Tracy's will seems so sensible and inoffensive, that we find it strange that two eminent men should have thought worth while to write in its defence : but so it was; so blind was the common opinion of the day, so great the need of enlightenment.

The other treatise which may belong to the year 1532 is on a far bigger scale, the *Exposition upon the Fifth, Sixth and Seventh Chapters of Matthew*. Many writers date this too early. It cannot have appeared before the latest months of 1532, because it uses Luther's exposition, which is described in October as one of the novelties of the season. Indeed, 1533 is a more likely date for Tyndale's book: later than that it can hardly be; for Thomas More is spoken of as in the full tide of prosperity. Two or three copies of the first edition survive.*

Tyndale expounds the sermon on the mount in such a way as to bring out those plain evangelical truths, which were being discovered anew by the reformation. The long sections into which he divides the treatise give him plenty of scope, and he writes with power and fire. In dealing with the practical questions that play so big a part in the sermon, his strong common sense shows to advantage, and in this treatise, as elsewhere, he is a stout champion of the poor. Nor is he a mere imitator of Luther. He borrows indeed some thoughts from the great German, yet he usually works them out in an

---

* The sermons making up Luther's exposition were preached from November 1530 to March 1532 (*Werke*, Weimar edition, 32, LXXVIII). As manuscript copies began to circulate, Luther put out a printed edition with a preface, and this is what Tyndale seems to use. The date 1532–3 is confirmed by these three facts: (1) In his *Exposition on I John* (September 1531) Tyndale speaks as if he were beginning his career as expositor. (2) More omits the work in the list of English Lutheran books in the preface to the *Confutation* (January 1532). (3) The fierceness of the attack on More for covetousness. The work seems first to be mentioned in Joye's *Apology* (February 1535). It was printed (so Miss Kronenberg tells me) by John Grapheus of Antwerp.

independent way, and the bulk of the book is entirely his own. Our first extract gives us an insight into his soul, and helps us to understand what it meant to a fine nature to be covered with scorn and contumely, slandered and vilified, treated as a pariah, cast forth from the visible society of the church, simply for doing a good deed from which every English-speaking Christian has benefited:—

> v. 11. (Blessed are ye when they revile you and persecute you.) " Here seest thou the uttermost, what a Christian man must look for. It is not enough to suffer for righteousness; but that no bitterness or poison be left out of thy cup, thou shalt be reviled and railed upon; and even when thou art condemned to death, then be excommunicate and delivered to Satan, deprived of the fellowship of holy church, the company of the angels, and of thy part in Christ's blood; and shalt be cursed down to hell, defied, detested, and execrate with all the blasphemous railings, that the poisonful heart of hypocrites can think or imagine; and shalt see before thy face when thou goest to thy death, that all the world is persuaded and brought in belief, that thou hast said and done that thou never thoughtest, and that thou diest for that, thou art as guiltless of as the child that is unborn.
>
> " Well, though iniquity so highly prevail, and the truth for which thou diest be so low kept under, and be not once known before the world, insomuch that it seemeth rather to be hindered by thy death than furthered (which is of all griefs the greatest) yet let not thine heart fail thee neither despair, as though God had forsaken thee, or loved thee not: but comfort thyself with old ensamples, how God hath suffered all his old friends to be so entreated, and also his only and dear son Jesus; whose ensample, above all other, set before thine eyes, because thou art sure he was beloved above all other, that thou doubt not but thou art beloved also, and so much the more beloved, the more thou art like to the image of his ensample in suffering.
>
> " Did not the hypocrites watch him in all his sermons, to trap him in his own words? Was he not subtilly apposed [questioned] whether it were lawful to pay tribute to Caesar? Were not all his words wrong reported? Were not his miracles ascribed to Beelzebub?

Said they not he was a Samaritan, and had a devil in him? Was he not called a breaker of the sabbath, a wine-drinker, a friend of publicans and sinners? Did he aught wherewith no fault was found, and that was not interpreted to be done for an evil purpose? Was not the pretence of his death the destroying of the temple, to bring him into the hate of all men? Was he not thereto accused of treason, that he forbad to pay tribute to Caesar, and that he moved the people to insurrection? Railed they not on him in the bitterest of all his passion, as he hanged on the cross, saying, Save thyself, thou that savest other; Come down from the cross, and we will believe in thee; Fie, wretch that destroyest the temple of God?

"Yet he was beloved of God; and so art thou. His cause came to light also, and so shall thine at the last; yea, and thy reward is great in heaven with him for thy deep suffering."

Tyndale never married, and we do not know whether he ever contemplated doing so: but he speaks of women and marriage with a noble tenderness unusual in those days. Thus here he writes on the breach of the seventh commandment (v. 27–30) :—

"The preciousest gift that a man hath of God in this world is the true heart of his wife, to abide by him in wealth and woe, and to bear all fortunes with him. Of that hast thou robbed him; for after she hath once coupled herself to thee, she shall not lightly love him any more so truly, but haply hate him and procure his death. Moreover thou hast untaught her to fear God, and hast made her to sin against God: for to God promised she, and not to man only: for the law of matrimony is God's ordinance. . . . Let every man have his wife, and think her the fairest and the best-conditioned, and every woman her husband too. For God hath blessed thy wife and made her without sin to thee, which ought to seem a beautiful fairness. And all that ye suffer together, the one with the other, is blessed also, and made the very cross of Christ, and pleasant in the sight of God."

In this book Tyndale returns to the question of the spiritual and temporal powers, and while he lays down that each has its due authority over the other, he makes it even plainer than in the *Obedience*, that the prince is by no means to be a spiritual dictator, or the lord of the consciences of men. Thus he writes:—

> " Though every man's body and goods be under the king, do he right or wrong, yet is the authority of God's word free and above the king: so that the worst in the realm may tell the king, if he do him wrong, that he doth naught [wickedly], and otherwise than God hath commanded him; and so warn him to avoid the wrath of God, which is the patient avenger of all unrighteousness. . . .
>
> " The king is as deep under the spiritual officer, to hear out of God's word what he ought to believe, and how to live, and how to rule, as is the poorest beggar in the realm. . . .
>
> " No king, lord, master, or what ruler he be, hath absolute power in this world, and is the very thing which he is called. For then they ceased to be brethren still, neither could they sin, whatsoever they commanded. But now their authority is but a limited power, which when they transgress, they sin against their brethren, and ought to reconcile themselves to their brethren, and to ask forgiveness; and they are bound to forgive."

That Tyndale was in favour of the state interposing to restrain the fearful evils of the church, is true. Who would not have been, that was suffering under those evils, and had seen the church refuse the task of reform? But he never taught that the prince was to be a spiritual lawgiver, or that he was to act merely at his own whim and pleasure; and he laid down in the bluntest and plainest way possible that if the supreme ruler violated the conscience of his subjects, they were to refuse him obedience.

Meanwhile the news from England became ever more painfully interesting. In January 1532 Thomas Dusgate or Benet, a graduate of Cambridge, was burnt in Devonshire. In March Hugh Latimer was haled before convocation, and after a delay of several weeks was forced to an ignominious recantation. The next martyr was James Baynham, a member of the Middle Temple, son of a Gloucestershire squire, and therefore sure to have been known to Tyndale by repute, if not in person. In December 1531 he had been lodged in More's house, and after a prolonged examination before Stokesley, in the course of which he confessed to owning five of Tyndale's books, he abjured in February, carrying a faggot at Paul's Cross, and paying a fine of £20. But his weakness was only for the moment. Full of remorse and contrition, a month afterward he entered the church of Austin Friars on a Sunday morning, carrying in his hand Tyndale's New Testament, and in his bosom the *Obedience*, and before all the people he withdrew his recantation weeping. Once more he was seized, condemned as a relapsed heretic, and burnt at Smithfield on the last day of April. Then in the early summer an aged man, named Thomas Harding, fell victim to the zeal of bishop Longland, and perished in the flames at Chesham in Buckinghamshire.

Thus in two and a quarter years there had been in England ten martyrdoms, and three, and perhaps five, of the victims were known to Tyndale, and one was a dear friend. But an even worse blow was at hand. In July John Frith, a young man who for his rare abilities, stainless life, and a gentleness of spirit unwonted in those days, won respect and sympathy even from his opponents, ventured once more into England.

Why he went, cannot now be ascertained. He journeyed to Reading, where he had some business with the prior of the abbey. Some thought that he desired the prior to relieve his poverty, others that he wished to take him into safety across the sea. The prior was a Lutheran of long standing, who had been active at the time of the Oxford troubles of 1528, and had been imprisoned for a year, until set at liberty by the king's desire. At Reading Frith was arrested, and refusing to give his name, was put into the stocks as a vagabond, and remained until he was well-nigh starved with hunger. In desperation he sent a messenger to the school master of the place, Leonard Cox, a man of learning, who enjoyed the friendship of Erasmus, and in later years that of Melanchthon. Cox talked with him, and finding him a good Latin and Greek scholar, and being above all charmed with his recitations from Homer's *Iliad* in the original Greek, went at once to the governors of the town, and persuaded them to release the sufferer.

From Reading Frith went to London, and thence into the neighbouring counties, hoping to make his escape abroad. But news of his presence in England had reached the authorities; a reward was set upon his head, and the roads and havens were watched. Though he changed his garments often, and shifted his place of dwelling, he could find no refuge, and at length—probably early in October— he was taken at Milton Shore near Southend in Essex, seemingly in the company of the prior and others. According to More, the arrest was made by Stokesley's servants, with the aid of the officers of the crown. Frith and the prior were lodged in the Tower of London, though the bishop had hoped and expected to have the keeping of them himself. This was of course the doing of Cromwell, whom we know to have visited the Tower within a few days, and who on October 21 received a report concerning the prisoners. He told the lieutenant of the Tower that it would be a pity to lose Frith, if he could be reconciled, and the lieutenant agreed. The other prisoners were placed in irons, but Frith was permitted to go unshackled; the lieutenant was much struck with his learning, his wit and pleasant tongue.

For five months Frith remained in the Tower, and no action was taken against him. Stokesley was powerless, and it is evident that neither Cromwell nor Cranmer desired to proceed to extremities. Shortly after his arrest, however, he all unwittingly did a deed which made his position doubly more perilous. His association with Tyndale, his book, now nearly two years old, against purgatory, were compromising enough; it would be hard indeed to save him if he laid unholy hands on the ark of transubstantiation. But this is what he now did. He was asked by a Christian brother for his views upon the Lord's supper. When he had given them by word of mouth, the other desired him to write them down, since they were overlong to retain in the memory. Unwillingly he consented. " Albeit," he writes, " I was loth to take the matter in hand, yet to fulfil his instant intercession, I took upon me to touch this terrible tragedy, and wrote a treatise, which, besides my painful imprisonment, is like to purchase me most cruel death." His friend unwarily lent it to one William Holt, a tailor (Halle and Foxe give us the name), who pretended friendship to the reformation. Holt, having obtained his prize, carried it straight to Sir Thomas More, who received also two copies through other channels; so efficient was the system of spying, of which this pious man did not disdain to avail himself.* Though Frith's treatise was not printed, More began to write a reply. He finished it on December 7; and Frith saw a printed copy of it in Gardiner's palace, when he was brought thither on December 26 for a private examination: for Gardiner had been his tutor at Cambridge. More begins his letter with the intention of treating Frith as a young man misled by evil counsellors, but he finds it difficult to keep up this rôle of gentleness, and ever and anon his hatred of heresy bursts out. The devil himself, he says, could not make a worse book than this; it outdoes Luther. Frith has heaped up in a few leaves all the poison contained in the works of Wycliffe, Oecolampadius, Tyndale and Zwingli; for he not only says that the sacrament is bread, as Luther does, but, " as these other beasts do," that it is nothing else but bread.

Although he had seen this book in print, Frith found it very difficult to secure a copy. At length, however, he obtained one in manuscript, and he set to work to compose an answer. But before he did so, he had received a letter from Tyndale, written about the month of January and directed to him under the name of Jacob. By that time Tyndale had evidently heard of the arrest of his friend, but he did not yet know that he had written on the sacrament, and was likely

---

* More himself speaks of these three copies (*Works* 833). Frith's reply is: If you have three copies of a work which I especially desired to keep secret, then indeed I must have traitors around me (Daye's folio 114–5). In the same way More speedily obtained copies of the two letters received by Frith in the first quarter of 1533 from Tyndale and Joye (*Apology* XXIV; *L. & P.*, VI., 303). More's use of underground methods springs from his one fatal mistake of regarding Lutherans as worse than the world, the flesh and the devil.

to be in trouble thereby. He therefore advises him to say as little about the matter in his examination as he can, and to content himself with pleading for the toleration of his own view. So he would not only avoid irritating the papists, but would also keep the ranks of the reformers together, some of whom took the Lutheran view of consubstantiation, while others followed Zwingli. The letter runs as follows :—*

"The grace of our Saviour Jesus, his patience, meekness, humbleness, circumspection, and wisdom, be with your heart. Amen.

"Dearly beloved brother Jacob, mine heart's desire in our Saviour Jesus is, that you arm yourself with patience, and be cold, sober, wise, and circumspect: and that you keep a-low by the ground, avoiding high questions that pass the common capacity. But expound the law truly, and open the vail of Moses, to condemn all flesh, and prove all men sinners, and all deeds under the law, before mercy have taken away the condemnation thereof, to be sin and damnable: and then, as a faithful minister, set abroach the mercy of our Lord Jesus, and let the wounded consciences drink of the water of him. And then shall your preaching be with power, and not as the doctrine of the hypocrites; and the Spirit of God shall work with you, and all consciences shall bear record unto you, and feel that it is so. And all doctrine that casteth a mist on those two, to shadow and hide them (I mean the law of God and mercy of Christ) that resist you with all your power. Sacraments without signification refuse. If they put significations to them, receive them, if you see it may help, though it be not necessary.

"Of the presence of Christ's body in the sacrament meddle as little as you can, that there appear no division among us. Barnes [a Lutheran] will be hot against you. The Saxons be sore on the affirmative; whether constant or obstinate, I commit it to God. Philip Melanchthon is said to be with the French king [a mistaken rumour]. There be in Antwerp that say they saw him come into Paris with a hundred and fifty horses; and

* The versions of Tyndale's two letters to Frith, given in Foxe (1563), Foxe (1570) and Daye's folio, differ slightly. Foxe (1563) is as a rule the most accurate.

that they spake with him. If the Frenchmen receive the word of God, he will plant the affirmative [the Lutheran view] in them. George Joye would have put forth a treatise of the matter, but I have stopped him as yet: what he will do if he get money, I wot not. I believe he would make many reasons, little serving to the purpose. My mind is that nothing be put forth, till we hear how you shall have sped. I would have the right use preached, and the presence to be an indifferent thing, till the matter might be reasoned in peace at leisure of both parties. If you be required, show the phrases of the scripture, and let them talk what they will. For as to believe that God is everywhere, hurteth no man that worshippeth him nowhere but within in the heart, in spirit and verity, even so to believe that the body of Christ is everywhere, though it cannot be proved, hurteth no man that worshippeth him nowhere save in the faith of his gospel. You perceive my mind: howbeit, if God show you otherwise, it is free for you to do as he moveth you.

"I guessed long ago that God would send a dazing into the head of the spiritualty, to catch themselves in their own subtlety: and I trust it is come to pass. And now methinketh I smell a counsel to be taken, little for their profits in time to come. But you must understand that it is not of a pure heart, and for love of the truth; but to avenge themselves, and to eat the whore's flesh, and to suck the marrow of her bones.* Wherefore cleave fast to the rock of the help of God, and commit the end of all things to him: and if God shall call you, that you may then use the wisdom of the worldly, as far as you perceive the glory of God may come thereof, refuse it not: and ever among thrust in, that the scripture may be in the mother tongue, and learning set up in the universities. But and if aught be required contrary to the glory of God and his Christ, then stand fast, and commit yourself to God; and be not overcome of men's persuasions, which haply shall say, we see no other way [i.e. but abjuring] to bring in the truth.

"Brother Jacob, beloved in my heart, there liveth not in whom I have so good hope and trust, and in whom mine heart rejoiceth, and my soul comforteth

---

* The counsel is evidently the seizure of ecclesiastical property by the English secular rulers.

herself, as in you, not the thousand part so much of your learning and what other gifts else you have, as that you will creep a-low by the ground, and walk in those things that the conscience may feel, and not in the imaginations of the brain; in fear, and not in boldness; in open necessary things, and not to pronounce or define of hid secrets, or things that neither help or hinder, whether they be so or no; in unity, and not in seditious opinions; insomuch that if you be sure you know, yet in things that may abide leisure, you will defer, or say (till other agree with you), ' Methink the text requireth this sense or understanding : ' yea, and that if you be sure that your part be good, and another hold the contrary, yet if it be a thing that maketh no matter, you will laugh and let it pass, and refer the thing to other men, and stick you stiffly and stubbornly in earnest and necessary things. And I trust you be persuaded even so of me. For I call God to record against the day we shall appear before our Lord Jesus, to give a reckoning of our doings, that I never altered one syllable of God's word against my conscience, nor would this day, if all that is in the earth, whether it be pleasure, honour, or riches, might be given me. Moreover, I take God to record to my conscience, that I desire of God to myself, in this world, no more than that without which I cannot keep his laws.

" Finally, if there were in me any gift that could help at hand, and aid you if need required, I promise you I would not be far off, and commit the end to God: my soul is not faint, though my body be weary. But God hath made me ill-favoured in this world, and without grace in the sight of men, speechless and rude, dull and slow-witted. Your part shall be to supply that lacketh in me; remembering that, as lowliness of heart shall make you high with God, even so meekness of words shall make you sink into the hearts of men. Nature giveth age authority; but meekness is the glory of youth, and giveth them honour. Abundance of love maketh me exceed in babbling.

" Sir, as concerning purgatory, and many other things, if you be demanded, you may say, if you err, the spiritualty hath so led you; and that they have taught you to believe as you do. For they preached you all such things out of God's word, and alleged a thousand texts; by reason of which texts you believed as they taught you. But now you find them liars, and that the texts mean no such things, and therefore you can believe them no longer; but are as ye were before they taught you, and believe no such thing; howbeit you are ready to believe, if they have any other way to prove it; for without proof you cannot believe them, when you have found them with so many lies, etc. If you perceive wherein we may help, either in being still, or doing somewhat, let us have word, and I will do mine uttermost.

"My lord of London hath a servant called John Tisen, with a red beard, and a black reddish head, and was once my scholar; he was seen in Antwerp, but came not among the Englishmen: whither he is gone, an embassador secret, I wot not.

"The mighty God of Jacob be with you to supplant his enemies, and give you the favour of Joseph; and the wisdom and the spirit of Stephen be with your heart and with your mouth, and teach your lips what they shall say, and how to answer to all things. He is our God, if we despair in ourselves, and trust in him; and his is the glory. Amen.

WILLIAM TYNDALE.

"I hope our redemption is nigh."

In his reply to More, Frith follows very much the lines laid down in Tyndale's letter. He puts forward with much ability his own view, which is not unlike Zwingli's, but he expressly refuses to condemn the two other views, and pleads that the theory of the sacrament is a thing indifferent, provided there be no idolatry joined with it. As a writer of controversy, Frith is easier to read than either Tyndale or More. His touch is lighter, he sticks to the point better, and repeats himself less. We need not follow him through his argument, but one passage cannot be omitted. More had denounced Tyndale as a beast and a false teacher; Frith springs at once to the side of his friend.

"And Tyndale, I trust, liveth, well content with such a poor apostle's life, as God gave his son Christ and his faithful ministers in this world, which is not sure of so many mites as ye [More] be yearly of pounds, although I am sure that for his learning and judgment in scripture he were more worthy to be promoted than all the bishops in England. I received a letter from him, which was written since Christmas, wherein among other matters he writeth thus:—I call God to record, against the day we shall appear before our Lord Jesus to give a reckoning of our doings, that I never altered one syllable of God's word against my conscience, nor would do this day, if all that is in the earth, whether it be honour, pleasure, or riches, might be given me. Moreover I take God to record to my conscience, that I desire of God to myself in this world no more than that, without which I cannot keep his laws etc. Judge, Christian reader, whether these words be not spoken of a faithful, clear, innocent heart. And as for his behaviour, [it] is such that I am sure no man can reprove him of any sin; howbeit no man is innocent before God, which beholdeth the heart."

That Tyndale should have inspired this veneration in so rare a nature as Frith's, is perhaps the best proof that can be given of his greatness of soul.

In this work Frith repeats the offer which Tyndale had made two years ago to Stephen Vaughan. More had complained of the flooding of the country with Lutheran books; if the brethren must write, why, he asks, cannot they keep their pernicious books to themselves instead of broadcasting them to all and sundry? Frith replies:

"Until we see some means found, by which a reasonable reformation may be had, and sufficient instruction for the poor commoners, I assure you I neither will nor can cease to speak; for the word of God boileth in my body like a fervent fire, and will needs have an issue, and break out when occasion is given. But this hath been offered, is offered, and shall be offered:—grant that the word of God, I mean the text of scripture, may go abroad in our English tongue, as other nations have it in their tongues, and my brother William Tyndale and I have done, and will promise you to write no more. If you will not grant this condition, then will we be doing while we have breath, and shew in few words that the scripture doth in many, and so at the least save some."

Frith's book was smuggled across to Antwerp for printing, but did not appear until after his death. But meanwhile a new champion with visor down had entered the lists. On April 5 was published, ostensibly from the house of Nicholas Twonson of Nürnberg, a treatise named *The Supper of the*

Lord, reinforcing Frith's arguments, and defending him with vigour and even bitterness from the strictures of Sir Thomas More. The writer was unnamed. Some said he was Tyndale, others Joye, others a third person. Foxe reckons the authorship doubtful, though he prints the treatise in Daye's folio. Thomas More also leaves the matter open, when he replies to the book in the autumn, and having in one place been dubbed by the author Master Mocke, he retaliates by labelling him throughout Master Masker. But he evidently suspects that he is dealing with Tyndale, and he was almost certainly right. Why then did Tyndale withhold his name? For Frith's sake probably. He wished to strike a blow for his friend and for the truth in the sacramental controversy, but Frith's chances of escape would not be bettered by the appearance of a work with Tyndale's name on the title-page.*

To the reader of to-day the most interesting part of the book is the description of the Lord's supper, as Tyndale would have it observed. The service is simple, communal and evangelical. All is to be said in the mother tongue. The curate addresses the people, showing the meaning of the sacrament, directing their minds to the spiritual truths that lie behind the form, and exhorting them to mutual forgiveness and love. He then comes down to the table, round and near which the people are seated. St John vi is read, and after more prayer and praises I Corinthians xi follows. After the creed has been recited aloud, each worshipper confesses his sins secretly to God, and prays for faith and grace; and the curate delivers a final word of warning. Then all fall upon their knees, and say the Pater Noster secretly in English, the curate kneeling before them. This done, he takes the elements, and " with a loud voice, with godly gravity " rehearses distinctly " the words of the Lord's supper," and distributes the bread to the ministers, who deliver it to the people, each man breaking it before he passes it to his neighbour: and the cups of wine follow in like manner. Meanwhile the curate reads aloud the words

* No doubt it was printed at Antwerp. The copies in the Bodleian and the Cambridge university library may belong to the first edition.

spoken by Christ at the supper table. When all have partaken, all fall upon their knees, and give thanks to God for the blessings of Christ, of which this blessed sacrament has been the symbol and the reminder: and so they depart, each man commending himself wholly to God. The rite here described is in sharp contrast to the customary service of the mass, and reveals Tyndale's radicalism of mind: but the tone is reverent in the extreme, and it might have taught More, had he been willing to listen, that his antagonist was something better than a mere spoiler of the past.

It will have been observed that Frith had a good deal of freedom in the Tower. He wrote two treatises on the sacrament, and two or three other little works as well, with one of which, the *Bulwark against Rastel*, he converted his opponent, who was brother-in-law to Sir Thomas More. He seems also to have been visited by friends, and by their means to have been able to distribute his manuscripts outside. From these facts we should judge that he had a complaisant jailer, and so we learn from another source. According to a manuscript, printed by Strype and formerly belonging to Foxe, the underkeeper, Phillips, would sometimes open the prison doors during the night, so that Frith might go out and visit a friend named John Petit, a grocer and a burgess of London, a generous helper of the reformers oversea, who had himself been in the Tower some time before, and who had then been permitted by the same underkeeper to remove a board in his cell, and to dine with Bilney, who was in the cell above.* Frith had indeed to be cautious of the superior officers. In his little book against Rastel he writes:

" I am in a manner as a man bound to a post, and cannot so well bestow me in my play, as if I were at liberty; for I may not have such books as are necessary for me, neither yet pen, ink, nor paper, but only secretly, so that I am in continual fear both of the lieutenant and of my keeper, lest they should espy any such thing by me; and therefore it is little marvel though the work be imperfect, for whensoever I hear the keys ring at the door, straight all must be conveyed

* Petit died within about three months of Frith's arrest; for his will was proved on January 24, 1533.

out of the way; and then if any notable thing had been in my mind, it was clean lost. And therefore I beseech thee, good reader, count it as a thing born out of season, which for many causes cannot have its perfect form and shape, and pardon me my rudeness and imperfection."

So matters went on for five months, but at length a certain royal chaplain named Dr Currein, at the instigation of Gardiner, succeeded in forcing a decision. Preaching in Lent before Henry, he said that it was no wonder that errors were current concerning the sacrament, seeing that there was even now in the Tower one who had been " so bold as to write in defence of that heresy, and no man goeth about his reformation." Upon this the king, who prided himself on his orthodoxy, sent for Cromwell and Cranmer, and gave instruction that Frith should be brought to trial. The archbishop therefore despatched one of his gentlemen, and a certain Welsh porter of his establishment, with a warrant to bring him to his palace at Croydon for examination. The three journeyed from the Tower by boat to Lambeth, and the gentleman, no doubt on his master's instructions, took the opportunity of giving Frith some good counsel: let him be prudent and draw in his horns for a while for the sake of his wife and children, yes, for the sake of the truth itself, which he would be able to preach later, if he temporized now; Cranmer and Cromwell indeed favoured him, but he had mortal foes who sought his ruin. Frith answered boldly that, come what might, he must utter his true belief at the ensuing interview; though he had twenty lives he would give them all, and in a score of years the more part of the realm would take his side of the matter.

Arrived at Lambeth, the three travellers refresh themselves with a meal, and then proceed on foot towards Croydon. Cranmer's gentleman now tries a second expedient to save his prisoner. Having first secured the consent of the Welsh porter, he proposes to Frith that he shall slip away near Brixton into the woods on the left-hand side of the road, and make for his native county of Kent, while his two guards after an interval will raise the hue and cry on the right hand towards Wandsworth, thus giving him ample time to escape.

To this plan, however, Frith will by no means consent. " If," he replies, " you should both leave me here, and go to Croydon declaring to the bishops that you had lost Frith, I would surely follow after as fast as I might, and bring them news that I had found and brought Frith again." Asked why he refuses his liberty now, when six months before he was straining every nerve to escape oversea, he replies that then he was a free man, and had no need to run his head into danger ; but now he is face to face with his enemies, and he must not refuse to testify to his faith, and so betray the cause of God.

At Croydon he passes the night in the porter's lodge, and next day is summoned for his examination, his old tutor Gardiner being also present. Here he stoutly upholds the Zwinglian view of the Lord's supper, alleging the fathers in its favour, but adding that he did not condemn transubstantiation, provided that it were held without idolatry. Needless to say this compromise did not content his judges. Three or four times Cranmer sent to him for private interviews to persuade him to " leave his imagination," but all was in vain, and the archbishop writes on June 17 : " We had to leave him to his ordinary,"—that is, to Stokesley, in whose diocese he had been taken. The end was now inevitable. On the 20th Frith was brought before Stokesley, Gardiner and Longland in St Paul's cathedral, and as he again proved obdurate, the bishop of London pronounced him guilty, and delivered him over to the secular power for punishment.

He was then taken to Newgate jail, where he remained for fourteen days in a dark dungeon, laden with irons, and spent the time in writing by the light of a candle. Gardiner sent two or three emissaries to convert him even at the eleventh hour, but although one of them, Germain Gardiner, the bishop's nephew, afterwards published to the world an account of his controversial triumph over the doomed man, Frith was not to be shaken, and on July 4 he went cheerfully to his death at Smithfield, having as his companion a young tailor's apprentice, named Andrew Hewet, who had also been betrayed by Holt. As the fire was preparing, a Dr

Cook, rector of a London church, who was present, addressed the people, forbidding them to pray for the prisoners—no more than for a dog: at which words Frith smiled, and desired the Lord to forgive the speaker. The two young men met their death with the greatest courage. As the flames drew near him, Frith embraced them with his arms, and although his sufferings were longer than those of his fellow, since the wind blew the fire somewhat away from him, he stood unmoved to the end, as though he felt no pain.

But before he perished, Tyndale had written him another letter, seemingly towards the end of May. This time he addresses him by his own name. It is clear that he has now given up hope that his friend will be saved from the flames, and it only remains to strengthen him for the coming ordeal. It runs thus:—

" The grace and peace of God our Father, and of Jesus Christ our Lord, be with you. Amen.

" Dearly beloved brother John, I have heard say that the hypocrites, now they have overcome that great business which letted them [i.e. the royal divorce], or that now they have at the least way brought it at a stay, they return to their old nature again. The will of God be fulfilled, and that he hath ordained to be ere the world was made, that come, and his glory reign over all.

" Dearly beloved, howsoever the matter be, commit yourself wholly and only unto your most loving Father and most kind Lord, and fear not men that threat, nor trust men that speak fair: but trust him that is true of promise, and able to make his word good. Your cause is Christ's gospel, a light that must be fed with the blood of faith. The lamp must be dressed and snuffed daily, and that oil poured in every evening and morning, that the light go not out. Though we be sinners, yet is the cause right. If when we be buffeted for well-doing, we suffer patiently and endure, that is thankful with God; † for to that end we are called. For Christ also suffered for us, leaving us an example that we should follow his steps, who did no sin. Hereby have we perceived love that he laid down his life for us: therefore we ought also to lay down our lives for the brethren. Rejoice and be glad, for great is your reward in heaven. For we suffer with him, that we may also be glorified: who

shall change our vile body, that it may be fashioned like
unto his glorious body, according to the working whereby he is able even to subject all things unto him.†

" Dearly beloved, be of good courage, and comfort
your soul with the hope of this high reward, and bear
the image of Christ in your mortal body, that it may at
his coming be made like to his, immortal: and follow
the example of all your other dear brethren, which chose
to suffer in hope of a better resurrection. Keep your
conscience pure and undefiled, and say against that
nothing. Stick at [maintain] necessary things; and
remember the blasphemies of the enemies of Christ,
' They find none but that will abjure rather than suffer
the extremity.' Moreover, the death of them that come
again [repent] after they have once denied, though it
be accepted with God and all that believe, yet is it not
glorious; for the hypocrites say, ' He must needs die;
denying helpeth not: but might it have holpen, they
would have denied five hundred times: but seeing it
would not help them, therefore of pure pride and mere
malice together, they speak with their mouths that their
conscience knoweth false.' If you give yourself, cast
yourself, yield yourself, commit yourself wholly and
only to your loving Father; then shall his power be in
you and make you strong, and that so strong that you
shall feel no pain: and that shall be to another present
death: and his Spirit shall speak in you, and teach you
what to answer, according to his promise. He shall set
out his truth by you wonderfully, and work for you
above all that your heart can imagine. Yea, and you
are not yet dead; though the hypocrites all, with all
they can make, have sworn your death. *Una salus
victis nullam sperare salutem.** To look for no man's
help bringeth the help of God to them that seem to be
overcome in the eyes of the hypocrites: yea, it shall make
God to carry you through thick and thin for his truth's
sake, in spite of all the enemies of his truth. There
falleth not a hair till his hour be come: and when his
hour is come, necessity carrieth us hence, though we be

---

† The words between the daggers are in Latin in Foxe (1563). So
also on the following page.
* *I.e.* The only safety for the vanquished is to hope for no safety.
(Virgil, *Aeneid* II., 354.) There are a number of classical allusions in
Tyndale's works.

not willing. But if we be willing, then have we a reward and thank.

" Fear not threatening, therefore, neither be overcome of sweet words; with which twain the hypocrites shall assail you. Neither let the persuasions of worldly wisdom bear rule in your heart; no, though they be your friends that counsel. Let Bilney be a warning to you. Let not their visor beguile your eyes. Let not your body faint. † He that endureth to the end shall be saved.† If the pain be above your strength, remember: † Whatsoever ye shall ask in my name, I will give it you.† And pray to your Father in that name, and he will ease your pain, or shorten it. The Lord of peace, of hope, and of faith, be with you. Amen.

"William Tyndale.

" Two have suffered in Antwerp *in die sanctæ crucis* * unto the great glory of the gospel: four at Riselles [Lille] in Flanders: and at Luke [Liège] hath there one at the least suffered; all that same day. At Roan [Rouen] in France they persecute; and at Paris are five doctors taken for the gospel. See, you are not alone. Be cheerful: and remember that among the hard-hearted in England there is a number reserved by grace: for whose sakes, if need be, you must be ready to suffer. Sir, if you may write, how short [soever] it be, forget it not; that we may know how it goeth with you, for our hearts' ease. The Lord be yet again with you, with all his plenteousness, and fill you that you flow over. Amen.

" If, when you have read this, you may send it to Adrian [otherwise John Byrte], do, I pray you, that he may know how that our heart is with you.

" George Joye, at Candlemas, being at Barrow, printed two leaves of Genesis in a great form, and sent one copy to the king and another to the new queen [Anne Boleyn], with a letter to N. for to deliver them; and to purchase licence, that he might so go through all the bible. Out of that is sprung the noise of the new

---

* *I.e.* May 3, the feast of the invention of the cross. Records still exist of the two martyrs at Antwerp and the one at Liège. Cf. *Antwerpsch Archievenblad*, VII., 188; *Histoire du régne de Charles VII en Belgique* (A. Henne) IX., 12, 17. On the five Paris doctors see *L. & P.*, VI., 507. Four were released by a royal order of May 18.

bible [report that there was to be a new translation];
and out of that is the great seeking for English books at
all printers and bookbinders in Antwerp, and for an
English priest that should print.

" This chanced the 9th day of May.

" Sir, your wife is well content with the will of God,
and would not, for her sake, have the glory of God
hindered.

" WILLIAM TYNDALE."

Whether Frith received this letter in time, we cannot say:
but to us it is very precious, as showing the noble simplicity
of the writer, and the close union of hearts between him and
his friend. The disciple was worthy of the master. There
was no fear of him recanting; he had learnt his lesson too
well. Nor did Tyndale's other disciple recant, John Rogers,
who twenty years later " broke the ice " as the first victim of
the Marian persecution, and went nobly to the fire, while his
wife and eleven children stood at the roadside, to strengthen
him to play the man.

It was probably about this time that Tyndale composed
his other work on the sacraments, which is variously named
A Fruitful and Godly Treatise and *A Brief Declaration*.* We
learn from Foxe that he held it up from publication, thinking
it not suitable for the times, and that it would be a breeder
of contention. No doubt it was found among his possessions
when he was arrested, along with the exposition of Tracy's
will, and was published by his friends at a suitable opportunity. No copy of the first edition is preserved. The work is
in places obscure and clumsy, as if it had not received the
finishing touches from its author. In tone it is moderate
and peaceable, and by a learned consideration of passages in
the Old and New Testaments it aims at showing the true
meaning and use of sacraments, that they are outward signs,
appealing to our bodily senses, and enforcing the inward
and spiritual truths of the gospel, but valueless to worshippers
who are blind in eye and hard in heart. It ends with a frank
review of the three kinds of sacramental doctrine, and an

---

* Foxe (1563) implies that it preceded the revision (1534) of the New
Testament. Bale (1548) first mentions it, as *De Sacramentis et Signis*.

appeal that all should be tolerated in the church. Let us have done, he says, with this endless brawling, and drink more deeply of those gospel truths, without which all external ordinances are nothing.

Meanwhile, despite stringent edicts from the emperor, Lutheranism had been steadily growing in the Low Countries. Prosecutions indeed were frequent, and martyrdoms were not uncommon, but they availed not to stem the tide. One or two preachers had adopted the new views and were expounding them in their pulpits; printers lent their powerful aid to the cause, defying the penalties of the law; part of the council itself was touched, and the rest were lukewarm, and unwilling to co-operate with the hierarchy in a determined effort to crush the rebels. There were, however, some humbler folk in Antwerp who were deeply pained at the trend of events, and early in 1533 they addressed to the chancellor of Brabant a letter, which has only recently been discovered, and which is of the highest interest to us, since it mentions Tyndale, though not by name.

The writers call themselves simple men, speaking out of the love of God. They describe the growth of Lutheranism in the town, the runaway monks and nuns who spread it, the preachers who go from house to house praying and holding services, the printers who contrive to issue bad books, the supineness or secret sympathy of the lords, the repeated slipping of offenders out of the net of punishment, even when it seems to be closing upon them. Then they come nearer home. Whenever they can, they give the names of the Lutheran leaders, the places where they might be found, the churches where false preaching was to be heard. The paragraph that is of the greatest interest to us runs as follows:—

" There is a printer at Antwerp, dwelling in the Camerstrate, within the old gate, next to the Vette Henne, on the same side, towards the churchyard of our lady. There shall you find books full of heresy in the English tongue, and also others; but you must go into the chamber within, and open the chests; there shall you find them. And the better to do so, take with you a Christian Englishman. And this printer will also show you a great heretic and doctor, who for his heresy has been driven out of England."

The letter ends with a strong appeal:—

We beg you to act. We have given you material enough. Do as they have done in Spain; purge the town. Strengthen the laws; make half-yearly searches after heretics. We write because our spiritual and lay heads have no care for these things.*

This document was received by the chancellor on January 28, and laid before the council. Then the queen-regent was informed, and she called for a report upon the matter. What further was done we know not: but that the letter was not without effect, seems proved by the names of the Lutherans that came under correction afterwards. In March a priest, named by the writers, was arrested, taken to Vilvorde castle, and in the following year burnt at Brussels. In May two laymen, who had attended one of the churches named, were beheaded in Antwerp. Two of the printers named found themselves in jeopardy during the ensuing two years; and in general the persecution seems to have become sharper and more active. Tyndale himself escaped for the time being, but no doubt this document made the authorities more vigilant, and more ready to exact the extreme penalty, when a couple of years later he was delivered into their hands. Whether the printer in the Camerstrate came into trouble, we know not. His house was named Roodenborch, and five years later an English New Testament was put forth by a printer dwelling there, named Willem van den Bergh (Montanus or Dumont), but there is no trace of his ever having been sentenced.

The great number of Lutherans revealed by this letter makes it easier to understand how it was that Tyndale avoided capture for so long. The refugees from England would of course hold together, but beside these there were not a few Flemings who were either thorough Lutherans themselves, or at least out of sympathy with the persecuting

---

* *De Gulden Passer* (1927), V., 4, p. 267. The letter is in Flemish, and is now at Brussels.

policy of the church. Such men would no doubt often give Tyndale a hint when danger threatened. It is evident too that Lutheran circles were being formed, in which a common religious life was fostered. Sir Thomas More several times taunts Tyndale with neglect of the services of the church. " For," he writes, " as they say that know him, he sayeth none [no service] at all, neither matins, evensong, nor mass, nor cometh at no church but either to gaze or talk." * It does not seem to have entered More's head that to Tyndale the meetings of brethren in private buildings, the breaking of bread from house to house after the New Testament pattern, might be a truer and holier form of worship than the grand rites of the Antwerp churches, where doctrines were taught which he believed to be untrue, where priestcraft came between the soul and its maker, and where the ministrants were only too often men of evil lives. It may well be that he sometimes attended the churches of the Lutheran preachers; we cannot say. But even if he did not (and More's evidence is of little weight), so marked a man as he could hardly be censured for preferring the closeness of private worship among well-wishers, to the dangers that must always have attended appearance in public places.

Of his doings in the remainder of the year 1533 we know very little. In the autumn he was approached by the opponents of the king's divorce, and asked to revise a treatise that had been composed against the recent marriage with Anne Boleyn; but he declined, saying that " he would no farther meddle in his prince's matter, nor would move his people against him, since it was done." So Vaughan reports to Cromwell from Antwerp on October 21. A couple of months earlier the same agent had informed his patron that Sir Thomas More had oftentimes lately been sending his books over to Antwerp for distribution, particularly the *Confutation of Tyndale* and the *Answer to Frith*. This was More's counterblast to the activities of the reformers: for he frequently complains of the floods of Lutheran books coming into England, and that the zeal of the brethren in spreading

* *Works*, 415, 432, 623, 711.

them abroad was so great that some were even given away free of charge.

In the following year (1534) Tyndale brought out the second editions of Genesis and the New Testament. Both were printed by Martin de Keyser, though only the latter carries his name. Genesis no doubt was the earlier of the two. About half a dozen copies survive to-day. It is printed in Roman letter, but the text shows few changes from that of 1530. The glosses, however, attacking the pope, three in number, have been removed, which seems to show that Tyndale was coming to disapprove the sharpness which he had shown four years before.* The other books of the Pentateuch were not revised; evidently the first edition had not been sold out; and the new Genesis was therefore bound up together with them. The revised New Testament came out in November, and to it several months must have been devoted. It will be discussed in the next chapter.

But before this book appeared, Tyndale had found a lodging in the English house, the residence which sixty years ago had been handed over by the town for the use of the merchant adventurers. That he gained thereby the legal rights and immunities of the merchants cannot be proved, though it is often asserted, but he would certainly enjoy a measure of protection, if only because the rulers of Antwerp desired to be on good terms with so powerful a corporation. His host was Thomas Poyntz, a member of the grocers' company and a distant kinsman of Lady Walsh of Little Sodbury, and here he dwelt for the nine months preceding his arrest. The merchants also offered him a stipend, so that for the first time in his life he was well off, or at all events had a secure income. His manner of life at this period is described in Daye's folio by Foxe, who no doubt got his information from Poyntz.

" He was a man very frugal and spare of body, a great student, an earnest labourer in the setting forth of the scriptures of God. He reserved or hallowed to himself two days in the week, which he named his pastime, Monday and

* So Rogers in Matthew's bible, while retaining some of Tyndale's glosses on the Pentateuch, omits all the sharp ones against the hierarchy.

Saturday. On Monday he visited all such poor men and women, as were fled out of England, by reason of persecution, into Antwerp; and these, once well understanding their good exercises and qualities, he did very liberally comfort and relieve; and in like manner provided for the sick and diseased persons. On the Saturday he walked round about the town, seeking every corner and hole, where he suspected any poor person to dwell; and where he found any to be well occupied, and yet over-burdened with children, or else were aged and weak, these also he plentifully relieved. And thus he spent his two days of pastime, as he called them. And truly his alms were very large, and so they might well be; for his exhibition that he had yearly of the English merchants at Antwerp, when living there, was considerable; and that, for the most part, he bestowed upon the poor. The rest of the days of the week he gave wholly to his book, wherein he most diligently travailed. When the Sunday came, then went he to some one merchant's chamber or other, whither came many other merchants, and unto them would he read some one parcel of scripture: the which proceeded so fruitfully, sweetly, and gently from him, much like to the writing of John the evangelist, that it was a heavenly comfort and joy to the audience to hear him read the scriptures; likewise, after dinner, he spent an hour in the same manner. He was a man without any spot or blemish of rancour or malice, full of mercy and compassion, so that no man living was able to reprove him of any sin or crime; although his righteousness and justification depended not thereupon before God, but only upon the blood of Christ, and his faith upon the same."

On the strength of this passage it has often been stated that Tyndale was chaplain to the English house. This is a mistake. The religious ministrations spoken of are private and unofficial, they are not the public services of the chapel; and although he received a salary, this is more likely to have been the spontaneous gift of a few admirers, such as Poyntz, than the official stipend of the society as a whole. We know that there were some merchants who were unfavourable to Lutheranism, and at a time when the imperial laws against heresy were growing in strictness, it is hard to believe that an arch-reformer like Tyndale could have held the post of chaplain, even if he had been willing to conduct the services after the old form. Besides, we know that Rogers was chaplain during the latter months of Tyndale's residence in the English house. From Christmas 1532 for about eighteen months Rogers had been incumbent of a church in London, his successor being instituted on October 24, 1534. Then he came over to Antwerp as chaplain, being still, as Foxe tells us, a papist. He must have had some leanings towards reform, otherwise he would hardly have commended himself to the merchants; but his decisive conversion took place in Antwerp, and was very likely due to the influence of Tyndale himself. Certainly he became his faithful companion and helper, and he may have been one of those two disciples, of whom Joye speaks so scornfully in his *Apology* of February 1535. Some time after Tyndale's death he gave up his post, and departed to Saxony, and dwelt there until he deemed it safe to return to England.*

So then Tyndale passed the last months of his liberty, occupied with expounding the scriptures and preaching, with deeds of charity, and with his scholar's tasks. He " gave himself to his book," says Foxe; this would be his translation of the scripture; and we may rejoice that it was so. Controversy has its uses, and Tyndale dealt many stout blows for truth and faith, yet it is well that the period before his apprehension was given to that work which he could do better than any other man, the rendering of the bible into his mother tongue. Within these nine months appeared his second and third editions of the new Testament, and we may suppose that he also bestowed some labour on that version of the books, Joshua to Chronicles, which he left behind in manuscript.

Meanwhile in England the sky was brightening. The old order was breaking down, and although there was as yet no reformation of doctrine, still the cruel tyranny of the hierarchy was tottering. Even the bishops were moving at last, and were feebly asking for the scripture in the mother tongue. On December 19, 1534 the upper house of the convocation of Canterbury passed a resolution, begging the king to have a new translation made. The petition came to nothing,

* He matriculated at Wittenberg on November 25, 1540.

partly (it would seem) owing to the unwillingness of the bishops chosen to perform the task, but it at least showed in which quarter the wind lay.   In October 1535 Coverdale's bible was published on the continent with the approval of Cromwell and with a dedication to the king, and was permitted to circulate in England.   The tide was turning at last, the hopes of the reformers were rising.   But it was just at this very season that Tyndale, who had borne the burden and heat of the day, had passed unscathed through the greatest perils, and escaped a score of plots against his life, fell victim to the machinations of his foes.

CHAPTER XII

In the postscript to his first New Testament Tyndale had excused the rudeness of the work, had begged his readers to correct any faults which they might find therein, and had held out the hope that he himself would later revise it and give it its full shape. That hope was not fulfilled for eight and a half years; for Tyndale, as we have seen, was busy with other matters. Yet during this long period the people was not wholly without the English testament. The six thousand copies of the first edition would take a year or two to dispose of, even allowing for the destruction of many through seizure and burning; and then there were the three thousand books of the Cologne fragment. Even when these were sold out, there was at least one enterprising publisher ready to take the risk of reprinting a work that was likely to find a ready market.

This was Christopher van Endhoven (or Ruremond) of Antwerp. George Joye in his *Apology* of February 1535 describes for us no fewer than four editions which issued from his press, all quite independent of Tyndale. With the first of these we are already acquainted; for it is none other than the little book which ambassador Hackett was tracking down in the Low Countries at the end of 1526, and which was condemned and burnt early in the following year. It is not likely that the whole impression was burnt; for New Testaments of a small size were coming over from Antwerp during 1527, and in the spring of the following year John Raimund, brother of Christopher van Endhoven, was in trouble in England for selling them, and was forced to abjure. In due course Christopher issued a second reprint, seemingly of octavo size and about the year 1530, and he is no doubt the person named " Christopher, a Dutchman of Antwerp " who (Foxe tells us) was in 1531 put in prison at Westminster for selling English New Testaments, and who there died. These two reprints were full of errors, because there was no Englishman to correct the press; they numbered between them about five thousand copies, and both were sold out by the end of 1533.

At this point Tyndale was "pricked forth to take the testament in hand" and to issue a revision, as he had promised "in the latter end of his first translation," but he "prolonged and deferred so necessary a matter." Such is Joye's account; but no doubt the truth is, that the printers saw that Tyndale's revision was likely to take six months or more, and were not minded to lose the market waiting in England: for with the recent anti-papal legislation the strictness of the laws against Lutheranism was beginning to relax. As Joye puts it, "now was there given, thanked be God, a little space to breathe and rest unto Christ's church after so long and grievous persecution for reading the books." The printers therefore approached Joye and asked him to correct a new edition. Joye agreed that a correction was desirable, but said that he supposed that Tyndale would himself put out a revision, and if so, Endhoven's would not sell. This answer shows that Joye knew quite well that Tyndale's second edition might be expected before long. However the printers persisted in their project, and brought out, seemingly early in 1534, an edition of about two thousand copies, in a small volume, and had shortly sold them all. This time the printing was even more faulty than before; and we need not doubt Joye's word on this point, though it was certainly to his interest to magnify the errors, in order to excuse his own intervention in the business of editing.

"All this long time," proceeds Joye, "Tyndale slept; for nothing came from him, as far as I could perceive," and the Dutchmen, seeing no one else in the field, began to prepare a fourth edition. They printed the first leaf, which had been corrected for them by another Englishman, and then came once more to Joye to ask him to carry through the remainder. He told them again that their edition would never sell against Tyndale's revision, if he amended it as

diligently as he had promised. They replied: Two thousand
of ours and two thousand of his will be a small number for
the whole of England; besides, we will sell ours cheaper
than his. Joye therefore, seeing that they were determined
to print, and forecasting that, unless an Englishman were
found to correct it, the new book would be even more faulty
than the last, agreed to undertake the business. " What
Tyndale doth," he said to himself, " I wot not; he maketh
me nothing of his counsel. I see nothing come from him
all this long while, wherein with the help that he hath, that is
to say one both to write it and to correct it in the press, he
might have done it thrice since he was first moved to do it."
Joye seems never to have asked himself whether it was a fair
or a kindly act to intrude into a work, in which Tyndale
certainly had the prior right, or to try to undersell the coming
revision of a man, with whom a few months later he was
professing to have been linked in familiar friendship.

The price finally agreed upon between Joye and the
printer was 3 stivers or 4½d. for each sheet of sixteen leaves,
which worked out at 14s. Flemish, or 12s. English money for
the whole [*i.e.* perhaps £9 in modern value]. But the copy,
says Joye, was so corrupt, especially in the table, that he
would not have done it for five times that sum, save that the
work was a good one. The edition appeared in August 1534,
three months before Tyndale's revision. One copy alone
survives, a beautiful little book of sextodecimo size, in the
Grenville library in the British Museum, the earliest copy
of any of the pirate editions to have come down to us. It
bears the somewhat pompous title, *The New Testament, as it
was written and caused to be written by them which heard it, whom
also our Saviour Christ Jesus commanded that they should preach it
unto all creatures.* There are no glosses or notes, but a
kalendar, references, and tables of epistles and gospels.
Joye's name does not appear in the book, nor does Tyndale's,
but the colophon states that it had been " diligently overseen
and corrected," and that it was printed by the widow of
Christopher van Endhoven.

Now if Joye had confined himself to amending the misprints of his copy, he would even so have been acting dis-

loyally towards Tyndale, and so Tyndale's friends regarded the matter. One of them even told Joye—seemingly in ignorance that he had the culprit before him—that it would be an alms to hang the man that was correcting for the Dutchmen. But Joye did more than this. He introduced a number of changes into the text, comparing it with the Latin Vulgate (for he was ignorant of Greek); and to crown all, in more than a dozen passages he altered Tyndale's quite correct translation *resurrection* into *life after this*, or some similar phrase. This it was that roused Tyndale's indignation, and stung him to insert at the last minute into his revised New Testament a second preface of violent protest against Joye.

But to understand this dispute we must go back a little. When the reformers denied the lawfulness of prayer to the saints, they denied also that the saints are already in heaven. Where then are they? What becomes of the departed souls between death and the resurrection of the body preceding the day of judgment? It was a frequent charge against the Lutherans that they believed the souls to be asleep during this period. Both More and Joye charge this upon Tyndale, but unjustly, for what he really says is that he does not know; that the state of the dead is a secret laid up in the treasure house of God, into which it becomes us not to inquire too curiously.* Still, though this specific charge was unjust, More and Joye undoubtedly believed that Tyndale's cautious ignorance came dangerously near to the doctrine that the souls sleep, while Tyndale on his part was equally sure that the belief that the souls are already in glory in heaven diminishes the need and the value of the bodily resurrection.

There had already been some contention upon this matter amongst the reformers both in England and in the Low Countries. In the first quarter of 1533 Joye received a letter from a brother in England, asking why in his published

---

* His earliest statement is in the *Answer to More*: " What God doth with them, that shall we know when we come to them " (III., 180, cf. II., 185). But of course he leaves the door open to the interpretation that souls sleep (III., 189). In fairness to More and Joye it should be added that the compiler of the index in the first edition of the *Answer* (whoever he was) refers to the above passage (III., 180) under the heading: Souls sleep.

works he had rendered Isaiah's prayer in two different ways, and in reply he took the opportunity of expounding his view of the resurrection. A copy of Joye's letter reached Frith, who was then in the Tower, and Frith, thinking that it was likely to mislead others, and to be a cause of dissension among the brethren, wrote to Tyndale to ask whether Joye could not be restrained from publishing such doctrine. He proposed also to write himself against Joye, but from this Tyndale dissuaded him. Tyndale appears, however, to have spoken to Joye, and requested him to cease writing; and Joye wrote a letter to Frith in justification of himself, to which he complains that he received no answer. In the discussions in Antwerp John Coke, secretary of the merchant adventurers, took a part against Joye, and a letter of his is still extant, addressed to a certain " brother William." This can hardly be any other than Tyndale. It runs as follows :—

" BROTHER WILLIAM,

" I heartily commend me unto you. I was not content that ye brake so suddenly away, and took not with you my letters, as ye promised me. Sir, I sent a letter as concerning the answer [Joye's] to him that would know, why the prayer of Esaie so varied in the primer and the prophet [two books of Joye's], and left myself no copy; of which letter [Joye's to the inquirer in England] it is thought that dissensions among the wise brethren begin to grow. I pray you in any wise monish him [Joye] unto whom ye delivered it [Coke's previous letter] of this folly, and bid him in anywise to send me the letter [Joye's to the inquirer] again, or else a copy thereof, and bid him, as ever I shall do, for him to take heed how they expound and descant upon so plain a matter, and bid him send Mr. Latimer a copy thereof [Joye's to England].

" Remember my wood and my cheese etc. God preserve you. The 29 day of April.

" Your JOHN COKE."

The reformers in Antwerp were always under the threat of danger, and written messages were liable to seizure; so this letter is purposely couched in vague terms; nevertheless its general meaning is clear. Tyndale must have delivered it to Joye on the same day; for on April 29 Joye wrote to Latimer, describing Frith's letter of complaint to Tyndale, and desiring to have his judgment on the controversy. He cannot, he says, send him a copy of his letter to the inquirer in England, for he has not kept one; but he tells him how he can obtain one in England. At the bottom of this letter Joye copies out Coke's letter to Tyndale, and this is how it has been preserved: for the messenger appears to have been seized by Cromwell's agents, and Joye's letter found its home in the treasury of the exchequer.

In his letter to Latimer Joye says nothing to the disadvantage of Tyndale, but after the conflict had broken out between the two men in the following year, he gives a highly coloured and most unflattering account of Tyndale's behaviour, whenever they talked together on this question.

" I reasoned with him, as we walked together in the field, more than once or twice, bringing against him such texts, as methought proved plainly against him. . . . But these plain testimonies of the scripture would take no place with Tyndale; for he wrested and writeth [?] them, contrary to his own doctrine, out of their proper and pure sense, with feigned glosses to shift and seek holes. He, after his wonted disdainful manner against me, filliped them forth between his finger and his thumb: and what disdainful and opprobrious words he gave me for so reasoning against him, I will not now rehearse, lest I should minish the good opinion that some men have in him . . . We never reasoned the matter, but through his impatience our disputation ever ended with chiding and brawling, in so much that afterward in his exposition upon John he stretched forth his pen against me as far as he durst, but yet spared my name; at the which challenge I winked, yet taking it not as meant of me, because I loved quietness, not willing that any man should know what hatred he did ever bear me since I came over."

It may be that Tyndale, who was by nature blunt and outspoken, showed Joye more plainly than he need have done, that he thought him a conceited and ignorant fellow: for such he was. At all events Joye himself would feel his own inferiority in learning, ability, and force of character; and, as is often the case with weak and foolish persons, the knowledge rankled within him. Thus when the task of correcting the New Testament for the press of Endhoven came into his way, he could not resist the temptation to assert himself, and to introduce his own view of the resurrection.

Tyndâle's protest, inserted into his November testament, was most pointed and forcible. It is headed: " William Tindale, yet once more to the Christian reader "; and then proceeds :—

" Thou shalt understand, most dear reader, when I had taken in hand to look over the New Testament again, and to compare it with the Greek, and to mend whatsoever I could find amiss, and had almost finished the labor, George Joye secretly took in hand to correct it also, by what occasion his conscience knoweth, and prevented me, in so much that his correction was printed in great number, ere mine began.

" When it was spied and word brought me, though it seemed to divers other that George Joye had not used the office of an honest man, seeing he knew that I was in correcting it myself . . . yet I took the thing in worth, as I have done divers other in time past, as one that have more experience of the nature and disposition of the man's complexion, and supposed that a little spice of covetousness and vainglory (two blind guides) had been the only cause that moved him so to do, about which things I strive with no man ; and so followed after, and corrected forth, and caused this to be printed, without surmise or looking on his correction.

" But when the printing of mine was almost finished, one brought me a copy, and shewed me so many places in such wise altered, that I was astonied, and wondered not a little what fury had driven him to make such change, and call it a diligent correction. For throughout Matthew, Mark and Luke perpetually, and oft in the Acts, and sometime in John and also in the Hebrews, where he findeth this word *resurrection*, he changeth it into *the life after this life*, or *very life*, and such like, as one that abhorred the name of the resurrection.

" If that change, to turn *resurrection* into *life after this life*, be a diligent correction, then must my translation be faulty in those places, and St Jerome's, and all the translators that ever I heard of, in what tongue soever it be, from the apostles unto this his diligent correction, as he calleth it ; which whether it be so or no, I permit to other men's judgments.

" But of this I challenge George Joye, that he did not put his own name thereto and call it rather his own translation; and that he playeth bo peep, and in some of his books [e.g. his translations of Isaiah, Jeremiah and Psalms] putteth in his name and title, and in some keepeth it out. It is lawful for who will to translate and shew his mind, although a thousand had translated before him. But it is not lawful (thinketh me), nor yet expedient for the edifying of the unity of the faith of Christ, that whosoever will, shall by his own authority take another man's translation, and put out and in, and change at pleasure, and call it a correction."

Tyndale then touches on the past controversies, on Joye's letter to England, and Frith's protest from the Tower. Whatever Joye's own opinion may be, still his " unquiet curiosity " and his " marvellous imaginations " about this word have led a number of people to deny altogether the resurrection of the body. Even if Joye's rendering gave a correct explanation of the meaning of the sacred writers, still the word is *resurrection*, and should be so translated.

" If the text be left uncorrupt, it will purge herself of all manner of false glosses, how subtle soever they be feigned, as a seething pot casteth up his scum. But if the false gloss be made the text, diligently overseen and correct, wherewith then shall we correct false doctrine, and defend Christ's flock from false opinions, and from the wicked heresies of ravening of wolves ? "

As to my own belief, it is that of the scriptures and the whole church, that the body shall rise before the judgment-day; but I do not think that the souls of the righteous departed are yet in full glory with Christ. Notwithstanding I am ready to believe this, if it can be proved by open scripture.

Then follows a moving passage, which reveals to us the process of the dispute in Antwerp, and gives us a glimpse of the personal attacks which Joye must have directed against Tyndale.

" Moreover I take God, which alone seeth the heart, to record to my conscience, beseeching him that my part be not in the blood of Christ, if I wrote, of all that I have written throughout all my book, aught of an evil purpose, of envy or malice to any man, or to stir up any false doctrine or opinion in the church of Christ, or to be author of any sect, or to draw disciples after me, or that I would be esteemed, or had in price, above the least child that is born, save only of pity and compassion I had, and yet have, on the blindness of my brethren, and to bring them unto the knowledge of Christ, and to make every one of them, if it were possible, as perfect as an angel of heaven, and to weed out all that is not planted of our heavenly father, and to bring down all that lifteth up itself against the knowledge of the salvation that is in the blood of Christ. Also my part be not in Christ, if mine heart be not to follow and live according as I teach, and also if mine heart weep not night and day for mine own sin and other men's indifferently, beseeching God to convert us all, and to take his wrath from us, and to be merciful, as well to all other men, as to mine own soul, caring for the wealth of the realm I was born in, for the king and all that are thereof, as a tenderhearted mother would for her only son.

" As concerning all I have translated or otherwise written, I beseech all men to read it for that purpose I wrote it, even to bring them to the knowledge of the scripture. And as far as the scripture approveth it, so far to allow it, and if in any place the word of God disallow it, there to refuse it, as I do before our saviour Christ and his congregation. And where they find faults, let them shew it me, if they be nigh, or write to me, if they be far off; or write openly against it, and improve [confute] it; and I promise them, if I shall perceive that their reasons conclude, I will confess mine ignorance openly."

Wherefore I beseech George Joye, and all others, to translate themselves, whether from Greek, Latin or Hebrew, or else (if they will) to take my translation and alter it, and publish their work under their own names, but not to play bo peep after Joye's manner. " For this I protest, that I provoke not Joye, nor any other man, but am provoked, and that after the spitefullest manner of provoking, to do sore against my will, and with sorrow of heart, that I now do. But I neither can nor will suffer of any man, that he shall go take my translation, and correct it without name, and make such changing as I myself durst not do, as I hope to have my part in Christ, though the whole world should be given me for my labour.

" Finally, that New Testament, thus diligently corrected, beside this so oft putting out this word *resurrection*, and I wot not what other change (for I have not yet read it over), hath in the end before the table of the epistles and gospels this title " (and here Tyndale quotes the colophon): " which title, reader, I have here put in, because by this thou shalt know the book the better. Vale."

This protest betokens keen feeling, but it rings true. Tyndale does not charge Joye, as many later writers have done, with casting out the word *resurrection* altogether, but only with altering it in some places, and when we compare his list of places with the book itself, the two exactly correspond. Nor does he charge him with denying the bodily resurrection, but only with using language that had led others to do so. Nor does he condemn the book in general; in fact, he is careful to say that he has not yet read it as a whole, but is basing his protest on this one ground alone. Whether Joye's answer is equally careful and precise, and has the same ring of truth, we shall see presently.

But if Tyndale had read the book through, his opinion of its author would not have been bettered. It was paraded as " diligently overseen and corrected," but the revision is of the most perfunctory kind. When Joye, in defending himself against the charge of covetousness, retorts quite fairly that the money he received was extremely small, he omitted to add that the correction was equally so. He seems to have done very little more than amend misspellings and misprints, introducing, however, the while some careless errors of his own. When he does aspire to play a more active part, he confines himself mostly to trifling changes, such as the writing of *unto* for *to*, or the insertion of *is* into *God with us* of Matthew i. 23. Occasionally, however, as if to justify his existence as a reviser, he bursts out into something of greater moment: but these corrections are rarely an improvement, and many of them are downright wrong.*

For the next stages of the contention we have only Joye's

---

* As a rule he keeps *seniors*, but also renders by *elders, bishops* and *priests*. Here are some of his most important changes:—John i. 21. *That* (*a*-Tyndale) prophet [An improvement]: Acts vi. 1. Their poor needy were neglect in the daily almose dealing [Wrong]: Acts vi. 9. *School* or *college* (*synagogue*): Rom. xii. 2. *Mind* (*wits*): Rom. xii. 19. Give *place* (*room*): Heb. i. 3. *His mighty word* (*the word of his power*): II Tim. iv. 7. Kept *promise* (*the faith*) [Wrong].

version: for Tyndale wrote nothing further against him. It would seem that, after the publication of Tyndale's protest, the friends of the two men interposed, and a treaty of peace was patched up. Joye was to withhold the defence of himself which he was preparing, and Tyndale was to recall his preface, and rewrite it for the fresh revision of the New Testament, which he was just putting into print. In fact, the new preface was to be a joint affair (this was Tyndale's own proposal), each man giving his reasons for his rendering of *resurrection*, and leaving the matter to the judgment of the learned, and saluting the readers with a common salutation as a mark of amity.

If this was the agreement, it was forthwith broken by Joye himself: for on January 9, 1535 he reissued from the same press his offending version of the previous August. In the text he made no changes of moment, but he added at the end of the book, under his own name, a translation from the Vulgate of the liturgical epistles of the Old Testament, and also a postscript dealing with Tyndale's attack. This edition was altogether unknown until thirty years ago, when a copy came to light, and found its home in the British Museum.

Now to reissue the book at all would seem to Tyndale an unfriendly act, but to add to his offence Joye uses his postscript as an opportunity of sharply reaffirming his own interpretation of the word *resurrection*, and of making further hits at his adversary. He starts off by speaking of Tyndale's " uncharitable epistle " and of the " lies and slanders " contained therein. He then describes the treaty of peace, and says that he does " gladly consent thereto."

But meanwhile (he begs) be not offended, reader, at the strife, nor think the worse of us two for engaging in it; our dissent is doubtless overruled to teach men that the dead are now alive with Christ, and in bliss in heaven, as the scriptures clearly testify. Better men than we have had contentions. This thing may teach others that all men are fallible, and may warn us " that we depend not whole upon any man's translation nor his doctrine, neither to be sworn nor addict to any man's learning, make he never so holy and devout protestations and prologs," but that we should measure all by the word of God.

After this renewed attack, Tyndale would certainly consider the treaty of peace to be at an end, if indeed there ever was one as definite as Joye alleges, and he went on with the printing of his third edition, and issued it in the early months of 1535. The book follows the same general plan as the second edition, but the preface against Joye is omitted.

But Joye was by no means minded to give up the struggle, and on February 27 he published his *Apology*, defending himself against Tyndale's attack, and giving his version of the reconciliation and its failure. Only one copy of this tract exists, in the library of Cambridge university. It is entitled: *An apology made by George Joye to satisfy (if it may be) W. Tindale, to purge and defend himself against so many slanderous lies, feigned upon him in Tindale's uncharitable and unsober pistle, so well worthy to be prefixed for the reader, to induce him into the understanding of his New Testament diligently corrected;* and its general spirit is well betokened by the text placed at the bottom of the page: *Lord, deliver me from lying lips, and from a deceitful tongue.*

Joye begins with an account of the interposition of the friends and the treaty of peace. He then goes on:—

After five or six days I came to Tyndale to see his correction of his epistle, but was told by him that he had never thought of it since. I departed, urging haste, and came again in five or six more days. This time he said that I should not be able to decipher what he had written, and though I told him I knew his handwriting, he refused to shew it to me. A third time I came, but now he had thought of a new cavillation: he would see my reasons and write against them, ere I should see his revocation. But I held that he ought not to write against them, till the learned men had had an opportunity of judging, and indeed not even then. Nevertheless I came a fourth time, but he again insisted on seeing my reasons and writing against them. He proposed, however, to submit the dispute to Doctor Barnes and his fellow Aepinus, pastor of St Nicholas, Hamburg, and he promised to revoke his charge that I denied the resurrection. As I could not get satisfaction, I informed two of the friends who had mediated between us, that if they could not persuade him to keep his promise, I would defend myself: and this I now do; for I see that Tyndale is half ashamed to make the necessary withdrawal.

The *Apology* is a long and rambling document with three main themes. The first is the dispute about the true doctrine of the resurrection. Joye describes his reasonings with Tyndale in the field, and how at length by a brilliant argument he drove him from his anabaptist heresy, that the dead sleep till doomsday. Christ is the head, he argued, and we are the body. Now the body must follow the head, and as Christ's spirit went into heaven, we also go thither at death.

" This reason," he exclaims triumphantly, " did so bite Tyndale, he could not shake it off," and now at last " in his goodly godly epistle against me " he has shifted his ground, and agrees with me. Yet rather than own his error, he is ready to hurt the church and delight the foe by covering me with perpetual infamy. " So proud and arrogant are they, that stand so high in their own conceit and false opinion," and defend what they know to be false, rather than seem " convicted especially of any simple, and one that appears not so well learned as they be themselves." It was to correct this false opinion of Tyndale that I altered my rendering of the word *resurrection*; my conscience moved me to do so. Not that I disbelieve in the resurrection; on the contrary I retain the word in many places of the New Testament.

The second theme is the general imperfection of Tyndale's first translation (and indeed of his second edition too), and the urgent need for a revision, not only because of slips and misprints, but because of misrenderings of the text.

Was it not a good thing, he asks, to correct a version that was negligent, I will not say false? Why, Tyndale himself asked his readers to correct what was amiss. I only corrected the copy, mending false words, and " when I came to a dark sentence," that was unintelligible, " whether by the ignorance of the first translator or of the printer," I made it plain by comparison with the Latin text. I restored phrases that had been omitted, and for the first time " gave many words their pure and native signification." My conscience compelled me, lest readers in England might be hurt. Does

Tyndale think his version cannot be improved? He must be the Almighty himself. The fathers corrected one another, and Tyndale is " far inferior unto them both in learning, judgment and virtue." We ought to give thanks to those who surpass us, and who amend our errors; for we are all born to profit one another.

I have made many changes, which Tyndale would have done, " if he had had such sight into the Greek as he pretendeth "; let him " look over his testament once again, and confer it a little better with the verity and Greek too." But in fact some of my changes he was himself compelled to adopt in his second edition. He should have mended more faults in the text, instead of putting so many vain and frivolous—yes, dark and obscure—glosses into the margin. For my part, I would omit glosses altogether; I would rather put the truth into the text. " I would the scripture were so purely and plainly translated, that it needed neither note, gloss nor scholia, so that the reader might once swim without a cork." His second edition does not fulfil " his so large promises, added in the latter end of his first translation to the reader; and I wonder how he could compare it with Greek, since himself is not so exquisitely seen [accomplished] therein."

The third theme of the *Apology* is Tyndale's faults of temper. On these Joye continually harps.

He stands " high in his own opinion "; and appeals to " his high learning in Hebrew, Greek and Latin." He is unwilling to believe that others may be able to instruct him. He has a party of supporters, who look on him as their master, and resent any disagreement with him; and he himself is only " patient, when every man say as he saith, and look up and wonder at his words." He has two disciples, " that gaped so long for their master's morsel, that they might have the advantage of the sale of his books "; and these were the men (I will not name them) that called me dishonest for correcting for the Dutchmen. He hints that I did it out of a spice of covetousness and vainglory. Why, I only received 12*s.* for it, and I hear his recompense has been £10; and if I were vainglorious, why did I not put my name to it? The fact is that he has long nourished hatred and malice against me, though outwardly he has feigned to love me. Malice and envy are his two blind guides. " For all his holy protestations, yet heard I never sober and wise man so praise his own works, as I heard him praise his exposition of Matthew v–vii; insomuch that mine ears glowed for shame to hear him: and yet it was Luther that made it, Tyndale only but translating and powdering it here and there with his own fantasies."

He cannot now restore my good name, of which he has robbed me. Even if I had been wrong, he should have corrected me privately first, and not been so hasty to judge me, " his brother that so well deserveth upon his work." His lying epistle has struck a blow at the gospel and hurt many simple men, causing them to cast their books away. Some good men wish that we two had never been born.

" Tyndale verily might never abide it that I especially (whether he so thinketh of other men, God knoweth) should translate, write or meddle with the scriptures, as though the Holy Ghost with his gifts were restrained unto only Tyndale, and might not breathe where him listeth, as though Tyndale was learned only, and none but he. Wherefore let every reader be warned and taught at this ensample and grievous temptation of this man, . . . lest, as Paul says, we be puffed up with cunning, void of all charity which edifieth. . . . Had it been my enemy that thus had unjustly reviled and vexed me, I could have borne him; and if my hater had thus oppressed me, I could have avoided him. But it was thou, mine own fellow, my companion in like peril and persecution, my familiar, so well known, unto whom I committed so lovingly my secrets, with whom gladly I went into the house of God. Wherefore methinketh he should have either borne and winked at the calling of this word *resurrectio* the life after this, since it so signifieth, or have patiently aboden other men's judgment, rather than with so slanderous a pistle so suddenly to have rent and torn my name with so perpetual an infamy and with so many feigned lies. Which, all God forgive the man, as I would be forgiven mine own self. Amen."

Joye's tract has been described at some length, because on the strength of it one or two writers have branded Tyndale as both shifty and quarrelsome. Yet one would think that a comparison of the attack with the defence shows plainly where the right of the case lay. Tyndale's chief complaint was perfectly precise; it was that Joye had no right to impose his own interpetations upon Tyndale's New Testament, and saddle his brother with renderings of which he strongly disapproved. But this is the one point which Joye carefully holds at arm's length. He exhibits a ludicrous medley of conflicting emotions. Spite, shame and injured innocence wrestle together within him. He enlarges upon many other matters: the misprints in the copies, the injury to the church, the proper rendering of *resurrectio*, the ignorance of Tyndale, and his many faults; and all this to escape from meeting the charge of dishonourable dealing. He is guilty of a flagrant untruth, when he affirms that Tyndale's exposition on the sermon on the mount was not his own work, but Luther's: for the two books exist, and we can compare them; and although Tyndale certainly used Luther's exposition, and draws from it a number of thoughts and a few sentences, yet the treatment is almost entirely his own. Nor does Joye's account of the treaty of peace hold together. If he was to put his side of the controversy into the joint letter of salutation, how was it unfair for Tyndale to do the same? and how could any joint letter be drawn up without each party seeing what the other had written? Moreover, the ignorance and levity of his attack upon Tyndale's translation leave a very bad impression upon the reader. He is ready enough to tell Tyndale that his rendering is wrong; but out of the dozen or so passages which he adduces (and he had the whole New Testament to draw from), he convicts Tyndale of error only twice or thrice, and he himself is palpably wrong six or seven times.

But if there had been any real doubt as to the merits of the dispute, it was completely removed by the discovery thirty years ago of Joye's second edition of January 1535. It is bad enough that he should, at the very time of the treaty of peace, repeat his offence, adding a spiteful postscript against the brother with whom he was now reconciled; but it is still worse that in his account of the controversy, given seven weeks later in the *Apology*, he withholds all knowledge of this fact from his readers. This want of candour puts him out of court, and clinches the verdict against him. No doubt Tyndale knew his man; he had not associated with him in Antwerp for six or seven years for nothing. He had found him, as we find him, well-meaning and zealous, but vain, shallow and untrustworthy, and probably he had no great confidence that Joye was in earnest, when the reconciliation was engineered by mutual friends.

We can now dismiss this unpleasant contention and turn to consider Tyndale's revised New Testament, his " noblest monument," as it has been called by Westcott. It was printed by Martin de Keyser, and bore its author's full name upon the title-page. The Worms edition had contained only the bare text, save for a short epilogue, but to this book were added references, glosses, tables, epistles from the Old Testament, and general and special prefaces. It opens with a long prologue, the beginning of which must be quoted :—

" Here thou hast, most dear reader, the New Testament, or covenant made with us of God in Christ's blood, which I have looked over again, now at the last, with all diligence, and compared it unto the Greek, and have weeded out of it many faults, which lack of help at the beginning and over-sight did sow therein. If aught seemed changed, or not altogether agreeing with the Greek, let the finder of the fault consider the Hebrew phrase or manner of speech left in the Greek words : whose preterperfect tense and presen t tense are oft both one, and the future tense is the optative mood also, and the future tense oft the imperative mood in the active voice, and in the passive ever. Likewise person for person, number for number, and interrogation for a conditional, and such like, is with the Hebrews a common usage. I have also in many places set light in the margin to understand the text by. If any man find faults either with the translation or aught beside (which is easier for many to do, than so well to have translated it themselves of their own pregnant wits at the beginning without an ensample) to the same it shall be lawful to translate it themselves, and to put what they lust thereto. If I shall perceive, either by myself or by information of other, that aught be escaped me, or might more plainly be translated, I will shortly after cause it to be amended. Howbeit, in many places methinketh it better to put a declaration in the margin, than to run too far from the text. And in many places, where the text seemeth at the first chop hard to be understood, yet the circumstances before and after, and often reading together, make it plain enough."

The books of the New Testament receive each a preface
of its own, except Acts and Revelation. These are mostly
very short, but before Romans is printed the long introduction, composed by Tyndale eight years ago at Worms.
Those on the epistles are generally taken, in substance if not
in words, from the prefaces in Luther's testament; but
Tyndale is no mere echo of the great German. He can go
his own way, when he has a mind; and with the three
crucial epistles, James, Jude and Hebrews, which Luther
put upon a lower plane than the rest, he breaks away from
his exemplar, and pronounces in favour of their full authority.
The prologue to Hebrews shows his sound sense, and may be
summarized here :—

> There has been much doubting concerning the author-
> ship of this letter, and I do not pronounce upon this
> question; I see no harm in such doubting. But some
> have refused it altogether " as no catholic or godly
> epistle," because of three texts therein, which seem to
> mean that sin after baptism cannot be forgiven. Yet
> these are not the only hard texts in scripture, and if they
> are properly expounded, they are found to be in full
> agreement with the doctrines of St Paul and the general
> articles of the faith. This epistle lays not the foundation
> of faith, but builds thereon pure gold, silver, and
> precious stones. Its teaching is excellent, and its author
> a true shepherd, and a faithful servant of Christ, and
> either an apostle or an apostolic man. Why then should
> it not be authority, and taken for holy scripture?

The text is accompanied not only by references, but
by a great number of glosses, almost all of them Tyndale's
own work, and written for this edition; scarcely one is
drawn from Luther. Many of them are simply headings,
but others explain or illustrate the matter in han . These
are admirably terse and pointed, and full of graphic touches,
which Luther himself never surpassed; yet they are mild
in tone, and in this fact we find yet another evidence, that
Tyndale had come to feel that the pungency of the glosses
of his first Pentateuch scarcely befitted the pages of holy
scripture. Maybe the death of Frith, or the humiliations
that were overwhelming Thomas More and his old enemies

in England, disposed him towards gentleness. Here are some of the glosses:—

Matthew xvi. 21. When aught is said or done that should move to pride [i.e. Peter's confession], he dasheth them in the teeth with his death and passion.

I Corinthians vii. 26. If a man have the gift, chastity is good, the more quietly to serve God; for the married have oft much trouble: but if the mind of the chaste be cumbered with other worldly business, what helpeth it? and if the married be the more quiet-minded thereby, what hurteth it? Neither of itself is better than the other, or pleaseth God more than the other. Neither is outward circumcision or outward baptism worth a pin of themselves, save that they put us in remembrance to keep the covenant made between us and God.

II Corinthians xi. 20. (For ye suffer, even if a man bring you into bondage, if a man devour you, etc.) Too much meekness and obedience is not allowed in the kingdom of God, but all must be according to knowledge.

I Thessalonians iv. 11. (Study to be quiet, and to meddle with your own business, and to work with your own hands.) A good lesson for monks and idle friars.

I Peter ii. 5. (A spiritual house, and an holy priesthood, for to offer up spiritual sacrifice, acceptable to God by Jesus Christ.) We be that church, and the obedience of the heart is the spiritual sacrifice. Bodily sacrifice must be offered to our neighbour; for if thou offerest it to God, thou makest a bodily idol of him.

I Peter iv. 8. (Love covereth the multitude of sins.) Hate maketh sin of every trifle, but love looketh not on small things, but suffereth all things.

Another novelty was the addition of the epistles from the Old Testament and Apocrypha, that were appointed to be read in the Salisbury service-book. These Tyndale translated from the original Hebrew and Greek, and not from the Latin of the missal. The reader now had all the liturgical epistles before him, and could use his New Testament for church worship. This was a benefit not only to the lay worshipper, but to the priests also; for they could, if they pleased, read out for the instruction of the people the translation of the epistle and gospel of the day. Tyndale chose the Salisbury rite, since that was most commonly used

in England, but it is interesting to observe that in the last
epistle of all—that for St Catherine's day—he prints the
lesson set in the Hereford book, which was likely more familiar
to him in Gloucestershire. But this mistake he amends in
his third edition.

Yet the chief glory of the second New Testament lies not in
its accessories, but in the text itself. This was thoroughly
and carefully revised. If it be true that Tyndale received
£10 for his work—and we have only Joye's word for this—
still, in proportion to the labour and skill used, his recompense was lower than the 12s. which was given to Joye for
his perfunctory correction. There are about four thousand
changes in all, and curiously enough these are more plentiful
in the gospels and the Acts than in the epistles. Very many
of them, perhaps half, are designed to bring the English
nearer to the Greek original. Connecting particles are
inserted,* loose renderings made more precise; sometimes a
new interpretation is adopted, or a sentence completely
rewritten, Thus he gives us:—

Matthew i. 18. Mary was *betrothed to* (*married unto*—1526)
Joseph.

For this proper alteration Tyndale is reproved by Joye.

Mark vii. 11. Corban, *which* (*that*) is: *That thou desirest of
me to help thee with is given God.* (*Whatsoever thing I offer, that
same doth profit thee.*)

Here Tyndale deserts the false rendering of the Latin
versions, and follows Luther.

Acts xix. 27. But *also that* (*that also*) the temple of the great
goddess (omit *goddess*) Diana should be despised, and her
magnificence (*majesty*) should be destroyed.

In rendering *magnificence* Tyndale rightly breaks away from
his three guides.

I Corinthians v. 11. But now I *write* (*have written*) unto you.

Here he agrees with R.V. against A.V.

II Corinthians iii. 18. But we all behold the glory of the
Lord with his face open, and are changed unto the same
similitude, from glory to glory, even of the spirit of the
Lord (1534).

---

* Mostly in the narratives: *e.g.* in Acts ix no fewer than seventeen
are inserted.

And now the Lord's glory appeareth in us all as in a glass; and we are changed unto the same similitude from glory to glory, even of the Lord which is a spirit (1526).

James v. 12. Let your *yea be yea and your nay nay* (*saying be yea yea, nay nay*).

I Peter ii. 19. For it is *thankworthy* (*cometh of grace*), if a man for conscience toward God endure grief suffering wrongfully.

Revelation xiii. 5. Power was given unto him to *do* (*continue*) forty-two months.

Here he agrees with the Vulgate and R.V.M.

But if Tyndale is concerned with amending the sense, he is no less careful to improve the style. Roughnesses are smoothed away, paraphrases are pruned, and a number of heavy or antique words disappear. Thus *senior* is banished in favour of *elder*, *health* gives place to *salvation*, *counterfeit* to *follow*, *proselyte* to *convert*, a rendering which might well have been kept in our king James' bible; and *verity* becomes much rarer than it was. Many small alterations are made in order to improve the rhythm and ease of the sentence, and sometimes Tyndale is not above taking a hint from his enemy, Thomas More. Here are some examples of stylistic emendations :—

Matthew v. 9. Blessed are the *peace makers* (*maintainers of peace*—1526).

The Lollard and Paues versions render *peaceable men*.

Matthew viii. 26. O ye *of* (*endued with*) little faith.

Matthew xi. 29. And ye shall find *rest* (*ease*) unto your souls.

John i. 1. In the beginning was *the* (*that*) word, and *the* (*that*) word was with God, and *the word was God* (*God was that word*).

In his first edition the order in the last clause is due to long familiarity with the Vulgate, and in writing *that* for *the* he follows Erasmus. Thomas More justly objects to both of these, saying that the order is against the English idiom.

John xx. 27. Be not *faithless but believing* (*without faith but believe*).

Acts vii. 60. Lord, *lay not this sin to their charge* (*impute not this sin unto them*).

Purvey had: *set not to them this sin*.

I Corinthians xv. 51. I shew *you a mystery* (*a mystery unto you*).

Ephesians v. 19. Speaking unto yourselves in psalms and hymns and spiritual songs, singing and *making melody* (*playing*) to the Lord in your hearts.

Philippians ii. 12. *Work out* (*perform*) your own *salvation* (*health*) with fear and trembling.

Hebrews v. 7. Was also heard because *of his godliness* (*he had God in reverence*).

It was left to the Revised Version to hit on the perfect rendering: *for his godly fear*: but Tyndale has *godly fear* in Hebrews xii. 28.

Hebrews xii. 16. Esau, which for one breakfast sold *his birth-right* (*his right that belonged unto him in that he was the eldest brother*).*

Hebrews xiii. 14. For here have we no continuing city: but we seek *one* (*a city*) to come.

That Tyndale has lost none of his love of variation, is shown by his capricious treatment of the angels of the seven churches of the Apocalypse. In his first edition he soberly called them *angels* in every place. Now they become normally *messengers*, but one is called a *tidings bringer* and one an *angel*. No doubt this diversity of rendering informs the reader that the word *angel* really means *messenger*, particularly as there is added a long note to that effect; but on the whole this is not one of the places where the translator's second thoughts are best.

Of Tyndale's second edition more than a dozen copies survive, and in this fact we may see a sign of the abatement of the persecution of the bible-readers. The British Museum alone has three, and to one of these, bequeathed in 1799 by a clergyman named Cracherode, a romantic interest belongs. It is an edition de luxe, printed on vellum, with capitals and woodcuts illuminated, and on its gold edges are inscribed in red paint, one on each face, the three words, now scarce legible, *Anna Regina Angliae*. It belonged to Anne Boleyn, who at the time of the printing was in the full flush of queenly

---

* The earliest use of *birthright* in the *Oxford English Dictionary* is by Coverdale (1535): but Tyndale had used it in 1530 in Gen. xxv. 31. Can he have coined it?

dignity, but ere many months was to come down to disgrace and a miserable doom. Her arms are emblazoned on the second title-page. The book contains the text only, the preliminary matter being omitted, but even so the thickness of the vellum makes it awkward and unwieldy to handle.

The unhappy queen is not perhaps noted for piety, though the menace from a common foe gave her a certain interest in Lutheranism. How came she to be possessed of such a book? Clearly it was a presentation copy, given by someone in Antwerp or closely connected therewith, since it had to be specially printed and prepared. But we are not left only to conjecture; an incident is recorded which throws light upon the matter. The queen had recently done a service to our old friend, Richard Herman, the English-born merchant of Antwerp, who in 1528–9 had been in prison for eight months on the charge, among others, of harbouring and supporting Willem Tandeloo. He was acquitted and set free, but it would seem that at that time he was deprived of his membership of the English house. At all events in 1534 he makes petitition to the queen for the restoration of his privileges, and she writes a letter to Cromwell, which is still extant:—

> " Anne the queen—Trusty and right well beloved, we greet you well; and whereas we be credibly informed that the bearer hereof, Richard Herman, merchant and citizen of Antwerp in Brabant, was in the time of the late lord cardinal put and expelled from his freedom and fellowship of and in the English house there, for nothing else, as he affirmeth, but only that he did, both with his goods and policy, to his great hurt and hindrance in this world, help to the setting forth of the New Testament in English, we therefore desire and instantly pray you that with all speed and favor convenient ye will cause this good and honest merchant, being my lord's true, faithful and loving subject, to be restored to his pristine freedom, liberty and fellowship aforesaid, and the sooner at this our request, and at your good leisure to hear him in such things as he hath to make further relation unto you in this behalf.
>
> " Given under our signet at my lord's **manor** of Greenwich, the 14th day of May."

It is likely that this vellum New Testament was sent to the queen from Antwerp as a thankoffering for this timely assistance, and perhaps also as a means of interesting her in the diffusion of the English scriptures. From whom then did it come? From Tyndale, say most writers; and it may be so. But it may equally well have been given by Herman himself, who had no doubt taken up his quarters again in Antwerp, and who would certainly be known both to Tyndale and to Martin de Keyser.

The November Testament must have sold rapidly: for within a month the third edition was in printing. This is the book with two title-pages of different dates. The printing began with the text of the gospels, and before this stands the second title-page, with date 1534. Later a first title-page was added, which reads: *The New Testament yet once again corrected by Willyam Tindale*, 1535. The second title-page bears a trade-mark with the initials G. H. These were long a puzzle to bibliographers. Some believed that they stood for Guilelmus Hychens: but it was proved fifty years ago by Henry Bradshaw, that they are the initials of the publisher, Godfrey van der Haghen, who doubtless bore the expense of the book, while the printing was done once more by Martin de Keyser.

In his second edition Tyndale had told his readers that if he found any faults therein, he would "shortly after cause it to be amended"; this promise he now fulfilled. Naturally there had been little time for the growth of those second thoughts in the translator's mind, out of which important amendments are made, and so this revision was less radical than the last; nevertheless there are more than 350 changes in the New Testament, and not less than 80 in the epistles from the Old Testament and the Apocrypha. The bulk of these indeed are rather slight, and there is little of that wholesale re-writing of sentences, which we find in the November book; still there are a number of decided improvements. Thus *resurrection from the dead* comes in half a dozen times in place of *resurrection from death*; and we find:—

John viii. 44. The lusts of your father ye will *do* (*follow*— 1534).

I Corinthians xv. 10. I laboured more abundantly than they all, *yet* (omit) not I.

Philippians ii. 4. Look not every man on his own things, but every man on the things of other men (1535).

And that no man consider his own, but what is meet for other (1534).

Hebrews ix. 22. Without *shedding* (*effusion*) of blood is no remission.

James i. 27. To visit the *fatherless* (*friendless*) and widows in their adversity.

Isaiah li. 3. The Lord hath *comforted* (*compassion on*) Sion.

This book was Tyndale's final revision of the New Testament, but it is only in the last half-century that it has come into its due honour. Only four copies exist, all imperfect; and but one of these contains the first title-page, which tells the reader that the book is a fresh correction of Tyndale's. But a careful comparison of the copies with one another and with other editions proves beyond question that this is indeed that New Testament which Joye speaks of as beginning to print in December 1534. This, and not the November edition, is the text which Rogers chose to put into his Matthew's bible, and thus it has become the foundation of our standard English version. Rogers would know very well where Tyndale's last correction was to be found; indeed, there was hardly time for him to make another; for within three months he was in prison.

Yet for many years the honour of being Tyndale's final revision was given to an ill-printed volume without glosses, which is described on its title-page as *diligently corrected and compared with the Greek by Willyam Tindale, and finished 1535.* The text of this, however, agrees broadly with the third edition, and is evidently taken therefrom, and with the re-discovery of the latter it has had to yield pride of place. There would be no need to mention it at all, were it not for the singularity of its spellings. Such forms as *faether, boeke, ruele, behoelde, waeye, hoow* frequently meet the eye of the reader. A hundred years ago learned scholars saw in this spelling the fulfilment of Tyndale's pledge at Little Sodbury, that ere many years had passed, the ploughboy should know more of the scripture than the great priest. Tyndale, it was

said, as his last gift to the world, put forth a New Testament
in the Gloucestershire dialect for the benefit of Gloucestershire rustics. Strange as this idea is, it is well matched by
another theory that was advanced by a philologist: Tyndale
was an enthusiast for spelling reform, and used his new
edition as a practical illustration of sound and rational
methods of figuring words. It is fatal to both these ex-
planations that the peculiar spellings are not constant
throughout the book; they appear capriciously, and in
some parts they are very rare, or even absent. The spellings
indeed smack much more of Brabant than of Gloucestershire;
and no doubt the book was a pirate reprint made after
Tyndale's apprehension, and carried through without any
Englishman to correct. It is full not only of misspellings,
but of misprintings and other blunders, which no Englishman could have passed; and from it we may perhaps form
some idea of those testaments of Christopher van Endhoven,
whose faulty state grieved the soul of George Joye.

In the following year, 1536, the year of its maker's death,
Tyndale's New Testament was first printed in England—a
sure sign that the tide was turning at last; and from that
time onward for thirty years a stream of English editions
appeared, besides others printed in the Low Countries. But
his influence is not to be measured by reprints of the testament alone; it is of even greater moment that his work was
caught up into Matthew's bible, and has passed into every
English bible that has since been printed. His labour was
earning its recompense, though he himself was away.*

* Tyndale's second New Testament has been reprinted in modern
times in Bagster's *English Hexapla*; his third has not been reprinted,
but the changes made in it are given in Francis Fry's *A bibliographical
description of the editions of the New Testament, Tyndale's version* (1878).
This book describes all the editions between 1526 and 1566.

CHAPTER XIII

EIGHT years ago Tyndale had foretold his martyrdom: I look, he said, for them to burn me also, if God will. The great ordeal was now at hand. An emissary at length was found to succeed in entrapping him. The story is told in full by Foxe, as he had received it from Thomas Poyntz.

"William Tyndale, being in the town of Antwerp, had been lodged about one whole year in the house of Thomas Poyntz, an Englishman who kept there a house of English merchants. About which time came thither one out of England, whose name was Henry Phillips, his father being customer of Poole, a comely fellow like as he had been a gentleman, having a servant with him, but wherefore he came, or for what purpose he was sent thither, no man could tell.

"Master Tyndale divers times was desired forth to dinner and supper amongst merchants; by the means whereof this Henry Phillips became acquainted with him, so that within short space Master Tyndale had a great confidence in him, and brought him to his lodging to the house of Thomas Poyntz, and had him also once or twice with him to dinner and supper, and further entered such friendship with him, that through his procurement he lay in the same house of the said Poyntz; to whom he shewed moreover his books and other secrets of his study; so little did Tyndale then mistrust this traitor.

"But Poyntz having no great confidence in the fellow, asked Master Tyndale how he came acquainted with this Phillips. Master Tyndale answered that he was an honest man, handsomely learned and very conformable [*i.e.* Lutheran in sympathy]. Then Poyntz, perceiving that he bare such favour to him, said no more, thinking that he was brought acquainted with him by some friend of his. The said Phillips, being in the town three or four days,

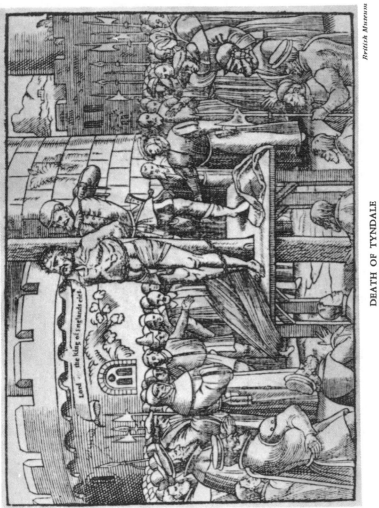

Facing p. 294

DEATH OF TYNDALE
(from Foxe's Acts and Monuments, 1563)

upon a time desired Poyntz to walk with him forth of the
town to shew him the commodities thereof; and in walking
together without the town had communication of divers
things, and some of the king's affairs: by the which talk
Poyntz as yet suspected nothing; but after, by the sequel
of the matter, he perceived more what he intended. In
the meantime this he well perceived, that he bare no great
favour either to the setting forth of any good thing or to
the proceedings of the king of England. But after, when
the time was past, Poyntz perceived this to be his mind, to
feel if he could perceive by him, whether he might break
with him in the matter, for lucre of money to help him to
his purpose [the seizure of Tyndale]; for he perceived
before that he [Phillips] was moneyed, and would that
Poyntz should think no less; but by whom [whence the
money came] it was unknown. For he had desired Poyntz
before to help him to divers things; and such things as he
named, he required might be of the best; for, said he, I
have money enough. But of this talk came nothing, but
that men should think he had some things to do; for
nothing else followed of his talk. So it was to be suspected,
that Phillips was in doubt to move this matter to any of
the rulers or officers of the town of Antwerp, for doubt it
should come to the knowledge of some Englishmen, and
by the means thereof Master Tyndale should have had
warning.

" So Phillips went from Antwerp to the court of Brussels,
which is from thence twenty-four English miles, the king
having there no ambassador; * for at that time the king
of England and the emperor were at a controversy for the
question betwixt the king and the lady Catherine, which
was aunt to the emperor, and the discord grew so much,
that it was doubted lest there should have been war between
the emperor and the king; so that Phillips, as a traitor
both against God and the king, was there the better retained, as also other traitors more besides him; who, after
he had betrayed Master Tyndale into their hands, shewed
himself likewise against the king's own person, and there
set forth things against the king. To make short, the said
Phillips did so much there, that he procured to bring from
thence with him to Antwerp that procurer-general, which
is the emperor's attorney, with certain other officers, as

* Hackett had died in October 1534; there was a very long interval
before his successor was appointed.

after followeth; the which was not done with small charges or expenses, from whomsoever it came.

" Within a while after, Poyntz sitting at his door, Phillips' man came unto him, and asked him whether Master Tyndale were there, and said his master would come to him; and so departed. But whether his master Phillips were in the town or not, it was not known, but at that time Poyntz heard no more, neither of the master nor of the man. Within three or four days after, Poyntz went forth to the town of Barrow, being eighteen English miles from Antwerp, where he had business to do for the space of a month or six weeks, and in the time of his absence Henry Phillips came again to Antwerp, to the house of Poyntz, and coming in, spake with his wife, asking her for Master Tyndale, and whether he would dine there with him, saying: What good meat shall we have? She answered: Such as the market will give. Then went he forth again, as it is thought, to provide and set the officers which he brought with him from Brussels, in the street and about the door. Then about noon he came again, and went to Master Tyndale, and desired him to lend him forty shillings; for (said he) I lost my purse this morning, coming over at the passage between this and Mechlin. So Master Tyndale took him forty shillings, the which was easy to be had of him, if he had it; for in the wily subtleties of this world he was simple and inexpert.

" Then said Phillips: Master Tyndale, you shall be my guest here this day. No, said Master Tyndale; I go forth this day to dinner, and you shall go with me, and be my guest, where you shall be welcome. So when it was dinner time, Master Tyndale went forth with Phillips and at the going out of Poyntz' house was a long narrow entry, so that two could not go in a front. Master Tyndale would have put Phillips before him, but Phillips would in no wise, but put Master Tyndale afore, for that he pretended to shew great humanity. So Master Tyndale, being a man of no great stature, went before, and Phillips, a tall comely person, followed behind him; who had set officers on either side of the door upon two seats, which, being there, might see who came in the entry; and coming through the same entry, Phillips pointed with his finger over Master Tyndale's head down to him, that the officers which sat at the door might see that it was he whom they should take; as the officers that took Master Tyndale afterwards told Poyntz, and said to Poyntz, when they had laid him in prison, that

they pitied to see his simplicity when they took him.*
Then they took him, and brought him to the emperor's
attorney or procurer-general, where he dined. Then came
the procurer-general to the house of Poyntz, and sent away
all that was there of Master Tyndale's, as well his books as
other things; and from thence Tyndale was had to the
castle of Vilford, eighteen English miles from Antwerp, and
there he remained until he was put to death."

So ends the first scene of the final act, and here we may
pause awhile. Who was this Henry Phillips? For a long
time nothing was known of him except what Foxe relates;
but it was assumed that he was a humble person, used as a
tool by men in authority. Of recent years, however, light
has been thrown upon him by the publication of the documents of Henry VIII's reign, and this fresh information is
for the first time gathered together here. He was the son
of one Richard Phillips, a man of note in the counties of
Dorset and Somerset, who in the course of a long life was
thrice member of parliament, twice high sheriff, and who
in 1533 was summoned to Westminster for the coronation
of Anne Boleyn. Richard lived at Charborough, five miles
from Poole, but he owned land in other places, and in
1538 he acquired an estate at Corfe Mullen, which remained
in the family for two hundred years. Other of his lands
were at Montacute, Somerset, and it was his grandson
Edward, the nephew of Henry, who, rising to wealth and
power in Elizabeth's reign to become master of the rolls,
built Montacute house, that glorious mansion which has
only lately (1931) passed from his family into the ownership
of the National Trust. Richard was also, as Foxe says,
customer of Poole, but he was no petty officer, as has been
supposed, but the chief authority; for he seems to have
leased all the tolls of the town and harbour. Henry, his
third son, had a good education and aspired to be a literary
man. Whether he was ever intended for the ministry of
the church is not clear, but he certainly had one or two

---

* In his preface to Daye's folio Foxe adds a further detail: " But
Tyndale, when he came near the door, espied the officers, and would
have shrunk back. Nay, said Phillips, by your leave you shall go forth;
and by force bare him forward upon the officers."

high ecclesiastical patrons. He is said to have been at Oxford, and no doubt he is the Henry Phillips who appears in the registers as taking the degree of bachelor of civil law in February 1533. But in the course of the next year or so he fell into disgrace; he robbed his father. Such at least is the ugly word applied to his deed by his enemies, but his own account, contained in half a dozen letters written to his parents and brothers in the early months of 1537, is scarcely more favourable. Having been entrusted by his father with a sum of money to pay to a person in London, he permitted himself on reaching that city to be tempted into play, and gambled away the whole. Not knowing whither to turn, and not daring to go home, he rode to court to take counsel with a Mr Semer—perhaps the Maurice Semer who was then incumbent of his father's parish of Charborough. Of his next movements he says nothing, except that ever since that date, three years ago, he has been in desperate poverty, and that now he is in the greatest extremity, about to sink beneath his adversities, unless his parents forgive him and hold out a helping hand. These letters are now in the Record Office, and were doubtless intercepted by Cromwell, ever on the look out for messages from traitors abroad. They have a false ring; their fawning, insincere tone gives us a base opinion of the writer.*

It was, then, a few months after he had grievously offended his father and brought shame upon himself, that Phillips appears in Brabant, and carries out a carefully conceived plan of apprehending Tyndale. He made Louvain his headquarters, a town devoted to the papal cause, and he is described as a student of the university. This may have been only a blind to cover his scheming,

---

* The letters, seven in all and undated, are misplaced in *L. & P.*, IX., 1138 ff. They cannot be earlier than the winter of 1536–7. They are addressed to his mother (from London), father, two brothers, two brothers-in-law, and Dr. Thomas Brerewood, chancellor of Exeter (all or most of these from Louvain). He says also that he has written to Dr Underhill, doubtless the prebendary of Sarum whose will was proved in 1538, and who seems to have been vicar of Axminster. In May 1537 he stated at Louvain that he had sent letters to his father baked in a loaf of bread (*L. & P.*, XII., (1), 1293). He spells his name Phyllypps, his father spells it Phelypps. What do the purists want us to do here?

but the place would be congenial to him; for he fancied himself as a scholar, and had a strong hankering after the life of the muses. At Louvain he was within easy reach of Antwerp, and could spy out the land at his leisure. The execution of his plot would indeed need money, both for his own expenses and perhaps for the payment of the officers, but with that he was well provided. Other witnesses tell us that, besides Poyntz. Whence came this money? One witness, Richard Layton, assumes that he was using the money that he had stolen from his father; but this seems to be a mere putting of two and two together; it is unlikely in itself, and it disagrees with Phillips' own story, that he gambled away the money, and found himself in poverty. Another witness, Thomas Tebold or Theobald, was told by Phillips himself in Louvain in July, that he held good benefices in the diocese of Exeter. This might have been brushed aside as a mere piece of boasting, or as a cover to conceal the real truth, were it not for the statement a few months later of a third witness, Robert Farryngton, that Phillips had had two benefices and a prebend, when he left England; and this information Farryngton seems (though the matter is not quite clear) to have received in England, and not from Phillips' own mouth in Louvain. Certainly the chancellor of the Exeter diocese was a patron of Phillips, and he may have helped him to these preferments; but if so, they must have run dry by the time he went oversea. No man with plenty of resources would need to rob his father, and if he foolishly gambled away money entrusted to him, he could replace it out of his own funds. In the above-mentioned series of letters he says no word of benefices—no, not even in that directed to his patron the chancellor. The tale is all of his own destitution and misery since his offence against his father; and those who met him after his departure from Louvain give the same account of his poverty. The conclusion seems irresistible. While in London after his theft, well-nigh in despair, not knowing whither to turn, he was approached by somebody, who, seeing in him a valuable tool, an educated man, hostile to the reformation, ready to turn his hand to anything, took advantage of his extremity, and offered him the job of entrapping Tyndale, supplying him also with money for the purpose. That there were great persons in the church behind Phillips, is stated by Poyntz and by Foxe; Theobald hints at it; and according to Halle it was a belief widely held at the time. Tyndale's betrayal, he writes, was accomplished " not, as many said, without the help and procurement of some of the bishops of the realm." Seven or eight weeks after the deed was done, we find Phillips in Louvain anxiously awaiting the return of his servant, whom he had despatched long ago with letters to England, and whose delay made him greatly afraid, lest he had been seized by Cromwell with the letters he carried. Clearly he had written something that he wished to conceal; what was it, and to whom? Likely enough a report to his employers of the successful accomplishment of his mission.*

We must not imagine that the bishops were too high-minded to stoop to such an intrigue. If Sir Thomas More used the traitor Holt against Frith, such men as Stokesley, Gardiner and Longland would not scruple to incite Phillips to treachery, if so they might put their arch-enemy out of the way. Can we then name the culprit? Unhappily not; but suspicion rests upon Stokesley. He was bishop of the capital city; he it was that was most active with Thomas More in the examination of Lutherans in 1531, when special inquiries were made about the lodging and appearance of Tyndale. It was his servant, John Tisen, an old pupil of Tyndale and therefore able to recognize him, who was seen in Antwerp about January 1533, but who kept away from the society of the Englishmen. Another servant of his, one Docwraye, a public notary, visited Antwerp for two weeks in the following July, as Vaughan reports.† All

---

* Foxe (1563) says that after the betrayal Phillips " procured and received more [money], wherewith to follow the suit " against Tyndale. Phillips himself told Theobald that he had a commission out to take Tyndale; the natural meaning of this is a commission from England.

† Doubtless Thomas Docwraye, a public notary, who became first master of the stationers' company. His will (1559) shows his strong papal sympathies.

this, together with the cruelty of his character, his zeal for persecution, his boasts on his deathbed of the number of heretics whom he had robbed of life, makes it reasonable enough to see in him the chief backer, if not the prime engineer, of the plot which destroyed Tyndale. But yet we cannot say that this is certain.

Whoever was the guilty person, it was not Henry VIII. Phillips detested the king and all his works, and was soon being searched for as a traitor and a rebel. Nor would Henry have employed as his tool such a good-for-nothing; he would have put the matter into the hands of an ambassador or other official agent, and left him to choose his own means. Cromwell too can be left out of account. On the whole he favoured Tyndale, and after his arrest made a vigorous effort to save him, not without the aid of his royal master. Indeed, the whole tone of the despatches from English agents abroad concerning Phillips during the next few years completely absolves the English government from complicity in the plot. He is spoken of throughout as an enemy to the state, and his betrayal of Tyndale, when mentioned at all, is made an aggravation of his offences.

Tyndale was arrested about the 21st of May, 1535, and remained in prison for more than sixteen months. There is still preserved among the archives at Brussels the entry of the payment to Adolf van Wesele, the lieutenant of the castle of Vilvorde, of the money expended by him, at the order of the procurer-general, in the " keeping of a certain prisoner, named Willem Tintalus, Lutheran, . . . for a year and one hundred and thirty-five days, at forty stivers the day." This entry stands under the heading: " Account of the confiscated goods of the Lutherans and heretical sects "; and therefore it would seem that Tyndale's imprisonment was paid for by himself and his fellow victims.

Vilvorde stands six miles north of Brussels, and is scarcely more distant from Louvain and Malines. It is a small town, but boasts an ancient history, and had been the residence of Edward III and other English kings. The castle, which stood upon the southern rampart, had been built in 1374 by one of the dukes of Brabant on the model of the Bastille, then lately erected in Paris. Its great strength must have pleased him well; for he designed it as a place of refuge for himself. It had seven towers, and was surrounded by a moat, spanned with three draw-bridges. In the eighteenth century it fell into ruins and was destroyed, but in Tyndale's day it served as the state prison of the Low Countries, and many notable men have lodged in its dungeons. Within this gloomy stronghold Tyndale would be safe enough, far away from the turbulent and free-thinking city of Antwerp, where the rulers winked at the advance of the Lutheran cause.

Whether the news of Tyndale's arrest reached the English house before the procurer-general came to seize the personal effects of the prisoner, we cannot tell. If it did, the wife of Poyntz would have a short space to secrete the more valuable of his possessions, if indeed she thought it wise to do so. Certainly some of his goods escaped seizure; for his book on the sacraments and that on Tracey's testament were found by his friends and printed: but these may have been already lodged in some hiding-place. We may, how-ever, be sure that when Mrs Poyntz heard what had happened, she would send post haste to her lord at Bergen. The news concerned not Tyndale only, but also the privileges of the English house, which might be considered to have been violated by the forcible entry of the officers; and the merchants probably made this a ground of complaint in the letter which they forthwith addressed to the government of the Low Countries. " Then incontinent," says Foxe, " by the help of English merchants were letters sent in favour of Tyndale to the court of Brussels." But such a request had small chance of being heeded. The rulers were becoming more severe against Lutheranism. Charles V seemed determined to make up for his impotence in Germany by wreaking his full vengeance on his hereditary dominions, where his writ still ran. Legally Tyndale was without doubt a heretic; and the laws against heresy were now more stringent than ever before. The merchants must have seen this well enough, and it is likely that they sent tidings of the arrest to the government of England also;

for it is from that quarter that the next steps on Tyndale's behalf came.   In all these activities Poyntz would be the chief mover; indeed, he was far from satisfied with the measures taken in Antwerp; he complains of the slackness of the governor of the English house, and believed that more vigorous action might have saved his friend.

But what might be expected from the intervention of the English government?   The outlook was not very promising. The king and the emperor were not on the best of terms. The days were long past when they were allies almost as a matter of course, and of late Henry had given his brother-sovereign much cause for displeasure.   For five years he had been laying ever heavier hands upon the church, and now was breaking once for all the tie that bound England to the papacy, and was building up a new order.   Fisher and More were even now being sent to the block as a warning to malcontents.   On the top of this, Charles conceived his honour to be touched by the divorce of his aunt Catherine.   Besides, Henry himself was lukewarm in Tyndale's cause.   He cared nothing for religious reform, and though he might wish to use Tyndale as a tool against the papal party, he would not press his cause, or risk anything to save him.   In fact he could not afford to favour him. As a set-off against his severity toward the papists, he was eager to prove that he was no Lutheran, and while sending some men to Tyburn for denying the royal supremacy, he was sending others to Smithfield on a charge of heresy against the sacraments.   Within a few days of Tyndale's apprehension fourteen Dutch anabaptists were sent to the stake in England.

In these circumstances it is hardly to be wondered at that Cromwell steered a rather slow and hesitating course.   It has indeed been thought that he instructed his godson, Thomas Theobald, whom he frequently employed as an emissary on the continent, and who was now setting forth for Nürnberg, to stop at Antwerp on the way, and to gather information about Tyndale; for at the end of July Theobald sends him a report from that city: but since this report deals with Phillips rather than with Tyndale, and is also very bare and meagre indeed, Cromwell's instructions cannot have been very ardent. Happily for us, however, Theobald wrote by the same post a second letter to Cranmer, with whom he was very friendly, and to him he imparts much more fully his news about Phillips and Tyndale; and we will therefore put this letter before the reader, leaving that to the secretary on one side. It is dated July 31, but the bulk of it seems to have been written about the middle of the month.

" Pleaseth it your grace to understand that I have delivered your letters unto Mr Thomas Leigh [a merchant adventurer]; which, according to your writing, hath delivered unto me twenty crowns of the [sum], which money, God willing, I shall deliver where your grace hath assigned within these sixteen days. I take my journey from Antwerp about the last day of July, and because, at my first arrivance to Antwerp, I found company ready to go up withal to Cologne, I went to see my old acquaintance at Louvain; whereas [where] I found Dr Bockenham, some time prior in the blackfriars in Cambridge [Latimer's old enemy], and another of his brethren with him. I had no leisure to commune long with them; but he showed me that at his departing from England he went straight to Edinburgh in Scotland, there continuing unto Easter last past [March 28]; and then came over to Louvain, where he and his companion doth continue in the house of the blackfriars there, having little acquaintance or comfort but for their money; for they pay for their meat and drink a certain sum of money in the year.

" All succour that I can perceive them to have, is only by him which hath taken Tyndale, called Harry Phillips, with whom I had long and familiar communication; for I made him believe that I was minded to tarry and study at Louvain. I could not perceive the contrary by his communication, but that Tyndale shall die, which he doth follow [urge] and procureth with all diligent endeavour, rejoicing much therein, saying that he had a commission out also for to have taken Dr Barnes and George Joye with other. Then I showed him that it was conceived both in England and in Antwerp that George Joye should be [was] of counsel with him in taking of Tyndale; and he answered that he never saw George Joye to his knowledge, much less he should know him. This I do write, because George Joye is greatly blamed and abused among merchants and many other, that were his friends, falsely and wrongfully.

"But this foresaid Harry Phillips shewed me that there was no man of his counsel but a monk of Stratford abbey beside London, called Gabriel Donne, which at that time was student in Louvain, and in house with this foresaid Harry Phillips. But now within these five or six weeks he is come to England, and by the help of Mr Secretary hath obtained an abbey of a thousand marks by the year in the west country.

"This said Phillips is greatly afraid (in so much as I can perceive) that the English merchants that be in Antwerp will lay watch to do him some displeasure privily. Wherefore of truth he hath sold his books in Louvain, to the value of twenty marks' worth sterling, intending to go hence to Paris; and doth tarry here upon nothing but of the return of his servant, which he hath long since sent to England with letters; and by cause of his long tarrying he is marvellously afraid lest he be taken, and come into Mr Secretary's handling with his letters. Either this Phillips hath great friends in England to maintain him here, or else, as he showed me, he is well beneficed in the bishopric of Exeter. He raileth at Louvain and in the queen of Hungary's court most shamefully against our king his grace and others. For, I being present, he called our king his highness *tyrannum, expilatorem reipublicae* [tyrant, spoiler of the commonwealth], with many other railing words, rejoicing that he trusteth to see the emperor to scourge his highness with his council and friends. Also he saith that Mr Secretary hath privily gone about matters here in Flanders and Brabant, which are secretly come to the knowledge of the queen of Hungary, the governess here, which she reckoneth one day at her pleasure and time to declare to his rebuke. What this meaneth, I cannot tell, neither I could hear no farther; but if I had tarried there any time, I should have heard more. . . .

"Written at Antwerp the last day of July by your bedeman and servant, ever to my small power—Thomas Tebold."

On the strength of this letter a belief has grown up, and now holds the field, that Gabriel Donne was hand in glove with Phillips in the betrayal of Tyndale, that he was an equal partner in the guilt, and that he was indeed the servant whom Phillips sent on messages to the English house before the arrest. Some writers even add that the gift of the abbey of Buckfastleigh in Devon was his blood-money, the reward of his successful treachery. But we have no right to paint him quite so black as this. It is very unlikely that he acted as Phillips' servant. Phillips certainly had a servant when Theobald wrote to Cranmer; for he was in England with his master's letters, and his return was daily expected. Why may not this have been the same servant, who was earlier sent to the English house? Phillips may well have employed him without letting him into the secret of the plot. Besides, Donne was a man at least as old as Tyndale, and probably older; he seems to have studied at both Oxford and Cambridge; and though we do not know that Tyndale had overlapped with him at either university, still it would be hardly prudent to send a man of his standing and education as a servant. If any-one recognized him, suspicion would at once be excited. That Donne knew of the plot is all that Theobald tells us. Certainly he must have approved of it, and he may have helped with his advice: but that is not quite the same thing as becoming an active partaker therein. Nor is it likely that the presentation to the abbey was a reward for the capture of Tyndale: for the news of the latter cannot have reached England much before June 1, and when it did, it would hardly be a passport to Cromwell's favour. Ecclesiastical preferment must have been much speedier in those days than in these, if a deed that was known only at the beginning of June was recompensed with a post of dignity by the beginning of July. It is true that Donne returned to England within a week or two of the betrayal, which is somewhat suspicious; but there may have been other reasons for this. Foxe says nothing of his guilt, and indeed does not even mention his name; and Phillips ever describes himself as the chief actor, and is so described by all his enemies. Donne truly was no heroic figure, but we must not outrun the evidence, and make him guiltier than we need.

The hopes entertained by Phillips of taking Barnes and Joye were disappointed. Barnes was now in England, and though he sailed for Antwerp at the end of July, it was only to touch at it on his way to Hamburg. Joye had left the Low Countries, and we find him at Calais on June 4, lodging in the house of Edward Foxe, the king's almoner, whom he had known at Cambridge, and through whom he now makes overtures to Cromwell, begging for permission to return to England, and promising not to speak against the current doctrine of the sacrament. There is reason to think that his request was granted, and that before long he was again in his native land.

But Theobald's mention of the threat to Barnes and Joye awakens our interest in another letter, which has hitherto escaped the notice of all writers upon Tyndale. This was written on May 1 from Antwerp by one George Collins, a mercer of London, who made frequent journeys to the continent. The receiver of it was another mercer dwelling in London, whose Christian name also was George, but his surname has been torn away. It runs as follows:—

" In Antwerp the 1st day of May, 1535.
" RIGHT WORSHIPFUL SIR,

" I recommend me unto you, trusting in God that you be in good health, which our Lord long for to continue to his pleasure and to your hearty desire.

" Sir, it may please you to understand that the stadholder of Barrow spake with Mr Flegge in the church, and he said : Mr Flegge, there is commission come from the procurer-general of Brussels to take three Englishmen, whereof one is Dr Barnes. Notwithstanding the stadholder said : We would be loth to do anything which were displeasure to the company [i.e. the merchant adventurers]. Wherefore he willeth Mr Flegge to give Mr Doctor warning : so that Mr Flegge took so great kindness withal, that he forgot to know who the other two persons shall be. By my next letter I shall write you what be the names of the other two persons.

I pray you, show Mr Doctor hereof; and thus our Lord preserve you in health. Amen.

"Yours assured GEORGE COLLINS."

Now this letter fits in uncommonly well with that of Theobald. In both three prominent Englishmen are to be taken; in both one of the three is Barnes—a singular thing, since Barnes had not resided in Antwerp for some three years.* It seems plain that by the end of April Phillips had persuaded the procurer-general to strike at the three ringleaders of Lutheranism, Tyndale, Barnes and Joye, and had offered his own assistance in their apprehension. The procurer-general therefore sent an order for their arrest to Bergen, thinking perhaps that one of them might visit the fair, which lasted till the end of April: but the stadholder gave a friendly hint to Flegge, who was one of the English merchants. This would explain why Joye is found at Calais at the beginning of June, and is so eager to make his peace and return to England. He had learnt of his peril, and fled from the Netherlands. But if so, how is it that Tyndale was not more upon his guard? Nay, why did Joye himself remain in Antwerp until the latter half of the month? for he reached Calais on May 20 at earliest, and perhaps even a week or ten days later.† In fact, it looks as if he were still in Antwerp when Tyndale was arrested; otherwise the merchants would hardly have suspected him of being a partner in the betrayal. To these questions we can give no certain answer. It can scarcely be that Flegge failed to make inquiry for the names of the other two Englishmen who were in jeopardy. More likely the reformers were well hardened in perils and alarms, and having friends upon the town council were confident of receiving timely warning, should the procurer-general send to Antwerp an order for their arrest. But however this

* He was in England from August 1534 to January 1535. Then he returned to Hamburg with Aepinus, and in March paid a flying visit to Melanchthon at Wittenberg. On May 27 we find him again in London. Perhaps he touched at Antwerp at the end of April.

† Edward Foxe landed at Calais on May 19 (*Chronicle of Calais*; *L. & P.*, VIII., 732), and writes on June 4 that "George Joye, ever since his coming to Calais, hath been lodged with me in my house."

may be, Tyndale remained where he was, and so delivered
himself into his enemy's hand.

We can well imagine the longing and impatience with
which Poyntz waited for the intervention from England.
He must have heard of Theobald's visit and of his intimacy
with Cromwell and Cranmer; for Theobald had discussed
with the merchants, and no doubt with Poyntz himself, the
arrest of Tyndale and the misdeeds of Phillips, and his
banker Thomas Leigh was a member of the English house.
But action must be speedy if it were to avail. When Theobald arrived, already nearly two months had passed since
the arrest, and however slow the process of law might be
in the Low Countries, each week that passed added to the
danger. After waiting a month, Poyntz determined to
bring private influence to bear. His elder brother John,
lord of the manor of North Ockenden in Essex, had been
for years in the royal household, and might be able to pull
wires at court, so as to press the matter upon the notice of
the authorities. Thomas therefore writes on August 25 a
long letter to his brother:—

> Brother, I write to you on a matter greatly con-
> cerning the king. My love of my country and my duty
> to my prince compels me to speak, lest the king be
> misled and brought into injury by men, yes traitors,
> who, under colour of forwarding his honour, seek to
> bring their own purposes to pass. I do not name
> them, but it is clear that it must be the papists who
> are at the bottom of it. " For whereas it was said here
> the king had granted his gracious letters in the favour
> of one William Tyndale, for to have been sent hither;
> the which is in prison and like to suffer death, except
> it be through his gracious help; it is thought those
> letters be stopped. This man was lodged with me
> three quarters of a year, and was taken out of my house
> by a sergeant-of-arms, otherwise called a door-warder,
> and the procurer-general of Brabant; the which was
> done by procurement out of England, and, as I sup-
> pose, unknown to the king's grace till it was done. For
> I know well, if it had pleased his grace to have sent
> him a commandment to come into England, he would
> not have disobeyed it, to have put his life in jeopardy

[i.e. even at the risk of his life]." But these privy lurkers, perceiving that the king meant to send for Tyndale, and fearing that he would hear him charitably, as no doubt he would, wished to hinder a thing so unfavourable to their interests, and therefore—so it is supposed—they have represented to the king or the council, that Tyndale's death in Brabant would be to the king's high honour and profit. In fact however Tyndale's death would hurt the king in several ways, as they very well know. Whatever be the method they have used, these crafty fellows ought to be ashamed of their deed: but they merely desire the king's favour and their own promotions and power, and are past shame. "But a poor man [i.e. Poyntz] that has no promotion, nor looks for none, having no quality whereby he might obtain honour, but of a very natural zeal, and fear of God and his prince, had liefer live a beggar all days of his life, and put himself in jeopardy to die, rather than to live and see those leering counsellors to have their purpose; for some men perceive more than they can express by words, the which sorrow it inwardly till they see remedy.

"And by the means that this poor man, William Tyndale, hath lain in my house three quarters of a year, I know that the king has never a truer hearted subject to his grace this day living; and for that he does know that he is bound by the law of God to obey his prince, I wot it well; he would not do the contrary to be made lord of the world, howsoever the king's grace is informed. What care these papists for that? For their pomps and high authority has always been holden up by murder and shedding the blood of innocents, causing princes by one mean or other to consent with them to the same."

Brother, twenty years ago the king received the style of defender of the faith, and right well has he lived up to this title, though in a way other than the givers imagined. God has entered him with the right battle, and I pray will give him victory. The death of this man will be a "great hindrance to the gospel, and to the enemies of it one of the highest pleasures. But and it would please the king's highness to send for this man, so that he might dispute his articles with them at large, which they lay to him, it might, by the mean thereof, be so opened to the court and the council of

this country, that they would be at another point with
the bishop of Rome within a short space. And I think
he shall shortly be at a point to be condemned; for
there are two Englishmen at Louvain that do and have
applied it sore, taking great pains to translate out of
English into Latin in those things that may make
against him, so that the clergy here may understand it,
and to condemn him, as they have done all others, for
keeping opinions contrary to their business, the which
they call the order of holy church.

"Brother, the knowledge that I have of this man
causes me to write as my conscience bids me; for the
king's grace should have of him at this day as high a
treasure as of any one man living, that has been of no
greater reputation. Therefore I desire you that this
matter may be solicited to his grace for this man, with
as good effect as shall lie in you, or by your means to
be done, for in my conscience there be not many perfecter men this day living, as knows God. Brother, I
think that if Walter Marsh, now being governor of the
English house, had done his duty effectually here at
this time, there would have been a remedy found for
this man. There be many men care not for a matter,
so as they may do aught to make their actions seem
fair, in avoiding themselves, that they be not spied."

Thomas Poyntz was, as he himself says, not very good at
expressing his meaning in words, but his heart was in the
right place. It may be, too, that he misjudges the position
of things, and over-estimates both the king's will to save
Tyndale, and his power to influence the government of the
Netherlands, but we forget this when we read his letter.
Out of all those concerned in the rescue of Tyndale, he
was the only man with a single eye, the only man willing
to risk himself in the cause. His letter indeed came too late
to be of use: for his brother forwarded it to Cromwell on
September 21, and by that time the secretary had already
taken action on behalf of Tyndale.

That he did not act without first consulting his master is
proved by a document preserved in the Record Office, and
described as one of Cromwell's *Remembrances*, a memorandum
paper for one of his visits to the palace, in which we find

the following entry:—" to know the king's pleasure for Tyndale, and whether I shall write or not." The document is undated, but other entries make it perfectly plain that it belongs to the latter part of August.* Henry must have granted his permission; for at the beginning of September Cromwell composes letters to two leading members of the privy council of Brabant. One is the president, by name Carondolet, who was archbishop of Palermo, and the other the marquis of Bergen-op-Zoom. With both men he had been in frequent touch, and less than a year ago he and the archbishop had become joint executors of ambassador Hackett. The letters have perished, but their tenor is plain to see. To claim anything of right would be useless, since Tyndale was being tried as an offender against the laws of the Low Countries. The only hope was to bring personal influence to bear, and to ask for Tyndale's release, and his despatch to England, as a matter of grace. When completed, the letters were sent to Stephen Vaughan, who was then in London, and he acknowledges the receipt of them on September 4 (" your two letters devised for Tyndale," as he calls them), and promises to forward them at once to Flanders. Whether he read them first, we know not; but he can hardly have been very hopeful of success, for he ends his letter with the words: " it were good the king had one living in Flanders, that were a man of reputation."

Vaughan sends the letters by the hand of George Collins to Robert Flegge, who was not unknown to Cromwell. Flegge received them on September 10, and on the 22nd wrote to the secretary, enclosing the answers of the two councillors.

I inquired at once, he says, whether the two lords were at court or not, and learnt that the marquis had departed two days before for Germany. As the letters were of importance, I sent one of our own merchants [Poyntz] after him, to deliver his letter and bring back the answer,

* *L. & P.*, IX., 498. One entry is: " touching the royal assent and congé d'élire for Hereford." The royal assent to Foxe's election was given on September 2.

and I wrote myself a letter to the marquis, desiring him to
commission one of his friends at court, to act in his stead
on your behalf in any matter of weight, of which your letter
may treat. His reply I have received; he writes that he
is very sorry to be absent from court, and so unable to
render the king's highness and you such service as he would
wish; but he has written to the bishop of Palermo, begging
him strongly to do everything to further your wishes; for
he can do most in the matter. This letter from the marquis
to the archbishop, together with your own letter to the
same, the messenger has presented, and begged for a
favourable and speedy answer. The archbishop spoke with
the queen and council, and has written you the answer
which I send by the same bearer. I pray God it may be
to the king's pleasure and yours.

Flegge's letter gives us the bare facts only; but we have
also, preserved in Foxe, the story of Poyntz himself, and this
must be set out in full, not only for its own interest, but
because his enthusiastic zeal landed him into the selfsame
danger from which he was trying to deliver his friend.

" Not long after, letters were directed out of England to
the council at Brussels, and sent to the merchant adventurers
[i.e. Flegge], commanding them to see that with speed they
should be delivered. Then such of the chiefest of the merchants as were there at that time, being called together,
required the said Poyntz to take in hand the delivery of
those letters, with letters also from them [Flegge] in the
favour of Master Tyndale, to the lord of Barrow and others;
the which lord of Barrow (as it was told Poyntz by the
way) at that time was departed from Brussels, as the chiefest
conductor of the eldest daughter of the king of Denmark
to be married to the Palsgrave; who after he heard of his
departure did ride after, the next way, and overtook him
at Akon [Alken], where he delivered to him his letters;
the which, when he had received and read, he made no
direct answer, but somewhat objecting said: There were of
their countrymen that were burned in England not long
before; as indeed there were anabaptists burnt in Smithfield; and so Poyntz said to him: Howbeit, said he, whatsoever the crime was, if his lordship or any other nobleman
had written, requiring to have had them, he thought they
should not have been denied. Well, said he, I have no

leisure to write; for the princess is ready to ride. Then said Poyntz: If it shall please your lordship, I will attend upon you unto the next baiting-place: which was at Maestricht. If you so do, said the lord, I will advise myself by the way what to write. So Poyntz followed him from Akon to Maestricht, the which are fifteen miles asunder; and there he received letters of him, one to the council there [at Brussels], another to the company of merchant adventurers, and another to the lord Cromwell.* So Poyntz rode from thence to Brussels, and then and there delivered to the council the letters out of England with the lord of Barrow's letters also; and received eftsoons answer into England of the same by letters, which he brought to Antwerp to the English merchants, who required him to go with them into England; and he, very desirous to have Master Tyndale out of prison, let not for to take pains, with loss of time in his own business and occupying: but diligently followed with the said letters, which he there delivered to the council, and was commanded by them to tarry until he had other letters, of the which he was not despatched thence in a month after [end of October]. At length, the letters being delivered him, he returned again, and delivered them to the emperor's council at Brussels, and there tarried for answer of the same.

" When the said Poyntz had tarried three or four days, it was told him by one that belonged to the chancery, that Master Tyndale should have been delivered to him according to the tenor of the letters; but Phillips, being there, followed the suit against Master Tyndale, and hearing that he should be delivered to Poyntz, and doubting lest he should be put from his purpose, he knew none other remedy but to accuse Poyntz, saying that he was a dweller in the town of Antwerp, and there had been a succourer of Tyndale, and was one of the same opinion, and that all this was only his own labour and suit, to have Master Tyndale at liberty, and no man's else. Thus upon his information and accusation Poyntz was attached by the procurer-general."

* Foxe (1563) is fuller: " And there he caused Poyntz to sup with him, and in the morning after breakfast, while his secretary was directing his letters, one to the lady his wife at Brussels, another to the council, etc., he talked very familiarly with the foresaid Poyntz of his journey, and of the company of men at arms which were there with him: for, said he, we know not whether we ride amongst our friends or enemies. And there he delivered me his letters."

So ended Poyntz' attempt to rescue his friend. His experiences as prisoner are described at length in Foxe's first edition, and as they throw light upon the procedure that must have been observed in Tyndale's case, it will be well to set them out here: but not in Foxe's own words; for his narrative is so rambling and obscure, that the reader will be glad to be spared the labour of extracting the meaning for himself.

Poyntz was arrested at the beginning of November. He was delivered not to prison, but to the keeping of two sergeants of arms, one of whom lodged him in his private house. The same evening the procurer-general with one of the chancery visited him, and swore him to make true answer to all questions that should be asked; for they wished to obtain a written statement of his opinions, so that there would be no need any more to examine him in person. The next day they came again, and every day for five or six days, and examined Poyntz in all upon more than a hundred articles, " as well of the king's affairs as of the message concerning Tyndale, of his [Poyntz] aiders and of his religion." From this lengthy inquisition the procurer-general drew up twenty-three or twenty-four articles in writing, and " declared the same," that is, formally put them in against Poyntz to the commissioners appointed to decide the case; and a copy was delivered to Poyntz himself, that he could make an answer; and he was permitted to have an advocate and proctor to help him. His reply was to be ready in eight days, and then after another eight days the prosecution would again reply, and so on by eight-day intervals, " till the process were ended." Meanwhile he was to send no messenger to Antwerp or elsewhere except by the post of the town of Brussels; nor was he to receive or to write any letters save in the Dutch [Flemish] tongue, so that they could be read by the procurer-general— a proceeding, as Foxe remarks, " contrary to all right and equity," since the procurer-general was party against him. Nor was any to talk with Poyntz in any language but Flemish, so that his keepers might understand what was being said. This last rule was indeed once broken, when the provincial of the whitefriars came to dinner in the house, and brought with him a young novice, an Englishman, who was encouraged after the meal to talk with Poyntz; wherein (says Foxe) " the purpose and great policy was easy to be perceived." Poyntz and the novice had " much pretty talk," as of Sir Thomas More and bishop Fisher, whose fate the novice greatly lamented, and accounted death in such a quarrel to be a martyrdom.

On the eighth day " the commissioners that were appointed " came to receive the answer; but Poyntz put them off with the pretext that he was a prisoner, and could not go abroad to visit the counsel whom he had named, and that they had not come to him, and indeed could not come to him, unless licensed by the commissioners to do so. They therefore gave him another eight days to draw his reply. This time Poyntz did compile a statement of his opinions, but only a general one, instead of answering each article singly. This they refused to accept on their next coming, and gave him another week's grace. Poyntz, however, was full of resource in making excuses, and by one means or another " he trifled them off from Hallowtide [November 1] until Christmas even, with dilatories from eighth day to eighth day."

On the morning of December 24 the commissioners came again for his answer, and not finding it—indeed, no counsel had come to him in all those weeks—determined to bring matters to a head. " Bring in your answer this day," they said, " or else ye shall be put from it." Poyntz, seeing that he should be condemned without answer, obtained with much ado the services of his advocate: and by his help drew up the document, and delivered it to the procurer-general; but only after eight o'clock, so long had the advocate been in coming.

But this was not the end of the matter. After an interval the prosecution made a further reply in writing, and then Poyntz replied again in his turn; and so it went on " with replication duplic, with other answers each to other," until the process was ended. If this phrase is to be taken strictly, there must have been at least two sets of attack and defence after Christmas eve; and these exchanges—all of them of course in writing—would account for another month, if we assume an interval of a week between each visit. Whenever the commissioners came to Poyntz, " that traitor Phillips accompanied them to the door, in following the process against him, as he also did against Master Tyndale, as they who had Poyntz in keeping showed him." When the two cases were completed, each party—viz. Poyntz and the procurer-general—delivered to the commissioners a bag, with his process in writing, and took in return an inventory of all the documents therein contained. These bags rested in the commissioners' hands, and doubtless would form the basis of their decision.

But meanwhile Poyntz had conceived the idea of escaping. At some time during the process he had asked to be set at liberty under surety. At first they granted his request, and he thereupon sent a post to the English merchants at Antwerp, thinking that they would not let him lack help, having themselves urged him to the work. Indeed, Poyntz claimed later to have written proof that they had promised to support him, and to pay his costs and losses, but this they denied. Whether they refused to stand security is not clear; for in this section Foxe has one of his worst fits of rambling: it looks as if they did; but in any case the commissioners withdrew their concession, and refused to take surety for the body of Poyntz.

But though they would not release him on bail, they demanded surety for the expenses of his imprisonment; for he was in private custody, and they reckoned the cost of his own keep, and of the victuals and wages of the two officers, to amount to 5s. a day. They made this demand when they received the last instalment of Poyntz' case, that is to say, on the visit preceding the delivery of the bags, and they ordered him to find the sureties within eight days. Poyntz, seeing their changeableness, and judging by the general trend of things (as indeed he had been secretly warned, doubtless by his warders) that his life was in danger, put a bold face on the matter, and promised to produce sureties—not that he expected to find any, but to gain time, fearing they would send him to a stronger prison. He also asked of them a messenger to send for the sureties, hoping to escape meanwhile. When therefore the commissioners came after a week, and took the bags, they demanded the sureties. Poyntz alleged in excuse that he had been unable to get a messenger, though he had more than once asked his keepers for one: which indeed he had done, but with no great urgency, for he desired to obtain another postponement. The commissioners sent him from the room, and conferring together, agreed to give him another week's grace; and then calling him in, instructed the officer to get him a messenger: which he did. Poyntz therefore wrote letters to the English merchants, who were now at Barrow, probably for the fairs; but he resolved in the meantime to break his prison. He had already been confined for twelve or thirteen weeks, and he saw well that his tarrying there meant death. If he were taken in escaping, it would still be only death. Without waiting for the return of the messenger, "in the night by a mean he conveyed himself" from the house, and at the opening of the town gate slipped out of Brussels; and although a hue and cry was raised, and horsemen were sent after him, knowing the country well, he escaped and came into England. Among the archives of Brussels there is still preserved the record of the heavy fine of £80, levied by the council upon John Baers for having "through breach of duty and negligence" permitted the escape of "a prisoner accused of Lutheranism, named Thomas Poyntz, an Englishman," who had been committed to his charge by order of the procurer-general.

But though Poyntz failed to save his friend, his failure wins him the greatest honour, and no biographer of Tyndale can withhold his tribute. He was the life and soul of all the efforts made in the Low Countries, and when he was removed from the scene, the other merchants did nothing. For two months he neglected his own business, travelling to and fro with letters, and even crossing the sea to England, where he kicked his heels for four weeks, while the great men made up their minds. That the task was hazardous to himself, he must have known; and so it proved. He gained thereby not only heavy financial loss, but three months' imprisonment, and came within an ace of death. Nor was this the full tale of his sacrifices. After his flight he was banished from the Netherlands, losing his goods and occupation there, and he never regained his old prosperity. Worse than this, his wife, Anna van Calva, who was a native of Antwerp, refused to join him in England, and for many years he was parted from his children. It is likely that she had property in her native land, which she was unwilling to abandon, and she may have thought him a quixotic fool for fishing in troubled waters, and risking his own interest and hers for the sake of a Lutheran. In due course indeed he succeeded, on his brother's death in 1547, to the ancestral manor of North Ockenden, but it is thought that he was too poor to live there; and four years later he was glad to obtain a royal order, authorizing collections to be made to defray his heavy debts and losses, dating from the time of his imprisonment. In a worldly way his life was ruined by his generous championship of Tyndale: but the lustre of his deed is his perpetual possession. The poor fools of this world sometimes turn out to have a higher wisdom than the prudent; and in the long line of tablets of the Poyntz family, which is the glory of North Ockenden church, none awakes so lively an interest in the visitor as that of this simple and warm-hearted man. His epitaph is in Latin, and runs as follows:—

" He, for faithful service to his prince and ardent profession of evangelical truth, suffered bonds and imprisonment beyond the sea, and would plainly have been destined to death, had he not, trusting in divine providence, saved himself in a wonderful manner by breaking his prison. In this chapel he now sleeps peacefully in the Lord, 1562."

Poyntz made his escape in the beginning of February.* We may suppose that on his arrival in England he did all

* He was arrested at Hallowtide, about November 1. He had been twelve or thirteen weeks in prison, when he wrote for his security less than a week before his escape. The matter is perfectly clear. It is strange to find Demaus dating it in the middle of March, and the editor of *Letters and Papers* (X., 222) in the first week in January.

that in him lay to spur the rulers into further action on behalf of his friend; but there is no record that Cromwell did anything more, no, not though he was pressed thereto by Stephen Vaughan, who returned to the Low Countries early in March, and was in frequent correspondence with his patron. Writing on April 13 upon other matters, Vaughan adds a postscript concerning Tyndale: "If now you send me but your letter to the privy council, I could deliver Tyndale from the fire, so it come by time, for else it will be too late." It may be that Vaughan was deluded by his sanguine hopes, and that Cromwell judged the position of things more truly than his agent. One would be glad to think that the secretary did all that was possible to save the great translator: but to Tyndale himself it mattered little. Had he been sent to England, he could hardly have escaped the fire for long. He was too prominent a man to be overlooked, and he had bitter and powerful foes. His radical opinions, his outspoken nature, his outstanding abilities would soon have brought him into trouble. He could not hedge nor trim, nor speak with a double voice. If Lambert and Barnes fell victims during the ensuing four years, Tyndale could not hope to be left in peace; and the stain would now rest upon his native land of doing to death one of the noblest of her sons.

But if Henry and his minister failed to save Tyndale, it is fair to say that they were no more successful in destroying their enemy Phillips, who in the security of Louvain was railing against the tyrant of England. Of his proceedings they received further tidings from Robert Farryngton, a scholar of Cambridge, who visited the town in the latter part of the year 1535. It has been hitherto supposed that he was sent thither by Cromwell as a spy, but this seems to be a mistake: for a fragment of a letter from Richard Layton to Cromwell, written early in 1539, makes it plain that Farryngton had been at Louvain for his own concerns, and on his return to England was introduced by Layton to Cromwell. Its opening words are of great interest to us:—

" When he [Phillips] departed out of England he robbed his own father, and so that time had more money than all the Englishmen that then were there [at Louvain]; and anon after Tyndale's taking he began to betray his country, as keeping certain Englishmen, students there at Louvain, prisoners. Which thing (as I suppose) I first opened unto your lordship myself, and brought with me a scholar, then returned from Louvain, called Farryngton, to declare unto you the circumstance and the whole truth of that traitor, his dealing and behaviour that time there."

Cromwell must have asked Farryngton to hold himself in readiness to make further inquiries; for on January 12 1536 the latter writes from Cambridge: " Pleaseth it your very good mastership that I might be ascertained . . . whether it may please you to command me any more service in the matter, that I did show your mastership when I came from Louvain; and I shall be glad with all my heart to give all diligence, to accomplish your pleasure therein "; otherwise he asks leave to go from Cambridge to his friends. At the end he puts a postscript:—" Pleaseth it your mastership, as I am credibly informed, Phillips had two benefices and a prebend when he went over the sea; what order his friends have taken with them since his departing, your mastership may have soon knowledge."

The news received by the king through this and other channels of Phillips' treasonable doings goaded him at last into striking at him direct, and at the end of March 1536 he writes to the queen regent and to the emperor, demanding the surrender of Phillips and of another criminal named Griffith, who had taken refuge in the imperial dominions. At the same time he writes to the consuls and senate of Nürnberg, asking them to seize the two men, if they should pass through the town on their way to Italy. Phillips, however, travelled through Germany in safety, though dogged by charges of treason, and reached Rome early in May. In the papal court he produced letters of commendation from the queen regent, and gave himself out as a kinsman of Sir Thomas More: but Henry's long arm reached him even here. The English ambassadors informed the cardinal, who had taken him up, that he was a scoundrel and a traitor, and so checkmated his schemes. From Italy he passed to France, and

here too was undermined by the same accusations.   In Paris
he is discovered " alto ragged and torn " by an old Oxford
friend, is helped by him with clothes and lodging, and is
said to have run away with some of the apparel of his bene-
factor.   Thence he returned to London, and fled abroad
once more to Louvain, and from these two cities he wrote
early in 1537 the seven letters of which we have already
spoken.   In the summer he is still at Louvain, trying
to insinuate himself into the entourage of cardinal Pole,
but in danger from the English ambassador who is on the
watch to entrap him.   In January 1538 he is again at Louvain, writing a cringing letter to his old patron, the chancellor
of Exeter; complaining that he has been driven by poverty
to take service with the imperial army, and asking him to
reconcile him to his parents and restore him to the muses.
In the autumn he arrives in Italy, clad as a Swiss soldier,
with German boots, having walked from Flanders.   He
comes to ask help from Pole, but is suspected of intending
to murder him, and is forbidden the territory of Venice.
Destitute and in great distress he sells his clothes, and
returns to Flanders.   Here early in 1539 he is persuaded to
give himself up to the English ambassador, so that he may
be sent to England, on a promise of pardon from the king,
but he thinks better of it, slips out of his confinement in the
ambassador's house, and is accused of robbing his captor.
His extradition is then demanded from the queen regent, but
she plays for time, and refuses compliance under various
pretexts.   At the end of April he is included in an act of
attainder, passed by parliament against a number of traitors
abroad.   The next year he is again in the Low Countries,
and once more in trouble and difficulty; and our final news
of him dates from the summer of 1542, when he is seized in
Vienna as a traitor against the king of England and the
king of Hungary, and is in peril of losing his eyes or his
life.   The latter sovereign, indeed, refused to deliver him
up to the English ambassador, and seemed disposed to champion him; but we do not know whether he proceeded against
him on his own account, or how Phillips escaped from his
predicament.   Thus we lose sight of him; and although the

rumour repeated by Foxe ("the saying so goeth," are his words) that Phillips, having for no long time enjoyed the price of innocent blood, "was consumed at last with lice," may be the invention of poetic justice, still we can hardly doubt that after so chequered a career he came to a bad end. We take our leave of him, disowned by his parents, cast aside by his friends, denounced by his country, shunned by the very party for whose sake he had marred his life, mistrusted by all, valued only as a tool, friendless, homeless, hopeless, destitute, fated to go down to history as the author of one perfidious deed.

But it is time to return to William, sitting in his cell at Vilvorde castle. Scanty as our direct information is, nevertheless by comparing it with the known procedure in heresy-trials in the Low Countries, we can draw a fair picture of the course of events. All was done in private until the very end of the process; there would be no public appearance of the prisoner until the time for sentence arrived, and even this could be pronounced behind closed doors, if the commissioners thought fit. The process proper seems to have begun with the drawing up of the formal accusation. To this end the Lutheran books seized in Tyndale's room would be a valuable weapon, and particularly those of his own authorship; but these latter were in the English tongue, which was little known in the Netherlands in the sixteenth century, and some time would be needed for their translation into Latin. But in any case the testimony of printed books would be no substitute for a personal examination of the accused, leading to a written confession of his opinions. Within a day or two of his arrest, therefore, perhaps even on the same evening, Tyndale would be visited by the procurer-general and the notary, would be sworn, and questioned about his life, writings and doctrines. This examination might be long or short. In Poyntz' case it lasted six or seven days, in the case of Enzinas, the Spaniard arrested at Brussels in 1543 for translating the New Testament into his mother tongue, it took more than a fortnight; but in Tyndale's case it may well have continued for an even longer period.

This first stage of the proceedings would not be under the

control of the procurer-general alone. As soon as the commissioners were appointed to try the case, they would take a hand, and one or more of them would be present at each examination. They were appointed by the emperor or his deputy, as soon as might be after the arrest of the prisoner, and they exercised undisputed authority; the ordinary tribunals of the law did not come into play at all. Such commissions were usually composed of four or five privy councillors, three or four theologians to act as advisers on matters of divinity, and a few local magistrates. The latter were thrown in as a sop to local feeling, which was rather restive at the overruling of the courts of justice, but in practice they were little better than shadows, when matched against the overwhelming prestige of the councillors. As Tyndale was a foreigner and had no local ties, it seems unlikely that any magistrates were put on the commission; at all events we hear of none: but the theologians played a big part. Strictly they may have been assessors rather than judges of the case; but in the trial of a clerk the difference would be of small moment.

The commission to try Tyndale was appointed by the queen-regent; and the account of the moneys paid to its members, and to others concerned in the case, is extant in the archives of Belgium. In this document are mentioned first the procurer-general; then the three theologians Ruard Tapper, James Latomus and Jan Doye, all canons of Louvain and doctors in divinity; then William van Caverschoen, who was secretary of de Lattre, the inquisitor-apostolic of the Low Countries; then four members of the council, seemingly lawyers, one of whom was named Godfrey de Mayers; and lastly follow nine names, of servants and messengers of the council. For his services in destroying the arch-enemy the procurer-general received £128, the three theologians and the inquisitor's secretary between them £149, Godfrey de Mayers £54, and none of the others more than £10: from which we may gather that the main burden of the inquiry into Tyndale's case fell upon Godfrey de Mayers, the procurer-general, the inquisitor's secretary, and the theologians. These seem large sums; but it was considered good policy to pay liberally, in order to stimulate the zeal for the hunting down of Lutherans.

The four privy councillors are no more than names to us; but of the theologians two are notable enough to be described to the reader. The first is the celebrated James Masson or Latomus, a tiny little man, now about sixty years of age, born in Hainault, who after taking his master's degree in Paris came to Louvain, where in 1519 he proceeded doctor of theology with the greatest brilliance, his scholars defraying the whole of his expenses. Since then he had been a valiant and constant champion of the papal religion against humanism and Lutheranism. He had crossed swords not only with Luther, but with Erasmus, whose liberal views were anathema to him. Erasmus, however, praises his learning, and in this very year he was advanced to the professorship. He was a scholastic of scholastics, and if his portrait does not belie him, with its thin and close-pressed lips, hard eyes, and cold and forbidding expression, he was a man of keen intellectual power, but of little warmth of feeling. We can well imagine how simple and uneducated persons, stronger in heart than in head, would tremble before his grim and merciless intellectualism: yet, as we shall see, in his dealings with Tyndale he shows himself not unkindly.

Even more famous was Ruard Tapper, commonly called Enchusanus from his birthplace Enkhuisen in Holland, a younger man, forty-eight years of age, who had spent all his academic life in Louvain, and graduated doctor at the same time as Latomus. He was now professor, chancellor of the university, and just becoming dean of St Peter's, the chief church of the town. Less combative than Latomus, he burnt with perhaps an even greater zeal for the extirpation of protestantism. In 1523 he had acted as theological assessor in the trial of the Augustinian monks of Antwerp, and had played the same part in many like cases since then; and nine months after Tyndale's death he was appointed by the pope inquisitor-general of the Low Countries. Here he had a wide field for his energies, and entered with ardour into the work. Enzinas and many another victim charge him with great cruelty, and though his defenders plead that it was the institution rather than the man that was to blame, still he seems to have done little to mitigate the severity of the inquisition. His principle is said to have been the following: " It is no great matter whether they that die on account of religion be guilty or innocent, provided we terrify the people by such examples; which generally succeeds best, when persons eminent for learning, riches, nobility or high station are thus sacrificed." Yet in the ranks of his own party he was held in the highest honour. Charles V consulted him constantly; the queen-regent looked up to him with the greatest veneration, despite her mild sympathy with Lutheranism: his house was called the oracle of Belgium, and when sent by the emperor to the second session of the council of Trent, his learning won him the most profound respect from the assembled fathers.

These three divines must have joined in the congratulatory letter, sent in 1528 to the archbishop of St Andrews by the theological faculty of Louvain, on learning the news of the martyrdom of young Patrick Hamilton. " We desire," they wrote, " to thank you for your worthy deed " in cutting off " the wicked heretic. . . . Believe not that this example shall have place only among you; for there shall be those among externe nations, who shall imitate the same. Certainly you have given us great courage." Alas! poor William. It will go hard with you now. You are like to be one of those, upon whom the externe nations were to prove their imitatory zeal. The great courage of the writers may well be directed against your body.

A word must also be said about Tyndale's accuser, the procurer-general. His name was Pierre Dufief, and he won a fearful reputation for cruelty among the Lutherans of the Low Countries: and indeed not from them alone: the Belgian scholar who has edited Enzinas' memoirs calls him " this terrible magistrate." No doubt he conceived it to be his duty to be ruthless with the sufferers, and it was certainly his interest, for he gained a share of the goods confiscated from them. For eighteen years more he wielded his awful authority, but then appears to have been deprived of his post for extortion and embezzlement. We have called

him Tyndale's accuser, and such he was in name: but in
these trials we repeatedly find him acting as if he were a
judge. He would be present at private examinations conducted by the commissioners, and of one such enquiry the
minutes are extant in his own hand. In Poyntz' case he
claimed the right of reading the defendant's letters. By
bringing pressure to bear upon the commissioners he could
often have the defendant sent to the torture chamber, so as to
extract fresh evidence. In one case described by Enzinas
he actually sits in the seat of judgment, and delivers the
sentence that sends two laymen of Louvain to the fire. Little
justice can be expected, when an accuser, even if not planting
himself upon the tribunal, is hand in glove with the judges.

The oral examinations would be conducted in Latin.
So at least it was eight years later with Enzinas—at his own
request indeed, for the commissioners began the conversation in French: and the learned language would be
even more fitting for so great a doctor as Tyndale. For the
same reason we may be sure that the theologians paid frequent visits to the prison. If Tapper and Latomus were
summoned to the cells of the humble martyrs of Louvain, how
much more needful was their presence to cope with the
renowned scholar from England; and indeed Latomus himself
makes it plain that he had met Tyndale face to face. And
behind the commissioners came ever Henry Phillips, accompanying them to the door of the cell, and remaining
at hand in case he could be of assistance. The present
purpose of his life was to destroy the man whom he had so
basely betrayed. He moved between Louvain, Brussels and
Vilvorde, and he was at Brussels " following the suit against
Master Tyndale," when Poyntz arrived from England with
his letters of rescue at the end of October. It is likely also
that he was one of the two Englishmen at Louvain who
(so Poyntz tells his brother in August) were translating
passages of Tyndale's works into Latin, as a handle for the
clergy to use against him. The other may have been
Buckenham, the blackfriar from Cambridge.

Thus three months had passed before even the business of
translating was concluded. The case would also be retarded

by the intervention of Cromwell in September, and the six weeks' correspondence with England that followed. A direct request from a powerful sovereign for the release of one of his own subjects could not be brushed aside. It would lead to anxious discussion within the council, and the decision must have been in doubt, otherwise Phillips would hardly have troubled to throw Poyntz into prison. It is likely, therefore, that it was not until the end of 1535, or even the beginning of 1536, that the articles of accusation were formally drawn up by the procurer-general.

Tyndale was offered the service of an advocate and a proctor, but he declined this assistance, saying that he would answer for himself. The great hour was come. Not for him to play for time, or to help himself with the subtleties and evasions of the law. His whole life had been a willing witness to the gospel, and he would not withhold his testimony at the end. We may be sure that, like his disciple Frith, he openly and joyfully avowed to all persons, whether by word of mouth or by writing, those truths, in the strength of which he had lived so long, and for whose sake he was now ready to die.

Then would begin the long and learned paper-warfare between the prosecution, or rather the theological assessors, and the defence, which is so singular a feature of heresy-trials in the Low Countries. " There was much writing," says Foxe, " and great disputation to and fro between him and them of the university of Louvain, in such sort that they all had enough to do, and more than they could well wield, to answer the authorities and testimonies of the scripture, whereupon he most pithily grounded his doctrine." Of these exchanges we should know nothing at all, were it not that Latomus' part in them has been preserved. Six years later he sent it to a friend with a foreword of explanation.

When William Tyndale (he says) was in prison for Lutheranism, he wrote a book on the theme: *Sola fides justificat apud Deum*, faith alone justifies before God ; this he called his key to the healthy understanding of sacred scripture. We replied in three books. In the first we took away his key, and put another in its place. To this Tyndale, " though he had no reasonable answer to make, yet preferred to make a show of replying rather than to acknowledge his error," and he wrote a second book against us, enlarging on the same theme, and also treating of nearly all the other matters of contention between us and them. We had therefore to answer him again in a second book of ours; and we plainly overturned his foundations and demonstrated the absurdity of his opinion. But we also added a third book, going shortly and clearly into the other points of dispute: "for this had Tyndale requested, that he might be able not only to hear, but also to read what we hold on these matters; and we were unwilling to decline any request of his." We feared indeed that our labour would not profit him: yet we hoped it might be a help to others.

After Latomus' death these books were printed by his nephew, along with other of his works, and the volume, a very rare one to-day, was dedicated to Ruard Tapper.

Latomus' treatises against Tyndale are singularly moderate in tone. There are almost no sharp words; he is simply the theologian arguing a piece of divinity, the dialectician joyfully using the weapons of his art. Would that all controversy in those days had been carried on in so cool a temper ! Demaus thinks that Latomus had been disarmed by Tyndale's nobility and candour, as he had witnessed them in his visits to the prison. There is something in this: but indeed all close personal contact tends to mitigate the furiousness of controversy. If you are talking with a man in the privacy of an inner chamber, for his ear alone, and not for the mob in the market-place, you cannot rail upon him perpetually, though he be your bitterest enemy; if you do, discussion becomes impossible: you must keep your mind at least in touch with his. Latomus nourished a faint hope of converting his notable prisoner, and Tyndale on his part would desire to put his case as carefully and strongly as possible to antagonists so famous as the professors of Louvain. Added to this, the seriousness of the issues involved, the feeling that a great man's life was at stake, and indeed that he was so far in their power that almost nothing could save him—all this might well sober the heated zeal even of the theological champions of the sixteenth century.

Latomus' first book is an able piece of work. You ask us, Tyndale, (he begins) to make a written reply to your thesis that faith alone justifies before God. We will try to satisfy you, so far as God grants to us. Let us first clear the ground by seeing where we agree together. And hereupon follows a list of seven or eight propositions, which both parties held in common. Then Latomus plunges into the thorny question of faith and works.

> Your use of scripture is onesided and unsound. If, as you write, you desire to be instructed, be careful not to regard the sacred text as a storehouse of arguments for your part. You omit passages that tell against you, and which imply that our good acts merit reward from God. It is true that St Paul says that our works have no merit and do not justify us, but he is speaking only of the time before we believe in Christ. Our first faith certainly is a free gift of God, in which we play no part at all, but as soon as we receive that faith and are justified through Christ, then we become for the first time capable of merit, partakers of the divine operation. You say that good works simply declare a man's goodness and do not make him good, just as the fruit of a tree shews, and does not create, the healthiness of the stock. The simile is a bad one; for the bearing of fruit weakens the tree, but good acts strengthen the mind: a fountain and its water would suit your purpose better. Our good works, you say again, are not needed by God nor do they benefit him, any more than the bitter draught, drunk by a patient, benefits the physician who prescribes it. I agree with you here: nevertheless God rewards us as if he needed our works, he rewards us merely for doing his will. Lastly, if good men merit no reward of God, what are we to say of sinners? Is it reason to say that a reward can be given only to an evil act and not to a good one?

Latomus' final argument is acute and striking. Nevertheless his treatment of the subject is vulnerable in one or two points, and Tyndale, so far from being shaken from his opinion, returned with vigour to the combat. His treatise has perished; but we can judge something of it from Latomus' reply in his second book. This latter is less strong and close knit than the first; and a touch of sharpness begins to creep into his words. You have written (he begins) at some length, *prolixe*, in support of your thesis, but you misunderstand the meaning of faith, and make it a weak and stunted thing, and you belittle the work of grace in the heart. You say indeed that you are unwilling to be contentious, or to raise verbal questions: would that you meant it! there would soon be an end of our controversy. And so the argument proceeds, Latomus showing plenty of dialectical skill, and growing warmer as he nears his conclusion.

Reflect upon all this, and you will clearly see the absurdity in which you are landed. Let me quote your statement of the case in your own words, so that " all readers may see its absurdity, and if you—which God forbid—shut your eyes, yet they may shun the mark of an obstinate heart. Works (you say) are the last things required in the law, and they do not fulfil the law before God. In work we ever sin, and our thoughts are impure. The love, *caritas*, which should fulfil the law, is colder in us than ice. Therefore we live by faith as long as we are in the flesh; and by faith we overcome the world. This is the victory which overcometh the world, even our faith (I John v), our faith in God through Christ; for the love of him who overcame all the temptations of the devil shall be imputed to us. By faith therefore is all the promise, that it may be firm to every seed of them that believe; for by the works of the law shall no flesh be justified before him. Thus far you recognise your own words. Here you seem to open the secrets of your heart." Yet when we come to examine this position, it cannot stand; it is riddled with difficulties. Consider, I beg of you, Tyndale, to what absurdity you are come by leaving the well trodden paths and the teaching of the fathers.

Then follows the third book.

" At the end of your treatise," begins Latomus, " you say that you have with a good conscience put forth your opinions. We believe that your opinions are even as you say. Wherefore if your belief is true, you are rightly displeased with those that imprison you in the name of pope and emperor, and treat you as a malefactor. Now since you ask to hear from us, nay to read, what our opinion is on the controversy, I will not disappoint your desire, in hope of thus recalling you from that error to catholic and true doctrine. Behold therefore, we put before you with a good conscience what we believe, what we hold, what we have learned in the catholic, orthodox, and, if you will permit the word, also Roman church.''

He then deals with the other matters which Tyndale had raised, the priestly order and the power of the keys, vows, fasting, images, worship of saints, sacraments, and the authority of the pope, propping his argument throughout with copious quotations from the fathers. '' I have written these opinions [from the fathers] at some length,'' he says, '' that you may see how great and of what nature are the men, whom you have deserted for Luther and Melanchthon; I would rather imitate the negligence of the former than the obscure diligence of the latter.''

In this general defence of the papal church Latomus is very much less at ease than when discussing the theological dogma of justification. He takes a stiff, even dogmatic, line, and has no lack of arguments; but they are abstract, logical, deductive. He dare not grapple with the practical evils that gave so much of its driving force to the reformation. The two men are at cross purposes. Latomus' hard and fast reasoning, his appeals to logic or authority, had nothing in them to still the cries of distress and rebellion that were arising from the hearts of thousands, who beheld the fair image of the church defaced, and longed to revive the living spirit that once had dwelt within her, and to call the free energies of all her sons into play. They asked for bread; Latomus and his like offered them a stone.

This controversy must have lasted some weeks. Latomus' first treatise consists of seven close-printed folio pages, and his second of eighteen pages; and we may suppose that Tyndale's contributions were of equal length, and as plentifully supported by quotations from the bible and the fathers. Besides, Latomus cannot have been the only champion who entered the lists. Tapper would long to take a hand against the great English heresiarch, and perhaps other theologians also. If we allot a fortnight to each treatise, a period of three, four, or even six months might well be accounted for by these exchanges.

That Tyndale was visited by other divines beside those on the commission, we learn from the sketch of his life, prefixed by Foxe to Daye's folio. The confinement at Vilvorde is here described as follows :—

" There he remained more than a year and a half; and in the meantime came unto him divers lawyers and doctors in divinity, as well friars as other, with whom he had many conflicts. But at the last Tyndale prayed that he might have some English divines come unto him : for the manners and ceremonies in religion in Dutchland (said he) did much differ from the manners and ceremonies used in England. And then was sent unto him divers divines from Louvain, whereof some were Englishmen ; and after many examinations at the last they condemned him."

This narrative is not very clear in its order of time, but it gives us several fresh pieces of information, which Foxe did not include in his *Acts and Monuments*. We should gladly know more of the visits of these English divines. No doubt one was Buckenham, who, as a former prior of a monastery, was a man of standing : but at this period Louvain was full of refugees from England who favoured the papal side.

But the most interesting fact concerning Tyndale's long sojourn in prison has only come to light in modern times. In the middle of the last century a letter from his own hand was discovered in Belgium, which had reposed unread amidst the archives of the council of Brabant for more than three hundred years. It is written in Latin to someone in authority, but bears no date nor name of place. It runs as follows—

" Credo non latere te, vir praestantissime, quid de me statutum sit. Quam ob rem tuam dominationem roga-tum habeo, idque per Dominum Jesum, ut si mihi per hiemem hic manendum sit, solicites apud dominum commissarium, si forte dignari velit, de rebus meis quas habet, mittere calidiorem birettum ; frigus enim patior in capite nimium, oppressus perpetuo catarro, qui sub testitudine nonnihil augetur. Calidiorem quoque tunicam; nam haec quam habeo admodum tenuis est. Item pannum ad caligas reficiendas. Duplois detrita est; camiseae detritae sunt etiam. Camiseam laneam habet, si mittere velit. Habeo quoque apud eum caligas ex crassiori panno ad superius induendum. Nocturna biretta calidiora habet etiam. Utque vesperi lucernam habere liceat; tediosum quidem est per tenebras solitarie sedere. Maxime autem omnium tuam clementiam rogo atque obsecro, ut ex animo agere velit apud dominum commissarium, quatenus dignari velit mihi concedere bibliam Hebraicam, grammaticam Hebraicam, et vocabularium Hebraicum, ut eo studio tempus conteram. Sic tibi obtingat quod maxime optas, modo cum animae tuae salute fiat. Verum si aliud consilium de me ceptum est, ante hiemem perficiendum, patiens ero, Dei expectans voluntatem, ad gloriam gratiae Domini mei Jesu Christi, cujus Spiritus tuum semper regat pectus. Amen. W. Tindalus."

" I believe, right worshipful, that you are not unaware of what may have been determined concerning me. Wherefore I beg your lordship, and that by the Lord Jesus, that if I am to remain here through the winter, you will request the commissary to have the kindness to send me, from the goods of mine which he has, a warmer cap; for I suffer greatly from cold in the head, and am afflicted by a perpetual catarrh, which is much increased in this cell; a warmer coat also, for this which I have is very thin; a piece of cloth too to patch my leggings. My overcoat is worn out; my shirts are also worn out. He has a woollen shirt, if he will be good enough to send it. I have also with him leggings of thicker cloth to put on above; he has also warmer night caps. And I ask to be allowed to have a lamp in the evening ; it is indeed wearisome sitting alone in the dark. But most of all I beg and beseech your clemency to be urgent with the commissary, that he will kindly permit me to have the Hebrew bible, Hebrew grammar, and Hebrew dictionary, that I may pass the time in that study. In return may you obtain what you most desire, so only that it be for the salvation of your soul. But if any other decision has been taken concerning me, to be carried out before winter, I will be

patient, abiding the will of God, to the glory of the grace
of my Lord Jesus Christ; whose Spirit (I pray) may ever
direct your heart.   Amen.   W. Tindalus."

What is the date of this letter?   It was written before
winter, but which winter?   Certainly that of 1535–6.
Tyndale was taken at the opening of summer, when the
days were long, and he would naturally ask for a lamp and
for warmer clothing at the approach of the first winter of
his imprisonment.   The date then will be the autumn of
1535, perhaps about the end of September.   By the following autumn he had already been condemned, and knew
quite well what was to become of him.   But to whom was
the letter directed?   To the procurer-general, some Belgian
scholars reply; and in that case the commissary is supposed
to be Tapper.   But Tapper was not yet inquisitor, and if
he had been, it is highly unlikely that the shirts and leggings
of a prisoner would be sent to his keeping to Louvain.   We
know that the procurer-general seized Tyndale's goods on
the day of his arrest; and no doubt he lodged them in a
safe place at Antwerp.   He then is the commissary.   The
person addressed in the letter is a man of high station, and,
as the first sentence shows, is not directly concerned with the
trial, but is in touch with those that are.   Demaus is surely
right in taking him to be the marquis of Bergen, the very
man to whom Cromwell about this time was sending petitions
for Tyndale's release.   He was not only a privy councillor,
but he was governor also of Vilvorde castle, and as such had
an interest in the welfare of the prisoners.   It is likely that
when Tyndale wrote the letter, there had been a lull for
some weeks or months in the visits of the commissioners
(this happened also in the case of Enzinas); otherwise one
would think that he would have made his requests by word
of mouth to the procurer-general.

   This is a beautiful letter, and it has often been compared
to St Paul's last words in the fourth chapter of the second
epistle to Timothy.   A noble dignity and independence
breathe through it.   There is no touch of flattery, much less
of cringing, yet it is perfectly courteous and respectful.

Tyndale accepts his present plight with an equal mind, though he will lighten its burden so far as he can. But through it all, his chief thought is for the gospel which is committed to him. A burning love of God fills his heart. In making his request he does not fear to remind the governor of spiritual things; in desiring warmth and light for himself, he longs still more for his Hebrew books, so that he may carry forward the work of translation, to which he has devoted his life.

Were his requests granted? Demaus feels sure that they were, and one would be glad to think so. Some writers even suppose that he translated in his cell the later historical books of the Old Testament, which were first printed in Matthew's bible. Again, one would be glad to think so. Yet if so, Tyndale must have found access in the castle to other books, beside the Hebrew volumes which alone he desires from the commissary: for in this version he uses the Greek, Latin and German translations as freely as he had done in the Pentateuch, when he was at liberty. In some prisons, indeed, he would have had little difficulty in obtaining books, and indeed all manner of other concessions. Discipline was often extremely lax, and a complaisant jailer would wink at many things for the sake of a prisoner who won his liking and respect, or who could afford to pay handsomely. Frith's friends brought him books in the Tower of London, though he had to whisk them away out of sight when the head-keeper appeared: and Enzinas treated the Vrunte prison at Brussels almost like an hotel; his visitors numbered more than four hundred, and he complained that they hindered him from his own literary labours. But the great state prison of Vilvorde cannot have been so easy going as this; if it had been, Tyndale's letter need never have been written. How was it that he could not get at least clothes and a lamp through his jailer? Poyntz or Rogers would gladly have supplied them. And how is it that Poyntz seems never to have visited him during the months of his own liberty? All this goes to show that the rules of the prison were strict. Perhaps the lamp and the clothes may have been granted him, if indeed the latter had not already been sold; but it is hard to believe that the procurer-general and the theologians, having him now so securely in their clutches, would help him to continue that very translation of the scriptures for which they were taking away his life. Foxe tells us of other manuscripts left behind by Tyndale at death, but he says no word of any biblical version, though this would be the most worthy of all to be mentioned. The picture of the heroic prisoner, working during the long nights of the winter at the books of the Old Testament, is so striking, that Poyntz could hardly fail to impart it to Foxe, if it were true.

It was not that the jailer was ill disposed towards Tyndale: far from it. The prisoner's noble and courageous nature moved him, as it moved so many others. Lutheranism was in the air, and penetrating into the hearts of many persons, who were not yet ready to avow it openly; and Tyndale did his part even at Vilvorde in spreading the good news. " Such," says Foxe, " was the power of his doctrine and the sincerity of his life, that during the time of his imprisonment, which endured a year and a half, he converted his keeper, the keeper's daughter, and others of his household. Also the rest that were with Tyndale conversant in the castle, reported of him, that if he were not a good Christian man, they could not tell whom they might take to be one." Nay, even his accuser, the terrible Dufief himself, was touched. He must have visited the cell many times, and he gave his testimony, as both Halle and Foxe relate, that the prisoner was *homo doctus, pius et bonus*, a learned, pious and good man. Although in confinement and cut off from the great world, Tyndale's last months of life were not without profit to his fellow-men.

And so the weary days dragged on, each week that passed making his doom more certain. When once Cromwell's plea in the autumn of 1535 had been rejected, and his messenger cast into prison, nothing could save Tyndale, unless it were some new and more forcible intervention from England; and of such a thing we have no record. The law must take its course, wicked and cruel though it might be; and at long last the process reached its inevitable end. Early in August 1536 Tyndale was condemned as a heretic, degraded from the priesthood, and handed over to the secular power for punishment.

We learn this from a letter of August 12, sent to Cromwell from Antwerp by John Hutton, agent to the English government in the Netherlands.

" So it is," he writes, " that as the tenth day of this present the procurer-general, which is the emperor's attorney for these parts, dined with me here in the English house; who certified me that William Tyndale is degraded, and condemned into the hands of the secular power, so that he is very like to suffer death this next week: and as to the articles upon which he is condemned, I cannot as yet obtain, albeit I have a grant [promise]; which once obtained shall be sent your lordship by the first. There was also another Englishman with Tyndale, judged the same time to return into his habit of St Francis' order, paying the charges of his imprisonment."

A trace of the ceremony remains in the archives of Brabant. Early in the present century a document came to light, which informs us that on September 1, 1536 there was paid to the procurer-general of Brabant, Master Peter Dufief, the sum of nineteen pounds odd, to make good " the cost of the hiring of carriages and the other little fees due to the serjeants and servants of the town; these charges having been incurred at the time of the degradation or unhallowing of Guillem Tindal, an Englishman, by the bishop suffragan and the two prelates assisting him; while other ecclesiastics and laymen were present at the said degradation or unhallowing; which took place in the town of Vilvorde."

The Belgian scholar who discovered the above document discovered also another, which forms one more link, albeit a small one, with the trial of Tyndale. On August 5 in the Falcon inn at Vilvorde a deed was signed, under which James de Lattre, inquisitor apostolic of the Low Countries, unable to cope with the work of his office, delegated his powers to Ruard Tapper. The deed was drawn up by William Cavertson, and the two witnesses were Latomus and Doye.* The date then of Tyndale's degradation was likely between August 5 and August 9.

* Cf. Paul Frédéricq, in *Mélanges d'Histoire offerts à M. Charles Bémont* (1913), pp. 476–7.

Thus a brilliant galaxy of stars assembled in the little town of Vilvorde for the casting forth of William from his priestly office. There was the bishop suffragan of Cambrai, in which diocese Vilvorde lay, and two other bishops; the names of all three are unknown. There was the inquisitor-apostolic and his secretary, and the three canons of Louvain. The procurer-general must be there, and doubtless the commissioners who had tried the case, as well as leading persons from the town and neighbourhood.

The condemnation for heresy, with the reading out of the articles of guilt, was distinct from the degradation, and often preceded it by some days. But in Tyndale's case one may perhaps suppose that the two were joined in a single ceremony. The degradation would be held in public, either in church, or more likely in the square of the town or some other place of general resort. The rite was somewhat as follows. The bishops sat upon a high platform, easily to be seen by all, and upon this the victim was led, clad in the vestments of the priesthood. He was made to kneel. His hands were scraped with a knife or a piece of glass, as a symbol of the loss of the anointing oil; the bread and the wine were placed in his hands and then taken away; and lastly his vestments were stripped from him one by one, and he was clothed in the garments of a layman. Then the presiding bishop handed him over for punishment to the secular officer, who in this case was the procurer-general.

To Tyndale himself all this business was of small matter. He was moving in loftier regions than his persecutors. What were these empty words that reached his ears? Separated from the flock? Unworthy to be a priest? Not so. No man had made him priest, and no man could rob him of his office. A thousand prelates could not separate him from the love of Christ, or take away his glory in the disciples whom he had made. His call had come from above, and it was even now ringing in his ears; nothing but death should stay his witnessing. This stripping off of garments was no more than a piece of play acting. It might be tiresome, it might even be insulting: but it carried no degradation. The true degradation rested on the heads of those who inflicted it upon a sincere and noble man.

Hutton had expected the execution to follow within about a week of the sentence, but it was delayed for nearly two months. It can hardly be that Cromwell interposed again. It was too late in the day; for the very letter which told him of the sentence, would lead him to suppose that it had already been carried out. Most likely there was some division of opinion within the council. Tyndale's bearing at the examinations and at the judgment may have moved some of the laymen on the commission, and made them anxious to save him, if a way could be found. Or it may be that before laying a finger on a prisoner so notable, a foreigner to boot, whose life had been strongly asked for by his government, it was deemed desirable to obtain the emperor's consent. But the emperor was now engaged in an unprofitable war in the south-east of France, and a week or two would elapse before a messenger could pass to and fro with letters.

The interval was no doubt employed by the papal party in an endeavour to break down Tyndale's resistance and to induce him to recant: for such was the custom. Relays of priests and monks would be sent to work upon the weakness or weariness of a condemned man. It was vain for the victim to beg to be left in peace, or to plead that his mind was fully settled; the unwelcome visitors were ruthless in their attentions, so zealous were they by hook or crook to snatch a soul from the everlasting fire. Against Tyndale these assaults and persuasions would break like waves upon a rock. The man that had given so heroic an advice to his disciple Frith, was not likely to blench when his hour came.

At length the day was fixed for the execution, one of the first days of October, so it would seem. Tyndale was not to be burnt alive—that punishment was reserved for the relapsed and for anabaptists—but to be strangled, and his dead body burnt. The time would be early in the day, perhaps as early as six o'clock, and hardly later than ten. The place would be some open spot, perhaps near the southern gate of the town. On the morning of his death, says Foxe, " he delivered a letter to the keeper of the castle; which the keeper himself brought to the house of the aforesaid Poyntz in Antwerp shortly after; which letter with his examinations [before the commissioners] and other his disputations [with Louvain] I would might have come to our hands: all of which, I understand, did remain, and yet perhaps do, in the hands of the keeper's daughter." In Poyntz' house the keeper spoke warmly of Tyndale, comparing his behaviour in prison with that of the apostles. *

Of the last scene of all we have only Foxe's meagre story: "He was brought forth to the place of execution, was there tied to the stake, and then strangled first by the hangman, and afterwards with fire consumed, in the morning at the town of Vilvorde, A.D. 1536; crying thus at the stake with a fervent zeal and a loud voice: Lord, open the king of England's eyes."

Yet perhaps we can draw a more vivid picture by the light of two executions—in Brussels and Louvain—described for us by Enzinas; one of which he witnessed himself. This is what he saw. A circle was enclosed with a barricade, which none might pass save the guards and the executioner. Inside, two great beams were set up in the shape of a cross, and this projected from the ground to a man's height. At the top were fastened iron chains, and there were holes in the wood, through which a rope of hemp was passed. Brushwood and logs lay heaped around. The procurer-general and his colleagues came and sat in a place prepared for them. The prisoner was brought in, and a last appeal was made to him to recant. He moved to the cross. His feet were bound to the stake, and round his neck was passed the chain, together with a noose of the hempen rope hanging slack. Next the brushwood, straw and logs, with gunpowder added, were packed close round the cross, forming as it were a little hut in which stood the doomed man. Then on a signal from the procurer the executioner, standing behind, quickly tightened the noose, strangling his victim. As soon as life was departed, the procurer seized a lighted torch of wax and handed it to the executioner, who set the wood on a blaze.

As he reached the cross, there was a short space for the prisoner to pray; and it must have been then, or more likely while he stood in the hut, that Tyndale uttered the cry which Foxe has recorded: "Lord, open the king of England's

* This point only comes out in full clearness in Foxe (1563).

eyes." Save for this, only one faint echo of the scene has reached us. Two months later, on December 13, Hutton writes to Cromwell: "They speak much of the patient sufferance of Master Tyndale at the time of his execution." That is the whole of our knowledge: but it is enough to show us—what indeed, knowing Tyndale, we might anyhow have forecast—that he bore himself nobly at the end, and did not disgrace the faith that was in him.

Blind though the eyes of the king of England might be to the deeper things of the spirit, nevertheless Tyndale's dying prayer did not lack all fulfilment. Within a year Matthew's and Coverdale's bibles received the royal licence. Within two years Cromwell in his master's name enjoined that the Great Bible be provided and set up in every parish church in the land, so that who would might come and read. Within five years this injunction was confirmed by a royal proclamation, visiting with very heavy fines all incumbents and churchwardens who continued to disobey. From those decisions England has never looked back. In 1531 Tyndale had proposed a bargain to the king: he would be silent, if the king would grant free course in his realm to an English bible, by whomsoever translated. Silent, did he say? Well, he is silent now, silenced by the stern halter of the executioner; his part in the bargain is now fulfilled. But neither will the king's part tarry long; the free and open bible stands at the door; the fight is all but won; William Tyndale has not lived and died in vain.*

* Foxe's text gives no day nor month for Tyndale's death; the accepted date, October 6, rests on the kalendar. But Foxe's kalendar only professes to give the *month* (arranging each month's martyrs chronologically by the year of death), except in those cases where the *day* of death is entered in a second column. Thus Frith has two dates, July 2 and 4; Rogers has two, February 22 and 4: Tyndale has one only, October 6, the second column being blank. Halle and Bale (*Illustrium Scriptorum*, 1548) say that Tyndale died in September *1535*; but it seems better to accept Foxe's month. If the date was about October 2, the arrest was about May 21, a year and 135 days before: and this fits all the evidence very well.

As to the spot, there is no evidence from the Belgian side, as I am assured by Mr. Jules Nauwelaers of Brussels, the great authority on the history of Vilvorde. The only English witness is Roger Ascham, who rode through the town from north to south in 1550, and writes four months later from Augsburg: " At the town's end is a notable solemn place of execution, where worthy William Tyndale was unworthily put to death."

APPENDIX A

I. *Likenesses.*

(1) In 1580 Beza published at Geneva his *Icones*, an account of leading reformers with portraits. Tyndale does not figure among them though his name is mentioned. In 1581 a French translation (by Simon Goulard) was issued from the same press, and by some oversight the icon of John Knox, given by Beza, was withdrawn, and quite another one put in its place. This is believed to be Tyndale, and certainly it is of the same type as the other likenesses which we have (see *Beza's Icones*; C. G. McCrie, 1906).

(2) Engraving in Holland's *Heroologia*, 1620.

This is the only likeness which gives us an idea of the man. The others are nondescript. The keen eye and sharp intelligent face fit him very well. In one of the copies of the *Heroologia* in the British Museum there is a manuscript list, telling whence the engravings were taken. That of Tyndale is said to have been taken from a picture in a shop in Fleet Street.

(3) Painting at Hertford College, Oxford.

This belonged to a principal of Magdalen hall, who bequeathed it to the hall in 1656. It cannot have been made during Tyndale's life. The inscription, and the hand pointing to the book, betoken a time long after his death: but it may have been based on a contemporary portrait. The Bible Society and the National Portrait Gallery possess copies or variants of this picture. (See Mrs R. L. Poole's *Catalogue of Portraits . . . of Oxford*, III., 270, 278.)

II. *Memorials.*

In 1866 a monument was erected to Tyndale on Nibley Knoll, Glos. In 1884 a fine statue (by J. E. Boehm) was erected in the Embankment Gardens, London: Tyndale stands in his academic robes, with a manuscript in his left hand, and a printing press beside him, copied from one in the Plantin Museum, Antwerp. In 1913 a monument was put up in one of the squares of Vilvorde, with inscriptions in English, Latin, Flemish and French.

APPENDIX B

(1) ERASMUS' *Enchiridion* in English (W. de Worde, 1533). This seems to be Tyndale's translation. It bears strong marks of his style, *e.g.* variation of renderings, use of *father and mother* for *parents*. I hope to put out the evidence elsewhere.

(2) *Exposition on 1 Corinthians vii* (Lufft-Marburg, June 20, 1529).

This was often ascribed to Tyndale, and in lists of books is also called *The Matrimony of Tyndale*. It is not Tyndale's: the writer sharply distinguishes himself from "the good man who translated" the New Testament. According to More (preface to *Confutation*) some ascribed it to Roye: but Roye was in England at the time of printing.

(3) *A Compendious old treatise how that we ought to have the Scripture in English*, printed at the end of *A proper dialogue between a gentleman and a husbandman* (Lufft-Marburg, 1530).

This is an edition of an old Lollard tract, but the editor silently adds much matter of his own in archaic language. Miss Deanesly ascribes it to Tyndale. This is unlikely. He is spoken of in the third person, as "Master William Tyndale." Tyndale never speaks thus of himself; nor does he elsewhere burst into poetry, as this writer does. The metre is that of some of the stanzas of *Rede me and be not wroth*, and the editor may be Jerome Barlow. Foxe, who prints it in his book, does not ascribe it to Tyndale.

(4) *Expositions on II and III epistles of John*, printed by James Nicolson, 1538, along with Tyndale's undisputed exposition on I John.

I thoroughly agree with Walter (against Demaus) in denying these to Tyndale. They are unknown to Vaughan (1531) and More (1532); Foxe omits them from Daye's folio. The earliest mention seems to be in Bonner's list of forbidden books (1542). The style and treatment are quite unlike Tyndale.

(5) *Examination of Thorpe and Oldcastle* [Hoochstraten, 1530].

An edition of the two Lollard documents in slightly modernized English. More ascribes it to Constantine, but Foxe (III., 249) says the editor is Tyndale, and that he himself is printing it from a copy in Tyndale's own handwriting. Bale also (Parker Society, p. 6) said in 1544 that Tyndale printed the book "fourteen years ago." The preface proves that it is Tyndale's; *e.g.* the following words: "Who can tell wherefore that good priest and holy martyr, Sir Thomas Hitton, was brent, now this year at Maidstone?" The closing passage is interesting: "This I have corrected and put forth in the English that is now used in England for our southern men, nothing adding to nor yet therefrom minishing [an allusion doubtless to the *Compendious Old Treatise*]; and I intend hereafter with the help of God to put it forth in his own old English, which shall well serve, I doubt not, both for the northern men and the faithful brethren of Scotland."

(6) *The prayer and complaint of the plowman*, February 28, 1531 [de Keyser].

Another old tract, edited by Tyndale: so say Bale (1548) and Foxe. The preface settles the matter; *e.g.* "that all the righteous blood may fall on their heads [the bishops] . . . from the blood of Stephen the first martyr to the blood of that innocent man of God, Thomas Hitton, whom William Warham, bishop of Canterbury, and John Fisher, bishop of Rochester, murdered at Maidstone in Kent the last year." Tyndale says: "I have put forth this old treatise in his own old English, changing therein nothing as far forth as I could observe it, either the English or ortographie," and he promises to edit other such old documents, should any come into his hands. He adds also a glossary of 30 " antiquate " words, among which it is curious to find *desert* (= wilderness), *doom*, *thrall*.

APPENDIX C

I. *Joye's evidence* (*Apology*, February 27, 1535) cf. pp. 70 f.,
268–71, 278, of this book.

(1) Tyndale's first New Testament, "a mean great
volume" with epilogue [Worms 8vo.].

(2) "Anon after, the Dutchmen got a copy and printed
it again in a small volume, adding the kalendar in the
beginning, concordances in the margin, and the table at
the end" [Endhoven 1; c. October 1526; doubtless 16mo.].

(3) "After this they printed it again . . . in a greater
letter and volume, with the figures [pictures] in the Apocalypse" [Endhoven 2; c. 1530; probably 8vo.]. "These
two prints . . . were all sold more than a twelve month
ago."

(4) "A small volume, like their first print;" it contained a table [Endhoven 3; early 1534; 16mo].

(5) Joye's revision. [Endhoven 4; August 1534; has
kalendar (running from 1526 to 1543, *i.e.* of Endhoven 1),
concordances and table; 16mo.]

To these we can now add:

(6) Joye's revision reissued; January 9, 1535; discovered
in 1904; 16mo. [Endhoven 5.]

II. *Scattered notices.*

(1) In 1531 "Christopher, a Dutchman of Antwerp . . .
for selling certain New Testaments in English to John
Rowe [a French bookbinder in London], was put in prison
at Westminster, and there died" (Foxe, V., 37). This
must be Endhoven, whose last book in the *Nederlandsche
Bibliographie* is dated May 14, 1531. These New Testaments were probably Endhoven 2, which therefore is dated
c. 1530.

(2) In 1528 "John Raimund" was abjured in London "for causing 1500 of Tyndale's New Testaments to be printed at Antwerp, and for bringing 500 into England" (Foxe, V., 27). This is Hans van Endhoven, brother of Christopher. Roemundt or Ruremond, near Endhoven, was the birthplace of the two men. Hans was printing in Antwerp in 1525, but then fell into trouble and seems never to have resumed there [Endhoven 1].

(3) On March 15, 1528, Tonstall writes to Wolsey that during the past year Theodoric, a Dutchman of Antwerp, had twice been in London, bringing "many testaments in English of the little volume, whereof many be come to my hands since" [Endhoven 1].

(4) On April 4, 1531, John Silverlink, acting for Hans van Ruremond, secured judgment in Antwerp against the heirs of the bookseller Francis Byrkman (who died in 1529 or 1530) for £25, being the balance of the £28 17s. 3d. owing to him for the supply to Byrkman of more than 700 English New Testaments (Pollard, 136: I cannot trace the original). If 729 books were delivered, the price was $9\frac{1}{2}d.$ apiece [Endhoven 1].

(5) Richard Herman, arrested on July 12, 1528 in Antwerp, makes two petitions to the emperor (*L. & P.*, IV., 4569). On the charge of selling bad books, he confesses "that a merchant out of Germany sent to the petitioner certain New Testaments in English without any gloss (*een coopman vuyt duytschlandt den supplicanten gesonden heeft gehadt zekere nyeuwe testamenten in engelssche talen zonder enighe glose*), which books the petitioner received, and sold them to a merchant out of England, and the latter conveyed them over to England." His second petition gives the same account in other words [Worms 8vo.]. Four letters from England (dated September 3, 1526, October 14 [probably 1526], February 20, 1527, and the fourth undated) were seized in his house, all speaking of the English New Testament (*L. & P.*, IV., 4693–4, 4714). Clearly he was engaged in selling them almost from the start.

(6) On April 28, 1528, John Tyball of Steeple Bumstead confessed that at Michaelmas 1526 he and Thomas Hilles

bought in London from Robert Barnes two testaments in English, paying 3s. 2d. each. Hilles' confession, however, says the price was 3s. and the time about Whitsun 1526 [Worms 8vo.]. Tyball also says that " about two years ago " he showed all his books to the curate of Bumstead, " that is to say the New Testament in English [Worms 8vo.], the gospel of Matthew and Mark in English [Cologne fragment], which he had of John Pykas of Colchester, . . . certain of Paul's epistles in English after the old [Lollard] translation, the four evangelists in English," *i.e.* the Lollard version.

(7) In 1530–1 Bayfield imported " the New Testament in English with an introduction to the Romans." This seems to be one volume, not two. It was denounced at Paul's Cross on December 3, 1531. It is probably Endhoven 2, though Joye says nothing of any introduction to Romans. On the other hand, when Francis Denham, an Englishman taken in Paris in June 1528, confesses that he has *novum testamentum Anglice cum introductione ad epistolam Pauli ad Romanos*, this is no doubt two books [both Worms 8vo.], but he may have bound them together. They were the only English books he had. He says he brought them with him in August 1527 from London, where he had lived in close touch with Fish and Constantine. Among his Latin books he links together in the same way (*cum*) two books of Luther which were never printed together.

(8) Demaus (1886, pp. 10 and 352) gives a facsimile of a New Testament title-page bearing date 1532, which was pasted into a copy (now lost) of the Mole testament (1536). This cannot be Endhoven 2. The order of books on the title-page follows Erasmus, and not (as Endhoven 4 and 5) Tyndale. Besides, the O.T. epistles are added at the end, and these were not translated by Tyndale or Joye till 1534. The wording and grouping of the page (cf. the misplacement of Jude) are clearly taken from the New Testament title-page in the Great Bible (1539–41).

III. *Confession of Robert Necton* [May–June 1528].

(1) " About a year and a half ago " he met in London vicar Constantine, who told him Mr Fish had New Testa-

ments to sell. Till then Necton had no testaments, "nor no other books except the chapters of Matthew" [Cologne fragment]. Then, however, "he bought at sundry times" of Fish "many of the New Testaments in English," five or ten at a time, "to the number of twenty or thirty in the great volume." Fish had them "of one Harmond, an Englishman, being beyond the sea." Of these books Necton "about the same time" sold seven in Suffolk "for 7 or 8 groats apiece" [2s. 4d. or 2s. 8d.]. He sold some also "about Christmas last" in the eastern counties and London; Richard Bayfield bought two unbound for 3s. 4d. Also "at divers times" he sold "15 or 16 of the New Testaments of the biggest" to Constantine, and in his turn would sometimes buy some of Constantine.

All these testaments of the great or the biggest volume were bought by Fish from Herman [Worms 8vo.]. Probably it was Necton's confession that led Wolsey on June 18 to demand Herman's arrest.

(2) "Since Easter last [1528] he bought of Geoffrey [Lome] . . . 18 New Testaments in English of the small volume," together with 28 (or 38; Necton's calculation varies) other books in Latin, and paid 40s. [10½d. a book, if there were 46, 8½d. if 56]. Of these 18 he left 15 unsold at King's Lynn, two "he hath in his own custody with another of the great volume," and one he has sold [Endhoven 1].

(3) "About Christmas last there came a Dutchman, being now in the Fleet" [John Raimund], and wished to sell him 200 or 300 English New Testaments; "for the which 300 he should have paid £16 5s. after 9d. apiece." He declined to buy. Necton's figures do not tally: if £16 5s. is right, the price was 1s. 1d. apiece [Endhoven 1].

IV. *Robert Ridley's letter*, February 24 [1527].

"As concerning this common and vulgar translation of the New Testament into English, done by Mr William Hichyns, otherwise called Mr William Tyndale, and friar William Roy, manifest Lutherans, heretics and apostates, as doth openly appear, not only by their daily and continual company and familiarity with Luther and his disciples, but much more by their commentaries and annotations in Matthew et Marcum in the first print [Cologne fragment], also by their preface in the second print [Worms 8vo.], and by their introduction into the epistle of Paul ad Romans, altogether most poisoned and abominable heresies that can be thought. . . .

" As for errors, if ye have the first print with annotationes in Matthew and Marcus and the preface, all is mere frenzy." Ridley then gives five loose quotations from the prologue to the Cologne fragment, cf. Arber, p. 53. " I have none of these books, but only I remember such things I read in the prefaces and annotations.

" As for the text of the gospel [the second print], first the title is heretical, saying that it is printed as it was written by the evangelists." [Tyndale's title-page must have had some such words.] Ridley alleges half a dozen examples of mistranslation in Matthew, John and the Pauline epistles, but his memory is so inexact that he usually misquotes the text. He also blames the translators for rejecting the words *church, penance, charity*, etc. " I would that ye should have seen my lord's books. . . . I certify you, if ye look well, ye shall not look three lines without fault in all the book: but I have not the book to mark them out." . . . Tell any doubter to " come hither to my lord, which hath profoundly examined all, and he shall hear and see errors, except that he be blind and have no eyes. Ye shall not need to accuse this translation; it is accused and damned by the consent of the prelates and learned men, and commanded to be burnt, both here and beyond the sea, where is many hundreds of them burnt " (cf. *Antwerpsch Archievenblad*, II., 319).

V. *Peter Kaetz' letter*, [c. December 1528].

A letter survives written in Flemish by Peter Kaetz to the Cambridge printer, John Siborch. From 1523 to 1525 Kaetz was settled in London as bookseller, but he then returned to Antwerp. He writes:—" I remain still in London, because my master [? Francis Byrkman] comes.

I await him from day to day. So I cannot even know when I cross over; but so soon as I cross over, I will do the best that is in my power. Item, I have spoken to Peter Rinck 3 or 4 times of the *Pater Noster*, but he tells me that he cannot find it; and Gei*b*kerken [the *b* is badly written and may be meant for *l*] has not given the ring to Jacob Pastor, but he wears it every day on his hand, and he will not give it to Jacob Pastor. Item, I send you 25 *Pronostication* and 3 *Novum Testamentum parvo*. The *Pronostication* cost one shilling sterling the 25, and the 3 *Novum Testamentum* cost 2*sh*. 6*d*. sterling; so there is still 6*d*. due to you, & I remain in your debt. I have no more *Novum Testamentum*, else I should have sent you more." (*Cambridge Antiquarian Society, Proceedings*, VII., p. 186.)

The date of this letter is late 1528 or early 1529: for Peter Rinck and Geibkerken are doubtless the son (Hermann) and the servant (Geylkirche) of Hermann Rinck, both of whom travelled from Cologne to London with John West in October 1528, and were ready to leave England in February 1529 (*L. & P.* IV., 4810, 4827, 5402, 5462). Young Hermann seems to have been known as Peter (*L. & P.* VI., 1082; XI., 1142). The testament mentioned may be Latin, but Kaetz would hardly run out of a book, of which six sextodecimo and three octavo editions were produced at Antwerp alone in 1525-7. Probably therefore we have here Endhoven's first (1526) English testament; for the price tallies, 10*d*. a book. The *Pronostication* was certainly English. The British Museum contains an *Almynack and Pronostication* for 1530 printed by Christopher van Endhoven, and he may have produced the same for 1529.

APPENDIX D

For the sake of completeness the following story is added from Foxe (1563).

" But among all other testimonies of his godly life, there is none more famous and worthy of remembrance than this, which was reported unto me by a grave merchant worthy of credit. The story whereof is this:—There was at Antwerp on a time, amongst a company of merchants as they were at supper, a certain juggler, who through his devilish magic arts would fetch all kinds of viands and wine from any place they would, and set it upon the table before them, with many other such like things. When as this good man Master Tyndale heard of it, he desired certain of the merchants that he might also be present at supper to see him play his parts. To be brief, the supper was appointed, and the merchants with Tyndale were there present. Then the juggler, being desired to shew his cunning, after his wonted boldness uttered all that he could do, but all was in vain. At last, with his labour, sweating and toiling, when he saw that nothing would go forward, but that all his enchantments were void, he was compelled openly to confess, that there was some man present at supper, who disturbed and letted all his doings."

In his second edition Foxe says that the story was told him " by certain grave merchants," some of whom were present on the occasion, and are still alive. This cannot be Poyntz, who died in 1562. The story is evidently embellished, but there seems no reason to doubt that there was in fact a juggler or dealer in the occult, whom Tyndale's presence disconcerted and threw out of his stride.

APPENDIX E

It has long been known that in March 1528 a Thomas Matthew of Colchester was in trouble for Lutheranism. We are now told that he was the editor of Matthew's bible of 1537. Dr. W. T. Whitley (*Essex Review*, 1934–5; *The English Bible under the Tudor Sovereigns*, 1937) finds from the Colchester records that this Matthew was a London fishmonger, who became freeman of Colchester in 1516, member of the second council in 1519, and member of the first council in 1528 : on which last body he sat until 1543, with a break of one year, Michaelmas 1536 to Michaelmas 1537. Why did he miss that year? Plainly (says Whitley) he was in Antwerp, whither he sped to take up the mantle of the dying Tyndale. He then edited the bible, and Rogers merely corrected the proofs.

This theory labours under great difficulties :—

(1) There is no shred of proof that Matthew was in Antwerp either this year or at any other time, nor that he was ever in touch with Tyndale's circle. If he missed a year on the council, the reason may be that he was ill, or absent in London or elsewhere.

(2) Even if he was in Antwerp, he cannot have edited the bible, though he might have helped it in other ways. The editor certainly knew Latin, French and German, and seemingly also Greek and Hebrew. He knew his ground in theology, and moves easily amidst the commentators and versions. His corrections of the text and his notes are sensible, and he never shows as a novice. Was Matthew equal to this? He read his English bible, but otherwise Dr Whitley can only say that as chamberlain of the city he had to keep records in Latin. Can we really believe that a fishmonger, pitchforked from the market place into the study, could pro-

354

duce so good a work in so short a time? for the book was in
England by August 4, 1537.

(3) If Matthew edited the bible, he had no right to claim
on the title page that he had " truly and purely translated "
it. Whitley indeed argues that translate can mean edit:
but of the two instances he quotes, one (Taverner's bible)
tells against him, and the other (John Hollybush) is merely
a dummy name.

(4) The ancient evidence on the matter, loose and inaccurate as it is, can only be explained, if Rogers edited the
bible as well as read the proofs.

(a) Bale (1548) says that Rogers " translated anew
faithfully " the bible from Genesis to Revelation, using
Hebrew, Greek, Latin, German and English copies, adding
prefaces and notes from Luther, and prefixing a letter of
dedication to the king " under the name of Thomas
Matthew."

(b) Foxe (Latin 1559, English 1563, etc.) says that
Rogers got to know Tyndale and Coverdale at Antwerp,
and joined with them in translating the bible, and the
book circulated under the name of Thomas Matthew.

(c) Elsewhere Foxe (1570, etc.) says that Matthew's
bible was printed at Hamburg about 1532 by Grafton
and Whitchurch; that Tyndale, helped by Coverdale,
had translated all the books save the Apocrypha; but
that when Tyndale was arrested, " it was thought good
to them that had the doing thereof to change the name
of William Tyndale, because that name then was odious,
and to father it by a strange name of Thomas Matthew;
John Rogers the same time being corrector to the print,
who had then translated the residue of the Apocrypha
[really Rogers translated only the Prayer of Manasses],
and added also certain notes thereto in the margin."

(d) When Rogers was in trouble in Mary's reign,
three official documents (1553, 1555) describe him as
" John Rogers alias Matthew " (*John Rogers*, J. L. Chester,
pp. 113, 418–24). It is true they do not call him *Thomas*
Matthew, but if the bible was known as Matthew's bible,
the Christian name might easily be omitted.

INDEX

A

ABINGDON, 16.
Adrian, 259.
Aepinus, 279, 308.
Akon (Alken), 313 f.
Alfred, king, 9, 75.
Amsterdam, 200.
Anabaptists, 303, 313, 340.
Anglia, 87.
Antonius Anglus, 53.
Antwerp, printers at, 123 f., 201, 241,
   252, 262, see Endhoven and
   Keyser; Lutherans at, 259, 261–
   3, 325; Tyndale at, 133, 146–9,
   153, 211, 248, 251, 272; see
   English house.
Antwerpsch Archievenblad, 133, 259, 351.
Apocalypse, translation of, 77.
Arber, E., 74, 351.
Argentine (Strassburg), 110.
Arundel, archbishop, 78.
Ascham, Roger, 342.
Athelstane, 9.
Atkyns, 24.
Augsburg, 162, 200, 342.
Augustine, 64, 189, 222.
Augustinian monks, churches, etc.,
   20, 25, 245, 325.
Authorised Version, 11; Old Testa-
   ment, 174 f., 177 f., 181–5; New
   Testament, 82–6, 88 f., 93, 96,
   100, 103 f., 106, 108, 287 f.
Axminster, 298.

B

Baers, John, 318.
Bagster's *English Hexapla*, 293.
Bale, John, 179, 260, 342, 346, 355.
Barckley, Alexander, 132.
Barlow, Jerome, 110 f., 130–4, 190,
   345; see *Rede me*.
Barnes, Robert, 20, 50, 248, 279, 320;
   recants, 111; and New Testament, 78, 349; *Supplication* of,
   201, 206, 223; safe conduct, 188,
   191, 207; in Germany, 52 f., 150,
   153; a plot against, 304, 307 f.
Bayfield, Richard, 154, 204 f., 227,
   349 f.

Baynham, James, 217, 227, 244 f.
Becket, Thomas, 166.
Bede, 64, 75.
Bell, John, 29–31, 36, 161.
Benet, Thomas, 244.
Bergen-op-Zoom (Barrow), 187, 196 f.,
   296, 302, 318; Lutherans at, 119,
   259, 307 f.; marquis of, 312–4,
   335.
Bergh, Willem van der, 262.
Berkeley, 1, 3 f., 6, 8, 11
Beza, 343.
Bible, the, fourfold interpretation of,
   14, 138; vernacular, 34 f., 42,
   75–81, 215 f., see Tyndale and
   England.
Bible Society, British and Foreign, 343.
Bibliographical Society, transactions of,
   124, 150.
Bilney, Thomas, 20, 254; recants,
   120, 259; burnt, 190, 204.
Boehm, J. E., 343.
Boek, Het, 124.
Bolde, Thomas, 225 f.
Boleyn, Anne, 142 f., 259, 263, 289–91.
Bonner, bishop, 345.
Borchling and Clausen, 62, 151.
Bordeaux, 65.
Boswell, 121.
Brabant, duke of, 301; council, etc.,
   of, 261 f., 302, 312–4, 340; see
   Brussels.
Bradshaw, Henry, 7, 291.
Brerewood, Thomas, 298 f., 322.
Bristol, 3, 11, 24–6, 67.
*Bristol and Glos. Archaeological Society,
   transactions*, 6.
British Museum, 46, 61, 67, 201, 270,
   278, 289, 343, 352.
Brussels, 39, 240, 295 f., 307; martyrs
   at, 160, 262, 341; archives at,
   262, 301, 318, 324, 333; prison-
   ers at, 314–9, 323, 336; see
   Brabant.
Buckenham, 304, 327, 333.
Buckfastleigh, 306.
Buckinghamshire, 17, 245.
Bugenhagen, John (Pomeranus), 52,
   61, 150, 153; letter to England,
   54 f., 58.